Jo̶̶̶̶̶̶̶̶̶̶sden is Professor of Modern History at Queen̶̶̶̶̶̶̶̶̶̶y University London.

Praise for *Don't Mention the War*

'A lucid, funny history of our attitude to the Germans since the Victorian age, encompassing everything from the Battle of the Somme to *Fawlty Towers*' Dominic Sandbrook, *Daily Telegraph* Books of the Year

'One of the many merits of John Ramsden's superb book is the calm and thoughtful manner in which he charts how British attitudes to our most significant neighbour have changed over 100 years . . . he is deft and expert at telling the story' Michael Gove, *Spectator*

'Cultural history at its most readable, crowded with insights, richly informative across a wide range of topics and skilfully organised to convey a sense of the contrasting characters of successive periods' *Times Literary Supplement*

'Ramsden deftly weaves together anecdote, film, snippets of government memos and tabloid stunts' *Observer*

'More than just a slice of socio-cultural history . . . A splendid testament to the fact that, though the British are often still beastly to the Germans, they are also their own best critics' *Literary Review*

'An engaging tour through Anglo-German relations' *Sunday Express*

'As amusing as it is enlightening' *Herald*

'Insightful and extremely well researched' *Times Higher Education Supplement*

Also by John Ramsden

DON'T MENTION THE WAR

The British and the Germans since 1890

John Ramsden

ABACUS

First published in Great Britain in 2006 by Little, Brown
This paperback edition published in 2007 by Abacus

A CIP catalogue record for this book is available
from the British Library.

ISBN 978-0-349-11539-9

Cartoons reproduced courtesy of the Centre for the Study of
Cartoons and Caricature, University of Kent.

Papers used by Abacus are natural, recyclable products made from
wood grown in sustainable forests and certified in accordance with
the rules of the Forest Stewardship Council.

Typeset in Garamond by M Rules
Printed and bound in Great Britain by
Clays Ltd, St Ives plc
Paper supplied by Hellefoss AS, Norway

Abacus
An imprint of
Little, Brown Book Group
Brettenham House
Lancaster Place
London WC2E 7EN

A Member of the Hachette Livre Group of Companies

www.littlebrown.co.uk

Contents

Introduction

Twenty years ago, my wife and I were marooned in an Italian hotel. Almost all of the rest of the hotel was filled with Italian teenagers continuously singing and shouting – *fortissimo*. The only other guests were a German couple who had arrived in a gleaming silver Mercedes. In sheer self-defence, we four grown-ups talked together for a couple of evenings. Two topics of conversation stand out in my memory.

On the first evening, having discovered a mutual love of opera, we discussed opera houses we had visited, but this produced real confusion. Our German friends, residents of Salzburg, asked if we had been to operas in Monaco, and when told that we had not yet done so expressed amazement: Monaco was among Europe's great opera houses, and so convenient from Salzburg, since they could drive there in ninety minutes. Desperately recalling my O-level geography and trying not to contradict someone I had just met, I expressed polite surprise: surely it was rather a long way to travel so quickly, and although German Mercedes drivers were famous for their speed on the autobahns, were not the Alps in the way? It soon became clear that 'Monaco' was actually Munich; not recalling the English name of the city, they had helpfully rendered it in Italian, since we were in Sorrento. Amusement all round left no doubt that these Germans had a very good sense of humour.

On the following evening, talk turned to places we had visited on previous holidays, and my wife and I were given authoritative guid ance on the best way to visit nearby Roman remains. (Being British, male and determined to make up my own mind, I ignored this well-meant advice and later arrived at Paestum to find the site closed.) After we had variously mentioned holidays in Europe and North Africa, our Mercedes driver asked if we had ever been to Russia. This being the final, nasty phase of the Cold War, not only had I never visited Russia, but I did not know anyone else who had been there. It seemed an odd question from someone who was demonstrably not an East German communist but a Western capitalist. After a pregnant pause, I politely asked if he had visited Russia. 'Well, just once,' he wryly responded. 'I went there in a tank in 1942.' Pause. 'To Stalingrad.' This was followed by a delightful smile and the whispered, 'I'm sorry. I know we are not supposed to mention the war.' The rest of the evening was fascinating, for I learned about the Russo-German War of 1941–2 from the first participant in those battles I had ever met; yet I had an uneasy feeling throughout that he really ought to be a bit more apologetic about the whole thing. There was, though, no reservation in my mind about the dramatic story he told: how his father, a general in Paulus's beleaguered Stalingrad army, ordered his own son to take a few men and cut their way out to safety, while the general himself remained to face death or Stalinist captivity; they never met again.

Many years later, the Cold War now over, the Mercedes driver offered the same reminiscences in a television documentary about battles on the Eastern Front. He was still a handsome, upright figure, the embodiment of the German army of former times. Yet, even in a documentary that balanced his testimony against brutal witness accounts from Russians, I remember feeling uncomfortable: did he and the other Wehrmacht veterans not feel even a twinge of *embarrassment* about being in Russia in the first place? However, by then half a century had passed. It had already become 'history'.

I offer this personal memory as a trailer for what follows, very basic examples of failures of communication and of the hang-ups that characterise Anglo-German exchanges. As it happens, I like the Germans I know about as much as their equivalents of other nationalities, although those whom I know well are, like myself, too young to have direct memories of war between our countries or any personal responsibility for it. I am, though, also extremely aware of having lived my life in a country in which Germans often feel unwelcome and unloved; in which they are sometimes abused and occasionally attacked in the streets; and at the very least are subjected to tasteless jokes that they find offensive. I am certainly not above making such jokes myself, though I hope not in circumstances where those present would take offence. We all do it, having developed a culture in which 'being beastly to the Germans' (as Noel Coward inimitably put it) is acceptable, in which there is indeed something of an obsession with Germany and Germans. I have therefore sought to analyse that process over the long term, beginning with the Victorian era, in which relations were warm and there were, in 1900, attempts to bring about an Anglo-German military alliance. From that point, I trace the way in which British – and especially English – concerns about Germany emerged in the Edwardian period, and were deeply re-inforced during the Great War, when, as Rudyard Kipling enthused, 'the English learned to hate'.

This was not a linear process of development. Between the wars, admiration for Germany was reasserted, with Bauhaus modernity and Brechtian freedom combining to make Weimar Berlin as attractive to intellectuals as Paris had been to earlier generations. That image of Germany as a vibrant, modern, free society did not outlast the arrival of the Nazis, but both it and the older memory of the culture of Goethe and Beethoven remained alive even in the desperate 1940s, when anti-German hatred filled the airwaves and the book-shelves. Belated awareness of the Holocaust then stunned Britain into a 'never again' mentality in 1945, in respect of Germany's ability to disturb the peace. (It stunned Germans too, though the British have never quite grasped that fact.)

In some senses, normality quickly reasserted itself in the 1950s, and when personal encounters took place dismal old stereotypes could be seen to make little sense. Bert Trautmann keeping goal in Manchester, Hardy Kruger starring in British films as a 'good' German, thousands of soldiers in the British Army of the Rhine, and British civilians meeting German prisoners of war, all provide evidence of that potential for normalised relations. Yet from the 1970s onwards, the process went into reverse: although diplomatic relations between the two governments remained as good as those that Britain enjoyed with her other allies, elsewhere resentment apparently increased, as is evidenced in television programmes, novels, tabloid newspapers, comedy routines, the chanting of football crowds and every other manifestation of our popular culture. It became not just acceptable but almost obligatory to refer to the Second World War, when 'we' beat 'them', when 'we' had right on our side and 'they' sold their souls to the devil in a Faustian pact with Hitler. As A. N. Wilson put it in the *Daily Telegraph* in October 1999, responding to 'the by now familiar German complaint' by their ambassador that the British were obsessed with 1939–45:

> the truly embarrassing thing about all this is the knowledge that many otherwise intelligent British people will read this lament and think that there is nothing to worry about. At more or less the same time as [Ambassador] von Moltke was taking his sad farewell of us, George MacDonald Fraser . . . told this newspaper last week why he didn't like the idea of the European Union. 'May I refer you to those wonderful people who gave us Belsen and Dachau,' he said. 'I'm not impressed at the idea of having their children influencing our laws and way of life.' Most people to whom I make bleating, pro-German noises whenever the subject crops up are decidedly of the George MacDonald Fraser line of thought. They probably know much more than I do about Goethe and Schinkel and Caspar David Friedrich and Hegel and Beethoven. But the hideous fact of Nazism will not, as far as they are concerned, ever leave the foreground.[1]

If this was the case among 'cultivated Brits', there was no ground for complaint about prejudices held and sometimes violently expressed by the masses. There is clearly a very real problem here, and if it were ever going to go away of its own accord, or through the magical processes of time, it surely would have happened by now. It hasn't.

I should add two explanations, and a number of thanks, before inviting readers to dive back into our allegedly shared Anglo-Saxon past. First, the reader may wonder whether I myself believe in national character. I should perhaps, like Len Deighton in *Winter, a Berlin Family, 1900–45*, quote James Jones, who warned readers to 'remember that the opinions expressed by the characters are not necessarily those of the author'. Many of my 'characters' utter hate-filled opin-

ions that I definitely do not share, but it would be trite to go to the
other extreme and deny altogether that different characteristics exist
between nationalities. That is not to say that all Germans behave in
the same way, or indeed that all the British do, merely that groups of
people – some of which are nations, though they can just as easily be
Yorkshiremen or Berliners, trainspotters or Millwall supporters – *collectively* behave in recognisably different ways from other groups,
conditioned to do so by cultural norms and majority expectations. It
would be foolish to deny that most of the British and the Germans,
to some extent at least, behave according to such different norms,
though none of these is fixed or eternal: the British of today are
more like the Germans of today than either nation resembles its own
ancestors in 1900, despite continuities of certain attitudes. They find
different things funny, exhibit distinguishable responses to authority,
and have distinct attitudes to work, to mention but three obvious
points. When, in 1971, John Mortimer translated Carl Zuckmayer's
'untranslatable' play *The Captain of Köpenick*, he was congratulated
by Zuckmayer himself for making his play about German reverence
for uniforms intelligible to English audiences. But Zuckmayer noted
too that Mortimer had made major changes, to reflect 'the difference
between English and German types and topics (like, especially, the
sense and the expression of humour)'. Kevin Brownlow, making the
film *It Happened Here* in the 1960s and aiming to show that, had
Germany conquered Britain in 1940, the conquerors would have
seemed much like the conquered, nevertheless noticed divergent
behaviour among his actors: whereas British veterans employed as
extras finished shooting a scene, threw down their helmets, unbut-
toned their tunics and rushed off to the pub, German veterans
brushed and put away their uniforms, replaced their helmets with
smart caps, and only *then* went for a drink. Some such traits seem to
endure as though they really are inbred into nations. In the 1780s the
traveller Thomas Brand thought Dresden, 'a beautiful town with a
magnificent bridge over the Elbe with sentinels who make you go on
one side and come back on the other, a restraint that Englishmen are
very refractory about. I must own I never had so violent a desire to
walk up and down the same side of a bridge in my life.' Two centuries
later it would be hard to improve on that succinct summation of one
difference between the British and German temperaments. It is,

though, all too easy to move from observational awareness of different behaviour to assumptions about innate incompatibility.[2]

In 1930, when Germany was a democracy, the novelist C. S. Forester, himself not particularly anti-German, reflected in *Plain Murder* how easy it was in Britain to inflict multiple deaths in suspicious circumstances, provided they were committed in different police districts. This was unavoidable, unless a new system were adopted, 'causing considerable inconvenience to individuals, as in Germany'. This was the book's only reference to Germans, but Forester went further: in Germany, 'every citizen with any notable event in his life history has that history filed at police headquarters and continually brought up to date – an objectionable system in practice, as it happens, because of its necessary consequences of police dictatorialism . . . and other encroachments upon individual liberty'. In 1930 this just seemed a peculiarity of life abroad, yet how sinister such bureaucratically invasive traditions would appear to be once the Nazis were running the show; and how long such perceptions then lasted. In the 1970s BBC television series *Secret Army* the SS chief policeman in Belgium insists on giving priority to his office files even over wounded soldiers when evacuating Brussels in 1944, since 'the structure of the Reich is founded upon accurate and thorough records'. When BBC radio first broadcast *The Captain of Köpenick* in 1933, *The Times* welcomed the chance to enjoy 'a hoax which convulsed a nation not normally inclined to laugh at its own weaknesses'; Hitler had just become Chancellor and few Britons would laugh at the German weakness for uniforms over the next dozen years, but nor would many Germans (Zuckmayer's play having been banned by the Nazis and the author driven into exile). When a German production visited New York in 1964 *The Times* thought the play dated: 'but then Mr Zuckmayer wrote his "German fairy tale" before the days of "horror comics" or he might have given his tale a different twist'.[3]

None of this implies predetermined or racially stereotyped conflict, or even dislike between the British and German peoples. The British have, after all, similar ways of distinguishing themselves from the French – differences that seemed highly relevant when the two countries fought in long-forgotten wars, and some of which remained popular even when they were on the same side in every twentieth-century conflict. Americans, against whom the British have not fought since 1814, and with whom many Britons feel close affinity, are equally differentiated by manner, custom and behaviour; as are Australians, against whom conflict has mercifully been confined to sports fields. What emerges here, though, is how relatively harmless observations of national behaviour, such as German respect for authority and valour, can become highly charged once they are linked to a genuine conflict; Germans in the age of Hitler, thought Field Marshal Lord Slim, were 'bloodthirsty sheep'. I may be taxed with exhibiting such a national characteristic myself, in that this work is unapologetically empirical, and observational. When addressing Wagner admirers in Lancaster in 1890, their speaker declined to go into the *Meister*'s philosophy, since it was 'as dry and irksome as German philosophy usually is'. He opted instead for the practical British approach, to 'abandon the methods and examine the results'. I have done much the same, and I trust that the result is as acceptable to my audience as it apparently was to his.

Such a wide-ranging book is necessarily dependent on many who have gone before, though I have resorted to originals wherever seminal texts like those by Jerome K. Jerome, J. M. Keynes and Robert Vansittart are discussed. My many debts to previously published works are indicated in the notes, which can be found on the Internet at www.johnramsden-dmtw.co.uk. I must, though, express personal thanks to friends and colleagues who have made invaluable suggestions or commented on parts of the text at an earlier stage. Among them are: Paul Addison, Paul Alkon, Peter Beck, Jim Bolton, Peter Catterall, Mark Connelly, Andrew Crozier, James Ellison, Peter Hennessy, John Miller, Daniel Pick, Paul Preston, Jon Smele, David Stafford, Dan Todman, Paul Ward and David Welch. Any errors that remain are entirely my own, but without such assistance there would have been many more. I am also grateful to librarians and archivists who assisted, especially those at the British Film Institute, the British Library, the Huntington Library, the Harry Ransom Center, the Berg Collection, and at local history centres in Walsall and Richmond. A number of the participants in these events found time within busy schedules to discuss the topic with me from their insider perspective, most notably Hardy Kruger. I owe even larger debts to Queen Mary, University of London, which facilitated the completion of the book through sabbatical leave, to the Arts and Humanities Research Council for a grant which doubled the length of that leave, and to the British Academy, whose grant enabled me to employ research assistants to look at German sources. To cover the German side of the story comprehensively is meat for a different historian, but it has been invaluable to set immediate German reactions to British opinions alongside key phases of the story. Lars Fischer and Arne Hofmann proved to be simply the most assiduous and reliable researchers, and I gratefully acknowledge my debt to them for this and for wider assistance. Richard Beswick, Steve Guise and their Little, Brown colleagues have been supportive and positive throughout, and I happily record my gratitude to a splendid publishing team to work with as an author.

It is very sad that Giles Gordon, the agent who encouraged me to write this book in the first place, did not live to see it come to fruition. As a proud Scot who commuted between the very different dominant nationalities of Edinburgh and London, I think he would have enjoyed it. I also regret no longer being in touch with my best friend as a small boy in early 1950s Sheffield; he had an ex-soldier British father and a German mother, paternal in-laws who strongly disapproved of his delightful mother and loving grandmother, and his second name, Carl, was *never* mentioned in the playground. There were so many like him in their personally negative experience of the difficult Anglo-German twentieth century, during which the British perceived Germans to be, as one of John Le Carré's characters puts it in *Call for the Dead*, 'carnivorous ruddy sheep'. That, of course, is a contradiction in terms.

John Ramsden
September 2005

1

'An amiable, unselfish, kindly people': Anglo-German perceptions before 1900

In 1890, fresh from the success of *Three Men in a Boat*, Jerome K. Jerome was asked by a friend, 'Well now, why don't you write a sensible book? I should like to see you make people think.' Despite initial scepticism ('Do you think it can be done?'), the next year Jerome published his *Diary of a Pilgrimage*, after visiting Oberammergau, promising to 'tell you all about Germany'. He travelled a good deal and had always 'yearned to be known as a great traveller', but had never visited Germany before 1890. The 'pilgrimage' in the book's title therefore refers to a personal journey as well as to the passion play that was its ostensible purpose. That first visit initiated a complex relationship with Germany for the rest of Jerome's life that typifies British ambiguity about Germans as the twentieth century began.[1]

Having told his readers all about Germany in *Diary of a Pilgrimage*, several years later Jerome was one of the first British journalists to highlight the threat posed by Kaiser Wilhelm. The mid-1890s were years in which, as his sub-editor later recalled, Jerome, 'with wonderful foresight, was telling the present ex-Kaiser what he really thought of him, and predicting his ultimate destination' – which was, in Jerome's opinion, hell rather than Holland. When first a magazine editor Jerome had had little to say about foreign politics, but this all changed with the diplomatic crisis over the Jameson Raid of 1895. Although he deplored British anti-German hysteria, he was convinced that Germany's leaders would not have allowed a near-war situation to emerge without having first made an alliance with a sea power like Russia, enabling them to transport their invincible army to Britain. The Kaiser might seem merely 'a hot-headed gentleman', but 'he comes from a race who have lived in the atmosphere of battles. The war instinct must be in his blood.' Thereafter, Jerome harped on about the German threat and the hostility of Germany's leaders, often reminding readers of the vast German military machine and the feebleness of the British army by comparison. He was in Germany himself in 1900 when Kaiser Wilhelm interfered during the Boer War, and sadly recalled in his memoirs the depth of hostility that was again engendered on both sides.[2]

Three Men on the Bummel (1900) was a second book on the nature of Germans, collecting together every existing British stereotype of Germans into one highly readable book, just as rivalry exploded between the two countries. Jerome demonstrated his own lack of chauvinism by living in Germany for four years, and was amazed to discover on his return to Britain that friends were talking about a probable war, which he thought quite ridiculous: 'you are all a hundred years behind the times, for there's never going to be another war'. Yet, despite his love of Germans, he was swept along by the tide, and when war came in 1914 he even tried to join the army. Since he was fifty-five, this was impossible, but he did serve as an ambulance driver in France ('*en qualité de conducteur, section Sanitaire Anglaise*'). He was, a newspaper reported, 'doing a lot of excellent Red Cross work at the front, although he is above military age to an extent which he probably would not feel very comfortable in admitting'. In that role he so over-exerted himself that he was invalided out, and on returning to London in 1917 promptly started working for a compromise peace, a far from popular cause.[3]

In the Great War, he says in his autobiography, he had done his bit, like 'all us literary gents', to use his pen for the British cause, for, although he now blushed for things he had written, which 'must have made the angels weep, and all the little devils hold their sides with laughter', he had indeed hated 'German militarism': 'I had seen German *Offiziere* swaggering three or four abreast along the pavement, sweeping women and children into the gutter . . . I hated the stupidity, the cruelty of the thing. I thought we were going to free the German people from this Juggernaut of their own creation. And then make friends with them.' This was, then, a complicated thirty-year relationship with Germans, and with national war-mindedness against Germany, informed by an unusual amount of personal contact with Germany and Germans.[4]

During Jerome's lifetime it was widely assumed that the British and the Germans shared a racial affinity, 'pan Anglo-Saxonism' being the creed of such different people as the imperialist Cecil Rhodes, the American President Theodore Roosevelt, the young Winston Churchill and many others; the inclusion of Germans as well as British and Americans among the first Rhodes Scholars is testament to the fact. A people regarding itself as Anglo-Saxon saw the original Anglo-Saxon colonists as Germanic tribes, bringing to Britain – and especially to England – lasting linguistic and cultural influences: among many other things, the English names for four of the seven days of the week reflect that influence. As a national sense of Englishness developed in late medieval times, distinct from the Latinate Norman-French regime after 1066, a highly skewed version of history reinforced that 'English' identity: a 'Norman yoke' had been placed on the free Anglo-Saxons. On such a reading, King Alfred and Edward the Confessor were English patriots, Harold died at Hastings defending freedom, and Hereward the Wake and Robin Hood resisted Norman tyranny for all freeborn men. Magna Carta in 1215 was the reassertion of traditional liberties against foreign autocratic government, feudalism an equally alien importation into free Merrie Olde England. T. H. White's *The Once and Future King* told the same tale in the twentieth century, also linking it to King Arthur. Such myths had remarkable staying power and adaptability: during the English Civil War of the 1640s, traditional freedoms suppressed by the Normans seemed to moderate Parliamentarians to be the upper classes' right to property, but Levellers thought them democratic rights, while all Parliamentarians agreed that Charles I was in this sense a 'Norman' who would overthrow 'Saxon' rights. 'O what mighty Delusion, do you, who are the powers of England live in!' wrote the Leveller Gerard Winstanley in 1649. 'That while you pretend to throw down that Norman yoke, and Babylonish power, and have promised to make the groaning people of England a Free People; yet you still lift up that Norman yoke, and slavish Tyranny, and hold the People as much in bondage, as the Bastard Conquerour himself'.

As a 'British' rather than a more narrowly English identity was popularised in the eighteenth century, the Norman yoke was again encountered right across the political spectrum, from Tom Paine to Edmund Burke. It was taken as a given by external admirers of the British parliamentary system like Montesquieu, the French philosopher who observed in *L'Esprit des Lois* (1748) that 'the English have taken their system of government from the Germans. Their fine system was found in the forests.'

Though Britain fought no wars against France after 1815, so no propaganda was needed to demonstrate the Saxon roots of British freedom, the myth was further popularised. Edward Freeman and J. R. Green tried to prove from documents that Anglo-Saxon society had rested more on consent than did the Norman regime; and there was a vigorous debate between pro-Saxons and pro-Normans among Victorian historians. As the 'Whig interpretation of history' predominated, Britain appeared not only as the birthplace of parliamentary government, but showed racial tendencies that made her people ethnically suitable for such a responsible role in history. But professional historians' influence lagged far behind that of popularisers like Charles Kingsley and Sir Walter Scott, who reached a huge reading public with fables of Hereward and Robin Hood as freedom-fighters. As Wamba the Saxon balefully intones in Scott's *Ivanhoe* (1819):

> Norman saw on English oak.
> On English neck a Norman yoke;
> Norman spoon to English dish,
> And England ruled as Normans wish;
> Blithe world in England never will be more,
> Till England's rid of all the four.

Fiction carries myths well beyond the parts reached by historians, often for generations after historians have comprehensively disproved them. Just how pervasive this particular myth could be is revealed in reminiscences about his childhood by the television historian Michael Wood:

The *Eagle* ran a wonderful series for half a year on the Norman Conquest – the story of King Harold and his faithful thegn Ulric of Glastonbury. Of course, it all ends in tears with the fascistic crop-haired Normans, the Battle of Hastings, and the tragic death of Harold. In the comic strip there was a wonderful last scene in which Ulric carried the body of King Harold down to the shore at Hastings. There he saw a vision in the sky: Tommies at the Somme and Alamein, Spitfires and Hurricanes, the Thin Red Line, Drake's drum and Nelson's *Victory*. The caption read: 'Saxon England was dead but a greater England would arise'.

That post-war *Eagle* comic inhabited exactly the same thought-world as Thomas Augustine Arne's opera *Alfred*, two centuries earlier, where King Alfred's victory over the Danes prompts a forward-looking final chorus, the debut of 'Rule Britannia' and the celebration of both British sea power and Saxon virtue. Alongside Scott's celebration of imaginary Anglo-Saxons, with implications for how the 'cousins German' might be viewed by his readers in the nineteenth century, was Elizabeth Gaskell's view of contemporary England. In her highly symbolic novel *North and South* (1855) the self-made Manchester manufacturer John Thornton explicitly separates his kind from cosmopolitan southerners, not just by policy but by race: 'I belong to Teutonic blood,' he insists, which has been

> little mingled in this part of England to what it is in others. We retain much of their language; we retain more of their spirit; we do not look upon life as a time for enjoyment, but as a time for action and exertion . . . We are Teutonic up here in Darkshire in another way. We hate to have laws made for us at a distance . . . We stand up for self-government and oppose centralisation.

Understanding perfectly well what all this implies, the southern clergyman Mr Hale responds that 'in short, you would like the [Anglo-Saxon] Heptarchy back', while the Oxford fellow Mr Bell thinks Thornton 'far gone in the worship of Thor'. Many later proponents of the view that the north somehow incarnated 'real' England, untainted by effete foreign influences, were often, sometimes unconsciously, making the same point. 'In an England cricket eleven, the flesh may be of the South, but the bone is of the North, and the backbone is Yorkshire,' declared the England captain (and Yorkshireman) Len Hutton in the 1950s. Half a century earlier the all-rounder Wilfred Rhodes had insisted that cricket was not a game played for fun. Over the Pennines in 1949, Manchester City's German goalkeeper was told by a fan not to worry too much about abuse from Fulham supporters, because 'those bastard Norman cockneys don't understand'.[5]

When 'Germany' and Britain began to interrelate as political enti-ties in the nineteenth century this shared racial inheritance had immediate application. Nobody influenced the Victorian admira-tion for Germany more than Thomas Carlyle. Citing Madame de Staël's *De L'Allemagne*, which had argued that shared ethnic roots explained why Britons took more interest in Germany than did Frenchmen, Carlyle viewed Germans as 'thirty millions of men, speaking the same old Saxon tongue, and thinking in the same old Saxon spirit as ourselves', a people which must be 'admitted into the rights of brotherhood which they have long deserved'. His contem-poraries were not afraid to discuss race as a core concept for the understanding of humanity, and most Victorians 'knew' that the Britons, Scandinavians, Germans, Austrians and some Swiss (and perhaps even the better class of Americans) shared a common racial affinity. Queen Victoria's daughter Vicky, married to the Prussian Crown Prince, thanked God in 1863 'that I was born in England, where people are not slaves', yet added the hope that Prussians too 'will soon prove that we come of the same forefathers, and strive for their own lawful independence'. She had no doubt inherited much of this from her Anglo-German ancestry, but would surely have read Carlyle's *Past and Present*, where he discusses Erasmus (born in Rotterdam) among the great 'Germans' of history (the Dutch and the Germans being to him one and the same people). In an earlier lecture he takes it as certain that the Germans and the British are also one people. Preaching to the assembled royal family, including the German Kaiser, just after Victoria died in 1901, Bishop Davidson of Winchester welcomed 'the two great kindred branches of our race'. The bishop did not know that Wilhelm had been so scandalised by his interventions around the royal deathbed that he had hissed to the new king, 'if I were dead and my pastor came into the room like that, he would be hauled out by the neck and shot in the courtyard'. Racial affinities notwithstanding, wide gulfs of understanding apparently remained. 'Our German cousins' was a popular conversational concept, but it had no etymological connection with the 'cousins-german[e]' from which the pun derived.[6]

The truth, however, was that for the millennium after the Anglo-Saxon invasions of eastern England, the 'British' and the 'Germans' knew very little about each other. Come to that, they had for most of the period only the foggiest of notions of their own national identities. When Londoners rioted against 'Germans' in the fifteenth century, they were exhibiting a chauvinistic dislike of foreigners in general and the desire to protect their economic self-interest against privileged aliens (often merchants who bought those privileges by lending money to the King), rather than displaying any particular hostility to Germanness. The attacked 'Germans' were as likely to be Dutch or Flemish as residents of the later 'German' territory, and Londoners often referred to the same aliens as 'men of the [Holy Roman] Empire' or 'Easterlings', so uncertain were they of who and what lay to the east of the North Sea. (There is, though, a nice irony, unappreciated by contemporary Eurosceptics, in the fact that the word 'sterling', so symbolic of British economic independence, derived from the medieval word for Germans as 'Easterlings', the then currency standard being measured in Cologne's Bohemian-mined silver.) Things began to change only with the Reformation, with an Anglo-German link becoming so traditional through regular practice as to be almost instinctive. The English Reformation (though not the Scottish version) owed something to German Lutherans as well as to Swiss Calvinists. German theologians like Bucer and Melancthon took refuge in London from persecution, with the former assisting Cranmer with the English Prayer Book; and there was by 1540 a 'German church' in London. The process should not be exaggerated, for the British connection with Dutch and French Protestants was generally stronger, especially when actual religious wars began in those nearer countries in the 1560s, but it did initiate a lengthy period in which northern Germany and parts of the Rhineland were viewed as potentially reliable allies in the lengthy international cold war between Protestants and Catholics.

This had effects right up to the nineteenth century: British tourists

loved to visit the grave of Martin Luther, and James Boswell thought
in 1764 that Frederick the Great of Prussia had been the 'great
defender of the Protestant cause, who was prayed for in all the Scots
kirks'. The same hero-worship had been seen in the noisy celebrations
of Frederick's birthday in British towns in 1758, and in his adoption
as the 'King's head' for inn signs. The Methodist evangelist George
Whitefield said prayers for Prussia in London churches, while both
the Wesley brothers made extensive use of German originals for the
hymns they wrote, which became central to Protestant worship. John
Wesley was partly converted by German 'Moravians' and the job was
finished by Martin Luther's preface to the Epistle to the Romans; he
was also impressed by the refusal to blaspheme of Rhine boatmen
(otherwise, he noted, proverbial for their wickedness). When Carlyle
visited central Germany in 1852 to gather material for his *Frederick the
Great,* he too visited the Luther sites, and in Eisenach kissed Luther's
table, saying to himself with tears in his eyes, 'here once lived one of
God's soldiers. Be honour given to him!' The more immediate consequence of Britons' feeling uncomfortable in Catholic Europe
during the Counter-Reformation was a greater likelihood that they
would visit Germany, as Sir Philip Sidney did in 1572, fleeing from
the St Bartholomew's Day Massacre in Paris. Hamlet was not the
only student to do his year abroad in Wittenberg, and Heidelberg was
also popular with British students. The diplomat Henry Wotton and
the Cambridge fellow Fynes Morison were among many who visited
Germany to buy books at Frankfurt, then the acknowledged centre of
the European printing and book trade. Familiarity may then have
reduced contempt. Some, like Sidney, came back with respect for
Germany, while Wotton concluded that law was far better taught at
Heidelberg than in Oxford, but not everyone liked what they saw in
what was regarded as a dangerous and backward land: Morison succinctly summed up his German experience as 'gross meat, sour wine,
stinking drink, filthy beds', and rhapsodised over his return to
English beer at Oldenburg, 'the goodness whereof made my companions speak much in honour of England'.[7]

This phase of Anglo-German discovery climaxed with the first
British dynastic alliance with Germany for centuries (Henry VIII's
unconsummated match with Anne of Cleves hardly counting): in
1613 James VI and I married his daughter to the Protestant Elector

Frederick of the Palatinate. The Elector made a remarkable impact on London during his nuptial visit, and several courtiers travelled back to Heidelberg with the happy couple to continue festivities there. 'The Admiral's Men', a crack touring company in Shakespeare's day, was re-branded 'the Palsgrave's Men' in honour of Frederick, as he and his 'winter queen' Elizabeth achieved great popularity; it was claimed that for every health drunk in London taverns to King James, ten were drunk to the newly-weds, while pamphleteers did a roaring trade with the latest news. For those worried about the Counter-Reformation, England and Scotland seemed now firmly anchored to the Protestant cause, allied to its leader in a key battleground, southern Germany. This, though, was not the King's intention: James was attempting the reunification of Christendom, which involved a highly unpopular Spanish marriage for his son, to match the Protestant marriage of his daughter. Such even-handedness ran counter to parliamentary opinion, especially when Elector Frederick's rash decision to accept the crown of Bohemia in 1618 plunged Germany into the Thirty Years War. His British spouse contributed to this over-ambitious stroke of policy, for Elizabeth announced that she 'would rather eat sauerkraut with a king than roast beef with an elector'. Pamphlets now announced *Victory of the King of Bohemia's Forces* (which was alas purely imaginary). British interest was enhanced by the fact that, until the future Charles II was born in 1630, Charles I being not physically strong, it was possible that Elizabeth would become Queen of England and Scotland, if not Bohemia. In the event she got neither: Frederick was evicted by Catholic troops from the Czech lands, and by 1621 from his Palatinate too, despite support from British troops, and James's desultory backing over the next few years failed to win it back. Throughout the thirty years of German war, British Protestants saw Germans as fighting a surrogate war for their own interests, much as anti-fascists felt about Spain in the 1930s, and some were imprisoned for speaking out in favour of intervention, though the chief hero of the war for Protestants was Swedish, Gustavus Adolphus. The government refused to intervene, though, and the absence of Parliament during Charles I's 'personal rule' from 1629 to 1640 deprived opponents of the means of pressurising it. Charles's briefly entertained 1628 plan to raise a thousand 'German horse' to impose his will on the country and enforce his taxes seemed later to have something in common with the use of 'Hessians' in American colonies in the 1770s, actually rather more with the longstanding preference for fighting wars with German soldiers and English money. Domestic affairs became the priority in the 1640s, but by then many Britons had experienced fighting in Germany as mercenaries or volunteers. When the English Civil War began, and especially after the Scots intervened in 1643, armies on both sides were officered by men who had learned their trade in Germany. Prince Rupert 'of the Rhine' and his brother Maurice (sons of the Elector Frederick) were only the most visible such imports.[8]

Despite official neutrality in the Thirty Years War, and although Charles II, when restored in 1660, pursued as pragmatic a foreign policy as his father and grandfather, England and Scotland nevertheless drifted at the end of the seventeenth century towards a Protestant alliance with Dutch and Germans against Catholic France and Spain (the groupings that fought in Marlborough's wars after 1700). By 1701, as a result of the flight of James II and the 'Glorious' 1688 Revolution which enthroned William and Mary, the improbable outcome was an act of Parliament bestowing the succession on a German prince whose distant claim derived from that marriage of Elizabeth and Frederick almost ninety years earlier. Prince George of Hanover had not particularly bothered to learn English, but why would he, for when born in 1660 he was twelfth in line of succession to the British throne, and had by 1679 fallen to nineteenth. Yet in 1701 Parliament named him next in line after the dropsical Queen Anne, her sickly son, and his own elderly mother. In 1714 he became George I, embodiment of the Vicar of Bray's 'illustrious House of Hanover and Protestant succession' (actually an Anglican succession, since George had to surrender his Lutheranism to become King, London being worth an Evensong), and was received with cheering crowds, bonfires and fireworks. Though he had visited London in 1680, he was thereafter kept at arm's length by jealous monarchs, but he did lead Hanoverian troops effectively in Marlborough's wars against France and was apparently respected as a soldier by the Duke. Meanwhile, another outcry had developed in 1709 against the 'poor Palatines', German refugees whose arrival was much resented by those whose jobs they might pinch, but once again this was more xenophobic than specifically anti-German, as earlier waves of Flemish and Huguenot migrants could have testified.[9]

Some real anti-German sentiment was occasioned by the Hanoverian succession; Lord Chesterfield, who thought the new king rather provincial, decided that Britain was simply 'too big for him' after his parochial little electorate. When George died during his sixth visit to Hanover in thirteen years, it was taken for granted that he would be buried there rather than in his adopted kingdom. But much of this was the consequence of his being any sort of foreigner, rather than a German. Similar xenophobia had greeted the Scots who arrived with James VI in 1603, and even Welsh Henry Tudor in 1485, while William III's Dutch friends stirred up far more hostility than George's Hanoverians. The 1701 Act of Succession was also 'for the limitation of the Crown'; since these clauses came into force only when George succeeded he had an attenuated role, could not make foreigners privy councillors, was prohibited from going abroad himself except with parliamentary approval, and could not even declare war in defence of his Hanoverian territories unless, once again, Parliament approved. Though the prohibition on foreign travel was repealed soon after he succeeded, its earlier existence was a reminder that Parliament could set such rules for an imported monarch who owed his title to its consent. Such restrictions reflected both MPs' memories of the way in which Dutch William had behaved – spending much of the 1690s on the continent fighting wars thought to benefit the Netherlands more than Britain – and the fact that Hanover was even further away and was largely unknown to British parliamentarians. In this context George I behaved sensibly, recognising that he must henceforth make his home in London and not visit Hanover often enough to upset his new (and much richer) subjects. Unlike his grandmother, he was thus able to eat roast beef as a king, while enjoying Electoral sauerkraut when on vacation. Though he continued to speak German for preference, he was capable of making himself understood in English, which he spoke better than his critics were ever likely to concede, commissioning and apparently enjoying performances of Shakespeare in English at Hampton Court. The hoary old myth that the British cabinet system only developed, independent of the monarch, because George I did not speak English and could not therefore be bothered to attend, was long ago disproved: he probably attended cabinets throughout his reign, and sometimes annotated cabinet documents in English; lengthier papers were translated for him into French, though this reflected his British ministers' reluctance to learn German as well as the international status of French in polite society. The growing power of ministers and the declining influence of the crown, a trend a century old when he arrived, rested on grounds other than George's linguistic skills: inadequate financial provision for the King's government further reduced his room for manoeuvre, while the fact that many Tories had Jacobite sympathies obliged him to choose Whig ministers throughout his reign, a factor that much enhanced their leverage. In 1719 chief minister Stanhope made a public demonstration of the King's weakness by forcing him to disown Hanoverian advisers who had meddled in British affairs, and shortly afterwards Walpole, whom the King deeply disliked, forced his way into office as the only man to manage Parliament.[10]

There were residual elements of anti-Germanism under George I and George II, inevitable in periods of sharp political strife when monarchs spoke less than perfect English. George I ran his court more formally than the Stuarts, setting fixed times at which ministers could discuss public business, and exhibiting a respect for regularity that was thought 'German'. Other complaints included ministers never getting close to him personally, his obvious preference for authoritarian princely government over Parliament (which he claimed never to understand), and his preference for old courtiers from Hanover, who were therefore thought to exercise unconstitutional influence. The very bitterness of party strife and his enforced alliance with Stanhope's (later Walpole's) Whig faction guaranteed that Tories and dissident Whigs would harp on his German origins, and in the robust terms in which politics were then conducted. A Tory pamphlet of 1714, for example, declared (in tones very like the 'welcome' to James VI in 1603):

> Hither he brought his dear illustrious House;
> That is himself, his pipe, his close-stool and his louse;
> Two Turks, three whores, and half a dozen nurses,
> Five hundred Germans, all with empty purses.

Several pre-existing German stereotypes, already widely reported by travellers, find their way into that nasty little quatrain: poverty begetting greed, uncleanliness, low morals, and indulgence in tobacco. Suspicion was increased when he ensured that his grandson Frederick receive a 'good German education' in Hanover, which seemed to suggest a German monarchy unto the third generation, while the necessity of British ministers accompanying the King on trips back home upset the smooth running of government. George II, who as his father's heir had started seriously to learn English when the crown was entailed to the family in 1701, and so by 1714 spoke the language well, was nevertheless mocked for his accent, and generally disliked for his irritability. There were complaints that he spent too much time in Hanover – in 1736 a wag affixed to the door of the Royal Exchange a notice announcing, 'It is reported that his Hanoverian Majesty designs to visit his British dominions for three months in the Spring'. Lord Hervey recalled in gossipy memoirs that in the 1730s the King had 'committed brusqueries to everybody by turn' and had been 'as much personally hated as Sir Robert Walpole' (which is saying a good deal), a fact greatly exploited by the Prince of Wales when, as usual among the Hanoverians, he was quarrelling with his father. The Queen was thought reasonably enlightened, the King something of a philistine, but then his mother had been seen by the philosopher Leibniz as 'the oasis in the intellectual life of Hanover', which rather indicates a cultural desert. When both King and Queen became staunch 'Handelians' in the battle between London opera houses, it was attributed to their German roots rather than their taste in music.[11]

George II's son Frederick, despite that German education, chose to oppose his father by taking the patriotically 'British' side in political intrigues, and as Duke of Cornwall used his influence in a county with more than its share of pocket boroughs to make life difficult for Walpole. This was an unconvincing pose, for Frederick spent most of his life in Hanover, had little sympathy for Britain, and once exclaimed (according to Hervey), 'the devil take the whole island, provided I can get out of it and go to Hanover'. The use of Hanoverian troops on British pay remained contentious, as did George II's occasional exercise of his right as Elector of Hanover to conduct diplomacy in Germany without consulting his British ministers. The King's victory at the Battle of Dettingen in 1743, well known as the last time that a British monarch personally led 'his' troops in battle, was fought in defence of Hanover against the French, while Britain itself was not yet even at war, though British troops made up part of his army. William Pitt had recently thundered that 'this formidable kingdom is considered only as a province of a despicable Electorate', but the King's victory over the traditional enemy occasioned bonfires, celebrations, and Handel's 'Fireworks Music', a rather finer piece than he managed for the defeat of the Jacobites in 1746. 'Butcher' Cumberland, the King's son who put down the Jacobite rising, was more criticised for his allegedly 'Prussian' efforts to modernise the army than for his reprisals in Scotland, while Pitt resumed his attacks on Carteret as 'the Hanoverian troop-minister'. Fears about Prussianising the army might have been deeper had there been awareness of the King's personal preference for Hanoverian government over the British version: as he explained to the Lord Chancellor in 1749, this was because in Hanover 'the government is military, as here it is legal'. Even a Germanophile like Boswell was moved in 1764 to write verses in memory of the first German soldiers he had seen, garrisoning Edinburgh against Bonnie Prince Charlie in 1745, and to compare them unfavourably with Scotsmen:

> Behold ye Hessians, from the Shire of Ayr
> A laird whom your moustaches have made stare!
> . . . While Arthur's seat resounded to your drums,
> I saw you buying breeches for your bums;
> But, with your breeches, you were not so stout,
> As the bold Highlanders who went without.

How unpopular German soldiers could be emerges from a dispute in Maidstone in 1756. Hanoverian troops were in Kent to defend the country against the French, but they acted in a high-handed manner when in dispute with local tradesmen. The Mayor of Maidstone had to be ordered by the government to release imprisoned German soldiers when their commander insisted that they were subject only to martial law, but the resulting outcry forced a climb-down, and the Hanoverian general was himself returned to Germany. The 'Norman yoke' was here evoked with a vengeance (though in reverse, the enemy being now Anglo-Saxon): one print appealed to 'Ye Men of Kent' to 'Recall to mind the Norman foe,/He didn't dare to use you so'.

Memories of such disputes encouraged George III and Lord North to ensure that German soldiers were not deployed (when desperately needed) to contain the anti-Catholic mobs that terrorised London during the Gordon Riots in 1780. In 1756, though, Pitt embarked on the war ministry that made Britain a world power, and had learned his lesson: it suited British interests rather well to have German soldiers paid by the British to keep the French occupied, while their own soldiers roamed the world by sea conquering French colonies. 'His Britannic Majesty's Army' in Germany during the Seven Years War therefore consisted mainly of Hanoverians and German mercenaries, and the key element in Germany was the subsidised campaigning of Frederick the Great, Britain's Prussian ally.[12]

George III's refusal to deploy German soldiers on the London streets in 1780 reflected a different national outlook as well as caution. He had been brought up in Britain rather than Hanover, spoke unaccented English, and when succeeding his grandfather in 1760 regarded himself as a British king who happened also to have German possessions, rather than the other way round; Alan Palmer makes the point that he was as much an absentee monarch in Hanover as in America. Over the course of his sixty-year reign, he never visited Hanover – never indeed ventured outside England – and became for a time rather more popular than either of the first two Georges (though, characteristically, English chauvinism still managed to detect an affront in his initial choice of a 'Scotch' minister, Lord Bute). As Horace Walpole put it, with the accession of George III, 'Hanover was no longer the native soil of our Princes . . . The prejudice against his family as foreigners ceased in his person.' This was though a matter of emphasis rather than a clean break, for when choosing a bride he never seriously looked beyond Protestant German princesses. Although he was banned from marrying a Catholic by British law, and from marrying outside a princely house by German law and so had little choice here, his personal preferences were to be seen by marrying eight of his children into German princely houses; within the family circle he spoke German to the Queen, sometimes referred

to the 'good German blood in [his] veins', and sent four of his sons
to university in Göttingen. The German connection remained fertile
ground for critics of the King's government, as Lord Byron showed
when he saluted Germany's most famous terpsichorean export:

> To Germany, and highnesses serene,
> Who owe us millions, don't we owe our Queen?
> To Germany, what owe we not besides,
> So oft bestowing Brunswickers and brides;
> Who paid for vulgar, with her royal blood,
> Drawn from the stem of each Teutonic stud;
> Who sent us – so be pardoned all her faults –
> A dozen dukes, some kings, a queen – and the Waltz.

Travel, however, usually tended to make British poets patriotic: it was
in Germany that Wordsworth hailed Britain as 'Freedom's impreg-
nable redoubt!' The Wordsworths did not much take to the military
side of German life (or to the inns), Dorothy being repelled by a
Gothic tale of blood and death told them by a soldier in Heidelberg,
which she thought 'of a kind specially pleasing to German imaginations'. Though only a matter of degree, and although anti-Germanism
like Byron's revived in Britain in the 1810s and 1820s, George III's
reign nevertheless inaugurated a pause between two phases of overtly
Anglo-German monarchy, 1714–60 and 1837–1901.[13]

Yet if the reign of George III indicated lesser British affinity with
German affairs, its final years provided the best example to date of
Anglo-German partnership, during the Napoleonic Wars. There was
surprising British hostility to Napoleon's seizure of Hanover in 1807,
and equally surprising warmth when celebrating the centenary of
the Hanoverian succession in 1814. There was a meeting of minds
between British and German opinion once a German national spirit
was aroused by French imperialism, in the campaigns of 1808 and
during the 'war of German liberation' in 1813–14. Most of all, while
Britain's freedom from Napoleon had been won by the all-British victory at Trafalgar in 1805, the freedom of Germany and Europe
depended on the polyglot army commanded in 1815 by Wellington at
Waterloo. Even while fighting 'alone' during the morning and afternoon of the battle, and wondering despondently whether the

Prussians would ever arrive, Wellington commanded at Waterloo forces containing fewer British soldiers than Germans, Belgians and Dutch, but Blücher's Prussians turned Napoleon's defeat into the final catastrophe for his empire. In the century of Western European peace that followed, Waterloo, a tale of historic Anglo-German co-operation, was taught to generations of schoolboys as the last great European battle, though it could also be a contested memory: in 1844 Thackeray visited the battlefield with English tourists and witnessed a prolonged argument: "'Ah, it was lucky for us that the Prussians came up!" says one little gentleman, in a particularly wise and ominous tone. "Hang the Prussians!" (or, perhaps, something stronger "the Prussians!") says a stout old major on half-pay. "We beat the French without them sir, as beaten them we always have."'" The Duke of Wellington was himself rather jealous about Waterloo, refusing even to take delivery of the vast Waterloo battle panorama presented to him after his victory until it had been reworked to play down the role of the Prussians, but the truth could not be more generally denied, and Wellington was happy enough to commission a portrait of himself for the Prussian military academy in Berlin, for which he wore the uniform of a Prussian field marshal. Germans came to be seen as Britain's 'natural allies' during the nineteenth century in part because the two countries actually had been allies when last at war. They had cohered, though, only in opposition to France, an eternal triangle that would now be central to all three countries' international diplomacy; at the conference that ended the Napoleonic Wars, Castlereagh's support allowed Prussia to seize parts of the Rhineland, a British policy designed to hedge in the French. Waterloo provided in due course a memory usefully evoked by Prince Albert, since it related to the Anglo-German link that he personally embodied; he assiduously attended annual Waterloo dinners, managed to win Wellington's respect, and, when he was choosing designs for the frescoes to decorate the new Houses of Parliament, opted for a huge mural depicting Wellington's meeting with Blücher as the memorial to Waterloo. Such sentiments worked only when not challenged by more immediate concerns – British inability to understand why Prussia had remained neutral during the Crimean War being a case in point. As interests diverged thereafter, Waterloo could be more useful as a stick with which to beat a former ally than as a demonstration of friendliness: in 1913, when preparations for the centenary began, men were already wondering how Britain and Prussia would be able to celebrate anything together by 1915; when war broke out the next year, the Kaiser raged that England had forgotten 'how we stood shoulder to shoulder at Waterloo'. He seems not to have noticed that Waterloo is actually in Belgium, which had by then acquired a very different significance for Anglo-German relations.[14]

Long before Waterloo, rather more Britons had gained personal experience of Germany by going to see it for themselves. The explorations of men like Sidney had been brought to an abrupt halt by the Thirty Years War, and the devastation wrought by that war ensured that Germany was not a favoured destination for almost a century. Even when Thomas Coryat visited the Rhineland in 1608, it seemed a land of 'freebooters', bandits likely to hold tourists to ransom; he took the precaution of travelling home with a party of students returning from Heidelberg, but the forces of order did not seem much more attractive, for he noticed the large number of gallows and 'execution wheels' visible from his boat as he sailed down the Rhine. That bloodthirsty reputation of Germans was also explored in *Robinson Crusoe* (1719). Defoe's hero is descended from a German family in Bremen ('Crusoe' being Yorkshire's attempt to pronounce Kreutzenaue), and when 'Man Friday' escapes from his cannibal captors, he cuts off one's head with Crusoe's sword, 'as cleverly, no executioner in Germany could have done it sooner or better'. The diarist John Evelyn did not visit Germany during his grand tour in 1643, since 'I had been assured there was little more to be seen in the rest of the civil world, after Italy, France, Flanders and the Low Countries, but plain and prodigious barbarism'. The classic grand tour, so popular with young aristocrats, restricted itself to France, Italy and Switzerland, and it was thought eccentric to venture further into Germany than a trip down the Rhine. Gradually, as the seventeenth century closed, this pattern changed, though when in 1698 the Duke of Bedford visited Hamburg, Berlin, Dresden and Nuremberg, he was thought almost as adventurous as a Victorian trekking into the African interior. The Hanoverian succession increased interest in western and northern Germany, but not until after the Seven Years War did many Britons venture into the German east. The heyday of the grand tour including Germany came between about 1763 and 1789, when it was undertaken by Boswell, Gibbon, Sterne and Smollett, among others. The belated recognition that Dresden offered a cultural experience for tourists in pursuit of art was evidence that until then Germany had been seen as a cultural wasteland, but Saxony was anyway more notable for the classical architecture tourists admired in France and Italy than was the rest of Germany. Dresden, which Lord Dartmouth thought a 'little London', was thus, like Vienna, valued for its artworks, but also thought less forbidding than the austere Prussian capital, Berlin; by 1797 Dresden had a significant British colony, as did Göttingen. Those few who visited Prussia discovered with amazement that Protestant as well as Catholic princes could be autocrats, but few found this aspect of Germany attractive. Germany seemed poor and backward in all the comforts of life regarded as normal by rich travellers (and few then travelled who were not rich).[15]

The most common British response to Germany related to travel itself: German roads and inns were proverbially the worst in Europe, and difficulties were increased by the multiplicity of princely authorities deciding customs, currency and the right to roam. Lord Burlington found in 1614 that the roads were too rough for his two coaches, being on one occasion stuck in the mud all night, and he needed guides even to find his way around the Rhineland (few educated Englishmen speaking German); it took nearly three weeks to get from Holland to Switzerland. Even the cities seemed barbarous by British expectations, and he noticed that in Cologne grass grew in the main thoroughfares. Rather later, Coleridge, who much admired German culture, was nevertheless scathing about Germany, especially about Cologne, the first city encountered by travellers going up the Rhine: 'I counted two and seventy stenches', he wrote, rhyming it unchivalrously with 'hideous wenches', and thought the city resembled venison 'kept too long', marvelling that such a place produced 'the most fragrant of spirituous fluids, the *Eau de Cologne*'. On his 'joyful departure', he penned another ode:

> As I am a Rhymer,
> And now at least a merry one,
> Mr Mum's Rudesheimer

And the Church of St Geryon,
Are the two things alone,
That deserve to be known,
In the body-and-soul-stinking town of Cologne.

Since Germany was simply not geared up for tourists, even aristo-cratic visitors were compelled to sleep in inns that offered no bed better than a table covered with straw; one traveller reported that he and his companions lay on straw 'like so many horses, in our clothes'. German cuisine was not so much disliked as found unfamiliar, compared with French cooking, often encountered in Britain, but the main complaint was that not enough food was offered, rather than that the taste was offensive; German wine and beer were also rejected as unfamiliar to palates trained on French and British beverages. In part, such dismissal of things German reflected a surge of British self-confidence during the seventeenth and eighteenth centuries, as naval and commercial power extended far and wide: a German pastor in London noted feelingly in 1780 that 'even an English beggar, at the sight of a well-dressed Frenchman, or any other stranger, still thinks himself superior and says within himself, I am glad I am not a foreigner'.[16]

Thanks to British industrialisation creating 'the workshop of the world' and the naval-enforced *Pax Britannica*, that complacent self-image did not moderate much during the next century: the boatswain in W. S. Gilbert's *HMS Pinafore* (1878) thanked his maker that the hero was an Englishman, and hence neither a 'Rooshian' nor a 'Prooshian' (though performance practice emphasised that the absolute pits was to be 'Hey-tal-eye-an', so far did Anglo-Saxon racial assumptions dominate even comedy). By then travel had extended rather further down the social scale. John Murray issued the first British guidebook to Germany in 1836, largely because of problems during his own travels, but it was not until the spread of railways across the continent that international tourism really took off. In the 1850s the Great Eastern Railway had a regular service to Antwerp, Cologne and Mainz, and Thomas Cook escorted his first party of tourists to the continent. The Rhineland was then an optional extra for a tour that concentrated on the Low Countries and Paris: as the first group sailed the Rhine, one recited appropriate cantos of Byron's

Childe Harold, so far did the British bring their cultural baggage with them. Cook initially had difficulty negotiating his usual discounts with German railway companies, and boldly promised five hundred passengers a year to get his contract, but he was soon sending that number every month. By 1868 Cooks were issuing hotel coupons for individual travellers; from 1873 a monthly continental railway guide and timetable; and from 1874 travellers' cheques. In the 1890s the company marketed several German tours, though prices beginning at twenty-five pounds would indicate an upper-middle-class market; in the Edwardian period travel became more democratic, with Cook's cheapest tours costing only five guineas. (When in 1992 Thomas Cook's was itself taken over by a German firm, the *Daily Star* cartoonist showed parties of British tourists being marched along a Mediterranean poolside, its officers looking like men of the Afrika Korps.) British travellers did not now need passports, and the creation of the German Empire with a single currency facilitated travel (just as the earlier *Zollverein* had simplified the customs). The imperial government set seriously about the improvement of roads and the rationalisation of railways, each of which enhanced tourism, while larger numbers of travellers forced inns and hotels to raise their standards: Carlyle stayed in 1858 at Berlin's 'British Hotel'; three years earlier Cook's first tourists had been booked into the Hotel Angleterre in Mainz, though they found there 'hard beds full of small intruders'. For Thackeray in the 1850s, tales of travellers had become hackneyed, the Rhineland 'as familiar to numbers of people as Greenwich', while formerly independent, proud cities had become artificial creations for the tourist, the sham chocolate-box soldiers of daytime 'Rougetnoirburg' magically transformed into croupiers by night. Sir John Forbes, advising on sightseeing in 1856, likewise assured readers that he would deal only with 'localities already well-known to travellers'. Fanny Trollope, the novelist's mother and a sensationalist travel writer, had a huge success with her book on America, but the sequel on Germany was a damp squib; potential readers had heard most of it before, and many had seen it for themselves.[17]

How did the new middle-class travellers respond? Often as British travellers invariably do, noting the colourfulness of life and the sheer size of physical phenomena: the Rhine seemed to British tourists a 'world-sized river' (as Carlyle put it), and German mountains impressively larger than anything in Britain; not everyone liked physical entities to be so *big*, but some were disappointed not to find them bigger (a view which Charles Lamb attributed to 'lying painters' who exaggerated even the Alps). As so often, travellers saw whatever their guidebooks had told them to expect: Thackeray thought John Murray's guides were 'the basis of most tourists' opinion of the continent', and in *The Kickleburys on the Rhine* he shows tourists utterly dependent on Murray. Since Germany was, they read, famous as a land of order and regimentation, visitors noticed that the trees, and even the cattle, stood in straight lines, though it is not likely that what they saw was different from rural scenes in France or Holland. They also noticed that cattle were rarely left to fend for themselves, and a children's book attributed this too to national character: 'I am sure, if you were a cow, you would much sooner be an English cow, ranging at will over the fields', than shut up in a stable by an authoritarian German farmer, or led about by the nose by one of his children. The tendency of elite Germans to congregate at spas rather than spend weekends at country houses was likewise attributed to fondness for being organised, while the fact that gambling was legal in Germany showed moral weakness: Cook promised those who went on organised tours that he would not let them be led astray in casinos. Noticing that German city-dwellers were more likely to live in apartment blocks than their British equivalents, tourists attributed it to German militarism, a preference for life in the barracks, with resident landlords the 'house policemen' who would probably report on them to the authorities. It was the absence of fortifications that led the publisher William Chambers to think that Frankfurt resembled an English city. Few travellers thought of Germany as a free country, assuming, like their guidebooks, that Germany was formal, hierarchical and over-regulated, but this involved only a narrow definition of freedom: the Congregationalist minister Henry Richard discovered with amazement in 1850 that it was actually compulsory to send your children to school in Hesse, and that the state ran all the schools, a position he thought woefully destructive of 'liberty', though the consequence was that Germany was more literate than anywhere else in Europe, and Britain lagged far behind, still 'freely' sending children out to work.[18]

Victorians had thus assembled from imagined history and the mediated experience of travel a series of stereotypes of Germanness. These were largely unchanged from centuries earlier, as Shakespeare's few allusions to Germans indicate: in the course of thirty-seven plays he makes only a dozen references to Germany and the Germans, stressing primitive characteristics and animal appetites, but not a lot more. Iago proclaims that 'your Dane, your German and your swagbellied Hollander drink' to excess, which is confirmed by Hamlet. Posthumous Leonatus in *Cymbeline*, tortured by his wife's apparent infidelity, imagines her willingly submitting to being 'mounted by a boar, a German one', strengthening the image of appetites boorishly slaked with the last three words. In *Much Ado About Nothing* Don Pedro, analysing Benedick's wayward character, declares him to be 'a German from the waist downwards, all slops', while Bardolph in the *Merry Wives of Windsor* reports three horsemen speeding away with stolen horses like 'three German devils, three Doctor Faustuses', to which mine host of the Garter responds ironically, 'Germans are honest men'. Finally, 'the young German, the duke of Saxony's nephew' who seeks Portia's hand in *The Merchant of Venice*, behaves 'very vilely in the morning when he is sober, and most vilely in the afternoon when he is drunk. When he is best he is little worse than a man, and when he is worst he is little better than a beast'. Such were the stereotypes which affected what the British saw when they then visited Germany and formed impressions of their own. Berlin, explained Sir John Forbes, was 'as everybody knows' full of 'colossal' statues, which all seemed to be 'in honour of military men . . . a striking illustration of the character of the Prussian Government'.[19]

During the nineteenth century, stereotypes remained at the heart of British views of Germans, but with the rise of Prussia and British employment of German mercenary soldiers, images of militarism had been added to the list, as Forbes's observation showed. Marietta Starke thought in 1798 that to visit Germany was to go back a century, 'as the dresses, customs and manners of the people precisely resemble our ancestors'. Having seen them at table in 1765, James Boswell was 'enlivened by seeing the hearty Germans' eat their supper. Drink was one aspect of over-indulgence much reported, though travellers were sometimes honest enough to admit that they enjoyed joining in, as did Joseph Addison in 1703, writing from

Hamburg that 'the great business of this place is commerce and drinking'. Defoe, allocating one sin to each nationality in *The True-Born Englishman* – pride to the Spanish, lust to Italians, 'ungoverned passion' to the French – had no doubt which fitted Germans:

> Drunk'ness, the darling favourite of Hell,
> Chose Germany to rule, and rules so well . . .

In the nineteenth century it was said that British travellers learned to 'eat a la Française and to intrigue a l'Italiene' but 'to smoke, take snuff and swear a l'allemande'; Forbes wrote of the 'eternal smoking of the people' as 'a perverter of the taste and a defiler of the imagination'. When Victoria announced her intention of marrying Prince Albert, the Prime Minister, her beloved Lord M[elbourne], told her that a German would irritate her with constant smoking and his reluctance to wash. Forty years later, meeting Bismarck in Berlin, Disraeli had to resume smoking in self-defence, 'the last blow for my shattered constitution'. Victorians perceived Germans, says Bernard Porter, as hard-working but ineffectual, romantic and dreamy, unattractive in appearance and habits: one traveller reported them 'fuming tobacco from every pore, hawking and spitting incessantly all over the floor', sweating, belching and 'unbuttoning' during meals. As a result of such over-indulgent simplicity, Germans were also thought over-ready to display their feelings, whereas, as Prince Albert told his brother, 'sentimentality is a plant that cannot grow in England . . . An Englishman, when he finds he is being sentimental, becomes frightened at the thought as having a dangerous illness and he shoots himself . . . I think the plant is smothered by reading too many newspapers.' Earlier in the century, and noting the same distinction, 'the Pedestrian' assured his readers that 'every tourist' made the same observation of Germans: that 'there is neither parade, nor pride, nor prejudice, flummery nor finesse. But there is manly feeling, open and sincere.' Charles Kingsley thought 'really this Germany is a wonderful country . . . and as noble, simple, shrewd, kindly hearts in it as man could wish to see'. These were noble savages, much like those that missionaries expected to find in Africa.[20]

Germans were also thought to be devoted to hierarchy and authority. In the 1740s George II had dubbed Frederick William of Prussia 'my brother the sergeant', and been called in return 'my brother the dancer'. Despite his admiration for Frederick the Great, Boswell decided after a few weeks at his court that 'this king is like a wild beast. I am quite out of conceit with monarchy.' He later dined 'with Prussian officers', and having heard of their service conditions 'thought them madmen to endure such fatigues'. He noted too that there was a great concern with formality at court, though the locals seemed not to mind; when dining in Berlin, he found it all 'quite German, for although this nation loves form, custom has rendered it easy to them'. Travellers certainly did mind all the repeated inspections of their baggage and documents in what the musicologist Charles Burney called 'the despotic states of Germany'; Hamburg had in 1772 'an air of cheerfulness, industry, plenty and liberty . . . seldom to be seen in other parts of Germany'. Travellers in the nineteenth century were reminded by Murray's *Handbook* that it was essential to report to the police on arrival in a German town, an expectation 'totally foreign to English habits'. They must remember that innkeepers were considerable persons locally and must be treated civilly; there was no point in complaining about the time at which dinner was served, for 'in Germany everything is done systematically', so no food for late arrivals. Nor should they object to the beds: 'an open wooden box' was normal for Germany, as was a 'bag of feathers' to cover the sleeper, the ancestor of the duvet, to which some British travellers never have accustomed themselves – Coleridge declared that he would rather 'carry my blanket about with me like a wild Indian than submit to this custom'. Since the government ran post offices and public conveyances, people who ran them were also superior to their British equivalents and expected respect. Regulations respecting charging for post horses were 'in the highest degree cumbrous, frivolous and vexatious'. Expounding 'Some peculiarities of German Manners', Murray's 1871 edition stressed once again order and formality: 'The German is scarcely happy until he can hang a little piece of striped ribbon from his button-hole', and extreme care should be taken to find the correct form of address for functionaries at each level of the bureaucracy, especially, once again, the post office. An aspect of this formality that imprinted itself on the British mind was the apparent dominance of 'dryasdust' professors in German intellectual life, the word coined by Carlyle, who met in Bonn some learned gentlemen he thought 'miserable creatures lost in statistics'. Germany, thought Palmerston, 'is a country of damned professors', and Wellington thought much the same.[21]

Children's books reduced stereotypes to bare essentials, but thereby reflected underlying assumptions. Germany was, wrote L. P. Meyer in a book many times reprinted in late Victorian Britain, 'the middle part of Europe', fearfully damp and cold. Its people 'work harder than any other people in Europe', but were subject to their appetites, being invariably heavy smokers, and generally over-indulgent; cherries were plentiful, and 'people sometimes eat several pounds at a time'. The picture is often positive, though: 'Like the English they can make beautiful things well. Like the Scotch they love reading and writing. They make clocks and watches, knives and swords, cups and plates. Like the Italians, they love music and singing.' Germans wrote and read more books than anyone else, a respect for learning reflected in all those streets named after Goethe or Schiller – why, the author asks, do we never name streets after Shakespeare? In view of the climate, little Britons would not wish to go to Prussia, 'yet it is a better country to live in than beautiful Italy . . . The people are taught to mind what is written in the Bible, and there are good laws. All the children are obliged to learn to read.' Young readers learned that Prussia had the most soldiers of any country in Europe, compared to population, with fierce discipline imposed on all men while they were conscripts, and women too knew their place: 'Can they do nothing but knit and cook? Yes, they can embroider very beautifully.' Since 1871 'Prussia and Germany are one': Prussian respect for guns had become universal, while Wiesbaden's Krupps armament factory was one of the great sights of Germany. Maggie Browne's *Chats About Germany* did not differ much. German schoolchildren had to start their lessons earlier than the British, with no time for boys' sports as in England. Since 1871 Germany had become 'one large kingdom' and was 'more powerful than ever'. The people thought very highly of warfare, and even children 'think a great deal about war'. Germany was proud of her language, her capital, and her growing power as a nation, devoted to the memory of Bismarck, who had 'made her what she is today'.[22]

No traveller did more to entrench stereotypes than Jerome K. Jerome. The most striking single image that he offers is of Germany as a military nation. His 1891 travellers pass a traditionally poor first night in what they hardly even recognise to be a bed, but next morning visit the station buffet.

> There were all sorts of soldiers – soldiers of rank, and soldiers of rank and file; attached soldiers (very much attached, apparently) and soldiers unattached; stout soldiers, thin soldiers; old soldiers, young soldiers. Four very young soldiers sat opposite us, drinking beer . . . and they each looked, also, ready and willing to storm a battery if the order were given to them to do it. There they sat, raising and lowering their mugs of beer, discussing military matters, and rising every now and again to gravely salute some officer as he passed.

His impression of exaggerated respect for order is reinforced by a discussion of railway guards, who seem over-fond of their authority: 'some people rave about sunsets and mountains and old masters, but to the German railway-guard the world can show nothing more satisfying than the sight of a railway ticket', a craving he shares with 'nearly all the German railway officials'. Whenever he sees a sad-looking railway official Jerome shows him a ticket (buying one specially if necessary) and cheers him up. When an English passenger mislays his ticket, he is escorted before 'a stern-looking gold-laced stationmaster, surrounded by three stern-looking gold-laced followers', all rather like 'a drum-head court martial'. The passenger displays English phlegm, asking that 'if the worst happened, to break it gently to his mother'. This is a country where you must continually prove that you 'have permission'.[23]

After his broader encounter with Germany, fictionalised as *Three Men on the Bummel*, this idea of Germany as an authoritarian state is carried much further, though he is careful now to note different types of German within the overall mass. There are elements here of the concept of Prussians as bad, power-crazed Germans, compared to Saxon and Rhinelander 'good Germans' that was to characterise so much British writing about Germany in the twentieth century. Hence Jerome likes Hamburg, Stuttgart and Hanover, and enjoys Munich as he had in 1891, but admires above all Dresden, and specially dislikes Berlin. Nuremberg he cannot quite decide about, since the half-timbered medieval and the boldly modern are inextricably together in the same parts of the city, whereas in Hanover both elements existed but in different quarters. A modern, thrusting Germany for the new century and half-timbered Germany for the tourist are just too hard to reconcile.[24]

His friend George's confusion of nesting boxes and letter boxes ('Why, in Germany, is it the custom to put letter-boxes up a tree?') prompts an extended fantasy on national character, when J[erome] replies,

> You must understand this nation. The German loves birds, but he likes tidy birds. A bird left to itself builds his nest just anywhere . . . He drops things on the grass; twigs, ends of worms, all sorts of things . . . The German householder is shocked. He says to the bird: 'For many things I like you . . . But I don't like your ways. Take this little box, and put your rubbish inside where I can't see it . . . Keep to the box and don't make the garden untidy.'

Dropping any pretence of a reported conversation, Jerome the narrator adds rhapsodically that,

> In Germany one breathes in love of order with the air . . . and in course of time every German bird, one is confident, will have his proper place in a full chorus. This promiscuous and desultory warbling of his must, one feels, be irritating to the precise German mind; there is no method in it. The music-loving German will organise him. Some stout bird with a specially well-developed crop will be trained to conduct him, and, instead of wasting himself in a wood at four o'clock in the morning, he will, at the advertised time, sing in a beer garden, accompanied by a piano. Things are drifting that way.

The fantasy continues with German gardeners teaching flowers to behave themselves and a claim that Germans prefer china dogs to real ones since they too are more orderly. Trees, lakes and rivers in Germany are all to be tamed, for 'in Germany there is no nonsense talked about untrammelled nature. In Germany nature has got to behave itself and not set a bad example to the children . . . It's a tidy land is Germany.'[25]

The human implications of this nonsense arise in incidents that beset the travellers during the journey from Nuremberg to the Black Forest, when all three have trouble doing things that would hardly be noticed in England. Harris gets into hot water for entering an art gallery through the wrong door, and is fined forty marks for calling the doorman a '*dummer esel*'; 'in Germany you are not permitted to call an official a "silly ass"'. J then inadvertently unloads from the train the wrong bicycle, and is rescued from prosecution only by knowing a senior railway official in the town, though 'my going scot free is regarded in police circles there to this day as a grave miscarriage of justice'. Finally George boards a train without the proper ticket, thereby committing eight separate 'sins' at once, as a result of which 'his journey from Karlsruhe to Baden was one of the most expensive perhaps on record'. None of these is an intentional offence, but 'in Germany . . . trouble is to be had for the asking', for there are so many things 'that you must not do that are quite easy to do'. These incidents are an excuse to list extracts from an alleged 'Police Guide of the Fatherland'. In Germany it is variously forbidden to hang your bed out of the window; to wear fancy dress in the streets (which might pose problems to a Highlander); to walk around the street 'in droves' (what is a 'drove'?); to break glass or china in the street – and if you do, you must pick up all the pieces, though the law does not permit you 'to throw them anywhere, to leave them anywhere, or apparently to part with them in any way whatsoever'. Nor can you shoot in a German street with a crossbow, for 'the German law-maker does not content himself with the misdeeds of the average man – the crime one feels one wants to do but must not; he worries himself imagining all the things a wandering maniac might do'. The section ends with an incident in which Jerome is reprimanded by a policeman after he has thrown things from his window at a howling cat. He tries sarcasm when the officer asks exactly which cat it had been, but 'the German policeman does not understand a joke, which is perhaps on the whole just as well, for I believe there is a heavy fine for joking with any German uniform; they call it "treating an official with contumely"'. The greatest offences of all are walking on the grass and otherwise transgressing rules regulating behaviour in parks. In this as in every other area Germans helplessly accept their subservience. Jerome decides that 'they are a law-abiding people the Germans', while George replies that 'anyone could rule this country, *I* could rule it.'[26]

After deeply negative accounts of the custom of duelling among students he proceeds to comparisons with Britain which render his observations all the more pointed. The German worships order, for 'the policeman is to him a religion, and, one feels, will always remain so', while, 'in England we regard our man in blue as a harmless necessity. By the average citizen he is employed chiefly as a signpost, though in busy quarters of the town he is considered useful for taking old ladies across the road.' The policeman is for German children partly Santa Claus and partly a bogeyman, for he represents the state, which provides all good things and punishes all transgression: 'the German citizen is a soldier and the policeman is his officer'. This is a comfortable state of affairs, since it relieves the citizen of personal responsibility for his own and anyone else's fate, but the lack of freedom troubles Jerome, even when paying compliments.

> The Germans are a good people. On the whole the best people perhaps in the world; an amiable, unselfish, kindly people. I am positive that the vast majority of them go to heaven. Indeed, comparing them with the other Christian nations of the earth, one is forced to the conclusion that heaven will be chiefly of German manufacture. But I cannot understand how they get there. That the soul of any single German has sufficient initiative to fly up by itself and knock at St Peter's door, I cannot believe. My own opinion is that they are taken there in small companies, and passed in under the charge of a dead policeman.

Quoting Carlyle's view of Prussians – but ominously updating him, 'and it is true of the whole German nation' – that their chief virtue lies in their 'power of being drilled', Jerome now understands why Germans make excellent colonists, once given their orders and an officer, but cannot imagine them as pioneers, 'not from any lack of intelligence, but from sheer want of presumption'. The same trait explains why 'the German has been so long the soldier of Europe', for 'the military instinct has entered into his blood', a worrying prospect since German education 'would appear to instil "blind obedience to everything in buttons"'. This political message is only partly undercut by a Gilbertian coda: 'The worst that can be said about them is that they have their failings. They themselves do not know this; they consider themselves perfect, which is foolish of them. They even go so far as to think themselves superior to the Anglo-Saxon: this is incomprehensible. One feels they must be pretending.'[27]

Three Men on the Bummel was reviewed coolly in Britain. The *Spectator* welcomed 'good-humoured satires of German docility', and the *Manchester Guardian*, acknowledging that 'there are certain aspects of German life that lend themselves very readily to caricature', thought Jerome had 'given a very humorous picture of some of those little peculiarities which attract most easily the foreigner's attention in Germany'. These were lukewarm plaudits, but the book nevertheless seems to have sold rather well, as the sequel to *Three Men in a Boat* was bound to have done.[28] In Germany, though, the book was a success which reinforced Jerome's growing reputation; it was republished by Tauchnitz and adopted as an English-language reader for German schools. Not everyone welcomed that decision, one reviewer arguing that although the book would 'undoubtedly find enthusiastic friends . . . schools could well and truly do without this text'. Others, even among its critics, conceded that Jerome was a friend of Germany giving an honest opinion. Heinrich Schmitz thought it 'of interest to learn of the opinion of a foreign author who is so familiar with our conditions in Germany and who has learned to love and respect the Germans to such an extent as Jerome'. Kurt Schladebach suggested that Jerome 'knows our characteristics quite well', even if he also exaggerated for effect. 'Hence, if we disregard certain exaggerations by the author, we can only be pleased with his judgement that is so very flattering for us.'[29]

When visiting Berlin the author found that a Jerome club had been founded, and in Dresden he received a message of congratulations from King Albert of Saxony. Several of his plays now had German productions, and there was renewed interest in his prose; a Swedish linguistics specialist who in 1911 examined the Jerome's works was able to find a dozen titles available in German editions. By 1930, the second German edition of *Three Men in a Boat* (1912) had sold eighty thousand copies. English humour, 'generally not received with particular warmth in Germany', thought Anselm Schlösser, had become primarily known through Jerome, whose works had received by 1937 fourteen new translations into German, two new editions of old translations and ten reprints. As a Dresden resident, he made many German friends – one of whom delivered tributes to him on German radio when he died in 1927. Although his autobiography recalls 'a kindly, simple folk, the Saxons', he also describes a visit from the Kaiser for military manoeuvres during which Wilhelm had unceremoniously had a private citizen's door battered down at 5 a.m. so that he could get a better view from upstairs, the owner and his wife being in bed at the time. 'Both were furiously indignant, but had to lie there until it pleased the Kaiser to stamp out again, without so much as an apology. He must have always been a tactless fool.' He also found that closer familiarity with 'the *Mensur* and all its bloody paraphernalia' made him even more hostile to duelling. When in Freiburg, he tried to introduce the students to soccer, but discouragingly discovered that German women preferred boyfriends who excelled in the court of honour and displayed its badges on scarred faces.[30]

Despite the pervasiveness of patronising or hostile stereotypes, the nineteenth century was also a period in which Germany became a country generally admired by British intellectuals. Indeed, in certain circles there was a veritable love affair with things German, reacting against traditional Francophilia that had never recovered from the Revolution, the Terror and the Napoleonic Wars. Though the early works of Schiller and Goethe made some impact on Britain in the late eighteenth century, the process effectively began with Madame de Staël, and was given force and continuity by Carlyle and Coleridge, Dickens and George Eliot, Matthew and Thomas Arnold. Germaine de Staël's book *De L'Allemagne* had been written in France as a deliberate provocation of Napoleon by a Swiss *femme fatale* who well understood that a preference for Germany would not go down well with the Emperor. Napoleon promptly banned it and tried to have the manuscript destroyed, but de Staël escaped with her copy, so the book was first published in London in 1813, where it made quite an impact. German Romanticism had previously been noted in only a disparate fashion, but *De L'Allemagne* proclaimed a whole system of intellectual thought to have come forth, and represented that German ferment as the wave of the future. Germany became the land of *Dichter und Denker* at exactly the moment when Germany was a British military ally of consequence. As Byron's poet Don Juan notes when touring Europe,

In Spain he'd make a ballad or romance on
The last war – much the same in Portugal;
In Germany, the Pegasus he'd prance on
Would be old Goethe's (see de Staël).

Key German texts, rarely translated into English in the previous generation, now began to pour from British presses, and the impact spread right across the country: admirers of German culture were as likely to be found in Edinburgh, Manchester or Norwich as in London, while German concepts increasingly appeared in English usage. The word 'philistine' as the ultimate opponent of art, soon a key concept for Matthew Arnold when discussing culture and its enemies, was first noted in Britain in 1827, and derived from *philister*, as used in German universities. In the same year, so great was the public's appetite for things distinctively German, six different anthologies of *Grimm's Fairy Tales* were published – incidentally reinforcing those stereotypes of Germans as innocents from the woods and forests, closer to Anglo-Saxon roots than the British, as Sir Walter Scott suggested when commending one of the translators on his work. The *Edinburgh Review* pointed out even in 1816 how remarkable was this change:

> About five and twenty years ago, all we knew about Germany was that it was a vast tract of country, overrun with Hussars and Classical Editors; and that if you went there, you would see a great tun in Heidelberg; and be regaled with excellent old hock and Westphalian hams . . . At that time, we had never seen a German name affixed to any other species of writing than a Treaty, by which some Serene Highness or other had sold us so many head of soldiers.

Now Klopstock was hailed as Germany's Milton, Goethe as the German Shakespeare and Schiller as a contemporary Homer. A sight-seer wrote in 1856 that 'it is something to see with one's bodily eyes the very table and desk and inkstand in which, and by which, emerged in material form, the *Wallenstein*, the *William Tell*, and those other noble productions which will live to delight mankind to the end of time'. The fact that Madame de Staël had not understood German Romanticism very well, and had little personal sympathy when she did, is beside the point: her book was timely and opportune, and the British ready for it. By 1830, Thackeray could note when visiting Weimar that 'old Goethe' acknowledged his fame in Britain with occasional tea parties for visiting British intellectuals, a favour not shown to other nationalities. (Goethe wrote in 1829 that 'no other nations plague me so much with visitors . . . as the English', though the reference to tea suggests that he accommodated himself to their presence.) At first the 'discovery' of Germany was limited to literature – except that German music was already well known – but soon German history-writing and documentary research methods, theology, science, classical studies and philosophy achieved equivalent respect, interrelated as much as separate achievements. Thomas de Quincey thought that 'German literature is at this time beyond all question, for science and philosophy properly so-called, the wealthiest in the world. It is a mine of riches.'[31]

Thomas Carlyle's first broad publication on German culture came in 1827, though he had written a life of Schiller two years earlier. In the preface to this anthology of 'German Romance', he warned his readers that these were German tales, and should not be judged as if they were written in English by British writers, but 'their Germanhood I have all along regarded as a quality, not as a fault'. As for learning German and delving more deeply into the culture, this was 'little more than a bugbear[:] to judge from the signs of the times this general diffusion of German among us seems a consummation not far distant'. A couple of years later, the Brontës' library at Haworth contained numerous German books, both in English translations and in the original German, while by mid-century legions of German governesses who helped bring up the children of the wealthier British ensured a yet wider permeation of the language. Carlyle's interest in Germany had been awakened by reading *De L'Allemagne*, but he had to learn the language for access to a full range of German writing, a process he then successfully recommended to others. Telling one friend to persist in his studies, for 'these people have some muscle in their frames', he added a fervent 'wish that Goethe was my countryman, I wish – O how I wish – he were my friend'. At first publishers did not share his enthusiasm for 'German mysticism', or believe that the public shared it either, but Carlyle persisted, and as his own influence grew, his ability to publish on German topics expanded along with his readership. As the tone of that letter suggests, Carlyle had surrendered body and soul to Goethe and his friends, finding their belief in instinct, patriotism and faith a powerful attraction as his own Calvinist convictions waned and as he was increasingly repelled by the rationalism associated with France: Richter's philosophy, he explained, sprang not 'from the forum or the laboratory, but from the depths of the human spirit'. How irrational was this leap of faith is revealed by Carlyle's response to Germany itself: when travelling there to conduct research on Frederick the Great, he found Germany less enthralling than he had anticipated, for 'the sight of actual Germans has hurt poor Fritz very much in my mind'. Though liberal thinkers like John Stuart Mill were critical of Carlyle's surrender, many nineteenth-century Britons followed his path, their own crises of belief matched by a drift towards conservatism, and by admiration for Germany rather than France: when the Duke of Saxe-Weimar asked Carlyle why German literature was not even more studied in Britain, he responded that it was 'because of our sulky, radical temper'. Carlyle was naturally ecstatic when in due course he made personal contact with Goethe, received his praise as a writer who understood German thought, and even managed to use him as a referee when applying for a chair at St Andrews (though he still did not get the job).[32]

It would be hard to exaggerate the significance of Carlyle in shaping perceptions of Germany in Britain, where he had a huge readership, and was accorded the status of a sage, a role he had deliberately carved out for himself. According to the critic R. H. Hutton, 'for many years before his death, Carlyle was to England what his great hero, Goethe, long was to Germany – the aged seer whose personal judgements on men and things were eagerly sought after, and eagerly chronicled and retailed'. As a writer, nobody – except Dickens and the moralist Samuel Smiles – could compete with him for sheer breadth of readership. The *Spectator* concluded, when his *Frederick the Great* began to appear and sold out several editions, that 'their appearance is not only the event of the publishing season, but is of lasting literary moment. All that Mr Carlyle writes at once takes its place among our standard English literature.' The same book prompted John Ruskin to call Carlyle the greatest historian since Tacitus (who had taken a rather more negative view of Germans). With

Frederick the Great, he achieved almost equal fame in Germany itself, fame that lasted surprisingly well, though not always in a positive manner: he received honours from German governments, but his celebration of hero-worship and the role of great men was later attacked as an intellectual ancestor of fascism – even though Marx learned from him too, as an Anglo-German model for indignant rhetoric. Much of this claimed linkage was nonsense, but lectures he gave in London in 1837 did contain references to Germans as 'the only true European people' – Britons being included in the master race by Anglo-Saxon descent, a people who 'have never been subdued, but been themselves by far the greatest conquerors of the world'; it was 'pretty clear that, in the progress of time, they must either occupy or hold rule over the greater portion of the earth'. This was no more 'fascist' in a twentieth-century sense than Wagner's prose writings, but such observations do explain why Hitler had Goebbels read *Frederick the Great* to him as the Red Army approached Berlin in 1945. Elizabeth Gaskell, for all her understanding of the Teutonic heritage of England, thought Carlyle's Germanic worship of the hero figure 'a poor, unchristian heroism, whose manifestation consists of injury to others'.[33]

It would be tedious to trace German influences on the mindsets of one Victorian after another, but Carlyle's Germanophilia should be placed in a broader context. Samuel Taylor Coleridge was another who learned German and visited Germany as a deliberate self-education in contemporary thought, a course that no Georgian poet would have considered for a moment; having then discovered Schiller's verse plays, he rhetorically asked Southey 'who is this Schiller, this convulsor of the heart . . .? I tremble like an aspen leaf . . . Why have we ever considered Milton sublime?' His reaction, like Wordsworth's and Southey's, was to attempt Schillerian historical drama himself, with respectable results. Time brought greater detachment, and he later observed with the eye of a professional poet that Schiller's verse 'moved no better than a fly in a glue bottle', using this even as the peg on which to hang a general reflection on underlying stereotypes: 'there is a nimiety, a too-muchness in all Germans. It is the national fault.' Nevertheless, when asked late in life from whence his philosophy came, he explained that all would be clear to anyone who read Kant and Fichte, for 'then you will trace, or if you are on the hunt, track me'. A similar heritage from German thought, in this case more theological than philosophical, can be seen in Thomas Arnold, and in a broader group of 'Germano-Coleridgeans'. At Oxford, German thinking entered into common discourse through the reading of Hegel and German theologians by Balliol's formidable Benjamin Jowett, and Hegelianism then enjoyed a broad and lasting popularity. William Hastie, introducing a history of German theology, argued in 1889 that German advances in the field had meant that British theologians had 'had to go to school again'; teachers in both Anglican and nonconformist colleges went to Germany with just that intention. For the influential cultural critic Matthew Arnold, there was a deep, pervading influence from Goethe, while his study of Prussian schools was influential in British educational reform.[34]

The popularity of German culture among intellectuals was such that it influenced both what was done in British domestic reform and the reputation it acquired. The creator of the Victorian Poor Law, Edwin Chadwick, was thought a 'Prussian' public administrator, since he both instituted a regime noted for systematic thoroughness and imposed within it a deliberately harsh life for inmates of workhouses. When a new university was proposed for London in the 1820s, so allowing nonconformists to evade the Anglican-only admissions policy of Oxford and Cambridge, the opportunity was also taken to create a modern institution, where the staff would actually teach and conduct research, along the lines that Alexander von Humboldt had developed in Berlin. University College came to be known not only as the 'Godless institution in Gower Street', but as the 'German' university, though it did not differ much from earlier Scottish practice. Hoping itself to avoid such progressive reform, Cambridge in due course elected Prince Albert as its chancellor, reasoning that a man who had to be non-political as the Queen's consort could hardly be 'political' in other roles. It found to its alarm – and great benefit – that he was as thorough a 'German' when modernising the university as any chancellor could have been. Germany viewed as 'modern' was a very different perception from the one brought back by travellers, but this opinion increasingly came to the fore as a key difference between the two countries; as Chancellor at Cambridge, Albert expressed amazement when the Vice-Chancellor argued that at least a century should pass before recent scientific discoveries were incorporated into the curriculum.[35]

Just what all this amounted to in terms of British perceptions of Germany is indicated in public lectures run by the University of Manchester in 1911. They were published in 1912 as *Germany in the Nineteenth Century* and twice reprinted to satisfy popular demand. After lectures on political and economic history, and explorations of overall intellectual and cultural life, the final three lectures covered theology, philosophy and music, each in awed tones. As the editor, the medieval historian T. F. Tout, explained, 'the student of Philosophy, or of Theology, who should neglect what Germany effected in these domains, virtually turns his back upon the Nineteenth Century itself. Of her music it would be superfluous to speak.' The lecturer on theology thought of Schleiermacher's *Speeches on Religion* that 'beyond any book published, it has moulded and stimulated men's thoughts on religion', and concluded that 'our own theology, where it has not been too deeply limited by insularity to learn from Germany, has in the past greatly profited by its teaching. It might profit very much more.' The lecturer on philosophy spoke in glowing terms of the dominance of German thought in his field, notably of Hegel and Kant, as did the specialist in music: Beethoven had placed Germany 'highest among musical nations', and showed that the symphony was 'peculiarly suited to the German temperament, since it demands besides inventive genius and imagination a sense of order and power of organisation – qualities in which Germans have ever excelled'. Wagner was the greatest creative genius of the second half of the century, as Beethoven had been in the first, but 'there is not one branch of music in which the Germans did not assume the lead' and retain it 'to the present day'. The entire series of lectures was an act of homage to German culture, and at times a process of British abasement.[36]

In no field was Germany admired more than in music, one area at least in which British self-confidence barely existed before the 1890s; despite multifarious concerts, festivals and amateur choral activity, Britain was widely said to be a *Land ohne Musik*, and it was no accident that this was expressed in German. Handel was considered a sort of honorary Englishman, in that he was naturalised and lived for forty years in London, but since he was a German economic migrant who came to London to put on Italian operas, Britain had produced no composer with a European reputation for two centuries. Handel's successor as London's most popular opera composer was another German, J. C. Bach; Angliciscd as 'John Christian', he was actually Johann Kristian, son of Johann Sebastian. Handel himself put his British counterparts in the shade, winning both royal patronage and a bourgeois audience, while the 'British' tradition of choral singing that he was supposed to have bequeathed was truly an international phenomenon. Visiting Germans felt that famous English provincial choirs concentrated more on volume than accuracy: well into the twentieth century it was the boast of the Huddersfield Choral Society that if it was not the best choir in the world then it was at least the loudest. The celebrity of German composer–conductors when they visited London – Haydn, Weber, Mendelssohn, Wagner – illustrates that sense of Britain being on the margin of the continent's musical life, as did London concert programmes, where both popular and elite performances were stuffed with German compositions. It was Beethoven and Mozart symphonies that Prince Albert and Queen Victoria played together as piano duets in the early years of their marriage, as the Prince strove to educate his wife's taste; after his death she tried hard but still preferred Gilbert and Sullivan. The Royal Philharmonic Society organised its programmes around works by Haydn, Mozart, Beethoven and Mendelssohn, and when the 'classical Monday pops' started in 1859, sixty-seven out of seventy-seven items played in the first season were by Germans or Austrians (and even that counts Handel as 'British'). In the thousand concerts staged over the next forty years, Bach, Beethoven, Spohr, Schubert and Mozart were joined in these popular programmes by Brahms and Wagner, with German/Austrian composers providing two-thirds of the works, even in the 1880s when a British musical revival began. London and the other major cities provided the greatest European market for the consumption of music, hence repeated visits by European composers and the readiness of Beethoven and Haydn to set Scottish folksongs for London publishers, but it was well down the league in respect of production. There were many German conductors and orchestral players in Britain, some of whom were, like Mendelssohn, critical in raising standards of performance, while August Manns at the Crystal Palace and Charles Hallé in Manchester were among the major impresarios. (Though, oddly, the Westphalian Carl Halle became the French-sounding Charles Hallé somewhere along the way, Lancastrians anyway pronounced him 'Hally'.) Such British composers as struggled through into concert and opera programmes were painfully indebted to German examples, since most ambitious British composers went to Germany to study, as did Arthur Sullivan with Mendelssohn in Leipzig.[37]

Nothing characterised British dependence on Germany more than the impacts of Mendelssohn and later of the very different Richard Wagner. Mendelssohn first visited in 1829, and was by 1837 already on his fourth extended tour of duty. So great was his appeal that musicologists still debate amid an aura of wounded national pride whether that influence was beneficial. Apart from his being rapidly taken up by the musical establishment, he was more widely popular, for example playing the organ to general acclaim at both Westminster Abbey and St Paul's Cathedral. He returned the compliment with works on British themes, notably the 'Scotch' Symphony and the 'Fingal's Cave' Overture (being especially popular in Scotland); he also composed in London a more Germanic work, the 'Reformation' Symphony, though this would at the time have been seen as involving the Protestant tradition that Britain also celebrated. In due course Mendelssohn came under attack by George Bernard Shaw for entrenching the oratorio at the core of British music-making, through the extreme popularity of his *St Paul* (1837) and *Elijah* (1846), both first performed in English in Birmingham; there were no great British symphonists or opera composers, Shaw argued, because they were too mired in religiosity and the annual round of commissions from choral festivals in the Midlands and North. It was though as a 'perfect Wagnerite' that Shaw attacked Mendelssohn, in the name of another German composer's more 'modern' approach to art. Wagner's operas never achieved the breadth of success that Mendelssohn had enjoyed, but orchestral excerpts were hits in Britain from early on, popularised by the great man's own concerts in London, while among those who took to the operas depth of devotion made up for lack of numbers. Wagner's music dramas were first played in Britain in the 1870s in Italian (that being London's provincial perception of the proper language for opera), but a visiting German company staged the *Ring* cycle in German in 1882, and thereafter Wagnermania took off. His disciples were soon writing indignantly to the musical press whenever a Wagner production departed by a scintilla from the Master's stage directions, unimpressed even by the 'perfect Wagnerite' Shaw, who assured readers that uncritical slavishness was a recipe for certain artistic decline. A Wagner society was formed in London in 1884, only a year after the composer's death, and a quarterly magazine, *The Meister*, launched in 1888, under the zealous editorship of a *Times* leader-writer, William Ashton Ellis. Its aim, he proclaimed, was to build bridges: German Wagnerians 'feel themselves at one . . . with those English thinkers who like Thomas Carlyle recognised the bond of union with the master-minds of Germany'. The journal would 'show the English-speaking world the many aspects of the genius of the departed Master', and carry Wagner's 'true faith . . . into ever-widening circles'. No doubt some members joined mainly to get tickets for the Bayreuth Festival, but most did so to carry the faith and support such projects as the translation into English of all Wagner's prose works. By 1890, even members of the distant Lancaster Philosophical Society were hearing an address on Wagner by a true believer who assured them that this was a European composer (not just a German), since he drew on Celtic and Scandinavian as well as Teutonic myth for his plots. Bayreuth had become a major international occasion each year, but was set amid the 'real Germany', in the heart of the best country-side; only Germans could play Wagner properly (even German bands 'rising to the occasion' when playing Wagner outside cafés). Was Wagner, he rhetorically asked his audience, 'the crowning point of musical art', with only decadence and decay to come? German music – and German culture more broadly – thus played its part alongside industry and commerce in shifting perceptions of Germany from a backward, underdeveloped country in the mid-eighteenth century to the epitome of the 'modern' by the end of the nineteenth. With the arrival of Richard Strauss and Gustav Mahler, British audiences began to wonder indeed whether German music had possibly become *too* modern, as they would do for most of the next century.[38]

One influence in the importation of German music into Victorian Britain was Prince Albert of Saxe-Coburg, the German prince who married Queen Victoria in 1840. Albert was a patron of Mendelssohn's music and wrote creditable music of his own in imitation of Mendelssohn's style; he also arranged the first British performances of

Schubert's Ninth Symphony and Wagner's *Lohengrin* (in the royal drawing room at Windsor). The marriage of Victoria and Albert epitomised the marriage of cultures, the view that Germany was simply not as foreign a country as France or Russia. There was some continuity here, for although George III had repatriated the monarchy and reaped advantages in popularity, he had never repatriated the family; no British sovereign between 1714 and 1901 was married to any consort except a German. As a result, elements of anti-German feeling about the monarchy also continued, beneath the surface for the most part under George III, more audible under his sons. Despite the ending of the direct link with Hanover in 1837, since Victoria could not as a woman succeed to a German throne, the early Victorian court was dominated by the Queen's German mother and her German governess, Victoria's ear ever open to advice from Baron Stockmar of Hanover and Uncle Leopold, the Hanoverian prince now reigning in Belgium. Neither government nor Parliament received the news that Victoria would marry a German with much enthusiasm. Albert was unlucky here, for his arrival coincided like George I's with a period of bitter party strife, and he was therefore attacked by Tories as a surrogate for the staunchly Whig Victoria, despite his own moderate sentiments: his proposed financial allowance was reduced by Tory pressure in Parliament which the Whigs dared not resist, and he was denied a proper title, while doggerel poets assailed the foreigner with old jokes: 'He comes to take, for better or for worse,/England's fat Queen, and England's fatter purse.' There were also disputes about Germans on the Prince's staff and his correspondence with German relations. In due course, though he had by then moderated the Queen's Whiggishness and accommodated both himself and her to a Conservative government, his determination to back Peel during the Corn Law crisis of 1846, even to the extent of sitting in the Commons gallery to demonstrate royal support, resulted in stern rebukes of foreign interference from Tories opposed to their own leader. When in 1853 he seemed to be obstructing Palmerston's warlike policy towards Russia, the press really tore into him, suggesting comparisons with historical favourites and pretenders like Piers Gaveston and Perkin Warbeck. There were widespread enough rumours that he would soon be arrested to produce an expectant crowd on Tower Hill, staring hopefully towards Traitors' Gate.[39]

Albert's tact and good judgement disarmed such criticisms over the years, and in 1857 he was finally made 'Prince Consort', the title suspiciously denied him for years past. He had though to strive continuously to avoid showing favouritism to Germans as a patron of the arts, and when disagreeing with Palmerston over foreign policy had to explain that he was not covertly pursuing the interests of Coburg. All this was more just than it may have seemed, for at heart he remained a German prince living in Britain, and was widely thought of that way, even after his early death made him 'Albert the Good'. At home Victoria and Albert spoke German, and his preference was for German rather than British newspapers; their family Christmas in 1844 seemed to the Prince 'German and *gemütlich*'. It is a myth that the Victorian Christmas was imported from Germany, though Albert did help popularise the German *Tannenbaum* already introduced by Victoria's German grandmother. Insistence on the Anglo-Saxon origins of Christmas revelries fitted nicely with the alleged racial character of the people, Yuletide being seen as essentially 'Teutonic', as was drinking too much over the festive season. Albert's rapprochement with Peel included correspondence about the *Nibelungenlied*, an unlikely topic of shared interest. One aspect of his alleged 'Germanness' that contributed largely to the whole mood of the court was moral earnestness, for he always approached his writing desk as if it were a pulpit, according to one observer; his descendant the Duke of Gloucester suggested in 1980 that 'to read of Prince Albert's life is like hearing a well-constructed but abrasive Sunday sermon'. What came later to be called 'Victorian values' owed more to Albert than Victoria, who in her youth at least was rather more light-hearted than her later 'we are not amused' image suggested: Wellington told the diarist Charles Greville in 1841 that it was 'the Prince who cared about spotless character (the queen not caring a straw about it)', like her uncle George IV and her son Edward VII. Albert himself thought the British aristocracy profligate and decadent, finding more virtue in the middle class, businessmen and craft-workers, and it was largely in deference to his sacred memory that Victoria became so stiffly moral as a widow.[40]

When Albert was directly involved in political matters, he was apt once again to run into assumptions that his efforts were 'German', or at least un-English, as he found when trying to modernise the

University of Cambridge. His effort to bring some system into the management of the royal household was long overdue, yet seemed to some of those whose comfortable lives were disturbed to exemplify a German fascination with efficiency and order – as compared with British pragmatism and corruption. Even the Queen decided that when once engaged on a subject 'Albert becomes a *terrible* man of business'. When he took up military reform, suggestions that he was introducing foreign practices were more pointed. *Punch* regularly lampooned him for having so great an interest in the army's uniforms, which it attributed to his German birth, likewise attempts to modernise its helmets; and when he sought during the Crimean War to enlarge the militia, Richard Cobden thought 'Prince Albert's rifle mania . . . mere Germanism', though Albert was actually urging voluntary enlistment, in direct opposition to the Prussian model. On the same basis, the seriousness with which he took music was regarded as 'true to the German type of race. He loved music with all a German's heart' (as an obituary put it). His accent and appearance seemed un-British, though, thought *The Economist*'s Walter Bagehot, 'his face was lit up by more than the mere manly virility which characterises the average German'. More negatively, for Lytton Strachey Albert resembled 'a foreign tenor'. His devotion to the Highlands around Balmoral was attributed to the German's love for mountainous scenery, his wearing of the tartan just another fad for uniforms. However often he claimed to have become one with the British, as when addressing the Royal Agricultural Society in 1848 as 'we agriculturalists of England', this rarely carried conviction in a man whose clothes and boots were German in style and who openly declared that no British tailor could cut a decent jacket.[41]

In Britain's relationship with the emerging German state, Albert's influence and legacy were ambivalent. He was a scion of the House of Coburg and a devoted constitutionalist, so apparently on the side of progress; as Germany drifted towards the 1848 revolutions he urged the King of Prussia to remember that the day had gone when monarchs could ignore the views of their people. Albert's own primary political objective, though, was German unity, and he was quite capable of expressing opinions of the type that made German nationalists an object of suspicion to their neighbours, as when he thought the Poles 'as little deserving of sympathy as the Irish'. Lord Aberdeen, who as Foreign Secretary and Prime Minister worked closely with Albert, thought that his only real weakness was his 'violent and incorrigible German unionism', and his failure to grasp that not all Britons shared that aspiration, but then Albert was unable to see British and German interests as being different anyway. He explained German neutrality in the Crimean War with the observation that 'if there were a Germany and a German sovereign in Berlin, it could never have happened'. As this suggests, he was realistic enough to expect German unification under Prussian leadership, but although he died before Bismarck embarked on that process through 'blood and iron', the previous history of Prussia did not provide much hope of constitutional monarchy arriving through a Prussian-led German empire. Nor did Albert's own idea of constitutional monarchy necessarily correspond to the British model; he explained on one occasion that the monarch should be a sort of permanent chairman of the cabinet, not quite Bagehot's idea in 1867 in *The English Constitution*. It was not always a compliment when British politicians suggested that 'he governs us in everything', while Disraeli mischievously suggested that if Albert had lived he would have reintroduced absolute monarchy.[42]

All this involved divided loyalties, beautifully illustrated in the marriage alliance that Victoria and Albert fostered between their eldest daughter and the heir of Prussia. Negotiations for the marriage became heated when in 1858 the Prussian royal family claimed that the marriage must take place in Berlin: Victoria wrote imperiously that this was 'too *absurd*', for 'it is not *every* day that one marries the eldest daughter of the Queen of England!' Nevertheless, even though important sections of opinion were hostile (led by *The Times* with its sneering question 'what is the King of Prussia to us?') the match was generally popular, and a verse was added to the national anthem to mark the occasion: 'God Bless our Prince and Bride,/God keep their lands Allied'. Thereafter there were exaggerated hopes that the marriage would harmonise the two countries' interests, while for English Vicky and Prussian Fritz, devoted as each was to Albert's teachings and Victoria's advice, the conflict was even greater. Suspected of being under the influence of his British bride, Crown Prince Frederick had constantly to confirm his Prussian, soldierly credentials, while Vicky found to her horror that even family letters were intercepted by the spies routinely infiltrated into their household. That same clash of political cultures was reflected in Prussian ministers' regular complaints that British police would neither pursue nor prosecute German socialists who had taken refuge in London, from whence they plotted to overthrow German governments. British ministers explained that this was simply a characteristic of freedom in Britain, and the exiles agreed, regarding Britain as a country where liberty meant more than it did in Germany; even for communists like Engels, Britain was 'the least unfree country' in the world. Prince Albert, visiting the happy couple in Berlin, had the impression of a country in 'perpetual uniform', wholly 'involved in playing at soldiers'. A few years later, he wrote to the King of Belgium that 'there exists a great Junker and bureaucrats' party in Prussia', and 'the King himself belongs to this party'. Nevertheless, Albert, until his death, and to an extent Victoria afterwards, never doubted that they had a special relationship with Prussia, and that once Fritz and Vicky became King and Queen all would be well.[43]

This placed too great a burden on Fritz's frail shoulders; he missed by fatal hesitation his one chance (if it ever existed) to halt the rise of Bismarck and the adoption of expansionist policies, and was kept waiting so long for the crown that his health could not stand the strain when he eventually succeeded, in a reign that lasted only a few weeks. Rather than the Crown Prince, 'that wretched B' (as Victoria dubbed Bismarck) therefore emerged as the key figure in the 1860s, and neither the British government nor the Anglo-German monarchy had enough leverage to retard his policies. The first sign was the signal defeat of Palmerston's foreign policy over the absorption of Schleswig-Holstein into Germany in 1863–5, at the expense of Denmark, to whose royal house the Prince of Wales was allied by marriage. Victoria could really not see what all the fuss was about, and strongly opposed military threats against 'our *natural* old allies . . . *Why* should we fear Germany's possessing Holstein? Germany is not likely ever to go against us; the French and Russian navies are the only ones we need ever fear.' This crisis was though the prelude to Prussian military victories over Austria and France which established a German empire in 1871 on Bismarckian terms. The defeat of Austria resulted in the destruction of Hanover's independence, and thus came close to British dynastic interests; royal disapproval was indicated when the fountain triumphantly installed at Windsor as a Prussian gift was quietly shoved off to Balmoral. But this was nothing compared to the tilt of opinion that took place when Prussia defeated France in 1870–1, humiliating the defeated foe by proclaiming the new German Empire at Versailles, from where two centuries earlier Louis XIV had planned his domination of Europe. At first British opinion strongly favoured Prussia, largely because of traditional dislike of France, and Waterloo was again much mentioned. Quick Prussian victories, however, tended to evoke sympathy for France: Napoleon III's empress went into British exile, imported British munitions helped the French continue the war, and once formal operations by the Emperor's army were replaced by republican guerrilla warfare, British volunteers fought in the French forces. Traditional British fear of any over-dominant power in Europe was reasserting itself.[44]

Disraeli thought Prussia's victory 'a greater political event than the French Revolution . . . The balance of power has been entirely destroyed, and the country that suffers most . . . is England.' The war of 1870–1 jolted then the Germanophiles' cosy assumptions. Carlyle might confidently assert that Prussian victory over France was 'the most beneficial thing that had been in the universe since he had been in it', a vindication of 'noble, patient, deep, pious and solid Germany' over 'vapouring, vainglorious, gesticulating, quarrelsome, restless and over-sensitive France', but even he worried that other Britons saw things differently. Queen Victoria worried too about the effect the Prussian victory seemed to be having on Britain: she and her court ladies had begun the war by sending to the German wounded bandages they made personally. Reminding her daughter Vicky, as the Germans neared the French capital, that 'the English are very fond of Paris', she counselled restraint, and when a German bombardment began she reported that 'to my despair the feeling is becoming more and more bitter here against the Prussians'. Vicky responded with a spirited defence of her husband's country and asserted that criticism was 'unjust', but her mother merely reiterated concern about British opinion:

To see the enmity growing up between the two nations – which I am bound to say began first in Prussia, and was most unjust and was fomented and encouraged by Bismarck – is a great sorrow and anxiety to me – and I cannot allow myself to be separated from my own people. For it is, alas! the people, who from being very German up to three months ago are now very French!

Such fears were serious but short-lived, for when the Franco-Prussian War had faded from immediate memory, Britain still had numerous colonial disputes festering with France but hardly any areas of conflict with Germany. As long as Imperial Germany stayed mainly out of the dash for colonies and limited her naval ambitions, there would be no reason for Britain to prefer France to Germany; while he retained the dominant position in Germany, Bismarck recognised that, saying in the Reichstag in 1884 that 'on no account do I want to act rashly towards a Government and a country with which we have such close and friendly ties and risk prompting a conflict with the English'. Despite the shocks administered to it in 1864–71, the assumption of a natural affinity between Britain and Germany was therefore re-established during the 1870s. Britain had diplomatic disputes with Germany in those years, but also with France and Russia, and in 1878 it was collective action by Britain and Germany at the Congress of Berlin that halted Russian expansion into the Balkans without war – that joint action whose absence Prince Albert had bemoaned as bringing war to the Crimea in 1854. To an extent, then, normal service was quickly resumed after 1871, especially at the dynastic level. During the heat of war fever, the Queen sensed the time not right for another German marriage, sadly noting that 'small foreign princes are very unpopular here'; her private secretary more bluntly advised that it was 'no use talking now of this or that Seidlitz Stinkinger. They are out of the question.' Yet in 1873 the royal family celebrated its seventh Anglo-German marriage of the reign, between Victoria's third son and Princess Louise of Prussia. There was some justice in the Foreign Secretary's private remark in 1876, that 'the royal family, being half-German, half-English by connection, think of the two countries as inseparably connected, and do not understand how those who are only German or English fail to see the relations between them in that light'. That was certainly the view of the radical journalist Henry Labouchere during the 1871 siege of Paris. 'Labby' thought Prussians 'saints' compared to Frenchmen: they had 'every sort of excellence', being 'honest, sober, hard-working, well-instructed, brave, good sons, husbands and fathers'. However, they ruined it all by being 'quite insupportable'.

> Laugh at the French, abuse them as one may, one cannot help liking them. Admire, respect the Prussians as one may, it is impossible to help disliking them . . . The only Prussian I ever knew who was an agreeable man was Bismarck. All others with whom I have been thrown — and I have lived for years in Germany — were as proud as Scotchmen, cold as New Englanders, and touchy as only Prussians can be. I once had a friend among them. His name was Buckenbrock. Inadvertently I called him Butterbrod. We have never spoken since.[45]

By the 1870s, a different concern about Germany was anyway being expressed, economic rather than political, as British confidence began to falter. Even in the 1830s, Germany's *Zollverein* had been regarded as inimical to the interests of free-trade Britain; the Privy Council's trade committee thought it 'an alliance conceived in a spirit of hostility to British industry and British commerce', much as Napoleon's 'continental system' had been, and as Germany's economic aims in the Great War would also appear. In 1841 the Foreign Office was concerned about 'the extent and perfection that has for some years been progressing in the manufactures of Germany'. Yet it was during the 1850s and 1860s, just as Germany was achieving unification, that its industrial revolution took off, and it was during the next four decades that the new Imperial Germany achieved an economic miracle of growth in population, urbanisation, industrialisation, production and commerce, making her the wonder of Europe: 'apprehensions of foreign competition . . . haunt us', lamented *The Times* in 1876, while three years later MPs were arguing in the Commons that Germany's 'excessive' tariffs were ruining the British economy. The German population, only ten million more than the British in 1871, was twenty million larger by 1913. This constituted a vital resource at the onset of a war in which casualties would be reckoned in the hundreds of thousands; in 1872 the British army was half the size of the German, but by 1914 under a third. In a key war commodity, British steel output was almost double that of Germany in 1880, but under half by 1913. Germany was thus outperforming Britain in economic growth, and especially in the most 'modern' products that characterised the 'second industrial revolution' of the last years of the nineteenth century: electrical goods, machine tools, optics and chemicals, each of which had military significance in modern warfare. In the short term, however, it was economic rather than military rivalry that seemed to matter most, it still being assumed that Britain and Germany need never fight: the volume of German exports, about half of Britain's in 1870, had caught up to near equality in 1914. As the economist J. M. Keynes wrote in 1919, in the years before the Great War, 'from being agricultural and mainly self-supporting, Germany transformed herself into a vast and complicated industrial machine'. If German culture being seen as modern confounded earlier stereotypes, so did German industrial wealth; no more would German soldiers be hired out to richer employers.[46]

Though the apprehensions of the 1870s died away when trade revived in the 1880s, worries about German economic expansion kept coming to the surface. Britain was gradually being squeezed out of European markets as every country became an industrial competitor, and was therefore increasingly dependent on her empire, to which more and more of her exports went, while Germany continued to trade well in Europe. In time, the rapid growth of Germany's ocean-going merchant fleet ensured that even the colonial market was not safe. Board of Trade reports and consular reports to the Foreign Office became increasingly pessimistic about trade rivalry with Germany, and the press too was inclined to blame slow British growth on Germany. More detached observers recognised that it had something to do with Germany's greater commitment to education, especially to the excellence of technical education there. The topic was much discussed following a royal commission report in the 1880s, one of the results being a wave of new university foundations in British industrial cities soon afterwards. A debate in the correspondence columns of *The Times* in October 1887 included complaints about the extent of German tariffs against British goods – while free-trade Britain still welcomed German products without duty – and pointed to the 'excessive' number of Germans working in the City of London, in banks and the Stock Exchange. As German industry surged ahead, Britain seemed to stand still. In 1886 a *Times* leader complained, in terms that strikingly prefigured how Germany would again be viewed in the 1960s, 'the Germans are beginning to beat us in many of the qualities which are the factors of commercial success. They are content with smaller profits; their clerks work for lower salaries; they speak all languages; they are bound by no hard and fast traditions.' The British consul in Samoa reported in 1886 that 'unless British manufacturers attack the colonial and foreign markets in the well-organised and energetic manner adopted by the Germans', they would continue to lose ground. Germany was better at providing customers with attractive credit terms and more ruthless at bullying other countries into extending commercial opportunities, while German commercial travellers never seemed to sleep: there were 3310 in Switzerland in 1894, compared to 69 from Britain and 633 Frenchmen, a fact celebrated in the German press. Germany's shift from mass-produced cheap products like the 'Dutch clocks' to be seen in Dickens' living rooms (proverbially always needing to be mended) into high-quality goods was even more threatening for the future. The British consul in Barcelona reported in 1886 that the Germans there lived 'in a style incredibly economical', some of them surviving entirely on bonuses for contracts won, while the salaried British had less motivation, were less educated technically, and seemed to live in restaurants and bars. Like the foreign sportsmen lampooned by Flanders and Swann in 1963, Germans 'argue[d] with umpires and cheer[ed] when they'[d] won,/And practise[d] beforehand, which ruin[ed] the fun.' As a result, while British complacency was often attributed to national character and history, so was German success: 'the Commercial Barbarossa is awake at last', warned *The Times* in 1898. Germans might have less 'dash' than the British, wrote an under-secretary at the Foreign Office in 1886, but 'they have a steady tenacity and habits of systematic application not less valuable in the long run'. This was James Bryce, of whom we shall here much more during the Great War.[47]

As Ernest Williams famously proclaimed in *Made in Germany* (1896), 'the industrial glory of England is departing, and England does not know it'. Yet the sensation that his book caused was short-lived, and the Colonial Secretary Joseph Chamberlain pointed out three months later that 'there is substantially no change of the slightest importance in the relative proportion of German and British trade'. As this indicates, such fears were in late Victorian times usually the temporary characteristic of periods of economic uncertainty, and a deep-rooted *Kulturpessimismus* – for only that German word will do – did not become characteristic of Britain until the Edwardian era. The Golden Jubilee of Victoria in 1887 is after all generally seen as the pinnacle of confidence in Britain as a world power, and even the Diamond Jubilee ten years later was a demonstration of the British Empire's might as well as of its fealty to an ageing matriarch. When Bismarck fell from power in 1889, having lost the goodwill of the new German Kaiser Wilhelm II, so far had he personally embodied the German bogey that few in Britain shed a tear; *Punch's* cartoon, 'Dropping the Pilot', in which the young Kaiser watches the old Junker go over the side before navigating for himself, was deservedly famous, but few who saw the original appear to have wondered whether a pilotless ship of state was a good thing for nearby shipping, and hardly anyone picked up on the significance of Germany venturing into the deep waters of *Weltpolitik* with so inexperienced a steersman. Wilhelm was the eldest son of the marriage of Fritz and Vicky, from which so much had been hoped, and had been brought up an Anglophile; Victoria could never forget that he was the only grandson who entertained real memories of Albert, or that the 'clever, dear, good little child' had been 'the great favourite of my beloved Angel'. True, she thought that Willy's treatment of his mother had been abominable, when on his accession he had seized her private papers lest they contain state secrets, but she was always ready to forgive a man who came out with such impeccably pro-British words and delighted in the uniforms of his honorary British military and naval ranks. She thought it only rather common of him to 'fish' so obviously for uniforms; others thought it rather 'German'. 'I am a good deal of an Englishman myself,' Wilhelm declared on his first official visit to Britain as Kaiser, though the strain of entertaining him had already prompted the Queen to warn the British ambassador in Berlin that 'regular annual visits are not quite desirable'.[48]

Wilhelm II's reign anyway began with a collaboration which marked the high point of Great Power partnership between Germany and Britain: following cooperation over Mediterranean issues, there was a 'colonial marriage' in 1890, when the two countries casually swapped possession of the islands of Zanzibar and Heligoland as if they were stamps. So close were relations that the German government was then conducting its foreign policy partly to strengthen the standing of the British Prime Minister, Lord Salisbury, while the Kaiser's Anglophilia had been reinforced by the warm reception he had when visiting England in 1889, when he was made an admiral of the fleet. On the British side, though Salisbury was criticised by Queen Victoria for surrendering too much in his dealings with Germany over Heligoland, newspapers generally praised the government for maintaining cordial relations with Britain's 'best friend'. The Tory *Morning Post* supported the exchange of Heligoland for Zanzibar, partly as a good deal in itself, partly because it would reinforce 'the good understanding' between Britain and 'her natural ally'. When the Kaiser next visited, *The Times* assured him that 'Germany does not excite in any class among us the slightest feeling of distrust or antipathy'.[49]

The history of British views of Germany before a military clash came over the horizon was thus a mixed one, but Britain had tended on the whole to treat Germans as more likely to be allies than enemies, partly because of the Reformation, partly because she had a more pressing enmity with France, whose colonial possessions offered more attractive prizes to be won in eighteenth-century wars than anything occupied by Germans. In the three-quarters of a century after Waterloo, despite growing travel and the appearance of a substantial German population in Britain itself, there remained a remarkable generalised ignorance on the British side: Bismarck was struck during his only visit to Britain by how few people he met had an informed understanding of Prussia, its politics, its people or its aspirations. Yet at the intellectual as well as the dynastic level profound admiration for Germany and Germans developed, and it was widely assumed in 1890 that because of race, religion and history, Germany remained the natural British ally. All that would very soon change. During Wilhelm II's Silver Jubilee in 1913, the *Daily Mail*'s Berlin correspondent summed up his reign so far: 'Twenty-five years of eventful sovereignty have brought his empire to the pinnacle of national greatness. Under his dynamic leadership the Fatherland has advanced to the front rank in the peaceful arts of commerce and trade, made herself the world's first military power and become

Britain's formidable rival for the mastery of the sea.' For all the awestruck tone of such tributes to the Second Reich, they did not by then reassure British readers, and they were not intended to, so that a mixture of fear and admiration became the cornerstone of British views during the twentieth century. If such a powerhouse was your natural ally, so much the better; but if it were not, what then? A perceptive German journalist argued in 1965, when Queen Elizabeth II visited Germany in the hope of harmonising relations that were now far more fraught than in 1890, that

> history teaches that in recent times no relations between peoples have been more deeply disturbed than that between the British and the Germans; and this precisely because there was so much sympathy, so much wooing, willingness to understand, even admiration involved on both sides. In this case the pain of disappointment corresponded to the degree of previously nurtured expectations.[50]

A jarring note in Jerome K. Jerome's autobiographical apologia for his pro-German sympathies is the phrase 'of their own creation', when applied to the German people's relationship to the 'Juggernaut' of militarism. He was not, though, far from the centre of British thought here, for throughout the twentieth century the British would generally find it impossible to decide whether Germans as a whole were responsible for German militarism. Jerome's memory as a mediator between Britain and Germany and his direct influence lingered on, largely because *Three Men on the Bummel* has been so often reprinted in the century since its publication. His intermediary role is, however, fascinatingly and more negatively nuanced in a recent poem by Gillian Bence-Jones:

> Goethe walked
> On the wild, romantic hill,
> Seeing an orderly world,
> Now the lion was caged,
> Lit softly by sweet reason,
> But he was afraid
> Of Frederick the Great's
> German over-order.

Jerome K. Jerome walked
In Germany;
Orders, cleanliness, kindness,
But he wondered:
'What if someone unpleasant
Was giving the orders?'

The hill where
Goethe walked
Became Buchenwald.[51]

2

'When will Germany strike? Who knows?': 1890–1914

In Britain's drift into antagonism with Germany, the historian continuously encounters the elusive William Le Queux, a popular writer but one whose life was as mysterious as his novels. His autobiography, *Things I Know About Kings, Celebrities and Crooks* (1923), was almost as fictional as his sensationalist writings, and David Stafford noted in 1982 that 'distant relatives to this day believe that he perished at the hands of the Bolsheviks while working as a secret agent for Winston Churchill in Soviet Russia'. Even his name was an uncertainty. One friend, remarking in 1921 that 'everyone knows William Le Queux . . . the bookstalls are always crowded with his exciting and mysterious romances', reported that he had acquired so many decorations from Allied governments that at formal dinners he was mistaken for a distinguished general. He also remembered 'coming up to town one day', before 1914, when

> a girl and her mother got into the train. The girl carried a book under her arm. When they were comfortably seated, the mother said: 'Give me that book of Le Queck's, my dear,' and the daughter replied: 'Excuse me mother, but I think you mean Le Kooks.' They appealed to me, and I said authoritatively that the proper pronunciation was 'Le Kew'; another man in the corner broke in with 'Le Kicks'.

His entry in *Who's Who* claimed in 1909 decorations from Serbia,

Montenegro, Italy and San Marino. Le Queux was San Marino's consul in Birmingham, though he never lived there or did the work, often dining out in the green and gold uniform and plumed hat of his mighty office, but otherwise 'an amiable and placid little man, who looked as if he caught the 9.15 from Ealing to the City every morning', as the *Morning Post's* obituary explained. He claimed to know all about spies, went about armed for self-protection, and may even have been a spy himself; he did not though reveal in *Who's Who* that he had had humble parents who cannot have afforded the private education he claimed. His address – changed frequently, as would any self-respecting spy – was listed as 'Villa Le Queux' in Tuscany, his interests as 'revolver practice, the study of palaeography and motoring'. He claimed to own 'a large and valuable collection of medieval manuscripts and codices', but it would have been a brave man who bought a codex certified as authentic by Le Queux. Nobody denied his capacity for work: in addition to short stories (reissued in thirty-five volumes) and a tidal wave of journalism, Le Queux published almost two hundred novels, and for his writing was usually paid twelve guineas per thousand words, which put him up with Thomas Hardy and H. G. Wells, and ahead of everyone else.[1]

Le Queux had a wide readership for his plain English prose, telling a journalist in 1904 that he had never written 'a single line that a child of twelve might not understand'. He gave even escapist thrillers reinforcement with 'facts' and 'documents' relating to the case, and sometimes graphic illustrations of familiar places in an unfamiliar light: in *The Great War in England in 1897* (1894) readers see Birmingham town hall flying the Russian flag while Cossacks carouse, a shocking image when Birmingham bestrode the British Empire in the person of Joseph Chamberlain. The title popularised the phrase 'the Great War', immediately adopted when it actually happened in 1914. In books as in life, Le Queux artfully blended fantasy with fact. When his characters boarded a train it was according to a timetable, using the right rolling stock and from the correct station, even if in Central Europe. He shamelessly flattered readers by suggesting they shared his characters' lifestyle ('You, dear reader, who have so often strolled down the Champs Elysées . . .') but managed to appeal at the same time to those for whom Paris was indeed familiar. Members of the Athenaeum argued with one another about new Le

Queux novels, and he was Queen Alexandra's favourite author, but he was popular too in the Salford slums and was among the most widely purchased authors for public libraries; a researcher in 1907 found twenty-eight Le Queux titles per library. Despite controversy over *The Invasion of 1910*, he claimed that 'my novels are at least as popular in Germany as in this country'. Yet Le Queux, 'a propagandist of almost pathological germanophobia', according to Stafford, helped to revolutionise British ideas: an Anglo-German war that seemed utterly fantastic in 1890 became inescapable in 1914.[2]

The quarter century between Kaiser Wilhelm's dismissal of Bismarck and the Great War was Le Queux's heyday, a revolutionary period in the Anglo-German relationship. The two countries began by viewing each other as best friends, and were as late as 1901 discussing a formal alliance, yet by 1914 they had become so mutually antagonistic as to embark on unlimited conflict, hoping that the other would get a historic bloody nose. The Great War then unleashed hatred that conditioned attitudes for the rest of the century. In the early twentieth century fear and suspicion dominated British views of Germany. As Le Queux's *Spies of the Kaiser* (1909) concluded: 'What will happen? When will Germany strike? WHO KNOWS?'[3]

In the early 1890s Britain had worse relations with other countries than with Germany, as colonial disputes on three continents came close to precipitating wars with France, Russia and the United States. Faced with problems in so many directions, the Colonial Secretary Joseph Chamberlain proclaimed in 1899 that 'the natural alliance is between ourselves and the great German Empire'. Kaiser Wilhelm explained not only that 'I desire to remain friendly to England', but that Britain needed his friendship, which was 'about the only one left her on the continent'. This being a great age of invasion literature, there appeared after the 1894 Franco-Russian alliance several such frightening tales as *The Sack of London in the Great French War of 1901* and Le Queux's *The Great War*. Plans to build a Channel tunnel reinforced scares, but largely because they gave *France* easier access to Britain. One author described how 'Great Britain stood face to face with France and Russia for the death-grip'.[4]

Nevertheless, during the 1890s the sense that Germany was Britain's natural ally declined, and in 1900 British readers had their first chance to read of a German invasion, T. W. Offin's *How the*

Germans Took London. German readers could explore the same fantasy in Karl Eisenhart's *Die Abrechnung mit England*. In part, the shift reflected reducing concern about Turkish decline, which had previously led Prime Minister Salisbury to work with Germany to counter French and Russian expansion; when the Anglo-German Mediterranean agreements expired in 1896, Britain chose not to renew them. By the mid-1890s, Salisbury was avoiding binding entanglement with any other power, keeping a free hand to deal with each bilaterally, as different colonial issues came to the boil, a policy nervously – or perhaps ironically – defended as 'splendid isolation'. The policy was not especially aimed against Germany, though as Germany became more interested in economic spheres of influence she joined France as a country with which Britain had too many points of friction for a continuous partnership. At precisely this time, a stridently patriotic popular press narrowed the government's room for manoeuvre in placating Germany: Heligoland could not have been ceded to Germany by 1896 without uproar in Fleet Street. Britain temporarily withdrew though from the carousel of European alliances just when Franco-Russian cooperation was giving Berlin fears of 'encirclement'. Of greater influence on deterioriating relations were changes within Germany, both politically and culturally. The 1890s, as Paul Kennedy puts it, was when radical nationalism first dominated Germany's public debate, as 'it acquired its chief characteristics: a hard-edged chauvinism, a proclamation of a cultural mission, an unwillingness to listen to arguments about diplomatic and political exigency, an open assault upon Liberal cosmopolitanism and Socialist "revolution", and a systematic sniping at the establishment itself'. The establishment adjusted to the new mood, but cannot be said to have created it, though Wilhelm II's ambition for colonies and warships was a powerful reinforcement of such currents of opinion. Kaiser and people were at one in pursuing *Weltpolitik*, even Napoleonic *Weltreich*. By 1897, the Kaiser was surrounded by new advisers committed to risky ambitions, notably Bülow as Chancellor and Tirpitz at the Admiralty. The *Daily Mail* warned in 1913 that the latter 'believes religiously in the superiority of German guns – that they will decide the issue to Germany's imperishable glory on the day when the Kaiser's Trafalgar is to be fought and won'.[5]

Increasingly, German diplomats ceased to bid for British friendship and began hoping for British setbacks, humiliations that would force Britain to ally with Germany. It was a short step from here to managing international affairs to *promote* British weakness, nowhere more than in South Africa. As the German ambassador in London reported after Wilhelm's 1895 'Kruger telegram', he had been shocked by anti-German feeling in Britain, especially by Britain's refusal to play the part expected.

> The general feeling was such – of this I have no doubt – that if the Government had lost its head, or on any ground had wished for war, it would have had the whole public behind it. The consideration that we could contribute essentially to England's difficulties in other parts of the world remained absolutely without effect upon the ignorant masses of the population. England's ostensible isolation likewise made no impression.[6]

Germans recognised an affinity with the Afrikaaner Dutch, but the discovery of gold in the Transvaal increased chances of a collision with Britain, especially after a German–Boer treaty of friendship in 1885. After Britain's clumsy 'Jameson raid' (1895), the *Neue Preußische Zeitung* proclaimed that 'Germany has considerable interests in the Transvaal which grow from year to year; it owns a blossoming colony in South West Africa which would also be affected should the Boer republic fall.' Germany was the Boers' international patron, much as Russia looked after the lesser Slavs, and a constant irritation to Britain. Britons thus viewed as purely mischievous the Kaiser congratulating Boer President Kruger after he had squashed Jameson's raid. The German ambassador in Paris thought this intervention 'a' match to set fire to the accumulation of . . . hatred', and *The Times*'s Valentine Chirol concurred: 'the German Government is . . . distinctly malevolent. I can put no other structure upon the Emperor's telegram to Kruger.' There was a press outcry, and Germans in London were personally vilified, British tolerance further strained by an anti-Jameson rally of German and Dutch socialists in Hyde Park, when the platform was stormed by a patriotic mob. The London correspondent of the *Neue Preußische Zeitung* reported that 'a particularly Jingo epidemic is currently rampant here . . . In the club and even in the street people have grabbed me by the collar and taken me to task.' There were boycotts of German goods and riots in the East End. Victoria urged her government to protect 'innocent and good German residents', but Salisbury replied that the telegram and press reactions had done 'infinite harm' to Anglo-German friendship. The *Hamburgischer Correspondent* reported unanimity in the German press, 'from the Social Democratic *Vorwärts* to the conservative *Kreuzzeitung*... we can barely recall an issue in which German public opinion in its entirety came to so unanimous and forceful a judgement of a foreign policy'. This was the zenith of German support for the Boers, it being recognised that the cost in British hostility was not worth the diplomatic candle: the Kaiser refused to receive Kruger and ensured that the Pan-German League did not welcome Boer generals to Hamburg. Yet as Anglo-Boer relations deteriorated, German consuls were rarely helpful to British interests, and when the Boer War began in 1899 Germany's government opportunistically fished in troubled waters. This again produced anger in London, even when Germany tried to be friendly, by stalling unhelpful French efforts to insist on international mediation, but then demanded 'compensation' for its trouble. A German diplomat reported that 'on no other occasion has Lord Salisbury voiced such displeasure as he evinced upon receipt of our notes on this matter'. Chamberlain observed that 'the policy of the German Empire since Bismarck has been always one of undisguised blackmail'.[7]

The Boer War occasioned a more personal breach. As a grim struggle of guerrillas, concentration camps and 'methods of barbarism' continued, Britain was widely criticised, but it was a German comparison that prompted a crisis. Chamberlain, conscious that 'Joe's war' was not going well, argued that 'we can find precedents for anything we may do in the actions of those nations that now criticise our "barbarity" and "cruelty", but whose example ... in the Franco-German War we have never even approached'. German newspapers screamed about slandered German honour, and Bülow demanded an apology, but Chamberlain was defiant: 'I withdraw nothing. I qualify nothing. I defend nothing. I do not want to give lessons to a foreign minister and I will accept none at his hands.' There was no national interest here, but Bülow responded in kind, publicly sneering at Chamberlain's 'crooked mind', and relations were never the same again. Lord Rosebery had sent his sons to school in Germany,

but they returned home 'rabid anti-Germans', having experienced
anti-British feeling personally. The Athenaeum exhibited anti-British
cartoons from the continental press, but Chirol noticed that 'both in
volume and in virulence the German section is *facile princeps*'. Within
the Foreign Office, the permanent secretary detected a revolution in
expectations:

> Whereas some time ago I had to explain often enough that there
> were certain things we could not expect of the Germans, however
> friendly they might be, I have now, whenever they are mentioned, to
> labour to show that the conduct of the German government has in
> some material aspects been friendly. There is a settled dislike of them,
> and an impression that they are ready and anxious to play us any
> shabby trick they can.

From Berlin, the British military attaché urged, '*we must go for the
Germans*, and that right soon, or they will go for us later'. One patriotic Englishman for whom the Boer War did change expectations was
Arthur Conan Doyle, who believed that Britain and Germany had a
natural affinity, so was deeply angered by attacks in German newspapers. Five years earlier, Britain would have rushed to war to prevent
German defeat, but 'now it is certain that in our lifetime no British
guinea and no soldier's life would under any circumstances be spent
for such an end'. This was 'one strange result of the Boer War, and in
the long run it may prove not the least important'. Even during 1900
the War Office telegraphed General Kitchener in South Africa to
ask how much cavalry he could spare if in a European war Britain
backed Germany. When Kitchener himself was War Minister in 1914,
British troops fought against rather than for the Fatherland.[8]

It is deeply ironic that Chamberlain should have been the cause of
estrangement, for he admired Germany more than anyone. After he
resigned from government in 1903 to campaign for tariffs, and was
arguing that the German economic threat to Britain necessitated
ending free trade, he was also sending parties of industrialists and
trades unionists to Germany to see for themselves how well things
were done there. But both his desire for a German alliance in 1899
and his lurch into tariffs in 1903 were products of a consciousness of
Britain's vulnerability if she remained economically isolated. As a

lifelong, self-appointed national prophet, Chamberlain was here doing what he had always done: moving faster and further towards extremes than others, but travelling in the same direction.

Despite a decade in which relations deteriorated, Britain and Germany conducted in 1899-1902 prolonged negotiations about a formal alliance. Chamberlain was the chief supporter, Salisbury the key opponent, but Lansdowne (Foreign Minister) and Balfour (Salisbury's nephew, and successor in 1902) hoped for a deal and could have counted on a cabinet majority had it come to a vote; but it never did come to a vote. There was no real possibility of an Anglo-German alliance, despite the best of intentions on both sides. Desultory talks lingered on only because neither side wanted to terminate them, so becoming the first to admit the impossibility of friendship. Much diplomacy was smoke and mirrors, as with the German diplomat Eckardstein, who promoted both understanding and his own career by telling each side that the other wanted a treaty. When the talks collapsed, there was mutual recrimination because this channel of communication had delivered such false intelligence, and Chamberlain's amateur diplomacy had similar effects. As P. J. V. Rolo puts it, 'every endeavour to improve Anglo-German relations only seemed to serve to exacerbate them', for there was a fundamental mismatch between the *type* of friendship discussed. For Germany, the minimum requirement was a formal treaty underwritten by Parliament, committing Britain to long-term support of Germany, Austria-Hungary and Italy. Even had that been possible, Germany offered only reciprocal support for Britain in Europe, not for the British Empire; as Salisbury pointedly told the German ambassador, 'you ask too much for your friendship'. It was the over-extension of Britain's world role that created feelings of vulnerability, not yet a European threat, so Britain wanted a looser arrangement, defusing existing frictions outside Europe, but committing neither side very far, like agreements made with Japan in 1902, France in 1904 and Russia in 1907, which only slowly developed into alliances. It has therefore been argued that if Germany had accepted what was on offer, habits of cooperation could have been established; as, critically, happened with France. That counter-factual argument mistakes a key point, though: military alliances, at whatever pace they emerge, rely on a common external threat, just as fears reinforced Anglo-

French rapprochement after 1904 (the threat being Germany). In 1899-1902 Britain was just starting to see Germany as the threat, and had fewer worries about France, Russia and America. There already was, then, no community of interest when Britain and Germany tried to make a deal.[9]

Salisbury's memorandum opposing an alliance stressed problems beyond the diplomats: an alliance 'would excite bitter murmurs in every rank of German society', while in Britain 'our popular constitution will not acknowledge the obligations of an engagement made in former years'. British opinion would some day reject the alliance as surely as Germans would oppose it now. After reading the memorandum, Balfour concluded that, apart from reluctance to trust Germany's word – which could hardly be said – the *only* argument against a German alliance was public opinion. In Germany it had been a cardinal principle of foreign policy that Britain must one day come to terms with Germany, since it was impossible to ally with France or Russia, colonial disputes remaining irresolvable. Bülow and the Kaiser would dictate the terms once Britain saw the light; when in 1901 Eckardstein optimistically told the Kaiser of Britain's desire for alliance talks, Wilhelm cabled Bülow, 'So, "they come" it seems – just as we expected'. The *Volks-Zeitung* had long taken the same view, urging Britain in 1896 'to ask itself what England could gain from strained relations with Germany. The English interests are so diverse that it *cannot do* without the moral support especially of Germany.' There was little awareness that if Britain feared Germany enough, then it would settle distant disputes so as to ally with France and protect the British Isles. In the first years of the new century ministers increasingly fixed their attention on the North Sea, entirely because of German naval expansion, but German leaders generally failed to understand the change. Hence, Germany's surprise when Britain allied with Japan and incomprehension when the Anglo-French Entente was signed. As Chamberlain had long ago explained, if the 'idea of a natural alliance with Germany must be renounced, it would be no impossibility to arrive at an understanding with Russia or with France'. Salisbury, less theatrical than Chamberlain throughout, had urged early on that the vital thing was not to antagonise France. The influential journalist H. W. Wilson now considered that 'it would be better to *rapproche* with Russia than with Germany. I used to be all the other way, but the more I see of Germans the more I distrust them.' Through the prism of failed negotiations with Germany an alternative future was glimpsed.[10]

From here it was downhill all the way to 1914, though the path was often indirect. The Anglo-French Entente (1904) was the hinge in the story, though initially a very limited agreement. It was Germany's determination to wreck the new alignment by provoking a 'Moroccan crisis' in 1905 – 'certain' that Britain could not support France in Africa – that drew the new allies closer together. When the Kaiser spoke belligerently at Tangier, as G. W. Monger described it, he 'put new life into the flagging entente'. The General Staff ran a war game to investigate how troops could assist France if Germany invaded Belgium, and Anglo-French naval and military talks followed. The Anglo-Russian Entente of 1907 was followed by another German attempt to disrupt the ententes in a second Moroccan crisis of 1911, initiated by sending a gunboat. The British ambassador in Berlin noted the Foreign Office view that 'the desp[atch] of the German ship to Agadir created a new situation – and that if . . . a German occupation was threatened we should be solid with France'. Britain and Russia now began to coordinate naval planning too. Wickham Steed, foreign correspondent of *The Times*, asking 'Is it War?' in December 1911, thought

> the goal of German policy is unchanged – to break, by menace or persuasion, the Anglo-French Entente that has, for seven full years, curtailed German power to reap, with unsheathed sword, the fruits of armed victory . . . The aim of German policy has not changed, will not change, cannot change until Germany puts her own affairs in order and lives, manufactures, trades and arms within her own means. Until then it behoves England to take counsel of France and to keep her store of powder not only dry but large.

In talks aimed at reducing tension, Germany's minimum demand was a prior statement of British neutrality in a Franco-German war, which was, as Premier Asquith put it, 'a promise we cannot give'. The cabinet decided in 1912 that, 'while we cannot bind ourselves under all circumstances to go to war with France against Germany, we shall also certainly not bind ourselves to Germany not to assist France'.

Since key ministers knew by then that France's military and naval plans depended on timely British aid, there were moral commitments to France building up, commitments that had not existed until Germany tried to wreck the entente. A consciousness was anyway emerging that Britain dare not in self-interest allow Germany to defeat France. Few had yet faced this logic, but once ministers accepted the premises in 1911–12, they would discover in 1914 where deductions from those premises must lead. By now, the German army had arranged exactly the attack on France which Britain could not allow to succeed, and made it the definite consequence of Germany going to war. As Kennedy puts it, 'the antagonism between Britain and Germany had emerged well before the Schlieffen Plan was made the only German military strategy; but it took the sublime genius of the Prussian General Staff to *provide the occasion* for turning that antagonism into war'. Martin Kröger concludes that 'rather than being encircled in consequence of some master plan, Germany, over a period of years, brought about its own "encirclement"'.[11]

Economic rivalry also grew, as Germany took Britain's place as Europe's dominant economy: analysing 'our German cousins' in 1909, the *Daily Mail* felt that 'no feat ranks so high in the building up of the [German] Empire as the declaration of independence against English industrial predominance on the continent of Europe'. Each time the British economy dipped into recession, anti-German articles appeared, and Chamberlain's tariff crusade railed against 'unfair' German competition. Yet it took recessions to create broad support for tariffs, which indicates how secondary an issue this was, except for industries and regions where international competition applied the greatest pressure. Germany had gained relatively, and was outproducing Edwardian Britain in chemicals, coal and steel, but in absolute terms Britain became steadily richer, profits were good and unemployment low. If British exports and the merchant fleet were less dominant than before, Britain still owned a third of the world's ships, carried half of the world's trade, and had four times as much merchant shipping as Germany. Salisbury told the Associated British Chambers of Commerce in 1901 that 'the spectre of Germany' did not induce British businessmen to 'despair of their country'; the German 'threat' had been invented by journalists 'under the necessity . . . of producing adequate copy'. This was not invariably clear to everyone else, given an increasingly defensive mentality in the commercial press, and the trend anyway indicated difficulties ahead: even Salisbury argued that Britain must be ready 'to meet adversaries of whom it is undoubtedly true that as every decade passes they become more powerful and dangerous'. So economic issues, though fragmented and discontinuous, mainly reinforced antagonisms that rested on other grounds. As Kennedy puts it, 'neither Prussian agrarians nor Birmingham machine-makers joined the various Anglo-German friendship committees, whereas Lancashire mill-owners and Hamburg bankers did'. The first group saw Anglo-German relations as rivalry, the second as mutual assistance.[12] It was not competing economies that pushed Britain and Germany into conflict, for there were in 1914 extensive commercial links, and if industrialists had any net influence it was to promote good relations rather than hostility. It was business interests that initiated the Haldane peace mission to Germany, and in August 1914 the City of London urged neutrality so strongly that the Foreign Secretary suspected German firms of protecting their interests through British partners. Nor was the economy seen as making war more likely at the time, for one of the era's best-sellers, Norman Angell's *The Great Illusion* (1910), was popularly (if erroneously) thought to have 'proved' that war had been made impossible, through the technical complexity of interdependent economies.[13]

Economic competition could not be separated from military affairs at a time when social Darwinists thought all indicators of national virility demonstrated a nation's prospects of survival against other races. When the press baron Lord Northcliffe visited Germany in 1909, he worried about 'the vast industrial strides made in practically every town. Every one of these new factory chimneys is a gun pointed at England.' His *Daily Mail* made much of the link, presenting Germany as 'no longer the land of thinkers and poets – it is a nation of business and battleships'. Though it backed tariffs, the *Mail* did not see them reversing British decline, which required the wholesale adoption of German methods, including 'primary education, technical training, military service, thrift, perseverance and patriotism. That is the German combination and it is a combination that must win.'[14]

Economic fears can also be seen in literature, as in books by Joseph

Conrad; for Conrad, the Boer War was 'not so much a war against
the Transvaal as a struggle against the doings of German influence'. In
'The End of the Tether' (1902) Captain Whalley reflects on the
decline of British shipping, challenged by 'a squad of confounded
German tramps' that 'prowled on the cheap . . . like a lot of sharks';
when Whalley declares that there is room for all, for 'the earth is big',
Captain Elliott replies, 'Doesn't seem to be much room on it since
these Germans came along shouldering us at every turn'. Though
Conrad admired Goethe and created sympathetic Germans like Stein
in *Lord Jim*, they were few and far between. His representative
Germans were painted in increasingly dark shades, especially the
recurrent Schomberg: in *Lord Jim* (1900), Schomberg is an eccentric
buffoon with a sideline in scandal-mongering; by *Victory* (1912–14),
he is a 'Teuton' who causes disaster through sheer malice. Hence, as
Conrad wrote, 'his grotesque psychology is completed at last . . . I
don't pretend to say that this is the entire Teutonic psychology; but it
is indubitably the psychology of the Teuton.' The good German
Stein went east to escape the repressive aftermath of the 1848 revolutions, so represents German liberalism, while Schomberg appears
after the Franco-Prussian War, incarnates German imperialism, and
is named Wilhelm.[15] For such social Darwinists, Germany's rise
necessitated Britain's decline. Kipling had reminded readers that some
day the British Empire would be 'one with Nineveh and Tyre', while
Chirol detected similarities between Britain and the senescent
Chinese Empire, around which colonising vultures circled. The
Observer's editor, J. L. Garvin, wondered in 1905 whether the
Trafalgar centenary celebrations would be celebrated imperially a
hundred years hence (he would not have liked the politically correct
'red' and 'blue' fleets of 2005). Such people were not reassured to read
of German patriots proclaiming that 'the German is again emerging
as the major people. If anyone is to be first among equals, it will not
be the Frenchman or the Briton.'[16]

If economics at most reinforced antagonism, naval rivalry had an
unequivocally negative impact: in 1909 the *Mail* thought the enlarged
German navy 'the greatest event of the Twentieth Century'. Although
the first naval 'scare' was in 1902, the Admiralty understood from the
start that German naval expansion's greatest impact must be on
Britain, since Tirpitz's 1898 plan had already raised Germany's battle

fleet from seven to nineteen ships. Lord Selborne, First Lord of the Admiralty, warned the cabinet in 1902 that 'the German navy is very carefully built up from the point of view of a new war with us'. Since Tirpitz had written that 'the military situation against England demands battleships in as great a number as possible', Selborne was not far wrong. Though he invariably denied that his fleet threatened Britain, the Kaiser was privately saying, 'in 20 years' time when it is ready, I shall speak another language'. Whatever was said diplomatically, anti-British rhetoric in Germany, mobilising support for naval spending, was reported in the British press. Naval building was worrying, Selborne thought, because of the 'intensity of the hatred of the German nation for this country'. When the War Secretary reported on Germany's 1902 naval manoeuvres, the cabinet concluded that the Royal Navy could not defend the country against Germany, France *and* Russia. No wonder they ended the country's 'isolation'. By 1905, friendship with France and the Japanese destruction of the Russian fleet concentrated attention on Germany, but since Germany had few colonies she kept her battle fleet at home, whereas Britain's was traditionally dispersed around the world. Growing friendship with America and Japan had the benefit of allowing Kipling's 'far-flung navies' to concentrate around Suffolk rather than Singapore.[17]

The Navy League, a pressure group for British naval expenditure, had been founded in 1893–4; once German naval building began in earnest its few thousand members rose to a hundred thousand by 1914. For, despite German enthusiasm, the rivalry mattered more to Britain. As Selborne argued, 'to us, defeat in a maritime war would mean a disaster of almost unparalleled magnitude in history. It might mean the destruction of our mercantile marine, the stoppage of our manufactures, scarcity of food, invasion, disruption of Empire. No other country runs the same risks in a war with us.' It did not require post-1918 hindsight to see that this was a one-sided viewpoint, for all those disasters could also happen to Germany when blockaded by the Royal Navy. Such a fate could though come only slowly, whereas for Britain, as Winston Churchill put it, the Royal Navy could 'lose the war in an afternoon'. The Prussian General Staff understood the distinction, planning a lightning attack to knock out France and a medium-quick campaign against Russia, both designed to be over before the Royal Navy could starve Germany.[18]

German leaders never grasped that their navy was different from Britain's. However well it played in the home market, Wilhelm's 'You have a fleet, why shouldn't we?' argument was misleading. For, as Kipling told Conan Doyle, while Britain might not win at sea, 'on land of course we haven't an earthly'. After 1870, there had been a European stand-off: Germany the dominant force on land, Britain at sea. Once Germany acquired a battle fleet stationed only a day's steaming from Britain's undefended east coast, that balance was terminally destabilised. The weakness of Britain's professional army now became highly relevant. Wherever Britain put her army, she had as always to maintain naval supremacy to remove the certainty of a land defeat within the British Isles. As the Kaiser proclaimed to British listeners at a 1901 dinner: 'We ought to form an Anglo-German alliance, you to keep the seas while we would be responsible for the land.' But actual policy already negated that historic possibility. Nor did Britain fail to bring the issue repeatedly to German attention. Foreign Secretary Sir Edward Grey told the Commons in 1911, 'if a nation has the biggest army in the world, and if it has a very strong navy, and is going on building a still bigger navy, then it must do all in its power to prevent what would otherwise be the natural apprehensions in the minds of others'. As put by the *Daily Mail*, 'the nation must be prepared to see the naval estimates rise annually or else make ready to surrender command of the sea and abandon the Empire'. There was never the slightest doubt which option would be chosen, even though Britain was run after 1905 by Liberal ministers who wanted to fight Lloyd George's 'war on poverty' rather than waste taxpayers' money on battleships.[19]

Fears were reinforced by the Kaiser's unguarded remarks, like his public ambition to become 'the Admiral of the Atlantic'; of the 1908 Naval Bill he gloated, 'Now Germany is in the saddle we can ride down our enemies'. Yet this was a race Germany could not win, since she also had to increase expenditure on an expanding army. By continuing to build ships, though, Germany reiterated the threat to Britain, and steadily widened the proportion of British people who believed in it. The fact that all discussions of future warship numbers were conducted against a barrage of newspaper exaggeration certainly did not help, as in the cacophonous 'We want eight [more battleships] and we won't wait!' campaign of 1909. When British

Liberal ministers sought room for manoeuvre by proposing disarmament talks in 1909 and a 'naval holiday' in 1913, they received discouraging German responses, for German public opinion had been educated to believe their navy need not be circumscribed by Britain. The Kaiser himself told a British diplomat that he would 'rather go to war than discuss naval limitations', which is in effect exactly what happened. When German responses to proposals for disarmament at the Hague Conference (1907) were unenthusiastic, British opinion rallied behind higher naval expenditure: 'Bülow has now come into the open, and we know where we are,' concluded Grey. Churchill and Lloyd George, who vehemently argued the case for social rather than naval spending in 1908, never did so effectively again, and once Churchill went to the Admiralty himself he advocated a bigger fleet. After 1911–12, partly because of the second Moroccan crisis but largely because of naval fears, middle opinion in the cabinet supported Grey, and in 1914 it backed him when going to war.[20]

The drive for a larger navy was reinforced by invasion novels, a thriller genre which, like the popular press, involved mass participation; with universal literacy, what had previously been books for military buffs now flooded the mass market. Invasion tales focused increasingly on Germany: between 1871 and 1914 there were sixty such novels, two-thirds of them identifying Germany as the threat, but of the thirty-one published after 1900 only five involved invasions by other countries and none of these appeared after 1904. Invasion narratives assumed a 'bolt from the blue', a German invasion without declaring war, so they also assumed German duplicity as a credible premise. 'It looks', remarked Bülow in 1904, 'as if a certain school of your publicists regards a paper war against Germany as the main object of its life.'[21]

Few such tracts had literary merit, but two made a special impact, Erskine Childers's *The Riddle of the Sands* (1903) and Le Queux's *The Invasion of 1910* (1906). Childers's heroes accidentally discover advanced preparations for a German invasion among the Frisian Islands near the Elbe, but Childers never knew that his guesswork was close to the 'Schröder Plan', devised when the Kaiser initiated planning against England in 1897. He was unhappy when his book was marketed as a novel, fearing that the message would be lost amid assumptions of its unreality, but *Riddle* almost single-handedly made a German 'bolt from the blue' seem a real possibility. That effect was largely fortuitous, for almost as soon as it appeared, the government announced a long-planned North Sea naval base, the timing apparently showing dilatory ministers forced unwillingly into action. The government inadvertently provided the smoke to prove Childers's claimed fire.[22]

Whereas Childers wrote well and expressed positive beliefs, Le Queux wrote to order, his most important invasion story commissioned by Northcliffe for the *Daily Mail*. Both of them had written earlier invasion tales, sensing that popularity, influence and money were to be made out of foreigners landing in England – *any* foreigners. Le Queux now signed up Field Marshal Lord Roberts to authenticate his German 'invasion', and claimed to have based his 'forecast' on 'all the available military and naval knowledge'. Roberts's advice was soon overruled by Northcliffe: the 'Germans' must pass through sizeable towns, not 'keep to one-eyed villages where there is no possibility of large *Daily Mail* sales'. Naming so many places, while giving graphic descriptions of havoc caused by Prussians, gave the novel immediacy, as did Le Queux's trademark inclusion of drawings of recognisable locations: here were civilian massacres at St Pancras Station, 'documents' issued by the Lord Mayor of London after capitulation, and German newspaper facsimiles reporting the *Triumph der Deutschen Waffen*. He allowed staunch British resistance, and for partisan warfare after the main battles, though this merely provokes German atrocities, 'as the bodies now swinging from telegraph poles on the various high roads in Essex testified'. The Germans take London, breaking through at Chipping Barnet after bombardment from around Chingford, during which famous buildings are destroyed: 'I saw Buckingham Palace attacked – Scots Guards did their best – short of ammunition – shot down like pigs', as a caption puts it, beneath a dramatic illustration. The British army rallies and the Germans are driven back, but they can still impose a harsh peace on the exhausted British. *The Invasion of 1910* caused a furore, partly because Le Queux's usual mixture of fiction and reality was reinforced by the *Mail*'s marketing, including men walking around London in Prussian uniforms. It was helpfully denounced by the Prime Minister, and the subject of daily reports to the Kaiser (or so the *Mail* claimed). Perhaps the greatest tribute was the publication in Germany of an unauthorised translation in which the Germans win the final battles. Most of the million copies sold worldwide were faithful to Le Queux's original, quite scary enough for British readers anyway. Censors initially refused to allow a film of the book, fearing German protests, but one was eventually made in 1914. By then, there was also a spectacular demonstration of fiction as alternative reality: when in autumn 1914 rumours circulated that the Germans had landed, the Officer Training Corps of the Inns of Court turned out, commandeered private vehicles and blocked the Great North Road to stop the Germans taking the capital 'again'. That was quite an achievement for a hack-writer whose surname no Briton has ever confidently pronounced.[23]

Alongside Childers and Le Queux were shoals of minnows, making a cumulative impression. They included a few of quality, like Saki's *When William Came* (in which George V flees to New Delhi), and parodies by A. A. Milne and P. G. Wodehouse. *Punch* wrote about Leo Maxse and William Le Queux invading Germany themselves, and satirised Le Queux when claiming that its author had 'wandered in search of local colour . . . from Shepherd's Bush to the Australian Bush', covering '1,932,102 miles' on the London underground, doing his research. But the genre was beyond parody, for 'serious' books had already hijacked the improbable, leaving no room for satirists. They were anyway supported in other media retailing similar romances, notably in boys' magazines and in the theatre. *Boy's Own* assured its million readers in 1906 that most German tourists in Britain were spies, its evidence being that they preferred the boots popular with German army officers during bad weather. After reading about the threat in *Chums*, Evelyn Waugh (aged eight) formed with his friends a 'Pistol Group', dedicated to drilling and preparing resistance to invasion; members pledged to 'knock down' any German they met, unless he was bigger than them (as they would all have been), in which case they would walk away and raise the alarm; they must 'never be polite to Germans'. The play *An Englishman's Home* by Guy du Maurier played to packed houses in 1909, while Territorial Army recruiting teams did a roaring trade in the foyer. Lord Esher, himself a military specialist, noted in his diary that it was 'a play of "Invasion" most excitingly acted'. Foreign soldiers (called

'Nearlanders' but wearing German helmets) invade an English middle-class home. Mr Brown, the householder, was originally executed by firing squad, but during the run a happier ending had to be substituted. The short story 'Germans at Meat' (1911) by Katherine Mansfield describes guests in her German *pension* discussing *An Englishman's Home*. One gloats that the British 'have no army at all – a few little boys with their veins full of nicotine poisoning'. Another offers double-edged reassurance: 'we don't want England. If we did we would have had her long ago.' Mansfield's narrator, repelled by coarse manners and beer bellies, stoutly maintains that 'we certainly do not want Germany'. Even a play seen only in London's West End could thus have a broader impact; there were photographs and reports printed by provincial newspapers, and excerpts were released on gramophone records (very likely 'made in Germany'). In Le Queux's *Invasion of 1910* one illustration shows a bus as a barricade in Tottenham Court Road, still bearing an advertisement for du Maurier's play. A variation on this theme was a season of live performances of Germans invading an English village, performed on summer evenings in the grounds of the Crystal Palace, while Londoners picnicked and cheered on the home team. As Cecil Eby despairingly concludes, 'formerly one had to be able to *read* in order to be spooked by invasion scares; now a blind illiterate had access to scaremongering literature'.[24]

There were German invasion books too, but in German accounts it is still usually Germany invading, reflecting the fact that in the overall geopolitical situation Britain was indeed defending the status quo, Germany trying to rebalance it in her favour. One was Karl Bleibtreu's *Die 'Offensiv Invasion' gegen England* (1907). In Germany too, with an expanding Royal Navy concentrating forces in the North Sea, there was genuine fear of invasion, though it was not known that in 1904 the British First Sea Lord, Sir John Fisher, had suggested a pre-emptive strike on Kiel before Germany's navy became too large. No such attack was ever planned, but Fisher's occasional public references to 'Copenhagening' (a pre-emptive attack, like the one employed against Denmark in 1801) worried Germans. Friedrich von Holstein in the German Foreign Ministry confessed in 1904 that he 'now believed in a war with England, in which the attack would come from England'. Explaining such fears, Kennedy suggests that Germany herself having plans to invade neighbouring countries made it easier for Germans to believe that Britain had similar intentions, though she never had an army capable of the job, not even in dreamland.[25]

Invasion books clearly affected British opinion, but did they change public policy? Here it is hard to separate the cultural context from specific military and diplomatic inputs, not least because diplomats and the military read the same books and newspapers as the public. Policy-makers were happy enough to use scares to strengthen their arguments: Esher assured Fisher in 1907 that 'an invasion scare is the mill of God which grinds you a Navy of Dreadnoughts'. In 1908 British service attachés in Berlin reported that Germany was planning a surprise landing on the east coast. This was more fiction than fact, but that year's naval manoeuvres practised repelling invasion from the North Sea, and when a German torpedo boat accidentally strayed into the area, it was assumed to be spying, so setting off another wave of novels – life influencing art as much as the other way round. The president of the National Service League, Lord Roberts, claimed that invasion literature confirmed his case for a larger army, but he had promoted Le Queux's best-seller himself. The first issue of Baden-Powell's *Scouting for Boys* (1908) was directed at recruits for the Territorial Army (which he helped launch) as well as boy scouts; its cover showed a scout watching for the invader, as Baden-Powell's Northumbrian 'terriers' would soon do. When the Committee of Imperial Defence (CID) was created by Balfour in 1903, its first task was to assess the feasibility of an invasion; when the exercise was repeated in 1908, it assumed Germany rather than France as invader. Balfour insisted that increased risk would exist only if Germany was more capable of invading than France, but decided that, since the vital issues were 'secrecy and speed', the risk *had* increased (the French being apparently incapable of keeping a secret or doing anything quickly). Naval manoeuvres only added to nervous risk-assessments, and since journalists were close to naval lobbyists, these assessments were not secret for long. In 1912, despite odds of two to one, the 'invaders' landed thirty thousand men in Yorkshire; 1913 was even worse, for the invaders had already landed twice as many when the exercise was called off as just too depressing. One consequence of such fiascos was declining faith in the Royal Navy to defend the homeland. It was consequently planned to leave significant forces at home, even during vital battles on the continent, as happened in 1914. Fiction and fiction-influenced fact had combined to make Britain very jumpy. Edward VII suggested in 1908 that the Kaiser might some day 'throw a *corps d'armée* or two into England', proclaiming that the loyal grandson of Queen Victoria would save Edward from 'the Socialist gang that is ruining the country'.[26]

The assumption that Britain would fight Germany in self-defence was reinforced by popular belief in German spies, ready to assist the invaders. Le Queux was again purveyor of the myth. He claimed that the Germans had for years maintained 'a civilian army' in Britain, men who, 'having served in the army, had come over to England and obtained employment as waiters, clerks, bakers, hairdressers and private servants, and being bound by their oath to their Fatherland had served their country as spies'. If so, they were a limited threat, for 'each man, when obeying the Imperial command . . . had placed in the lapel of his coat a button of peculiar shape, with which he had long ago been provided, and by which he was instantly recognised as a loyal subject of the Kaiser'. The author of *The Enemy in Our Midst* (1906) described how British topography had been minutely surveyed: 'the railways were known to a truck; the tubes were understood throughout every yard of their length, and the possibilities for an appalling sacrifice of the English people calculated and put down on paper'. Such nightmares were given superficial plausibility from the fact that Germans were, after the Irish and Russo-Polish Jews, the third-largest immigrant community, totalling about fifty thousand men, women and children. Roberts made this '80,000 Germans in the United Kingdom, almost all of them trained soldiers', while another inflated it to '350,000 living in our midst'. The Liberal MP who fantasised about '66,000 trained German soldiers in England', with '50,000 stands of Mauser rifles', hidden 'within a quarter of a mile of Charing Cross', was thus being rather cautious. The CID's secretary, Colonel Hankey, worried about attacks on the government by 'half a dozen desperate men armed with knives or clubs', never mind fifty thousand riflemen, and was disappointed not to interest Asquith in the risk. War Secretary Haldane was initially sceptical, but seems to have half believed in a spy network once he heard the experience of the Mayor of Canterbury, after arresting two Germans in his grounds. After dinner, 'their tongues loosened by port', they confessed to reconnoitring for an invasion. The public was astonishingly gullible: a German 'spy' was convicted in just four min-utes by an Exeter jury in 1911, the only evidence being that he was an avid reader of the local press; but he was hardly working undercover, for he flew the German flag over his house. Foreigners studying rail-way timetables or buying phrase books – what tourists do the world over – were frequently suspected of treachery. Though there was a sustained attempt to ridicule the scare, the stories were impossible to refute, since they discussed things that would be invisible if they existed, equally invisible if they did not. Le Queux wrote in 1906 that what he alleged was 'well known to the authorities', who could not say so publicly for fear of jeopardising counter-intelligence work: 'I have refrained from giving actual names and dates, for obvious rea-sons, and have therefore been compelled, even at the risk of being again denounced as a scaremonger, to present the facts in the form of fiction – fiction which, I trust, will point its own patriotic moral.' In this case 'the authorities' kept the scare going; it suited those who wanted money for counter-intelligence to exaggerate the threat they would contain. Lieutenant Colonel James Edmonds headed in 1907–8 the 'Special Section' MO5 at the War Office, much regretting that newspapers committed more resources than the government to finding spies, but he was convinced of the reality of a German net-work. Edmonds collaborated with novelists as well as policemen, and Le Queux passed over all the letters from cranks and paranoids received after he published *Spies of the Kaiser*, a process much assisted by the promise of ten pounds for every story the *Mail* printed. Edmonds then used this 'evidence' to persuade the CID to set up an inquiry into German espionage, a process that produced the Secret Service Bureau, which begat MI5 and MI6. Its first director, the legendary 'K', corresponded with Le Queux and holidayed on the Norfolk coast himself, to discover 'if there were any German activities going on'. Haldane advised Edmonds to 'lay stress on the anarchist (demolition) motive' when addressing the CID committee, which Haldane chaired; the committee gave Edmonds and Haldane the report they wanted and resources were increased. Unlike invasion scares, the British were here imputing to Germany what they were themselves doing, for examination of future battlefields was exactly what the army intended. General Henry Wilson later recalled seventeen cycling tours of future battle zones made with friends during pre-war 'holidays'. Childers urged in 1906 that the Admiralty should likewise send officers to explore unofficially the coastline described in *The Riddle of the Sands*; in 1910 two British officers were convicted of espionage when caught doing exactly that, while on a 'walking tour' around German naval installations, their luggage full of notes and photographs.[27]

The spy scare was often ludicrous. The *Daily Mail*, arguing that 'it is not obvious why we should tolerate foreign pigeon cotes', demanded a moritorium on pigeon-flying near defence facilities. So excited was the public that reporting imaginary agents seemed even to scaremongers to hamper the hunt for real ones. The public mood is caught by the Ordnance Survey cartographer who was arrested as a spy in almost every East Anglian village where he worked. Again, parody was hardly possible when the originals were so improbable, and the scaremongers alternately gloried in the opprobrium heaped on them by sceptics and hinted that truth was suppressed by traitors in high places. Naming real places again conveyed spurious authenticity: 'Do you know, Jack,' says one of Le Queux's heroes, 'that Beccles has been decided upon by the Germans as the headquarters of the Army Corps which lands at Weybourne? It's a natural position, standing upon high ground and commanding the surrounding countryside. Signals made from that church tower yonder could be seen very far afield.' Again there are fictitious documents, printed with typography chosen to enhance the sense of actuality. One such was a draft 'German proclamation' to be issued by the 'Governor General of East Anglia', which had been 'found . . . in the secret store of arms in Burnham-on-Crouch'; any resistance would be instantly 'PUNISHED BY DEATH'. Germany did have spies in Britain, but not many. 'K' had about two hundred people under observation in 1914, but only around sixty were arrested when war began – a long way from the nine thousand 'enemy agents' reported to the police in London alone that autumn. Few even of those arrested during 1914–18 were ever prosecuted, and the Germans executed as spies numbered a mere eleven patriots shot at the Tower of London. Asked to explain how they could have been so wrong, the spy-mongers cheekily argued that they must have been misled by false stories circulated by

Germans, and 'K' proceeded as if a major threat still existed: by 1918, his 850 staff had 38,000 personal dossiers on British residents, with over 100,000 cross-referenced index cards, kept up to date by an army of clerks. Germany had had few spies, but Britain acquired armies of spy-catchers.[28]

All these developments relied on belief in German duplicity, a conviction that steadily permeated Britain in the generation before 1914. Even in 1896, Colonel Swayne, military attaché in Berlin, had decided that the great failing of every German, 'whether he is an exalted personage, a diplomat, or of the lower classes', was that 'he lies and lies without blushing'. Among Swayne's culprits was the Kaiser, whom he knew to have lied to Victoria and the Prince of Wales. British ministers were equally certain when it emerged that Anglo-German alliance negotiations, held under a pledge of secrecy in 1900, were being reported to the Tsar by the Kaiser to create discord between London and St Petersburg. The German press was thought, exaggeratedly but with reason, to be officially inspired in its views on foreign policy, so that official denials added to British suspicion of duplicity.[29]

Kaiser Wilhelm encapsulated such suspicions: his boasts seemed to give the game away, his capriciousness produced uncertainty as to Germany's intentions, and his medal-bedecked uniforms embodied Prussian militarism. An imperial visit to Hatfield House in 1891 produced as a thank-you present a thirty-by-ten-foot portrait of himself in uniform, a painting so vast that it filled an entire wall of Salisbury's drawing room, and the Prime Minister rarely entered that room again: Wilhelm was, he wrote, 'mad enough for anything'. A diplomat noted in 1895 Salisbury's view that Germany's demand for the Upper Volta 'must have been the idea of the Emperor himself, as no responsible statesman could have put it forward'. Three years later, the permanent secretary at the Foreign Office, hearing that Wilhelm claimed to be 'like a man with a pail of water', trying to put out the Anglo-French fire over Fashoda, remarked acidly that he was more like 'someone running about with a lucifer match and scratching it against the powder barrels'. During the Edwardian decade 'Edward the peacemaker' and Wilhelm the warlord incarnated the collision of their peoples: Wilhelm was, thought the *Daily Mail*, 'the very type of impulsive, aggressive, energetic, omniscient Germany'. In 1896, when he visited Grandma Victoria on the Isle of Wight, he had, as John

Grenville put it, 'already become an obstacle to the development of good Anglo-German relations, although, paradoxically, he ardently desired Britain's friendship'. He could still be personally popular in Britain and was widely praised for his dignity at Victoria's deathbed and funeral. Crowds cheered him at King's Cross (dressed in his new rank of British field marshal), and a band played *Heil dir im Siegerkranz*. As the train moved off, he leaned out to grasp the King's hand, a gesture Edward thought as dangerous as it was tasteless. When the two monarchs met again for the funeral of the Kaiser's mother, the Empress Vicky, Edward was again unimpressed; after a four-hour train journey, refreshment was delayed for a military display that kept him waiting for his lunch. So it continued, boastful speeches and militaristic gestures continuously undermining the Kaiser's intention to be helpful. He gave an unwise interview for the *Daily Telegraph* in 1908, in which he spoke excitedly about how much his subjects loathed Britain. Liberal newspapers called him a fool in an attempt to limit the damage, while the Tory press thought him both a knave who had inadvertently told the truth *and* a dangerous fool too. Belligerent speech-making in Germany ensured that efforts to persuade Britain that he was her friend but hampered by German opinion did not impress British observers convinced that he inflamed the hostility personally. As early as 1896 the socialist paper *Vorwärts* suggested that the Kruger telegram could not be just 'a personal initiative', since he was head of state, but, 'given the gagging of the press', there would never be a proper public debate about such things. Discussing Anglo-German relations with Edward VII in 1901, the Kaiser himself explained that 'I am the sole arbiter and master of German foreign policy, and the Government and country *must* follow me. May your Government never forget this.' Wilhelm's association with naval expansion and the army made him the embodiment of threatening Junkerdom. This popular view was reinforced in January 1914 when a military court acquitted officers who had behaved brutally towards protesters against German occupation in Alsace, an acquittal condemned by the Reichstag; that vote would, wrote the British ambassador, 'make no difference'. A *Times* leader argued that the incident proved Germany was a militarised autocracy. This was an exaggeration, but it was true that neither the monarchy nor the military had in Britain a fraction of the influence it exercised in

Wilhelmine Germany; in 1914 the Reichstag was informed that Germany was at war, while Britain's government nervously awaited a Commons vote before taking the plunge. The last peacetime chancellor, Bethmann Hollweg, had, thought the *Mail* in 1913, 'singularly failed to emancipate himself from the shackles of the "Black and Blue" alliance which . . . stands for reaction'. German people 'identifie[d] him with the caste which stubbornly withh[eld] from enlightened Germany that great ideal of all genuinely liberated nations – parliamentary institutions and truly representative government'. When Edward VII speculated on a German invasion, he assumed that the Kaiser would establish for him 'autocratic rule as a feudatory of Germany'; his horror at the prospect of absolutism indicates the gulf between them. Lansdowne wondered of the Kaiser 'what may not a man in such a frame of mind do next?' while Grey compared him to a battleship going full steam ahead with a faulty rudder. In the German Foreign Office he was known as 'Wilhelm the Sudden', while Berliners joked that he fair-mindedly approached every problem with an open mouth.[30]

Suspicions were widely shared by British politicians, the press, the Foreign Office and the Palace. British royalty had quarrelled with Wilhelm soon after he became Kaiser, annoyed by his insistence on being called 'His Imperial Majesty' within the family, which Victoria thought 'dreadfully *vulgar*'. Edward VII, thought his confidant Lord Esher, 'felt towards Germany as 999 Englishmen out of 1000 do, very considerable distrust'. Though making few public statements expressing distrust, Edward was a willing sponsor of the Anglo-French Entente, and intervened personally to encourage diplomats who shared his views. During the naval-building controversy of 1909, he insisted that 'as long as Germany persists in her present programme of shipbuilding we have no alternative but to build double'. Queen Alexandra never forgave Germans for what they did to Denmark in 1863–4, despising 'nasty, *Pickelhaube* Prussians', but her son George V was closer to Cousin Wilhelm, as demonstrated at the funeral of Edward VII in 1910. In 1914 George was in Prussian uniform reviewing 'his' German regiment. He much preferred harmony, used family connections to facilitate warmth, and supported the Haldane mission. There is though no evidence whatsoever that he opposed his government's response to German naval building. As

Harold Nicolson put it, in 1914 the King's 'relations with Sir Edward Grey were of unclouded mutual confidence . . . The cabinet knew that the King would support and further their policy by every word and deed.'[31]

Grey had sensed a threat even in 1903, thinking Germany 'our worst enemy and our greatest danger. I do not doubt that there are many Germans well disposed to us, but they are a minority; and the majority dislike us so intensely that the friendship of their Emperor or their Government cannot be really useful to us.' He therefore welcomed the Japanese Treaty and the Anglo-French Entente, even before becoming Foreign Secretary. Though some radical Liberals thought Grey's German policy provocative and Conservative diehards thought it weak, the bulk of both parties were supportive. Some Conservatives considered it ideal to have a Liberal government taking such a stand with Conservative support, since any Conservative minister doing the same would have been barracked by Liberals. When it briefly seemed possible that the Liberals might split rather than join the war in 1914, anti-war radicals soon realised that any alternative government would anyway support France at war, which greatly reduced their influence. The entente that Grey signed with Russia in 1907 was, he thought, 'necessary to check Germany'. It was therefore a more explicitly anti-German arrangement than Lansdowne's earlier entente with France. Thereafter, Grey strove for better relations with Germany from a position of strength, but he was deflected by disputes over Egypt, Persia, Morocco and Turkey, and especially over armaments. Though prepared to negotiate flexibly about commercial matters and diplomatically over distant problems like Balkan wars, he declared at the same time that '*the* test of whether an understanding is worth anything' would be Germany's naval plans. For, as Paul Kennedy put it, 'the real reasons for British estrangement from Germany in the years before 1914 lay in the North Sea and along the river Meuse, not in Central Africa and the Euphrates valley', a major shift from 1890 when Salisbury's offices had been papered with maps of Africa. German diplomats in London reported this shifting focus, but provoked only withering asides from Wilhelm about 'the "blindness" of his diplomatic corps'. The Kaiser was thought typical of Teutonic myopia rather than a special case. Lord Sanderson, at the Foreign Office, wrote in 1907:

The German Foreign Office hold to a traditional view of negotiations, that one of the most effective methods of gaining your point is to show how intensely disagreeable you can make yourselves if you do not. They are surprised that the recollection of these methods should rankle, and speaking generally the . . . Germans combine intense susceptibility as regards themselves with a singular inability to appreciate the susceptibilities of others.

Responding to a call for greater British armaments from the *Spectator*, Grey supportively replied that 'our attitude towards the Germans is not unfriendly but they have forced us to make it defensive'. Just how defensive was revealed in 1907, when Grey practically threatened to resign the Foreign Office if the Coldstream Guards' band toured Germany, for such a visit would send misleading signals to both Germany and France.[32]

Though the Foreign Office has not been conspicuous over its long history for any determination to upset foreigners, Grey had unflinching support from his advisers. An influential 1907 memorandum, by the senior clerk Eyre Crowe, argued that Germany's 'intention to become a great naval power' involved not only a major conflict but many lesser ones too – over coaling stations, for example – which could well bring on a war in which British interests would necessarily be involved. Britain, having acquired similar assets over a longer period, did not seem to Crowe to pose such a threat. That defence of the international status quo, casting Germany as the active aggressor, suited British interests as a declining economic and imperial power very well indeed. Most British commentators viewed British pre-eminence as beneficial, and expected an alternative German hegemony to be violently disruptive, but Germans naturally saw this as double-talk. As Bülow put it, when Britain told Germany to limit her *Weltpolitik* it was like a father saying to his son, 'If only you would not grow, you troublesome youth, then I would not need to buy you longer trousers!' The *Pax Britannica* had, Crowe thought,

harmonize[d] with the general desires and ideals common to all mankind, and more particularly . . . with the primary and vital interests of a majority, or as many as possible, of the other nations . . . It might be deduced that the antagonism is too deeply rooted [to be] . . . bridged over . . . On this view of the case, it would have to be assumed that Germany is deliberately pursuing a policy which is essentially opposed to vital British interests, and that an armed conflict cannot in the long run be averted, except by England either sacrificing those interests, with the result that she would lose her position as an independent Great Power, or making herself too strong to give Germany the chance of succeeding in a war.

Germany's approach had been 'that of a professional blackmailer', and 'History' suggested only one safe response. From the same perspective, Kipling wrote about Ethelred the Unready for a children's book in 1911: 'if once you have paid him the Dane Geld,/You never get rid of the Dane'. So,

> We never pay *any*-one Dane-Geld,
> No matter how trifling the cost;
> For the end of that game is oppression and shame,
> And the nation that plays it is lost!

Similar views were held by ambassadors abroad and by successive chiefs at the Foreign Office, but the idea that it was sensible and manly to fight for one's rights permeated the whole culture. P. G. Wodehouse, whose *The Swoop, or How Clarence Saved England* (1909) did an effective job in ridiculing invasion scares, could not resist it when he turned away from humour. In *The White Feather* (1907), a public-school novel, the cowardly Sheen is liberated from lack of moral fibre by a chance meeting with Joe Bevan, former world boxing champion. Bevan teaches Sheen to defend himself and win boxing trophies for his house, redeeming him with his friends, but he also changes his outlook on life. Sheen begins

> to understand that the world is a place where every man has to look after himself, and that it is the stronger hand that wins. That sentence from *Hamlet* which Joe Bevan was so fond of quoting practically summed up the whole duty of man – and of boy. One should not seek quarrels, but 'being in' one should do one's best to ensure that one's opponent thought twice in future before seeking them.

So, even Bertie Wooster's creator thought it necessary to fight one's corner, and thousands of boys learned about white feathers from Wodehouse, a lesson that became horribly relevant in 1915.[33]

The government could stand firm against Germany because it had active support in the press. There were critics, notably such Liberal papers as the *Manchester Guardian*, but neither in vehemence nor circulation could they compete with the barrage from the other side. In any case, the impression that the British Left took a feebler collective view was ruined by Northcliffe's 'inspired' choice of the socialist Robert Blatchford to write viciously anti-German pieces, columns that appeared in a million and a half daily issues of the *Mail* during one week of 1909. Blatchford was earlier credited with 'making more socialists' through his *Clarion* magazine than anyone else, but he had also sold two million copies of the patriotic manifesto *Merrie England* (1894). Summing up his articles, which provoked official protests by the German Embassy, Blatchford concluded with seven propositions:

I have tried to show
1. That Germany aims at European domination.
2. That to attain her ends she must break the power of Britain.
3. That all attempts at conciliation and compromise are foredoomed to failure; nothing will deter Germany but a demonstration of power.
4. That if France falls we shall be unable to hold our own.
5. That France is not generally regarded as a match for Germany.
6. That we are not in a position to help France.
7. That unless the British people make greater sacrifices than they are at present prepared to make, we shall lose our Empire and our independence.

The slightest hint of ministerial 'Potsdamism' (sympathy for everything included in the spiritual home of the Prussian army), and abuse rattled about them from the most talented pens in Fleet Street. Northcliffe's *Daily Mail*, the biggest-selling newspaper of the day, was vociferous in describing a German threat, backed up by other large-circulation titles like the *Daily Express* and the *Daily Mirror*, but also by the quality press, notably *The Times* and H. A. Gwynne's *Morning*

Post; by the most respected Sunday paper, Garvin's *Observer*; and by influential Conservative weeklies, St Loe Strachey's *Spectator* and Leo Maxse's *National Review*. Though Maxse and Strachey were deadly foes in domestic politics, they were united over Germany. There was no pressure from this influential nexus of papers to moderate British policy, just steady advice to stiffen it. No doubt chasing sales was one motivation, especially for Northcliffe, but the fact that he could sell papers by exploiting this story tells us much about the public's views; Northcliffe himself explained (as would Rupert Murdoch, seventy years later) that 'we don't direct the ordinary man's opinion; we reflect it'. Circulation wars fail anyway to explain the equivalent obsessions of Maxse, Strachey, Garvin and Gwynne, and even for Northcliffe influence was important, too. When he bought *The Times* in 1908, he pledged never to interfere with editorial independence *unless* it failed to warn readers about Germany. This was unlikely, for *The Times* had already come to an independent conclusion about Germany by 1902 and never then deviated from its suspicions.[34]

Not everyone in Britain swam with the anti-German tide. Just as individuals pointed out absurdities in spy scares, there were efforts to foster closer relations. In 1905 a deputation of county councillors visited Germany; when the mayors of five German cities returned the compliment in 1906 they were received by the King, and London's Lord Mayor called for friendship between the peoples, while the junior minister for the colonies, Winston Churchill, denounced 'attempts of alarmist journalists to set up strife between the nations'. Two thousand people helped launch an Anglo-German friendship committee, followed by a similar meeting in Berlin. Chambers of commerce in both countries joined in, and the Churches launched their own committees to promote personal contact, as did newspapermen. The Liberal journalist J. A. Hobson, in *The German Panic*, pointed out that Britain's economic rivalry with Germany was no worse than with others, and that Germany's were not the highest tariffs that British exports faced. Some were still impressed by the 'common racial stock' to which the Kaiser appealed, or by the Reformation heritage. The Goethe Society operated among cultural organisations that exemplified respect for Germany, a literary-ambassadorial role like that accorded to Shakespeare in Germany; and a deferential working relationship continued between British and

German academics, and among musicians. It did not take much to bring out peaceful opinions in the Liberal press: the Kaiser's tearful demeanour at the funeral of Edward VII ('that old hen Uncle Eddy') persuaded the *Daily News* that even the 'most nervously distrustful politician' must 'be convinced of the baselessness of the fears they have sought to plant in our minds'. The Society for Anglo-German Friendship was active, led by former ambassador to Berlin Sir Frank Lascelles, and an Anglo-German union club was formed by businessmen, publishing the *Anglo-German Courier*. Within the government, Lord Chancellor Haldane entertained the Kaiser to lunch, and lectured at the University of Oxford on 'mutual suspicions' being 'largely due to mutual misunderstandings' (for which he was hotly denounced as leader of the 'Potsdam party'). In the tense mood of 1911, MPs in the Anglo-German Friendship Society, together with pacifists, socialists and those who simply wanted to spend taxpayers' money on social policy, harried Grey and pressed for concessions to maintain the peace. Even in July 1914 peacemakers issued a manifesto printed in most newspapers, and circulated masses of leaflets through volunteers in London and the provinces; there were big meetings in Trafalgar Square and provincial cities, MPs were lobbied, and three hundred men with placards demanding peace stumped around London. That final doomed campaign was supported, Norman Angell later remembered, by 'professors, peers, bankers, journalists, newspaper-owners, lawyers and bishops'.[35]

There were, though, three problems confronting apostles of understanding: fighting a more powerful opposing current, opposing the *Zeitgeist*, and the fact that their optimism had no bearing on British security. Organisations devoted to improving relations were created only because their founders themselves noticed rising hostility; in this sense all such organisations, visits and well-meaning resolutions demonstrated antagonism rather than latent harmony. Angell later recalled that he had been 'drawn into the work' because he had become 'convinced to the point of chronic sleeplessness that we . . . were headed for war'. Despite their best intentions, the peacemakers never dented the lead in popular opinion already established by scaremongers. Nor were they well placed to argue that time was on their side; apart from businessmen defending personal interests, friendship societies were generally led by men who had been active in public life before 1900, when relations had been warmer: the Anglo-German Friendship Society's leaders were in 1905 all over sixty. While the ex-ambassador Lascelles remained active, aged sixty-six, the current ambassador was urging toughness towards Germany, and Lascelles himself had warned from Berlin in 1902 that 'we cannot safely ignore the malignant hatred of the German people or the manifest design of the German Navy'. Like its supporters, the case for peace seemed simply out of date. Most important, proponents of better relations had no answer to the question of naval rivalry; when British members of joint organisations urged German counterparts that Germany must not frighten its neighbours, they made little headway. The point was well made by J. L. Garvin (whose library was a shrine to German culture, with volumes by Kant, Ranke and Mommsen): 'Nothing will break the bonds between me and these old friends, and they testify that on my part there is no lack of an initial good will. But of course next to these stand all the volumes . . . which remind me *daily* that the second-largest fleet in the world has been created in scarcely ten years and so far no limit has been placed on its expansion.' Every effort towards Anglo-German harmony was wrecked on the sandbanks of the North Sea, for it did not – as peacemakers necessarily claimed – take two to make a fight. Angell remembered, two world wars later, the ingenious couplet that Hilaire Belloc devised to expose the weakness of his argument: 'Pale Ebenezer thought it wrong to fight,/But Roaring Bill (who killed him) thought it right.' Belloc chooses an Old Testament name, redolent of unworldly Primitive Methodists, for peace. The Kaiser's name incarnates war.[36]

Increasingly, the debate acknowledged an inevitability: if Germany did not abandon the naval race, and Britain dared not do so, then war would occur, probably quite soon. Crowe, welcoming friendship with France through settling peripheral disputes, and urging in 1907 a similar understanding with Russia, added that 'for an Anglo-German understanding on the same lines there is no room, since none could be built on the same foundations'. In the same year the Berlin *Post* argued that 'nobody in Germany doubts England's abhorrence of war, but abhorrence of war has nothing to do with Anglo-German relations. The conditions of Germany's development and her rivalry with England for world power would of themselves bring about a fatal collision.' In 1911 Grey's secretary wrote that 'after six years experience' he thought the only thing Germany 'wants is the hegemony of Europe', which Britain *could* not concede. For the *Morning Post*, there was 'a vague feeling that Germany may in the twentieth century play the role that Spain played in the sixteenth and France in the seventeenth and eighteenth'. Leo Maxse was assured by a correspondent that the Kaiser aimed to be 'the dictator of Europe. We are face to face with the same state of things which existed in Europe under Charles V, Louis XIV and Napoleon.' Also in 1911 the German colonial lobbyist Karl Peters wrote that 'Germany is for the normal John Bull what Spain was in the Sixteenth Century, France in the Nineteenth, and Russia in the Twentieth'. Alongside this paragraph, Wilhelm minuted, 'Correct'.[37]

For British people brought up on the history of 1588 and 1805, identifying Wilhelm II as Philip II or Napoleon was quite enough to show where both their duty and the national interest lay. Few British school histories omitted Napoleon's remark in the year of Trafalgar: 'It is necessary for us to be masters of the sea for six hours only, and England will have ceased to exist.' Kipling's poem about the Dutch in the Medway in 1664 and his short stories about the Norman Conquest and its aftermath reflected the same dark memory. If the Kaiser understood that Germany was seen that way and thought it 'correct', his irresponsibility was all the more culpable, unless his ambition really was Napoleonic. Assessing responsibility for the Great War, we can endorse the verdict of Paul Kennedy's magisterial *Rise of the Anglo-German Antagonism*:

> It was the unstable Wilhelmine leadership, which, by actions such as cutting the 'wire' to St Petersburg [in July 1914], tariff wars, the Kruger telegram, the *Flottenpolitik*, the Tangier landing, the Bosnian ultimatum and the *Panther*'s 'spring' in 1911 – what in other words Crowe called 'the generally restless, explosive and disconcerting activity of Germany in relation to other states' and Bethmann Hollweg described as 'a strident, pushing, elbowing, overbearing spirit' – had built up in the minds of its neighbours a cumulative impression of Germany's ambitious aims and irresponsible power such that older antagonisms with other powers had to be suppressed in order to meet the new danger.

When Britain launched into her most terrible war in August 1914, there was no doubt in the minds of her government, press or citizens that she had sought friendship but been forced onto Grey's 'defensive'. Belloc's 'Roaring Bill' had created the Frankenstein's monster of the Great War, as William Le Queux's fantasy also became fact. Naturally, the indefatigable Le Queux was in September 1914 one of the first to produce a book 'proving' that Germans committed atrocities against women and children. That instantaneous gearing up of hatred was the ugly face of things to come.[38]

3

'When the English learned to hate': 1914–18

Rudyard Kipling was well qualified to hate for England, and in 1914–18 he did just that. He was also, though, the most widely read British author and a man whose popularity with the public was so secure that he could turn down the poet laureateship (three times), knighthoods, peerages, the Order of Merit (twice) and all other marks of official favour. His appeal rested on two factors: the easy accessibility of his verse, as comprehensible as music-hall lyrics; and the broad acceptance of his attitudes among middle-class readers. As George Orwell noticed, this gave to Kipling an immense influence, for he both reflected and shaped opinion for two generations. But in *A Diversity of Creatures* (1917) Kipling included a poem that few even of his admirers relish. 'The Beginnings' is cool in its narrator's apparent state of mind, but coldness makes the content more deadly, as it describes anti-German hostility attributed with relentless iteration to 'the English':

> It was not part of their blood,
> It came to them very late,
> With long arrears to make good,
> When the English began to hate . . .
> It was not preached to the crowd,
> It was not taught by the state.
> No man spoke it aloud,
> When the English began to hate.

Kipling's poem was a propagandist's response to the German *Hymn of Hate* by Ernest Lissauer which earned its author an Iron Cross that Kipling would have refused, but there is little doubt that it represented views he really held. As he wrote in a 1918 pamphlet, 'the Hun has been educated by the State from his birth to look upon assassination and robbery, embellished with every treachery and abomination that the mind of man can laboriously think out, as a perfectly legitimate means to the national ends of his country'.[1]

Kipling was far from alone in holding such views by 1918. The stress of a nation undergoing a war of industrialised mass killing provides partial explanation, but the degree of race hatred commonplace during the Great War is nevertheless shocking to the modern reader. As Peter Buitenhuis summarises opinion, British writers blamed Germany alone for starting the war, 'which was a product of German militarism and lust for conquest. The Germans, Huns of ancient memory, left behind them in the invaded territories a trail of ruins, blood and terror, murder and rapine.' All the Allies 'were united in the belief that it was necessary to fight the war to victory, regardless of cost, so that German militarism could be finished for ever'. The novelist Arnold Bennett, having seen the destruction of French cultural treasures, argued that 'if, at the end of the war, Cologne were left as Arras was when I visited it, a definite process of education would have been accomplished in the Teutonic mind'. Henry Jackson, Regius Professor of Greek at Oxford, exploded, 'What pigs the Germans are! It is a sacred duty to hate them.' 'Kill Germans! Kill them!' was the Bishop of London's message: 'not for the sake of killing, but to save the world . . . Kill the good as well as the bad . . . Kill the young men as well as the old . . . I look upon it as a war for purity.'[2]

Such hatred may be comprehended only with awareness of the way in which the Great War was perceived to have started, the way in which fighting was understood, and the deep British commitment to victory. Hardly any British people doubted Germany's responsibility for the war (and therefore for the slaughter that followed); if Kipling was not quite right in declaring that such hatred 'was not taught by the state', it remained true that in propaganda as in every other aspect of war-making, war prompted a huge voluntarist effort in a deeply pluralist society. The idea that Germany had started the European war was a respectable opinion to hold and one that was still being put forward half a century later by professional historians. The American historians Robin Winks and R. J. Q. Adams recently decided that 'when one asks which nation finally disturbed the status quo in Europe sufficiently to bring on the war, it is difficult to answer with any other name than Germany'. Whether this was true is beside the point, but the fact that it was possible for rational men to believe it to be true was of great importance. The need to find a cause at all is worth emphasising, for despite what now seem to have been years of mounting tension, few anticipated an actual war with Germany. H. G. Wells, who could legitimately claim greater foresight than most, confessed, 'I was taken by surprise by the war. I saw long ahead how it could happen, and wove fantastic stories about it, but at the bottom of my heart I did not believe it would really happen.' Having not quite believed in it, Wells, like others, had to find a human 'cause'.[3]

The Prime Minister, Herbert Asquith, proclaimed in September 1914 that 'Responsibility for all the illimitable sufferings that now confront the world belongs to one Power, and one Power only, and that Power is Germany.' On 6 August not one MP had voted against supporting the war on these grounds; only a handful had abstained; and no national newspaper had opposed the war. At the other end of the social and age scales, a teenager who later went in for nursing, munitions work and the Women's Land Army wrote, 'I believe that we're fighting for an ethical truth, and that the war is a struggle between civilisation, and all that it stands for on one side, against German barbarism . . . which isn't based on a solid civilisation.' One of the thousands of household debates was so forceful that a young girl in Barking vividly remembered it almost ninety years later:

My brother, indeed the whole family, were conscientious objectors . . . We were in mid-discussion when my brother suddenly stood up and said, 'You know, Mother, supposing people were to come into this room . . . and attack you and Emily . . . I shouldn't sit here and let them do it . . . I've got to go, the Germans are coming here, we all know the stories they are telling. I've got to protect you from them . . .

I'm here as a defender and I've a right to defend you' . . . We did not want to go and fight anybody, we wanted to live in peace. However, we weren't allowed to because of Germany, it wasn't our fault.

As the *Wipers Gazette*, produced by and for soldiers at the front, decided alphabetically,

> H is for the Hun who lives over the way:
> His future is black and his present is grey;
> Yet a Hun is a Hun, and as such he must pay
> For making us live in the trenches.

Even opponents of the war effort conceded that Germany was cul-pable. The headmaster of Eton, after preaching a 1915 sermon on 'Love your enemies', agreed that 'the German spirit, as now manifest [was] an utterly dangerous and abominable thing [so] the hope for peace and honour among mankind rests, so far as I can see, in a decisive victory for the allies'. Christian charity must wait until the Armistice. Goldworthy Lowes Dickinson, a staunch opponent of the war, vig-orously contested the view that Germany had long ago planned to start a war in 1914, an opinion he nevertheless thought to be 'univer-sally held in England'. Even Bertrand Russell, who opposed the war with such vigour as to lose his job and end up in jail, was at least ambiguous about war guilt: 'the sins of England [would] sink into insignificance beside the German treatment of Belgium'.[4]

Critics of government policy adopted the same language, as well as sharing its assumptions. Germany had been traditionally associated with efficiency, organisation and militarism, so efforts to make Britain too a warrior state seemed to go against everything the coun-try was fighting. The government response, that it was necessary to fight fire with fire, only confirmed the critics' diagnosis. As the his-torian R. H. Tawney argued, Britain had to achieve 'a form of national concentration' that was as effective as Germany's, but in a manner 'consistent with the ideals which led us into the struggle'. Lloyd George was particularly vulnerable to attack as a pre-war rad-ical who had opposed the Boer War, especially when in 1915–16 the main issue was recruiting for the army: 'Is it conscription? Not nec-essarily in any ordinary sense.' Former Liberal and nonconformist allies were unconvinced: 'Admit conscription', thundered the Baptist leader John Clifford, 'and the Kaiser is not far behind. He will come, and you will be Prussianised.' Free churchmen condemned reprisals for Zeppelin raids as 'Prussian' techniques, which would in effect mean that the enemy had won. This tactic enabled war resisters and those with tender consciences to get their own back on super-patriots who labelled them 'pro-Prussian apologists', a tactic that worked even after the war. C. E. Montague wrote in *Disenchantment* (1922) of the Versailles peacemakers doing 'the Prussian goose-step by way of *pas de triomphe* in the streets of Paris'. Sometimes the carry-over from anti-Germanism to war criticism was subtler, as when Edward Thomas attacked Britain's 'fat patriots', profiteering from the war, an image drawn from caricatures of the stereotypical Krupp. The oppositional message was that it was vital that the British should not become 'Huns in their own country', but this literary strategy rested entirely on shared assumptions about how 'Huns' behaved elsewhere.[5]

Previous links with Germany must be severed, a view found as much in the elite as among East End louts who stoned dachshunds as 'German dogs'. There certainly were riots, even in so unlikely a place as Aberystwyth, and much victimisation of individual Germans: one child, overhearing her parents discussing the governess, asked piteously, 'Oh Mummy, *must* we kill poor Fräulein?' After a German submarine sank the *Lusitania* in 1915, the prejudice became really bad: German-born butchers were driven out of their trade at Smithfield Market; German brokers were expelled from the Baltic Exchange; German shops were attacked in Kentish Town and 150 looted; and three nights of riots followed in Liverpool. A favourite ploy was to throw German pianos into the street, where they accompanied patriotic songs. British children no longer learned 'German fingering' during piano lessons, and 'German measles' became 'Belgian flush' (however odd it may seem to name a disease after an ally). Boots assured customers that their *eau de Cologne* was not from Cologne, and C-B Corsets pledged to put the squeeze on *all* non-British firms in its specialised market. Faced with a march by stockbrokers on Parliament to demand tougher action, the government capitulated. Asquith reluctantly announced the internment of male enemy aliens and the King withdrew the knighthood of the

Garter from several relatives. Many interned Germans were unceremoniously deported at the war's end, though charged with no
offence, and the German community in 1920s Britain was less than
half what it had been in 1914. In Edwardian times there had been
German communities from Brighton to Dundee, though concentrated in London, where there was a German hospital, a German
chapel, and a strong presence at University College; there were also
substantial German commercial communities in Manchester and
in the textile areas of Yorkshire. This was now all swept away, and
when in the 1990s Bradford local historians researched the 'Little
Germany' district where Frederick Delius grew up, they found no
evidence of German connections except a name that was by then
more than half a century out of date; the oldest traceable memory,
listing men who worked there in the 1920s, contained barely a
German name – though at least one, Mr Stafford, had once traded
as Stavert. Sylvia Pankhurst witnessed an anti-German riot after an
air raid on Hull in 1915, in which she saw a stout man dragged along
by a crowd, 'his clothes whitened by flour, his mouth dripping
blood'. Nor did such things happen only early in the war, for a 1918
petition demanding the internment of naturalised ex-Germans
attracted over a million signatures. Unlike the fastidious Asquith,
Lloyd George played to the gallery at such moments: his secretaries
assured demonstrators that their petition would be taken seriously,
and he himself told the Commons that whenever British troops suffered setbacks, he received exultant 'anonymous letters written by
Germans in this country . . . Where are they? I feel that that sort of
thing has got to be stopped.'[6]

Sir John Brunner and Sir Alfred Mond, chemical industry tycoons
but suspect because of foreign names, sued a rival who called them
'German swine'. Even Sir Eyre Crowe was attacked because of his
German mother, protesters demanding his replacement by someone
'of purely British blood'. Brunner and Mond won their case and
Crowe survived, but others were less lucky in the court of public
opinion. Prince Louis of Battenburg, First Sea Lord, was hounded
out because of his ancestry, his father being a serving officer in the
Austrian army. Though it took longer, so was Haldane, who had
been the cabinet minister most favourably predisposed to pre-war
Germany; a cabinet colleague noted in July 1913 that Haldane 'as

usual wanted us to accept the German point of view'. Being a student of German philosophy, cartoonists drew him surrounded by books, labelled 'Cant'; Wilhelm II had called Haldane his 'good friend'; and Haldane himself called his dog 'Kaiser'. The idea that he was pro-German in wartime was ridiculous: the Postmaster-General, Charles Hobhouse, noted in August 1914 that although several ministers supported 'peace at any price', 'the PM, Haldane and I were for war if there was even a merely technical breach of the Belgian treaty'. Though an energetic war minister who had prepared the army to fight, Haldane was now condemned: Kipling had recently invented the words 'Boschialist' (a pro-German socialist) and 'Hunnomite' (for lesser offences, but 'a beautiful word' that he preferred, since it 'verges on the obscene'), and now pronounced Haldane 'indubitably a Hunnomite'. The *Daily Express* deplored employing 'elderly doctrinaire lawyers with German sympathies' and the *National Review* denounced him as 'a very clever German' (some even absurdly claimed that he was an illegitimate brother of the Kaiser). In May 1915 the Conservatives made Haldane's removal one price for joining the government, so Asquith sacked him. When the Tories' own elder statesman Lansdowne appealed for peace talks in 1917, and was generally execrated, Bertrand Russell joked that it would 'soon be discovered that his great aunt was born in Kiel, or that his grandfather was an admirer of Goethe'.[7]

There was a complete breach among the Churches, academics and socialists. The war liberated academics from a sense of inferiority to German scientific method – or, put more negatively, pedantry – under which they had long laboured. Lord Acton had worried as early as 1886 about 'the familiar German scholar . . . the man who complained that the public library allowed him only thirteen hours a day to read, the man who spent thirty years on one volume', but in 1915 an Oxford historian rejoiced that 'the age of German footnotes is on the wane'. Support for the war by almost the entire German professoriat seemed grounds for lamenting the decline of moral standards in German universities, a trend generally attributed to Hegel and Nietzsche, and to professors' employment as civil servants. German-born teachers were removed as summarily from British universities as were the German bands in cafés – though some of the latter ingeniously reappeared as 'Serbian' allies. German waiters who got the sack were less fortunate, largely because the *Daily Mail* urged a million readers to refuse service by a German, and even to demand to see the passport of any foreigner claiming to be Swiss.[8]

If British academics celebrated liberation from Teutonic role models, others severed more personal links. The biographer of Ford Madox Hueffer suggests that his readiness to write propaganda that paid little regard to either fact or previous conviction was a conscious assertion of the non-German over the German side of his ancestry. Hueffer did not do anything so obvious as changing his name (until after the war), but many others did. The conductor Basil Hindenburg could be forgiven for re-christening himself Basil Cameron, but this was a common trait even when the Germanness of names had no political connotation: the composer Gustav von Holst discreetly dropped his 'von', though Ralph Vaughan Williams continued mischievously to refer to him as 'v'. At Oxford, the Vice-Principal of Brasenose changed from Sonnenschein to Stallybrass, Cambridge's Professor Waldstein became Walston, and the Orientalist Arthur Schloss became Arthur Waley. Pubs changed their names – East London's 'Frederick the Great' becoming the 'Edward VII', so blotting out the Protestant alliance from the Seven Years War – and so did street names: Leicester's Hanover Street was Anglicised into Andover, Saxe-Coburg into Saxby, and Gotha into Gotham. All these streets had been named for the royal family, which could not withstand the tide itself. Neither Asquith nor Lloyd George was impressed by royal apologies for the war service of German cousins, and Lloyd George privately called the King 'my German friend'. Kipling was equally unimpressed when Princess Victoria of Schleswig-Holstein asked of the Kaiser, 'Who would have thought he would have turned out like *this*?' When H. G. Wells wrote disparagingly of Britain having 'an alien and uninspiring court', George V angrily responded, 'I may be uninspiring but I'll be damned if I'm an alien.' Whispers about the King's ancestry continued, though, and in 1917 he condoned witch-hunting by renaming his clan 'the house and family of Windsor' ('of' here conflating place and surname). Royals had to renounce German titles in favour of new-minted British ones, as the Duke of Teck became Marquess of Cambridge. Kaiser Wilhelm at least saw the funny side, instructing his court theatre to perform *The Merry Wives of Saxe-Coburg-Gotha*, but George V was never afterwards happy in the company of Germans. Though he opposed the Kaiser's trial as a war criminal, he refused ever to communicate with Wilhelm in his post-war Dutch exile.[9]

One of the most violent severing of ties was in music, where generations of inferiority brought out the worst in the British. A Proms concert in August 1914 should have included music by Richard Strauss, but Tchaikovsky's *Capriccio Italien* was substituted, an ally replacing an enemy. There were demands for 'no-German-music' concerts and more British music was played, also more 'allied' music by Russian and French composers. But while Tchaikovsky presented no problem, British composers were a different matter; Arnold Bennett went to one such concert and pronounced it 'rotten'. As George Bernard Shaw crowed, when British music was advertised 'Everyone applauded the announcement. But nobody went to the concerts.' Equally it was noticed that if *all* 'German' music were banned then Handel's *Messiah* and Mendelssohn's *Elijah* would have to go, and this was unacceptable. Concert promoters therefore developed a compromise, continuing to programme dead masters but refusing music by living Germans. One clever solution was to ban Wagner's *Kaisermarsch* but play his 'Rule Britannia' Overture instead, subjecting Germans to friendly fire. The ideological implication was that Beethoven characterised acceptable Germany in the past, Richard Strauss contemporary Prussian militarism. The *Musical Times* thought 'Bach, Haydn, Mozart, Beethoven, Mendelssohn had nothing to do with Twentieth Century mad German megalomania. Both England and Prussia were on the side of the angels in Beethoven's time' (against Napoleon, as 'allied' French critics may have noticed). The 'two Germanies' was redefined, as chronology rather than geography.[10]

Nothing illustrates British ambivalence about German culture better than the Great War record of Sir Edward Elgar. Germans had admired Elgar's music from an early stage, and German audiences rallied to some works better than the British; one of his most 'British' works, the enigmatic variation 'Nimrod', was punningly dedicated to his German friend Jaeger. Indeed, the conductor Thomas Beecham, when asked in wartime 'Where have all Elgar's friends gone?', replied, 'They are all interned.' Elgar himself had enrolled in the Special Constabulary, thinking it 'a pity I am too old to be a soldier'. Alice

Elgar's wartime diary evidences hostility to the 'diabolical Germans', and, though she was more a patriotic imperialist than her husband, they rarely differed about the war. He set wartime lyrics in support of Belgian and Polish allies, and music written for patriotic recitations like *Le Drapeau Belge* suggests personal sympathy with their denunciations of black German hearts. Elgar's largest wartime work, a setting of Laurence Binyon poems as *The Spirit of England*, is mostly grieving music, but one of Binyon's verses caused Elgar difficulty. This asserted that Germany's was 'the barren creed of blood and iron, vampyre of Europe's wasted will'. He could not find music for such words, until he hit on the idea of accompanying them with the 'Demons' Chorus from his own *Dream of Gerontius*, confirming that Germans were literally 'diabolical'. When challenged the composer was unrepentant: 'Two years ago I held over that section hoping that some trace of manly spirit would show itself in the direction of German affairs; that hope is gone forever & the Hun branded as less than a beast for very many generations.' Since he could not imagine music so frightful, he had linked it musically to the circle of hell reserved for the 'great intellects' that 'gibber and snarl *knowing they have fallen*. This is exactly the case with the Germans now.'[11]

If Elgar remained always an outsider, Hubert Parry was an establishment figure – married into the aristocracy, Oxford professor and the Royal College of Music's director – but it was an alternative establishment: he hated hierarchy, loathed his wife's relatives, and was relieved when his daughter married the radical Liberal (later Labour) Arthur Ponsonby MP. Parry was passionately fond of German culture: as a young man he sought lessons with Brahms and was overwhelmed by Wagner and his music; he counted the pianist Edward Dannreuther and the conductor Hans Richter as close friends, and even when at the forefront of a definitively British voice in music continued to pay homage to the German masters. When Brahms died, Parry told his students that he had been 'the last of the great German heroes of musical art', from whom 'the English race' should learn.[12]

When the war began, it came home to Parry at once, for his assistant, George Schlickenmeyer, was interned as a suspected spy, and not even Parry's elite connections could secure his release. Yet if he thought Schlickenmeyer worth saving, he had reversed his view of Germany, likening her in his esteem to the fall of Lucifer, a beautiful thing gone rotten. As Jeremy Dibble puts it, 'he was at a loss to understand how a nation so pre-eminent for its contribution to artistic ideology and creativity' could unleash the greatest war in history, and he sought a cultural explanation in the 'bitter spite' infiltrated into the German mind by Nietzsche. Though he retained personal doubt, his public utterances were uncompromising: as he told his students during a formal address late in 1914, he had his 'own confession to make. For I have been a quarter of a century and more a pro-Teuton.' He had so worshipped German art as not to see clearly Germany itself, but 'we know now that it is arrogance run mad. We know it is the hideous militarism of the Prussians that has poisoned the wells of the spirit throughout Germany.' Horror of the bombing of civilians reinforced this initial view, 'all owing to the militarism and the vile fury of forceful domination which is the German creed'. Though convinced that 'we now know that if we cannot scotch the war-fiend the world will not be worth living in', Parry remained a troubled man. He worried about German friends and recognised that they were undergoing similar spiritual torment. Hence he did his bit for war charities and argued with his son-in-law about the war, but when Hans Richter resigned his British honours to demonstrate support for Germany, Parry sent a message of love and respect. Just how moderate this was appears in the reaction by the Irish Tory composer C. V. Stanford to a similar provocation. As Parry's Cambridge counterpart, Stanford also admired German musical culture, but when Max Bruch resigned his Oxford honorary degree he detected a national insult. Adopting a sneering, anti-Semitic tone, Stanford sent Bruch an open letter linking the degeneration of German music to the ethical downfall of Germany. 'As a modern German you have forgotten the meaning of self-reliance . . . Initiative is to you and Germany a sealed book. England has opened it.' Deploring the sheer scale of Richard Strauss's orchestral works, and noting that 'the essence of German militarism has been reliance on numbers', Stanford argued that 'Strauss is the counterpart of Bernhardi of the General Staff'. Nevertheless, 'neither Wagner nor Brahms had any truck with the Prussianised crew who have arisen since their day' and deserved no blame for the 'the beastliness' of modern Germany, or the 'modern muck' produced by Strauss. Deeply suspicious of such jingoism, Parry nevertheless wrote during the war his best-known and most patriotic work, setting 'Jerusalem' for the pro-war pressure group 'Fight for Right'. This contains, thanks to Blake, no hostility to anything except capitalism, and was about as harmless a patriotic song as it was possible to produce in wartime. Parry was delighted that 'Jerusalem' became at once a suffragette anthem, but his death in 1918 meant that he never saw its wholesale adoption by Women's Institutes in the 1920s, nor its popularity at internationalist rallies. Its rebranding as the English cricket anthem eighty years later would surely have seemed a mystery; as would its annual rendition, accompanied by flag-waving frenzy, at the Last Night of the Proms.[13]

Parry was certainly no imperialist, and there is much debate about the extent of Elgar's imperialism: in view of his Catholicism, his humble origins and the reluctance of the hierarchy to accept him, it is plausibly claimed that his clipped tones and military moustache concealed uncertainties. If so, in rallying to the wartime consensus Elgar and Parry were by no means the only oppositional figures to do so. Nonconformists had recently thought war belonged 'to the dark ages; it is not fit for our time', as Clifford proclaimed in a New Year message to Baptists for 1914. *Peacemaker*, magazine of the Associated Councils of the Churches of the British and German Empire for Fostering Friendly Relations between the Two Peoples, proclaimed even in June 1914 that it was 'almost difficult to realize that there are still unsolved problems affecting the relations of the two countries.' When war broke out, nonconformist leaders were at a fraternal conference in Konstanz and needed the intervention of the Kaiser's favourite preacher to get them home. But the invasion of Belgium changed them into holy warriors; this would be, proclaimed the *Christian World*, 'a war against War-Lordism'. Nonconformists were among the super-patriots of the Great War: men like Geoffrey Shakespeare, who led his congregation in prayers for Germany's utter destruction. Even those who had self-righteously denounced the Boer War supported this one: the *Spectator* could not resist poking fun at 'our Grand Old Man' Clifford for having become 'a Cromwell Ironside, taunting the shirkers and urging that the war should be pursued with our whole force'. Old antagonisms with Anglicanism were largely set aside, and nonconformists did not demur when an Anglican bishop referred to the Allies as 'the pre-ordained instruments to save the Christian civilisation of Europe from being overcome by a brutal and ruthless paganism'. Nor did they dissent when, in response to a patriotic manifesto by eighty German theologians, the Archbishop of Canterbury led the British Churches' counter-attack, asserting that the destruction of Louvain proved who were the barbarians.[14]

Suffragette leaders were hardly less militant than they had been in the campaign for votes, especially those who followed Mrs Emmeline Pankhurst. It was claimed that she called off the suffragette campaign as a tactic to prove women's fitness for political rights. Since votes for women arrived in 1918, it worked out that way, but no such theory is needed to explain her views. Back in the 1870s, she had written a play about the Paris Commune in which a character rages about France's German occupiers: 'You will see them marching with their odious goosestep through our beloved Paris. Oh their brutal heavy jaws and those cold, prominent eyes, cold and hard as the eyes of a snake, damned Prussian savages.' When 1914 produced what she referred to as the 'GERMAN PERIL', she denounced it with the best of them: Germany was not a real democracy, even though the right to vote happened to be more widely available there than in Britain, and was anyway backward about women's rights, its military system 'masculinity carried to a point of enormity and obscenity'. (Kipling too wrote of Germany counting on England's 'feminism'.) The fight against Germany was the continuation of pre-war suffrage agitation rather than its denial, the struggle 'in which all fighters for freedom have been engaged'. Pankhurst would 'rather die a thousand deaths than see my country a province of Germany'. She campaigned for interning aliens, supported the distribution of white feathers, and demanded the dismissal of officials of German blood. 'If the Germans came here, they would outrage women and children, shoot the men to force submission, and then they would Germanize us.' Her daughter Christabel proclaimed that 'the men who talk of peace by negotiation have lost any idea of what it is to be a British citizen'. They were 'foxes without tails. Men who do not resent the Germanisation of Britain, because they are Germans already.' The Pankhursts were not the entirety of the suffrage movement, and there were voices raised in support of different views (including daughter Sylvia's), but they were easily the best-known figures in the organisation. Millicent Fawcett's rival wing of the movement also backed the war effort, if rather less stridently anti-German in tone, while Annie Kenney plumbed new depths after visiting a spiritualist who claimed contact with the reincarnated spirit of Voltaire, angrily denouncing the dead man's 'pro-German pacifism'.[15]

Socialists also believed before 1914 that the age of peace had dawned, through workers' power to ensure that a war government was halted in its tracks. Within days of the war's onset, though, the Socialist International split and British socialists denounced German comrades for voting funds for the war. Having so few seats, British Labour MPs had less influence, but they would certainly have done the same. Trade unions and the Labour Party both argued that war must go on until Germany was utterly defeated, but there were individuals like H. M. Hyndman and Robert Blatchford who lobbied for an even stronger effort; Blatchford thought Germans 'a race of militaristic bandits' who wanted to come to London to murder everyone. In 1915 they formed the Socialist National Defence Committee to counter the influence of the few British socialists who opposed the war. Resigning the Labour leadership to campaign for peace, Ramsay MacDonald acknowledged that it was 'the most popular war this country has ever fought'; on this basis Labour joined Asquith's war government in 1915 and Lloyd George's in 1916. Defending his ministerial record in 1917, party leader Arthur Henderson stressed that it had always been the majority Labour view that the war should be supported, for a German victory would mean defeat for democracy. Fabians like Sidney Webb supported the war 'to overthrow aggressive militarism', and assured his wife Beatrice that 'the Great War will seem to future generations a landmark of progress'. Even Shaw was only half hearted in opposing war, cynical debunkings of false morality camouflaging his belief that Germany must be defeated. Tawney took a more detached view, having been a pre-war admirer of German social relief, from which Britain had much to learn. However, just like the guild socialist G. D. H. Cole, he thought after 1914 that 'a German victory would be a disaster for Europe'. Tawney became not just a supporter of the war but an army sergeant adept at shooting Germans. After the invasion of Belgium, he never wavered in the belief that only German defeat could advance the left-wing causes that were the mainspring of his personal beliefs. To Tawney, Germany was, as J. M. Winter puts it, not so much a country as 'a state of mind', and it was in opposing the 'Might equals Right' approach that he fought her.[16]

A final group to review is soldiers. As Martin Stephen argues, one of the 'minor myths' of the Great War has been that 'soldiers sympathised with their opposite numbers in the German trenches, and felt bonded to them by a universal horror of experience'. This illusion has rested heavily on the writings of junior officers who appointed themselves spokesmen for their men. There were certainly occasions that indicated lack of hostility to German soldiers as individuals, notably the unofficial Christmas truce of 1914 and the 'live and let live system' in quiet sectors of the front. Once Germans had been captured, it was noticed that British soldiers shared water and cigarettes with them, sometimes for the newsreel cameras. Occasions when prisoners were shot out of hand were undocumented and unphotographed, but more consistent with an officer's later recollection that 'We all knew that the Germans were as anxious to kill as many of us as possible . . . and we all to a man felt we should ourselves kill as many Germans as we could in return.' Many private soldiers thought of Germans without deep hatred, and 'Fritz', 'Jerry' or 'the Alleyman' were commoner epithets than 'Huns' and 'Boches', labels used by officers and civilians. Richard Holmes recently concluded that there was great respect for the German soldier and little personal animus; he also records, though, that there were 'striking exceptions' to this pattern of behaviour, and that few British soldiers had strong views because few ever met Germans until they surrendered. A 'two Germanies' view existed in respect of Prussians being soldiers you really would not want to be up against in a fight while there was lesser fear of Saxons, Württemburgers and Bavarians, but Germans had similar respect for Highlanders and Australians, less for the Welsh and the southern English. None of this was evidence either of a lack of patriotism among British soldiers or of pro-German sympathies. Ian Hay's novel *The First Hundred Thousand*, a breezy account of an enthusiastic volunteer battalion of 1914, with its assumption of atrocities committed by beastly Teutons, remained popular reading-matter in the trenches right up to 1918, although by then many readers were conscripts. Soldiers were part of the national consensus about the war, and since they had even more reason than civilians to hate those who caused such horrors, they too laid the accumulating blame on the enemy.

Trench newspapers were not as full of unreasoning hatred as the *Daily Mail*, but nor did they preach international brotherhood. Even those who tried to maintain perspective found that it vanished during fighting: the humane Tawney recalled that 'the sight of the Germans drove everything else out of my head'. Siegfried Sassoon, for all the 'anti-war' views claimed for him later, was writing in his diary in 1916 that he just wanted to stick his bayonet into Germans by daylight. Neither Sassoon nor Wilfred Owen won the Military Cross for their passive suffering; nor were they decorated for feeling *angst* on behalf of their men.[17]

With such a firm national consensus about the evil represented by 'Germany', the British government had no need to force its views on the people. The state did extend its activities into mind control for the first time in 1914–18, but slowly and for the most part indirectly, with greater emphasis on influencing neutral America than the British. The most famous posters of 1914–16 were commissioned by the Liberal Party for the Joint Parliamentary Recruiting Committee, and celebrated propaganda stories came from newspapers off their own bat. Even in 1917–18 the information war was run ministerially by conscripted press lords, while such non-governmental bodies as the British Empire Union propagated more anti-German venom than the cabinet. Michael Paris argues that official films 'avoided the hysterical and deeply chauvinistic "propaganda of hate" that was so dominant in the wartime propaganda constructed by the press and the innumerable private patriotic organisations that sprang up'. In any case, the number of cameramen working for the government was never more than a single newsreel company would have employed on the Grand National, so their capacity for influence was strictly limited. No doubt greater government interference would have emerged, or emerged earlier, had it been needed. It never was. The historian of wartime theatre reports that there was no difficulty with 'the mobilization of hatred against the enemy' because of 'the tide of patriotic enthusiasm that swept the country in 1914'; when in 1915 it became a different task for the long haul, 'the authorities had the theatre's continued backing'. Unlike 1939–45, this was not among British theatre's finest hours, one standard history comparing 1914–18 to the Puritans' closing of the theatres in 1642. Theatre provided escapist entertainment for civilians and soldiers on leave, with a steady diet of war plays with patriotic messages. Over two hundred of these were licensed for performance by 1916, while over a hundred dramatised German espionage. The censor played little part in shaping these violently anti-German performances, and where he did intervene it was more often on grounds of taste than politics. He would not pass the stripping and beating of a mother superior by German soldiers, but allowed in the same play a speech about them burning eyes out with a red-hot iron, since it took place offstage. Several plays showed German officers condoning mass rape, for the assumption was that atrocities comprised part of the German army's normal behaviour. It was during the Great War that theatres and concert halls began to play the national anthem at each performance, a practice then continued for half a century.[18]

War plays were generally welcomed in the press, or reviewed unfavourably only because they were bad plays rather than for their content. The press itself, without much need for censorship or state control, threw itself into propaganda with enthusiasm – especially such mass-market titles as the *Daily Mail* and the pictorial *Daily Mirror*. Populist campaigners like Horatio Bottomley and Pemberton Billing owed a great deal to press support, in spreading dark fantasies about sinister networks of homosexual pro-Germans in high places, for Bottomley mainly through his own paper *John Bull*, which enjoyed a circulation of between one and two million copies. Newspapers went well beyond the government in orchestrating hatred, notably so in ridiculing Asquith's wife for sending food parcels to German prisoners of war (POWs). Such papers could not be ignored, however, for in many cases they had shown more prescience than the government about a German war. The *Daily Mail* and the *National Review* proudly reprinted in 1914 'scaremongering' stories from past years, and reaped obvious benefit: the *Mail*, describing itself as 'the paper that persistently warned the public about the war', added 15 per cent to its daily sales. The *Daily Express*'s circulation went up by over 30 per cent once it had assured readers that its editor, R. D. Blumenfeld, 'is not and never has been a German', that the newsprint used 'is not and never has been made in Germany', and that 'there is not one German who works on the staff'. As the philosopher Gilbert Murray wrote, explaining his conversion from philosopher to propagandist.

I have derided all scares and loathed all scaremongers and breeders of hatred. I have believed (as I still believe) that many persons now in newspaper offices might be more profitably housed in lunatic asylums . . . And I now see that on a large part of this question – by no means the whole of it – I was wrong, and a large number of people whom I honour most were wrong.

It was impossible, whatever such men believed about the sanity of Fleet Street's warriors, to sustain any demand for a return to reason.[19]

Since newspapers were the only mass medium in 1914, they largely set the tone for the debate, but writers of stature retained freedom of expression, and were likely anyway to read liberal papers that continued to value rationality over emotion. However, eminent literati like Thomas Hardy and Henry James rushed to lend their pens and reputations to the cause. The biggest impact of this writers' war was outside Britain, where independence from the British government allowed their personal followings to influence neutral opinion. The depths to which even a literary war could descend appear in the identification of Shakespeare by one playwright as 'Wilhelm the Third', whose characters dramatically invade the bloodstained dreams of Wilhelm II. Another writer, conceding that in 'the *Goethe*' Germans had at least one literary 'super-dreadnought', thought it 'hardly the equal in guns or speed to the *Shakespeare*'. Oxford's Professor of English, Sir Walter Raleigh, recalled in 1918 that a German poet had thought Germany Hamlet, 'urged by the spirit of her fathers to claim her inheritance, vacillating and lost in thought, but destined before the Fifth Act ends to strew the stage with the corpses of her enemies'. Raleigh, though, was not content to have Shakespeare a German colony, for 'only a German could hit on the idea that Germany is Hamlet . . . But if these clumsy allegories must be imposed upon great poets, Germany need not go abroad to seek her destiny. Germany is Faust; she desired science and power and pleasure, and to get them on a short lease she paid the price of her soul.'[20]

On the home front, more impact was made by middlebrow writers like John Buchan and Arthur Conan Doyle, for if Shakespeare was conscripted for the duration, Sherlock Holmes was volunteered. Conan Doyle signed the 'Authors' Manifesto' of 1914, becoming a 'literary tourist' who published bland pamphlets after visiting the trenches ('occasionally there were patches of untidiness'). In one such account he contrasted Australian soldiers' keen, manly and clear-cut faces with German prisoners, 'heavy-jawed, beetle-browed, uncouth louts with ox-like stolidity and dullness'. Though fifty-five in 1914, he volunteered for the army and when rejected formed a volunteer defence force, being photographed as a private on guard duty. His unique contribution was though to bring Holmes and Watson back from the dead for one last adventure, in the short story 'His Last Bow: An Epilogue of Sherlock Holmes'. This assumes a longstanding German war plot and brilliant British intelligence thwarting it. German spies long knew that August 1914 would be the date, and organised the 'devil's brew of Irish civil war, window-breaking furies and God knows what' which kept pre-war Britain distracted (rather a shock to Mrs Pankhurst). The evil Van Bork, 'the Prussian', pretended to be 'a sportsman' and was welcomed by the generous English. Not knowing that these English (Holmes in disguise) are on to him, he confidently expects a German invasion and massed attacks by Zeppelins within a week. Once trapped by Holmes, however, he becomes boorish, letting loose 'a furious stream of German invective'. Holmes recapitulates earlier services to a more civilised Germany, and is sure that antagonism between the two countries is caused by Germany – it must be if they had August 1914 marked in their diaries in advance. He also refers obliquely to the British mood, assuring Van Bork that if he flees he will add 'The Dangling Prussian' to the repertory of English inn-signs. Finally, the plot defeated, Holmes resumes beekeeping, though Watson rejoins his old regiment. (But how will dear old Watson cope with shell-shock?) Before that, though, the moral is driven home by Holmes telling Watson of the better world to come when the German 'east wind' ceases.[21]

Though an older and more experienced writer, Conan Doyle offers here a story more reminiscent of John Buchan than his own earlier tales. Buchan had dabbled widely before the war – journalism, soldiering, public administration and the law – but really made his name through his 'Richard Hannay' stories, which began with *The Thirty-Nine Steps* (1915) and continued with *Greenmantle* (1916) and *Mr Standfast* (1919), each dedicated to a friend or unit in the army. He wrote conventional propaganda and war histories too, but saw thrillers as the real contribution to the war effort he could make in no other way, being in poor health. His 'shockers' were widely read, not least by soldiers: *The Thirty-Nine Steps* quickly sold twenty-five thousand copies in 1915, and was reissued in a pocket edition for 'Tommies'. Buchan's Germans are ruthless aggressors, devoid of moral scruple. In *The Thirty-Nine Steps* they murder, bludgeon and blackmail their way across Britain to steal naval secrets that will neutralise the Royal Navy on the outbreak of war. Though they exhibit patriotism ('in a foul way'), they are a devilishly evil foe. By *Greenmantle*, Hannay has done good service with the army; now he thwarts 'the whole ugly mechanism of German war' in the Near East, and von Stumm's death is 'God's judgement on the man who had set himself above his kind', like Germany itself, also 'a brute and a bully'. By *Mr Standfast*, set when British forces defeat the final German offensive of 1918, Hannay is a brigadier with the DSO and Legion of Honour (not to mention 'Matabele and South African medals') to his name. He is an authentic war hero as well as a master of counter-espionage, a fictional T. E. Lawrence (on whom Buchan's 'Sandy Arbuthnot' was based). As the title suggests, black and white characterisations of British and German have become even sharper; the final pages describe the death of Hannay's South African friend Peter Pienaar, sacrificing his life to prevent the German air ace Lensch escaping. The book closes with reference to *The Pilgrim's Progress*, explicitly linking Britain with Christianity and Germany with satanic evil; Hannay knows the foe cannot triumph, for 'by the grace of God that gate was barred for ever'. Kipling would have enjoyed the reference, for in his poem 'A Tinker out of Bedford' he too enlisted *The Pilgrim's Progress*:

> Two hundred years and thirty.
> Ere Armageddon came,
> His single hand portrayed it,
> And Bunyan was his name.

Bunyan, thought Kipling, would have 'thoroughly understood the Hun'. He would certainly have appreciated the wartime poster showing a parting of the ways: one signpost pointing to 'German peace', the primrose path leading to hell ('peace before victory'), while the steep, uphill pathway arrives eventually in the sunlit uplands of 'victory before peace'. Defeating Huns is God's work.[22]

In forming and retaining such negative views of Germany, Britons placed emphasis on 'atrocities' committed by German armed forces. While these were exaggerated, they were not entirely fanciful: from August 1914 onwards the German government and army adopted military policies acknowledged as risky for Germany's image abroad, but thought justifiable in the pursuit of victory, after which the victors would write the history. German propaganda agencies were less effective than the British, notably so in the crucial United States, but then they had a far more difficult product to sell. When it was later claimed – and widely believed – that British propaganda, rather than naval blockade and the Allied armies, had won the war (a convenient evasion from the viewpoint of pacifists and Nazis alike), the factual basis of British propaganda largely faded from sight too. But to understand the British war mentality in these years it must be put back in its proper place.

When the *Daily Mail Yearbook* for 1917 turned to 'German outrages against humanity – a diabolical record', it listed eighteen categories as 'a few of the worst outrages'. For most Britons, the worst was the treatment of Belgians in August and September 1914. Britain would have to have declared war anyway, in defence of France and the European balance of power, but the invasion of 'gallant little Belgium' enabled the country to fight without serious internal divisions. The German view, that Britain was hiding behind the Belgians and her treaty with them, had a good deal of validity, but the insolent claim of the German Chancellor that Britain had gone to war for 'a scrap of paper' ruined the argument, for it appeared to show that Germany regarded treaties as waste paper. (Though he protested that too much had been made of one offhand remark, Bethmann Hollweg never denied he had said it.) Never slow to play the populist card, Lloyd George invited the audience at one of his meetings to burn their five-pound notes, which were also scraps of paper, but carried 'the whole credit of the British Empire [loud applause]'. That view was doubled in trumps by Germany's response to Belgium's protests: Belgians had only themselves to blame for they could have let the German army walk over them and so avoided bloodshed. Here, to British eyes, was a refusal to accept that small countries had any rights. Henceforth, British people knew they were at war for a moral cause. As with the view that Germany had caused the war, this conviction ensured that blame for later suffering would fall on Germany. Kipling wrote that 'when Liege falls the German army will make such a ghastly "example" of it (with a view to striking terror) as will send every available male in England scuttling into the ranks in order to get a gun to have a pot at the Germans. That's where the policy of "striking terror" breaks down as applied to English folk.' A recruiting song gibed of the Kaiser that 'naughty nights at Liege quite upset this dirty dick', while *Punch* depicted 'The Triumph of "Culture"' as an aggressive German officer gloating over a defenceless Belgian woman and her daughter; their menfolk killed and their house burning, Belgium was being raped.[23]

Belgium therefore occupied a warmer place in British hearts than ever before or since. John Galsworthy was prepared to argue the case even when other views of the war had changed. In *Maid in Waiting* (1930) a sceptical American asks if the British ever really believed in 'Belgium', and receives an answer he thinks 'mighty well put':

> Speaking for oneself, yes. I don't suppose it made any difference to the Army people, Navy people, big business people, or even to a large section of Society, political or otherwise. They all knew that if war came they were practically committed to France. But to simple folk like myself and some two-thirds of the population not in the know, to the working classes, in fact, generally, it made all the difference.

Back in 1914, the National Relief Committee produced 185,000 posters and a million Belgian flags for display in Britain, and raised £160,000 for Belgian war charities; Belgian artists, musicians, painters and cartoonists achieved fame; and crowds turned out for Emil Cammaerts's *Carillon*, declaimed to Elgar's stirring accompaniment. Such feelings were reinforced by the universal view that the German army had outraged decency by its descent into barbarism at the expense of Belgian civilians. Among the chaos of fleeing refugees, a rapidly advancing army on a tight timetable, and inadequate press coverage by neutrals, lurid stories of murder and desecration circulated, inevitably more the product of rumour than fact when it was not easy to tell one from the other. They certainly included events that never took place at all, and others exaggerated out of all proportion. August 1914 provides the *locus classicus* of the dictum that 'truth is the first casualty of war', though reality was terrible enough. Asquith privately told a correspondent that 'there are stories of the Germans killing [wounded Belgians], which one prefers not to believe. The burning of Louvain is the worst thing they have yet done. It reminds one of the Thirty Years War . . . and the achievements of Tilly and Wallenstein.' (Even sceptics went back to German history for a precedent.) Preferring not to believe such tales, he cross-examined a wounded soldier who claimed to have personally seen Germans advancing behind screens of Belgian civilians. When he could not shake this testimony, his verdict was 'Pretty bad!' But if Asquith was unconvinced, when he told a cabinet colleague the story was noted in his own diary as fact. By the end of September, Asquith believed in atrocities himself, writing of the Belgians' 'piteous appeals for help . . . one cannot be surprised or blame them, for the Germans have been unusually active these last few days in burning their villages and shooting the inhabitants'. Kipling, living near the Sussex coast, had no need of third-hand testimony, for he met Belgian refugees and was shocked by what they told him. His wife wrote:

Rud tries to see as often as possible a young Belgian refugee who was a teacher at Liege . . . Such a charming young fellow who they fear will go crazy. He saw the Germans cut the throat of his father and mother and sister of 12, after they had raped the latter, and he cannot be got to close his eyes because he says that he can see it all again.[24]

Since most of Belgium remained under German occupation for four years, and was treated with exemplary harshness, this initial view of barbaric treatment remained central to British perceptions of the war. The systematic theft of civilians' property for military use was not well known, but the deportation of a hundred thousand Belgians to work as slaves in German war industries attracted attention. That record was the basis for the British film that invited viewers to imagine a German occupation of Chester, and what would happen to its inhabitants. It was also cited as evidence by the Wimbledon clergyman who argued in 1916 that a German invasion of Britain would be followed by the killing of 'every male child', and his yet more improbable claim that British girls would be removed to 'human stud farms in Germany'. Atrocity claims were sensationally revisited when in 1918 the government commissioned D. W. Griffith to make *Hearts of the World*, in which Lillian Gish barely escapes onscreen rape by a German officer. None of these wilder tales would have been credible without awareness of what had happened in Belgium.[25]

But *had* it happened to Belgium? The question arises only because of the best-known episode in the propaganda war, the report of a commission under Lord Bryce which concluded that Germany committed atrocities, a report generally accepted as final in Britain because of the impeccable reputation of Bryce himself: there had been, concluded Bryce's committee, 'a deliberate campaign of terror-isation', so that 'innocent civilians, both men and women, were murdered in large numbers, women violated and children murdered'. But it has been clear since the 1920s that Bryce's report was highly unreliable, that the committee went out of its way not to check the evidence, or even to question witnesses on oath. As a result, it has been popularly believed that *all* the 1914–18 atrocity stories were fabricated. However, close reading does not lead to that conclusion, and nor does research in the German military archives. Robert Graves's *Goodbye to All That* was scathing about atrocity stories, claiming that by 1915 soldiers 'no longer believed highly-coloured accounts of German atrocities in Belgium', but continues that 'by atrocities we meant specifically rape, mutilation and torture – not summary shooting of suspected spies, harbourers of spies, *franc-tireurs*, or disobedient local officials'. It is doubtful if many Britons would in 1914 have accepted the distinction between these two types of crime and labelled only the first as 'atrocities'. Nor would they have been likely to accept Graves's corollary: that all armies committed crimes of the second type. Germany alone of the Western combatants occupied large tracts of inhabited foreign territory, so competing claims are impossible to confirm anyway. John Horne and Alan Kramer confirm that the German army did indeed shoot civilians, burn towns and commit other *military* outrages, which these prize-winning Irish authors consider 'atrocities'. The practice arose from panic, from expectations of guerrilla resistance not actually there, but also as a conscious military intention to terrorise Belgians into submission.

Saxons as well as Prussians were among the offenders. Nobody, though, claims to substantiate the generalised accusations of rape, mutilation and torture that were so popular in 1914. Trevor Wilson fascinatingly suggests that Bryce, a Liberal supporter of the war only because of Belgium, faced up to exactly this distinction. Knowing that to clear the German army of one category of atrocity (for which it was at best non-proven) would lead public opinion to acquit it of the type of atrocity of which it was guilty (as it largely has done ever since Bryce's report was discredited), he may have chosen deliberately not to allow this to happen, by 'confirming' the wilder stories. Such judgements had significance in the long term, but hardly at all in 1914–18. For the duration, the mass of British people concurred with Kipling, believing that the Germans had raped Belgium and would do the same to Sussex.[26]

Establishment of German guilt over Belgium in the first weeks of war facilitated belief in later examples of German 'frightfulness', often labelled *Schrecklichkeit*, as if such methods were describable only in German. When implausible claims were circulated about Germany rendering human corpses to make margarine, the government argued that 'in view of the many atrocious actions of which the Germans have been guilty, in defiance of all the dictates of civilisation and humanity', there did not 'appear to be any reason why [this] should not be true'. Kipling, in a poem even he dared not publish, with the heroine cheekily derived from Goethe's *Werther*, gave recycling human remains a comic twist:

> Charlotte, when she saw what Herman
> Yielded after he was dead,
> Like a well-conducted German,
> Spread him lightly on her bread.

In cases involving new weapons or new tactics of war, neither ignorance nor black comedy was needed. Germany was not only the first country to use poison gas, but pretended otherwise by claiming a week earlier that its troops had been poisoned by gas from the Allies. Use of gas was explicitly outlawed by pre-war conventions that Germany had signed. (The Allies then used gas too, claiming historic rights of retaliation once Germany had incurred the odium of setting the precedent.) Much the same was true of the flamethrower, again an outlawed weapon that Germany used first, and of the indiscriminate bombing and shelling of civilians. Conan Doyle wrote of his 'feeling of loathing' for using gas, 'an incident by which warfare was degraded, and a great army . . . became in a single day an object of horror and contempt'.[27]

When German warships shelled Whitby, Scarborough and Hartlepool in December 1914, killing 133 people, the news shocked the British public, not least because it appeared to show the reality of earlier invasion scares. One Hartlepool woman remembered it in the 1990s as 'a terrible thing to do, we were angry, not afraid, more angry. Why had little children been killed going to school? Why had that lady in Thirlmere Street, so close to my own home, been killed? The poor soul was only cooking her breakfast. I think that put a hatred of the Germans into us.' The *Daily Mirror* wrote of 'German Ghouls Gloating over Murder of English Schoolboys'. Churchill, embarrassed that his navy had not prevented the attack, wrote angrily of the 'Scarborough baby-killers'; so angrily that the Prime Minister thought he had gone too far in 'cheapish rhetoric and an undertone of angry snarl'. Asquith, though, was out of touch with the growing fury. Lady Elgar told her diary that it was 'low, barbaristic to shell a defenceless watering place'. After the *Lusitania* was sunk, it was a 'truly German deed', and when Kitchener was drowned after HMS *Hampshire* hit a mine she suspected 'some horrid treason and German murder'. When Yarmouth was bombed by Zeppelins, she noted that the Germans were 'engulfing themselves more deeply in crime than ever. Brutes.' Such air raids, reported the *Daily Mail*, were 'an attempt, without an excusing circumstance, to wage war on the lines of a sheer terrorism'.[28]

Zeppelin attacks continued to produce such reactions, even when the Royal Flying Corps retaliated against German cities. There was much reference to a German postcard celebrating Zeppelins in the act of murdering babies, and there was a poster in which the Kaiser is saying, 'Look Hindenburg! My German Heroes!' as hospitals are bombed. The ironic reference to the bombers as 'Knights of the Air' contrasted with popular descriptions of Zeppelins as 'baby-killers' and gibes about their 'bravery', as they bombed from a thousand feet. A *Punch* cartoon showed the Kaiser rebuking aviators for not having killed children: 'Well, then, no babes, no iron crosses.' In total, 1413 British civilians were killed in air raids and 3000 injured, a drop in the ocean compared to the Western Front, but shocking to those who inherited a centuries-old security in their own homes. Security was snatched away by, as the *War Illustrated* put it, 'the Kaiser's Air Pirates'.[29]

More logically described as pirates were submariners: another British poster contrasted the Union Jack representing 'freedom of the seas' with German leaders: 'What would these pirates and pledge-breakers do?' The special hatred felt for German submariners was reflected in their segregation in POW camps, away from 'honourable prisoners of war' and subject to 'special conditions'. As the war ended, most of the Germans that the British government hoped to try as war criminals were U-boat commanders. The sinking of the *Lusitania* occasioned special anger, and reignited volunteering for the army. That extra outrage was partly because so many lives were lost, and partly because of reported German glee – a special medal was struck to honour the submariners. If this was ironic German humour in which the British could not see the joke, it was also in poor taste. Selfridge's sold 300,000 copies of the *Lusitania* medal at the sugges-tion of naval intelligence, the accompanying literature describing it as 'proof positive that such crimes are not merely regarded favourably but are given every encouragement in the land of *Kultur*'. So, despite the fact that the ship was carrying war goods (which the British gov-ernment denied), the sinking became another German own-goal, as was the widely quoted editorial in the *Kolnische Volkszeitung* about the death of a thousand passengers: 'With joyful pride we contem-plate this latest deed of our navy . . .' There were German critics of unrestricted submarine warfare: Princess Bluecher noted that some of the loudest enthusiasts for the *Lusitania* sinking soon had second thoughts, not because they disliked the tactic but because they had recognised its effect on neutrals. It can be argued indeed that Germany got the worst of both worlds, setting submarines on then calling them off, so offending neutral opinion without winning the naval war. A similar hesitancy was seen in individual incidents: when a submarine torpedoed the Channel steamer *Sussex* in March 1916, the commander first claimed that he thought it a minelayer, and then that it was a war transport. The British press believed neither explanation, but nor was it ever claimed as a straightforward act of war. The same confusion surrounded the most celebrated submarine-related 'atrocity', the execution of Captain Fryatt, whose 'only crime' was to ram the U-boat sinking his ship.[30]

In attacking the German submarine campaign as piracy and ignoring the British blockade that had the same aim of starving civilians, the British applied double standards. By the end of the war, the German ration was barely sufficient to sustain active life and German civilians were literally starving, better rations being reserved for the army. Meat, potatoes, sugar and soap were all rationed, in Berlin coal was almost impossible to find, and milk could be bought only for children and invalids; 1917 was the 'turnip winter' when even potatoes became unobtainable. Blockade swept the German merchant marine from the seas and German colonies were occupied, so that by 1917 all German economic activity was within Europe, while Britain's aspirations for a post-war settlement lay across the oceans. This generalised blockade was as 'illegal' in international law as Germany's submarine activity, justified by the British government as a belligerent's right of 'retaliation'. It was only after unrestricted submarine warfare began that the British 'reprisal' of stopping all supplies, not merely war goods, was introduced, so making the economic war much like the use of gas, a lowering of the standards of warfare for which Germany could be blamed. The press endorsed this explanation, and the public would hardly have had the legal skills with which to challenge it. Crucially, submarine attacks drowned identifiable sailors and passengers (some of whom were, helpfully, neutrals), while the British blockade killed unseen Germans miles from the sea. It was easy to notice one and ignore the other.[31]

The war finished as it started, with the German army accused of atrocities in retreat, exactly as it had been pilloried during the initial advances. As a deliberate military tactic (and hardly an original one), retreating troops implemented a scorched-earth policy, both in the 1917 withdrawal to the Hindenburg Line, and after Germany's 1918 defeats. The difficulty for Germany was that, unlike the Russians doing the same thing against Napoleon, they laid waste foreign territory rather than their own. As the Allies advanced, soldiers were shocked by the destruction, with not only bridges and railways blown up, but non-military destruction gratuitously thrown in too. Gilbert

Murray was now writing of 'the great criminals and semi-maniacs in Germany and Austria'. Noting that the destructive operation was officially called *Alberich*, after Wagner's malevolent troglodyte, the war correspondent Philip Gibbs was equally depressed to note that it had been inflicted on villagers by the same soldiers who had lived among them for two years: 'Karl was a nice boy. He cried when he went away . . . But he smashed up the neighbours' furniture with an axe.' Geoffrey Malins, an army cameraman not easily shocked by scenes of devastation, was deeply upset by what he saw in 1917:

> Houses burnt, horses taken away, agricultural implements wilfully smashed, fruit trees and bushes cut down, even the hedges around their little gardens, their cemetery violated and the remains of their dead strewn to the four winds of heaven. Their wells polluted with garbage and filth; in some cases deliberately poisoned, in others totally destroyed by dynamite. Their churches used as stables for horses and for drunken orgies. All the younger men deported and the prettiest of the girls.

Asking 'Is this war?', Malins answered, 'It is the work of savages, ghouls, fiends.' The liaison officer Edward Spears, witnessing similar devastation, noticed how German 'organisation' had been devoted to destruction and offered another supernatural description: 'it was as if Satan had poured desolation out of a gigantic watering can'.[32]

Beyond these unrelentingly negative images, how did 1914–18 change perceptions of Germany itself? Propaganda was targeted personally at the Kaiser, a tactic which had previously been officially discouraged, though the press had not always been successfully warned off. The ban on his portrayal on stage and in films, which he had enjoyed as a member of the royal family, ended in May 1915; the censor was having just too much difficulty with plays like *Gott Strafe England*, which lampooned the Kaiser to the great enjoyment of the audience simply by putting a character with a German accent on stage and then having him strut about making a fool of himself. As cartoonists knew, a spiked helmet and upturned moustaches instantly made 'the Kaiser'. The chief beneficiaries were entertainers in the music halls, though the legitimate stage was not slow to question Wilhelm's parentage too. J. M. Barrie, whose 'Captain Hook' in

Peter Pan (1904) was already based on the Kaiser – invader from the sea, fierce moustache, damaged arm, constant worry about behaving correctly, and a fantasy claim to the British throne – now cast off pretence: in *Der Tag* he put the Kaiser on stage as himself, proclaiming, 'The Day! We sweep the English Channel . . . Dover to London is a week of leisured marching, and London itself, unfortified and panic-stricken, falls in a day!' And this was the playwright of whom Jerome K. Jerome could write even in 1920 that 'he alone has the genius to force the public to listen to kindliness, tenderness and pity'. Another essentially kindly man driven to write war drama as propaganda was the poet Alfred Noyes, whose *Rada* effectively restaged *An Englishman's Home*, the heroine's mother shooting Rada and herself to save her daughter from being gang raped by bestial Germans whose brutalities include hanging a revolver on the Christmas tree.[33]

A recruiting song, 'Belgium Put the Kibosh on the Kaiser', captures the mixed message, in turn seeing Wilhelm as a funny foreigner, an urchin schoolboy, a madman with delusions of grandeur, and a threat to world peace. He is 'a silly German sausage', who 'dreamed Napoleon he'd be', but like all naughty boys he must be taught his lesson.

> Though the Kaiser stirred the Lion,
> Please excuse him for the crime.
> His lunatic attendant,
> Wasn't with him at the time . . .
> We shall shout with victory's joy,
> Hold your hand out naughty boy,
> You must never play at soldiers any more.

The Liberal minister Charles Hobhouse, meeting the actual Kaiser in 1914, had thought him 'vivacious, restless . . . well informed, uncertain, a remarkable individuality, but not a commanding personage . . . only dangerous because he was unstable'. Not a very different perception, once a wartime tone was added.[34]

At a more serious level, the Kaiser's posturings led to similar doubts as to whether he was a fool or so wicked a man as to merit trial as a war criminal. His new title, 'All-Highest War Lord', had to

English ears the sound of both the satanic and the ridiculous; a pre-war court circular reported that on Sunday the 'All-Highest' had presented his compliments to 'The Highest'. Stephen Phillips's play *Armageddon* achieved the same mixture of the diabolical and the absurd when Satan gives orders to his German generals. Kipling meanwhile wrote in 1918 a whimsical story about the trouble caused by traffic jams at the Pearly Gates, the result of the increased wartime death rate. This is for Kipling an unusual exercise in compassion, for among those who help out St Peter are historic sinners, including Judas Iscariot; there is no mention though of any German casualties getting in. The Kaiser's symbolic status repelled as much as it fascinated; for the sociologist Graham Wallas, the war was necessary, to destroy 'a medieval aggressive dynasty wielding the whole material force of a fully conscious national machine-industry'.[35]

The Kaiser was inseparable from Prussian Germany, all equally to blame in the Liberal Ramsey Muir's paranoid view: 'the whole policy of Germany during the last five and twenty years is of one piece', a planned 'great bid for world power which was made in 1914 on so slight a pretext'. Another historian, G. W. Prothero, thought that to avert the threat of social revolution at home, 'the great capitalists, the military party and the Emperor himself' had made common cause in the bid for world power, though Wilhelm was 'already inclined on other grounds to war'.[36] Prussia, its king and its Junkers remained then the chief targets. Kipling's poem 'A Death-bed', in which he reacted to rumours that the Kaiser had throat cancer, compared his tumour to the 'State above the law' which Wilhelm had previously embodied, with the murderous implication that he would get only his deserts. For Tawney in 1914, 'the scale of values which horrifies us' was precisely 'the claim of some Prussians to have a right to determine the future of "weaker" or "inferior" nations'. The political scientist Ernest Barker, aware that comparisons might be made between British policy in Ireland and Prussian colonisations of Slavs, affirmed that Prussia still did what Britain had given up long ago: 'While Prussia has been evicting the Poles, Great Britain has been settling the people of Ireland on the land.' It was Prussia that Arnold Bennett had in mind when he spoke of Germany as one vast military camp, a modern Sparta with 'every male citizen a private soldier and every private soldier an abject slave'. Gilbert Murray thought that the 'specialised soldier' was a deplorable Prussian invention, whereas other countries had 'the human soldier, the Christian soldier, the soldier with a sense of civil duties', so they were nowhere near as 'militarist' even when at war. Those who took this view were deeply resentful of Shaw's impish claim that Britain had its own Junker class, its Navy League and its Krupps, a theme he had already investigated in *Major Barbara* (1905). Yet as Paul Kennedy points out, the habit from Bismarck onwards of Germany's civilian leaders' 'flaunting of the uniform' on public occasions had no counterpart in Britain: 'the very idea of Gladstone, Campbell-Bannerman or Asquith in uniform appears absurd; Salisbury, who had little respect for the military, would have snorted in derision; Balfour would simply have felt uncomfortable'.[37]

R. W. Seton-Watson, doyen of British historians of Eastern Europe, thought that the difference lay in 'the very names of the two countries . . . 'Germany means the country of the Germans, as England means the country of the English. But the name Prussia commemorates the subjugation and extinction by German conquerors and crusaders from the west of the Prussians or Bo-Russians, a Slavonic tribe akin to the Russians.' The rising man in British politics, David Lloyd George, took a similar view of 'Prussians', writing, 'I like the Germans, but I hate the Junker caste'. Speaking for the government, he proclaimed in September 1914 that 'the Prussian Junker is the road-hog of Europe . . . Were he to win it would be the greatest catastrophe to have befallen democracy since the day of the Holy Alliance.' Two months later he promised a fight to the finish, until 'the military domination of Prussia is wholly and finally destroyed'. At the end of 1917, now Prime Minister, he asserted that 'the Allies entered this war to defend themselves against the aggression of the Prussian military domination' and must go on until there was 'no possibility of that caste ever again disturbing the peace of Europe'.[38]

Opponents of Prussia (especially those who thought it racially semi-Slav) had to explain away the uncomfortable fact that Russia, the greatest autocracy of all, was a British ally. It was easy enough to claim Tchaikovsky and Dostoevsky as evidence of Russia's contribution to European civilisation, and Diaghilev's Russian ballet helped too, but the political issue required intellectual gymnastics. Tolstoy offered better ammunition than Dostoevsky: the Shakespeare scholar

John Dover Wilson portrayed Russia, as Roland Stromberg puts it, as 'a kind of bucolic paradise inhabited by simple but sweet, religious peasants and kind-hearted landlords, living "in close communion with nature"'. It was 'the most Christian country in the world', with its 'fundamentally democratic spirit'. Stephen Graham wrote rhapsodically of 'Mother Russia', while British historians disingenuously discovered that Russia was democratic, but in some deeper sense than mere elections and parliamentary government. If there were in Russia imperialism, anti-Semitism and a police state, this was due to the 'Germanisation' of the bureaucracy in the last century. The revolutions of 1917 ended such nonsense, and made it easier for those on the British Left to support war against Germany. The vengeful peace that Germany then imposed on Bolshevik Russia provided new evidence of Prussian aggressive tendencies.[39]

In the denunciation of Prussia there was frequent reference back to two Germanies. Walter Raleigh, when reflecting that Germans had 'made a religion of war and terror', added that 'they were not always like that'. C. H. Herford, Manchester's Professor of English, supported 'the usual explanation of dividing the German people into two alien hosts', on one side the sensible people, writers, intellectuals, musicians 'and the millions of kindly men and women', on the other 'the brutally aggressive military caste'. While this usually separated Prussia from the rest, he did not think the distinction quite worked in that way. Sir Michael Sadler agreed, telling a friend that the Germany 'that you and we love is not responsible for this wickedness, except so far as it has not had the physical or moral courage to stab the Junkers in the face long ago'. Nobody believed in German duality more than James Bryce, who personally identified 'frightfulness' with Prussia (though his famous report was less discriminating). By 1916, Bryce was making a more limited point, arguing that Britain had to fight against practices that elevated the state above morality, but that 'our quarrel is with the German government'.[40]

By then, such distinctions had become rare, for support offered to Germany's war effort by the pre-war friends Herford thought of as 'kindly men and women' made it hard to avoid a tougher view. In October 1914 ninety-three leading German scholars announced that 'the German Army and People are one, and today this consciousness fraternises 70,000,000 Germans, of all ranks, positions and parties being one'. Herford regretfully concluded that 'the things we honour and the things we abhor' in Germany were now so inextricably mixed as to make distinctions meaningless. Elgar wrote sadly in 1917 that Germany was 'the horror of the fallen intellect – knowing what it once was & knowing what it has become – is beyond words frightful'. Others were not slow to find words. The historian E. H. Benians, writing in 1915, had decided that Germany (as a whole) was 'a nation of machines' which could never grasp the importance of individuality to democracies like Britain. Increasingly the battle lines were drawn in this crude way, between opposed national characters, British gifted amateurism (including volunteer soldiers) contrasted with Teutonic 'deadly concentration of mind'. For Ramsey Muir the contrast was between 'science over against sportsmanship; discipline over against self-government'. Raleigh thought Germans a 'highly emotional and excitable' people, 'organised and regimented like an ant-hill or a beehive', compared to the sensible, independent British.[41]

Such analyses raised a philosophical question: 'Can a whole nation be fundamentally immoral?' asked Ramsey Muir. Ford Madox Hueffer answered clearly enough: 'I wish Germany did not exist, and I hope that it will not exist much longer. Burke said that you cannot indict a whole nation. But you can.' Later in the war British opinion had come largely to that conclusion, faced with accumulating evidence of Germany's 'crimes', too widespread to have been imposed on an unwilling nation by the Junkers. Larry Collins has noted that in early war plays the villain was usually 'a Prussian or a Uhlan', but soon, 'as the public's sense of abhorrence and outrage became more widespread, the feelings of hatred encompassed all Germans'; by 1916, any stage German was hissed. Caricatures by Will Dyson exhibited in 1915 show the same trend, for his drawings ridiculed German professors, science and art: in one, Heine greets Krupp, and in another ('Kultur Protector') Wagner, Beethoven and Goethe kneel before him and exclaim, 'Hail, Saviour Krupp, how can we ever thank thee?'[42]

It was a short step to envisage Germans through sheer racism, a nation of 'Huns', with all that implied about wanton destroyers of civilisation. This too was a German own-goal, for the reintroduction into political debate of the concept of Germans as 'Huns' derived from the Kaiser's speech in 1900, delivered to German soldiers off to fight in China: 'Once, a thousand years ago, the Huns under their King Attila made a name for themselves, one still potent in legend and tradition. May you in this way make the name German remembered in China for a thousand years so that no Chinaman will ever again dare to *even squint at a German*!' It was Kipling who two years later introduced 'Hun' into the British vocabulary of Germanophobia. In wartime usage the concept deprived Germany of two millennia of progress: Sir Gilbert Parker thought that 'the German of today is the same as the German who strove and conquered in the Teutoberger forest in the dawn of our era. He is still in most essentials a primitive man.' Writing prematurely of German defeat in 1914, G. K. Chesterton explicitly removed Germany from Christendom: 'the empire of blood and iron rolled slowly back towards the darkness of the northern forests'. It was contradictory to view Germany as innately backward but at the same time to accuse her of unleashing the terrors of modern science on the battlefield, but this was routinely done: for Arnold Bennett, Germany's approach to war 'added all the resources of science to the thievishness and sanguinary cruelty of primeval man'. For Kipling, the *unfrei* people of Germany were 'the Middle Ages with modern guns'. Mrs Humphrey Ward argued complacently that 'we are terribly right in speaking of the Germans as barbarians; that, for all their science and their organisation, they have really nothing in common with the Graeco-Latin and Christian civilisation on which this old Europe is based'.[43]

Lord Bryce, despite his positive pre-war experience of Germany, condoned the version of his atrocities report abridged by J. H. Morgan, of which a million and a half copies were printed. For Morgan, Germans showed the same tendencies as the barbarians who destroyed the Roman Empire. Prussians were not even Teutons, but 'a "throw-back" to some Tartar stock', while Germans as a whole were a 'hybrid nation' with only a veneer of European consciousness masking the atavism of 'of some pre-Asiatic horde'. For good measure, he added that many Germans were innate sexual perverts, specially fond of sodomy and child rape. Morgan claimed to have discovered this from official surveys of Berlin's 'moral distemper', but it probably owed more to pre-war court scandals than statistics. Sometimes the overt racism of such views did not flatter Britain's

Russian allies in its casual assumption of the depraved appetites of Slavs. Crucially, though, claims of Prussians' Slavic ancestry cleared Britain's own Anglo-Saxon heritage of a similar taint. Sir Walter Raleigh noticed that a portrait of the Kaiser with his generals included only 'two European faces – the others are Kalmucks' (medieval Mongols). Another writer argued that Prussians, though seen by German patriots as 'the quintessence of the German race', were in fact mongrels, 'at bottom either Germanised Slavs or at the most the result of a mixture between Germans and Slavs'. There was, conceded Muir, an 'element' of the Teutonic in the British, which 'has given us the framework of our language [but] the Germans themselves have a large admixture of Slavonic blood, in which we have no share'. The ultimate point of racial theorising came in picturing Germans as less than human, more like apes and so further down the evolutionary chain than the British and French – or indeed than the Slavs that many Germans despised on similar grounds. The most famous version of the image came in the American poster 'Stop This Mad Brute!' *Punch* depicted Germany as an ape-like ogre by mid-1916, and in a cartoon by the Australian David Lindsay a spike-helmeted German ape reaches with dripping, bloodstained hands for the globe. There were now, argued Kipling in 1915, 'only two divisions in the world . . . human beings and Germans'; the humans 'desired nothing more than that this unclean thing should be thrust out from membership and the memory of the nations'.[44]

It is thus hardly surprising that few in Britain supported the idea of a compromise peace while the war lasted: Germany must admit its guilt and return the booty gained in 1914. The Archbishop of Canterbury argued in 1917 that 'so long as the enemy are committed irrevocably to principles which I regard as absolutely fatal to what Christ taught us . . . I should look on it as flimsy sentimentality were I to say that I want immediate peace.' A commercially made documentary, *Our Empire's Fight for Freedom*, proclaimed that 'this war must continue! To save the *civilised* human races, to save the universe.' Lack of support for peace initiatives suggests that these were still widely held opinions during the second half of the war, as does popular hostility to the few like Russell and Lansdowne who supported them. In the 1918 general election, all who had flirted with peace movements were summarily swept out of Parliament by the newly democratic electorate. D. H. Lawrence, persecuted in wartime for his German wife Frieda, wrote in *Kangaroo* (1923) that 'no man who has really consciously lived through this can believe again absolutely in democracy . . . During the crucial years of the war, the people chose, and chose Bottomleyism. Bottom enough.' To explain this, we must also remember how Germany reacted to peace feelers, what Germany's war aims were, and how little they moderated between 1914 and 1918. Whether or not they had played any part in the war's origins, popular demands for German colonisation of *Mitteleuropa* were official policy within a few weeks of its outbreak. The Pan-German League demanded that Germany pledge itself to annex Belgium to the Reich, along with French ironworking districts, and the Channel coast down to the River Somme. The German government's objectives in September 1914 were more modest, but the door was left open for additions later, and although the Reichstag majority moved in 1916–17 towards supporting peace without annexations, such men as Stresemann, the leader of German democracy in the 1920s, remained among the annexationists. As the triangular battle between moderates, Pan-Germans and the army developed, official war aims hardened; increasingly the army demanded a Carthaginian peace, as was imposed on Russia in 1918. Bethmann Hollweg lamented even in 1915 that this debate was impossibly unrealistic, since 'the psychology of our people has been so much poisoned by boasting during the last twenty-five years'. By early 1917, he recognised that with army leaders he was 'dealing with men who no longer intended to discuss the decisions they had made'. As late as August 1918, with total defeat just weeks away, the generals insisted that the acquisition of France's ironworks was an essential demand. By 1917, when terms for peace were published as a response to American President Wilson, it was, as Gerd Hardach puts it, 'clear that the annexationist war aims of the Pan-Germans had prevailed'. Given the centrality of Belgium to British views of the war, that part of the package had special resonance; in April 1917 Germany's leaders agreed that after victory Belgium would be militarily occupied until it accepted a subservient alliance with Germany, and that in any case it would be occupied for an 'interim period' determined by Germany. Together with Germany's policy in occupied Belgium since 1914, these brutal proposals seemed to confirm what Arnold

Toynbee had argued in a propaganda pamphlet: that Germany would 'suck the life blood out of any nation' it controlled. Britain would be deprived of trade access to most of Europe, an economic catastrophe. It is necessary to note these points to establish the fact that for Britain to fight on in 1917–18 showed awareness of where the nation's cardinal interests lay. Facing during the next world war a claim that nobody really wins in wars, the Labour politician Hugh Dalton responded robustly: 'No difference between victims and vanquished? A foolish fable. The Germans didn't believe it after 1918. We shouldn't have believed it if they had won.' Though he had famously protested in 1917 against the continuation of the war, which had become a (British) 'war of aggression and conquest', Siegfried Sassoon later agreed that 'in the light of subsequent events it is difficult to believe that a Peace negotiated in 1917 could have been permanent. I share the general opinion that nothing on earth would have prevented a recurrence of Teutonic aggressiveness.' Sassoon volunteered to return to the front in 1918, as did Wilfred Owen. British resolution during the war's final crisis remained firm, and there was renewed xenophobia when in spring 1918 it seemed that Germany might win. This was, as Michael Paris has put it, xenophobia 'more passionate, more hysterical than anything that had gone before, and that xenophobia dominated the public mood through to the very end. In November 1918 the people's determination to defeat Germany was perhaps even more passionate,' and it had little to do with propaganda.[45]

Britain's own war aims were, as Sassoon claimed, territorially less ambitious but psychologically just as impossible for Germans to accept: Germany should admit her guilt, make reparation and restore the 1914 boundaries. The Allies implicitly also demanded regime change in Germany: Field Marshal Sir Evelyn Wood told readers of the *Daily Mail* that no peace would work unless massive armaments continued for years ahead, 'while the brutal faithless government of the Hohenzollerns exists'. As Foreign Secretary, Grey advised the cabinet that 'peace without victory' was unacceptable, for the German military autocracy could then start another war just as it had started this one. This was a difficult issue for a British government, not least because George V was understandably sensitive to claims that monarchs were responsible for their governments' actions, but also because insistence on the removal of the German figurehead might weaken a possible German peace party. From the Right, Kipling denounced belief in a peace party: 'I do not believe the Germans can be converted.' From the Left, the government was suspected of timidity about the Kaiser's future through solidarity of the boss-class. For a variety of reasons, therefore, but especially when a German peace party failed to emerge, ministers increasingly talked about the need for a different regime in post-war Germany, explicitly democratic, without a privileged role for the army, and without the Hohenzollern monarchy. Such arguments were consistent with optimistic hopes, like the poet Charles Sorley's in 1914, that this would be a war of German liberation, since 'the best thing that could happen to them would be their defeat'. An unforeseen consequence was that such rhetoric gave Germany's successor government grounds for complaining in 1919 about the peace terms the Allies imposed; in trying to reject Germany's 'war guilt', her negotiators argued that the German people could not be held responsible for the errors of its former, overthrown government.[46]

These protests did not deflect the peacemakers, who insisted that the 'war guilt' article was included in the Treaty of Versailles. Diplomatic claims of non-responsibility did though help to launch Germany's subsequent campaigns against the treaty and provided a peg on which Hitler hung heavy arguments later. They never cut much ice with the French or the Belgians, but in Britain too they could not have been effectively deployed between 1914 and 1919. The far from vindictive *New Statesman* carried in January 1919 an article by a correspondent in Germany, reporting

> hardly any recognition of the crimes Germany has committed. The German people as a whole do not in the least understand why they are hated. They realise the fact, only to be bewildered by it. Never having been a democratic country, they have not that sense of common responsibility for the acts of their government which with us is instinctive.

Maybe so, but had it been 'their government'? And since British people had come to the conclusion that all Germans were collectively culpable, it was largely beside the point. Many agreed with Mrs

Pankhurst that Germany should have her mineral resources and armaments confiscated, so that the country could never wage war again, whatever system of government it adopted. Others would at least have wanted to see hard evidence of German conversion to democracy before abandoning the moral high ground occupied in wartime. Even among the most judicious commentators, the experience of 1914–18 left its mark: the diplomat Elizabeth Wiskemann wrote in 1938 that 'egalitarian principles' between nations were not instinctively popular among 'Germans . . . as a whole, in whom historical circumstances appear to have fertilized the notion that some races are born to rule others'. There is a strong flavour here of 'Once a Hun, always a Hun', the opening title of the government propaganda film *The Leopard's Spots* (1918). That message in turn matched the poster produced by the British Empire Union, 'Once a German – Always a German!' This depicted in parallel drawings a German army officer and the same man as a post-war civilian salesman, the background filled in with burning buildings, sinking ships, a bayoneted baby, the shooting of Nurse Cavell, and a German officer enjoying champagne and a cigar while ogling a captive woman. 'This man, who shelled Churches, Hospitals and Open Boats at Sea; This Robber, Ravisher and Murderer' and 'This Man, who after the war will want to sell you his German goods, ARE ONE AND THE SAME PERSON'. *John Bull* urged the same case against post-war magnanimity: 'If by chance you should discover one day in a restaurant that you are being served by a German waiter, you will throw the soup in his foul face; if you find yourself sitting at the side of a German clerk, you will spill the inkpot over his foul head.' No wonder that German residents put up so little resistance when so many were pointlessly expelled in 1919. It was, however, very unhelpful that individual British people would be less likely to meet Germans, now there were far fewer German waiters, barbers and butchers with whom they could experience routine commercial intercourse.[47]

Which brings us back to Kipling, whose dislike for Germany had long preceded the Great War, but was nevertheless deeply reinforced by the events of 1914–18. He was, as Lord Birkenhead puts it, 'a connoisseur in the study of Germanism', and was from the 1890s prescient about the threat that Britain might face. Even before 1900 he was predicting in a private letter a 'big smash' with the Germans, 'lesser breeds without the law'; and in the same year he told an American friend to remember 'when Armageddon comes' that, however many sins Britain had committed, she would have been 'kicked into this war'. Another Kipling influence was his advance use of 'Armageddon' for the Great War, a popular term once it arrived. (Armageddon will be, according to the Book of Revelation, the battle between good and evil before the Last Judgement.) In 1908 he was writing that 'the Teuton has his large cold eye on us, and prepares to give us *toko* [ritual execution] when he is good and ready'. He fantasised in 'With the Night Mail' about the world in 2000: war has ended for ever in 1967, but he cannot resist upbraiding Danes for buying German goods. In 1913, in 'The Edge of the Evening', house-party guests rehearse the Great War; they witness a German reconnaissance plane taking photographs, arrest the intruders when the plane is forced to land and kill the occupants. Having got the plane airborne, the corpses loaded aboard, they unconcernedly watch it heading for a crash-landing in the Channel, a drowned 'invasion'.[48]

When the war began for real, Carrie Kipling wrote in her diary, 'My cold possesses me', and her husband added, 'incidentally, Armageddon begins. Britain declares war on Germany.' Kipling's poetic response was to urge the British to 'Stand up and take the war. The Hun is at the gate.' His articles and speeches were larded with anti-German rhetoric, especially after his son was killed in 1915. In a recruiting speech he urged volunteers to 'check the onrush of organised barbarism'. He predicted, when most thought the war would be 'over by Christmas', that it would last for three years (actually four, of course) and that Germany would suffer five million casualties (it was six million). In Kipling's wartime fiction his sympathy is not with the hated, but with those who hate. In 'Swept and Garnished' an elderly German lady is visited by the ghosts of Belgian children maimed by 'her' army; the visitation brings home the meaning of the war and wrecks her mind. In 'Sea Constables' a British captain refuses to help a sick American skipper to hospital; he is too busy on war duty, and the neutral had been blockade-running oil for German submarines. The 'hero' casually adds that the neutral skipper died. The epitome of engendering hatred through literature, though, is 'Mary Postgate', thought by Kipling's cousin Oliver Baldwin 'the wickedest story ever written'. The spinster Mary, companion to an elderly lady, becomes fond of her employer's nephew, who is then killed in the war. She also sees children killed in an air raid. Mary agrees to remove the child-hood belongings of the dead nephew, but is interrupted by a wounded German airman who pleads for help. She calmly fetches a revolver to protect herself, but brings no water for the German, and when the nephew's toys have burned on their 'pyre' and the airman has expired, she says briskly, '*That's* all right,' and runs a bath. Some commentators have tried to explain away 'Mary Postgate' as an inspired exploration of psychological feelings under pressure (which it certainly is), but no more (which it is not). There is no reason to doubt Kipling's identification with Mary or the endorsement of hatred that it offers – in stark contrast to British posters that claimed that only a *German* nurse would refuse water to a dying man.[49]

Though Kipling's hatred for Germans cost him the esteem of lib-erals, it seems to have had no impact on broader opinion. The same went for John Buchan and other such writers, like Dornford Yates and 'Sapper'. Yates, in *Lower than Vermin*, a 'Berry and Co.' book not published until 1950, has his hero call Germany 'a cad'. For Yates, there was no harsher epithet, but it seems that Germany was also – even worse – *lower class*. Before 1914, as

> the gorgeous years slid by . . . a neighbour was biding his time, wait-ing to ease his hatred, waiting to blast the beauty of the English way. Jealousy knows no law. The *Hymn of Hate* was the anthem of the greatest explosion of class-hatred the world has ever seen. Such was the occasion of the first world war – class hatred, and nothing else. The poisonous cad of Europe hated the peer.

Sapper wrote less polished prose: his German villains 'gutturally' utter such barbarities as 'hold him the arms of, and I will tear the throat out'. He too was widely read for several decades from the twenties onwards.[50]

Kipling's post-war books also sold well, *The Heart of a Dog* a hun-dred thousand copies in six months in 1930. Every post-war Kipling collection contained at least one short story or poem about the war, and none was forgiving. J. I. M. Stewart, reviewing Kipling's reputa-tion in 1972, and conceding reviewers' low opinion of his later work, nevertheless concluded that 'the ordinary reader, one suspects, has never very drastically written him down'. Angus Wilson vividly remembered both the popularity of Kipling in middle-class families and the hatred of Germans that he had been taught from the age of five, in the year the Great War ended. For the actor Roger Moore, a Kipling fan born into an Anglo-Indian military family in 1927, Kipling was familiar by the age of eight, 'a heroic writer for me', and he studied the author for examinations: 'people of my age know their Kipling from school'. Like Stewart, Moore thought in 2004 that 'in the 70 years since he died, the literary establishment has been unstinting in its sneering – probably because he is so popular . . . Let them sneer. The politically correct . . . will always revile him.' Kipling continued then to be widely read while he was writing new anti-German polemics, predicting the Second World War as surely as he had foreseen the First. He thought in 1932 that 'the Were-Wolf has got tired. He's been a man for twelve years and has got all out of mankind that he needs. At least he can't get any more – so it is time for him to change shape. In less than a year he will be clamouring for the return of his colonies as "necessary for self respect". You wait and see.' Hitler seized power in 1933 and did just that.[51]

About the time he wrote 'The Beginnings', Kipling wrote privately that it had 'taken the Hun two years to teach the English how to hate, which is a thing we have never done before'. (How dare he? He had rarely done anything else!) 'It will take us two generations to stop.' Or, as the poem detachedly puts it,

> It was not suddenly bred,
> It will not swiftly abate,
> Through the chill years ahead,
> When Time shall count from the date
> That the English began to hate.

4

'The Germans are unchanged':[1]
Good Germans and Nazis in the
age of Adolf Hitler

Fighting stopped on 11 November 1918, and the war formally ended when the Treaty of Versailles was signed on 28 June 1919. In the following December, however, six months after the treaty and only a year after the Armistice, a brilliantly effective attack was mounted on the peacemaking process by the economist John Maynard Keynes in *The Economic Consequences of the Peace*. Though some newspapers castigated Keynes as a 'pro-German', the British view of Versailles was permanently shifted onto different lines, with Germany coming to be viewed as a victim of 1914–19, rather than a nation of aggressors. This development then affected British attitudes to Germany for the next quarter century, with negative consequences when the country struggled to respond to Hitler in the 1930s.

Keynes was a Germanophile from childhood, brought up in an intellectual Cambridge household where German scholarship was highly regarded and German governesses ensured knowledge of the language. When he watched Queen Victoria's funeral, he was much impressed by the demeanour of the Kaiser and was 'most pleased with the small band of picked Germans'. He thoroughly enjoyed a first visit to Germany in 1904, and, already a connoisseur, regarded Dürer, Holbein and Cranach as 'most to my taste'. Despite reservations among his Cambridge friends in 1914, Keynes supported the war and regarded it as Germany's responsibility. He told the philosopher G. E. Moore that recent events had 'destroyed his opinion of

Germans; he didn't think they would seriously act and believe on such absurd principles, as war had shown they do'. Even that opinion was though no more than half hearted, and in an article in the *Economic Journal* a year later he noted that German wartime writing on economics was characterised by 'moderation, sobriety, accuracy, reasonableness and truth', five nouns by then rarely applied to anything German. Although Keynes never opposed the war like his friend Bertrand Russell, and worked for the war effort in the Treasury, he was increasingly uncertain about Britain's case, especially after Lloyd George became Prime Minister: 'I work for a government I despise for ends I think criminal,' he told a friend in December 1917. When he accompanied Lloyd George to the peace conference in 1919, as the Treasury's official representative, Keynes was burning to expiate a personal guilt.[2]

What he saw for himself between the Armistice and the signing of the treaty confirmed this view, surely compounded by wounded pride, for Keynes knew his own worth and took pride in the young science of economics, for which he saw himself as an ambassador in the world of politics. He was personally affronted when lesser men pursued political expediency and personal popularity, rejecting his better technical advice; worse, when considering the crucial issue of how much Germany could and should pay for war damages, Lloyd George sidestepped Keynes and put his faith in a banker and a judge. Neither had a fraction of Keynes's grasp of finance, but both were more worldly wise in public affairs. After discussing it all with the Labour minister George Barnes, Tom Jones (Deputy Secretary of the Cabinet), noted that Lloyd George had deliberately appointed these 'stony-hearted men' to see off Keynes's more generous approach to German reparations. That conflict between the economist and the politicians also emerges in the diary of Lord Riddell, the newspaper proprietor taken to Versailles by Lloyd George to manage the press. Riddell reported in May 1919 that he had written a paper on German indemnity payments, and secured one from Keynes: 'According to him, the Germans can pay not more than two thousand millions. The publication of his paper as issued would have been disastrous. Consequently I deleted a large number of the paragraphs. I issued the two papers to the Press' (after getting the approval of Lloyd George's secretary). Seeing the way the wind was blowing, Keynes resigned from the Treasury before the treaty was signed, hoping to persuade the South African leader Jan Smuts to lead a public campaign against it, with Keynes himself supplying the ammunition. Smuts was though a close associate of Lloyd George and had been personally implicated in dubious manoeuvres at the peace conference. He signed the treaty on behalf of his own country, and declined the role that Keynes had assigned him.[3]

According to *The Economic Consequences of the Peace*, the treaty-makers had a simple duty: 'to honour engagements and to satisfy justice; but not less to re-establish life and to heal wounds. These tasks were dictated as much by prudence as by the magnanimity which the wisdom of antiquity approved in victors.' Keynes thus linked the tight economic reasoning in which he was pre-eminent with an appeal to self-interest, fair-play, tradition and morality, a dual approach that gave the book its impact. 'My purpose in this book', he wrote, 'is to show that the Carthaginian peace is not *practically* right or possible', words that again linked informed pragmatism with principle. Against this combination of wisdom and technical competence, the peacemakers appear prejudiced, incompetent, amateurish. France's Clemenceau was, for Keynes, the 'foremost believer in the view of German psychology that the German understands and can understand nothing but intimidation, that he is without generosity . . . that he is without honour, pride, or mercy'. America's President Wilson was all principle and no practicality, though his principles were undermined by being 'foolishly and unfortunately sensitive' to claims that he was 'pro-German'. Lloyd George was all pragmatism and no principle, furnishing in December 1918 election speeches merely 'food for the cynic', offering promises (such as the hanging of the Kaiser) which he had no intention of keeping, but then having to manoeuvre deviously to allow them to be dropped. Between them, Keynes concluded, the statesmen ignored the key issues, which were the economic ones, lost in self-absorption, 'Clemenceau to crush the economic life out of his enemy, Lloyd George to do a deal and bring home something which would pass muster for a week, the President to do nothing that was not just and right'.[4]

Keynes points out early in the book that Britain and Germany had been major trading partners in 1913, and goes on to argue that

German economic recovery was vital for Europe and Britain. Prudence should have made this the peacemakers' clear aim, but the huge reparations bill foisted on Germany would be a deterrent to economic progress for decades. Beyond imprudence, they had indulged in dubious law and questionable morality, confiscating wholesale the property of individual Germans, and making Germany pay war debts even for her allies. His analysis of the size of Allied claims on Germany was authoritative, refuting the French and Belgians with their own statistics, and demonstrating that there had been no demands for payments on such a scale until after the Germans had surrendered and were powerless to resist them. The peroration of this part of the book has enormous force:

> The policy of reducing Germany to servitude for a generation, of degrading the lives of millions of human beings, and of depriving a whole nation of happiness should be abhorrent and detestable – abhorrent and detestable, even if it were possible, even if it enriched ourselves, even if it did not sow the decay of the whole civilised life of Europe. Some preach it in the name of justice. In the great events of man's history, in the unwinding of the complex fates of nations, justice is not so simple.

Britain should help Germany resume 'her place in Europe as a creator and organiser of wealth'. In that paragraph alone, Keynes had briskly dismissed many wartime assumptions: the collective guilt of the entire German nation, the necessity of punishment, and the convergence of revenge with self-interest.[5]

He dedicated his book 'to the formation of the general opinion of the future', for though he thought that wartime chauvinism ensured that 'never in the lifetime of men now living had the universal element of man burnt so dimly', yet 'the true voice of the new generation has not yet spoken, and silent opinion is not yet formed.' However, he can hardly have expected his book to be so persuasive; but it was so well written that its failings tended to be overlooked. It was a publishing sensation, and, thought the *Manchester Guardian*, 'not merely an act of conspicuous courage and public spirit; it is an infinitely more important event than any speech that has been made on the peace by any of its authors'. *The Economist*, well qualified to judge Keynes's practical arguments, thought his case 'unanswerable' and called for 'a change . . . of heart in every Allied country'. Even *Punch* concluded that

> . . . he's not merely a slinger of partisan ink,
> But a thinker who gives us profoundly to think,
> And his arguments cannot be lightly dismissed
> With cries of 'Pro-Hun' or of 'Pacifist'.

Right-wing newspapers sometimes thought he had betrayed those who had died in the war, a treacherous act by a public servant, but there was near-unanimous praise from the Left and Centre. What could not be denied was the stir that the book caused or the sales it achieved: by the middle of 1920 it was in print in twelve languages and had sold over a hundred thousand copies. Nor, despite criticisms of his motives and his ethics, had anyone managed to refute his key technical argument: Germany's actual ability to pay. By November 1920, he could assert in the introduction to the Romanian edition that 'the treaties of the Paris conference are crumbling politically and economically because they had no solid foundations'.[6]

Visiting Cambridge during publication week, Hugh Dalton found 'much talk of Keynes's book', though one don had sourly dubbed him 'Jeremiah Malthus Keynes'. Keynes himself told Lytton Strachey that his book was being 'smothered . . . in a deluge of approval; not a complaint, not a . . . line of criticism; letters from Cabinet Ministers by every post saying that they agree with every word of it'. Ironically, he expected Lloyd George to join the chorus and Clemenceau to offer the Legion of Honour. The book certainly did attract the great and the good. The Chancellor the Exchequer, Austen Chamberlain, told his sister that 'you must get Keynes' book [for] it is ably & indeed brilliantly written . . . I wish I could say that I differ seriously from Keynes' examination of Germany's ability to pay . . . [but] there is only too much truth in Keynes' gloomy picture'. His half-brother Neville thought the book 'a brilliant piece of writing', and his descriptions of the 'Big Three' (Lloyd George, Clemenceau and Wilson) 'masterly', though since he had read somewhere that Keynes supported a capital levy, Neville also wrote him off as having 'mental aberration of a dangerous kind'. Nor were the Chamberlains Keynes's only Conservative admirers: in 1923, when Tom Jones was shown around Stanley Baldwin's library, his host specially pointed out the Greek text of *The Odyssey* he had used at Harrow and his copy of *Economic Consequences*, which quoted anonymously Baldwin's own phrase about 'hard-faced men who looked as if they had done well out of the war'. Labour and Liberal opinion was unanimously favourable. Asquith's daughter, Lady Violet Bonham Carter, sent Keynes's book to a friend for Christmas, as '*quite* brilliant – an unanswerable indictment'. Lord Bryce and Lord Cecil, who, like Keynes, had bad consciences about the war, had disliked the peace treaty from the first, but now found intellectual support for the view they wished to hold, as did Labour internationalists like Philip Snowden. Cecil, who as Minister of Blockade had helped to starve Germans but was now an internationalist supporter of the League of Nations, wrote, 'I am quite clear that we shall have to begin a campaign for the revision of the Treaty as soon as possible.' More ominously, while Keynes's book made little impression on France, it 'caused a sensation in Germany', as Gerard Schulz puts it; here was a former enemy, prominent in organising British warfare, denouncing as unfair the treaty Germans had been forced to sign.[7]

How, though, had British opinion turned around so fast, and how had a peace been made that so many British people quickly disowned? The root of the problem was the suddenness with which the war ended, and the confused transition from Armistice to peacemaking, a period complicated by a long-overdue British general election. Germany's military collapse in October 1918 had taken the Allies by surprise, for they had themselves struggled to avoid defeat as recently as June. It was sometimes said in the 1930s that the Allies ought to have refused anything short of total surrender, marching on until Germany's defeat was visited inescapably on her civilians, and demands for 'unconditional surrender' in the Second World War were an attempt to avoid making the same 'mistake'. Lloyd George did consider fighting on to make Germany's defeat more visible, but after the mass killings of 1916–18 it would have been impracticable for the Allies to reject any reasonable German offer to stop fighting, and nobody at the time seriously suggested such callousness. The second problem was that Germany made its initial approach to the USA, which was not formally part of the wartime alliance but an 'associated power', clearly hoping for a warmer response than from vengeful Europeans. Neville Chamberlain was 'terrified lest we should somehow get cheated out of the peace we ought to have & the Germans escape the punishment they so richly deserve'. Wilson refused to negotiate alone, but the Armistice was nevertheless agreed on the basis of his 'Fourteen Points', to which Britain and France had previously given only partial acquiescence and to which they now added vague riders. As Keynes put it, 'the enemy had laid down their arms in reliance on a solemn compact as to the general character of the Peace, the terms of which seemed to assure a settlement of justice and magnanimity'. Third, the Germany that surrendered was very different from the regime that had fought the war, for the Kaiser's departure preceded the Armistice; since so much Allied propaganda had been directed at Wilhelm, this removed the obvious link between guilt and the retribution that peacemakers would discuss. The Armistice was not a surrender but a pause in the expectation of negotiations, and yet its terms prevented Germany from keeping armed forces available for a renewal of fighting, while the Allies retained forces ready to enforce a treaty, and occupied the Rhineland anyway. Fourth, specifically for Britain, the general election in the hour of victory was a raucously patriotic affair, as pro-war politicians exploited their sudden popularity and exacted vengeance on liberals as well as Germans. A humane man like Churchill, magnanimous in victory and hoping to recruit the Germans as allies against Bolshevism, found that electors even in radical Dundee demanded vengeance. Rather than educating public opinion, for example in respect of Germany's ability to pay war damages, most winning candidates just went with the flow, as did the Prime Minister. Ministerial promises to hang the Kaiser, and to squeeze Germany like a lemon, 'until the pips squeak[ed]', epitomised generally uninhibited electioneering. When the results came in, moderates had been almost wholly swept away, and the Commons had a majority who would denounce as 'pro-Hun' anything less than a vengeful settlement. It was impossible to understand the peace conference, wrote Elizabeth Wiskemann twenty years later, 'unless one is willing to consider the terror and havoc which had gone before it'. Keynes's rational arguments fell at that hurdle, though Lloyd George never seriously tried to get his British nag to jump it.[8]

In this sense, the peace conference was doomed from the start, for it was soon under the domination of just three men, the leaders of Britain, France and America; caught between Clemenceau's determination to remove any chance of German recovery and Wilson's yearning for a principled settlement, Lloyd George usually engineered the compromises, but his own position was continuously bedevilled by the need to watch his back against Tory assassins. When it seemed that he would shift from demanding of Germany the full cost of the war to all the Allies – an absurd demand to which he ought never have been committed – he was rudely reminded of his vulnerability by a telegram signed by over three hundred government MPs, and shifted tack accordingly. As he told Tom Jones, he returned to England to consult the Conservative leader Bonar Law, and 'they decided to capitulate to the mutineers as there was no time to educate the public to accept the lower figure'. Not by then, there wasn't, but there had been four months earlier.[9]

Lloyd George was certainly aware of the dangers of a draconian peace, for his own 'Fontainebleau Memorandum' drawn up in advance had argued that a lasting peace for Europe could be achieved only if it did not leave Germany with permanent reasons for resentment; he continued to resist proposals to put Germans under foreign governments for the same reason. In the conference every concession wrung from France was gained at a high price, and he was compelled to agree much that he thought unacceptable in order to broker a deal and get through any treaty at all. He accepted, for example, a total bill for the war that he privately thought to be 'wild and fantastic', but in order to bolster support in Britain and the Empire then increased that total, so that the latter would get a share of the swag. He was then compelled to justify all this by reasserting the idea of punishment for Germany's past sins: Riddell noted on 9 April that when the Prime Minister spoke about indemnities, 'I thought his tone very changed. Today he said the Germans would have to pay to the uttermost farthing. He pushed aside the economic difficulties and said that if the Germans decline to fulfil their obligations, we can compel them by an economic blockade.' Wilson and Lloyd George did get concessions from France, for example stopping the Rhineland becoming a buffer state between Germany and France, but the resulting hybrid treaty was neither punitive enough to keep Germany down (were such a thing possible) nor generous enough to make Germans content. As Keynes privately put it shortly before he resigned, 'the Peace is outrageous and impossible and can bring nothing but misfortune . . . Certainly if I were in the Germans' place I'd die rather than sign such a Peace . . . Anarchy and Revolution is the best thing that can happen, and the sooner the better.'[10]

Peace terms eventually put to the German government were unacceptable in both form and content. Huge antagonism was caused by the Allies presenting Germany with a *fait accompli*, refusing to allow proposals to be renegotiated; they countenanced no delay before they were accepted, and threatened reprisals if they were not. There was universal outrage in the German press, opposition from every political party, and massive demonstrations of protest. In content the proposals confiscated German territory and the property of German citizens and companies, made Germany alone responsible for the war and for its entire cost, refused Germany the right to do as she wished within what remained of her sovereign territory, and outlawed German armaments and fortifications. Germany in the 1920s had no air force, virtually no warships and barely enough soldiers to keep order. The principle of self-determination, enshrined in the Fourteen Points that Germany accepted, was applied wholesale across Europe but not to Germany: German citizens were pushed into the Polish and Czech states, Austrians were forbidden to join Germany, and when a plebiscite was held in Silesia the result was not wholly honoured. Germany was saddled with a war bill of twenty billion pounds, ten times Keynes's technical assessment of what was justly owed and what Germany could pay. The German government had little option but to sign, but made its dissent clear, so that the 'war guilt' clause acquired no legitimacy when imposed by the Allies rather than freely accepted by Germany. Its government announced, even as it signed the treaty, that it was 'yielding to overwhelming force, but not on that account abandoning its view in regard of the unheard-of injustice of the conditions of peace'.[11]

Though the German government formally accepted the war guilt clause along with the rest of the treaty, in a few months many in Britain, with Keynes in the lead, were more convinced of their own country's 'peace guilt' than of Germany's responsibility for the war, and bluster by Wilson and Lloyd George about the German representatives' gracelessness when accepting their terms ('Those insolent Germans') was a fairly obvious cover for nagging consciences. Keynes's alternative view was that the Germans had demonstrated in responses to the proposed terms that the Allies had committed since November 1918 'a breach of engagements and of international morality comparable with their own offence in the invasion of Belgium'.[12]

After 1919 German historians devoted themselves to exposing the fallacies involved in the idea of Germany's sole responsibility for the war, their work reinforced by Americans and by historians of other nationalities. Since the treaty was founded on the claim of German guilt, every published document undermining that claim also weakened the other clauses. By 1925, Gilbert Murray, chairman of the League of Nations Union, could remark to a German friend that 'hardly any reasonable person in England continues to talk of Germany as solely responsible for the war'. Politicians' memoirs, like Churchill's *The World Crisis* (1923–9), contributed too, stressing the anarchic state of pre-war diplomacy rather than discussing one country's guilt. Keynes reviewed the volume in which Churchill described 1919, and regretted that it assigned no guilt for the treaty, for this had been 'a situation where an investment of political courage would have been marvellously repaid in the end'. Lloyd George's *War Memoirs* (1933) blamed the now safely dead Sir Edward Grey for 1914, while his *The Truth about the Peace Treaties* (1938) made little attempt to claim that the peacemakers had got it right, rather blaming the equally dead Clemenceau and Wilson for getting it wrong. Revisionism in the 1920s also extended to the best-known atrocity stories. As was argued in Chapter 3, by disproving the most outlandish claims many writers assumed that all claims of German atrocities were equally false; by then, alleged brutality by French colonial troops occupying the Ruhr in 1923 had anyway put that jackboot on the other foot. When Nazi aggression began in the 1930s, the British response was heavily conditioned by recognition that Germany had been ill-treated in 1919, in many of the exact places where Hitler now made demands. This explains in part why British governments were initially more exercised by Mussolini than Hitler, though Germany was the greater threat: Italy had been one of the victors in 1919, Germany a victim. The new consensus was clear enough when a revised *Encyclopaedia Britannica* appeared in 1928–9: articles on the peace treaties were edited by J. L. Garvin, a staunch anti-German from 1900 to 1918 who now concluded that 'in the height of triumph and wrath' the Allies had decided in 1919 on 'a new and unnecessary humiliation' (the war guilt clause) and a generally unwise treaty.[13]

The changed view of Germany was confirmed by a history published in 1925 by G. P. Gooch, ex-Liberal MP and 'one of our most distinguished living historians', as the former education minister H. A. L. Fisher described him. This was, thought Fisher, a 'surprisingly dispassionate' book from the man chosen as joint editor of British diplomatic documents for 1898–1914, a project intended to bolster Britain's original claims about 1914. Gooch concluded that 'no evidence . . . has appeared to indicate that the German Government or the German people had desired and plotted a world war'; the worst he could accuse them of was recklessness during July 1914. 'Each country accused its enemy of atrocities,' he added, the implication being that all claims were equally false, a regrettable effect of modern warfare. On the peace conference, Gooch time and again took the German side in stressing the Allies' failure to carry out in 1919 what they had promised in 1918, Britain in particular being responsible for the provocative insertion of clauses about war criminals. Not everyone accepted such a liberal outlook, *The Times* guardedly greeting it only as 'a very valuable and very remarkable book on modern Germany', but most reviewers thought that it was about right.[14]

The shift can be seen at ambassadorial level, too. When Lord D'Abernon went to Berlin as Britain's first post-war representative in 1920, he was not confident about his role, and his wife was altogether dismayed, for 'except for German music I have never felt attracted by German things, and to try and re-establish relatively pleasant normal relations will require a mountain of effort'. Her husband was soon urging a more generous policy, championing German entry into the League of Nations, for 'to some extent you make the virile Teuton what you assume him to be'. By 1922, when Lady D'Abernon compiled 'Memoranda on Germany and Germans', she too had become more sympathetic, and thought Germans were 'possessed of many virile and outstanding qualities'; she was even prepared to say that 'the young are naturally *frohlich* . . . and are easily amused'. When they left Berlin in 1926, she was moved by the warmth with which many Germans had come to regard them, and regretted her original 'ungenerous feelings . . . generated by harsh and difficult circumstances (the inevitable aftermath of a great war)'.[15]

It is therefore hardly surprising that, socially, the 1914–18 breach between Britons and Germans was quickly healed. When Ernest Bevin led British trades unionists to an international meeting in Amsterdam in April 1919, the British and German delegations met by chance across a canal bridge. After momentary embarrassment, they advanced and shook hands, but although Bevin excused Germans from responsibility for the recent war, he nevertheless complained that they should have protested against such crimes as the sinking of the *Lusitania*. Formal mechanisms for maintaining hatred were quickly wound up. In the cinemas that produced rapid results. *Hearts of the World* was re-edited as a generalised lament about war, rather than an attack on Germany, and 'The National Film' in production throughout 1918 was never released (all copies collected by envoys from Downing Street in return for cases of used notes). The reading public took a similar turn towards tolerance, for while Buchan's novels recounting Red plots against the British Empire sold well, William Le Queux's suddenly dated tales of German spies now made no impact. (Le Queux died in obscurity in 1927, his funeral attended by only a handful of people.) Another sign of popular opinion was the League of Nations Union, with around 600,000 members in the early 1920s. The LNU was a constant advocate of normal relations between Britons and Germans, campaigned for Germany's admission to the League, and when its leaders faltered briefly in 1923 the entire German sub-committee resigned in protest. Individuals took a more activist line: Rolf Gardiner toured Germany in 1922 with a party of British folk singers, following up with an Anglo-German festival of music and dance in the north of England; although, since Gardiner detected racial affinities between Britons, Germans and Scandinavians, he may better be seen as a precursor of the fellow-travellers of the Right who operated in the 1930s. More typical was 'Miss Kilman' in Virginia Woolf's *Mrs Dalloway* (1925), a Quaker teacher turned out of her previous post for refusing to pretend that she hated all Germans, but now not only employed by the fashionable Dalloways but allowed to teach history to their children.[16]

Sympathy continued to be enhanced by awareness both of Germany's economic circumstances and of the need to revise the peace treaty. Even during peacemaking, the shortage of food in Germany had been used as a weapon by both sides – Germany offering the surrender of her merchant fleet only if the Allies promised food, the Allies threatening further blockade if Germany did not sign. Tom Jones thought in March 1919 that 'there really is an appalling state of affairs in Germany. The question is: can we get through the preliminaries of peace in sufficient time, and in such form, as to save Germany?' Food shortages, inflationary pressures and their social consequences were constant themes of British reports from Germany: one diplomat noted in 1919 that 'there is real want. Feeling is that we are murdering women and children unnecessarily.' Those who feared communism were especially concerned, Churchill telling Lloyd George that his approach was 'Feed Germany; fight Bolshevism; make Germany fight Bolshevism'. Self-interest had a wider implication too, it being argued by the Foreign Office in 1923 that 'the illness of Germany is indeed in danger of growing into an international pestilence; the disease is fast becoming endemic among the stricken nations', much as Keynes had foreseen. So bad did things become that in January 1924 *The Times* carried an appeal for relief funds for Germany, signed by several bishops and the Chief Rabbi. Economic privation remained a factor in Anglo-German relations throughout the Weimar Republic.[17]

British guilt could be assuaged only by revising the 1919 treaty, Ernest Bevin reporting to his TGWU in 1922 that 'statesmen seem incapable of cutting the knot they tied at Versailles: neither trade can revive nor peace be established while the present lopsided position remains'. Those on the Left were most frightened of a right-wing backlash in Germany if just grievances were not addressed, but many liberals took the same view, Lloyd George now among them. In 1928 he made a big speech in which he argued that Britain had gone to war for a scrap of paper, but had not then carried out its own disarmament obligations. It was hard to criticise Germany's refusal to observe the treaty's military clauses when Britain and France were ignoring them too. Increasingly, even those who had supported the peace in 1919 began to demand its revision. Lord Birkenhead did so in 1928, and Harold Nicolson's *Peacemaking 1919* joined in five years later, an insider's account that further damaged the reputation of the peace-makers. There was also concern that an angry Germany might get into bad company, linking itself with other defeated powers like Russia. When this actually occurred at Rapallo in 1922, the same people were less sympathetic: 'only the Hun can do these things', observed Lloyd George's secretary. Keynes, on the other hand, kept up his campaign for treaty revision through newspaper articles, and by facilitating contacts between British and German bankers and economists, hoping to broker agreement on reduced reparations. For this he was sometimes still labelled 'pro-German', and Robert Skidelsky thinks there was truth in the claim, for 'he may have been wrong in thinking that the Germans were willing to pay anything'. In 1932, attending a conference that effectively ended reparations amid a world slump, he reflected that 'it is a long time since June 1919 when I resigned from the British delegation in Paris in an enraged and tormented state of mind. The waste over the intervening years has been prodigious.'[18]

To a large extent, waste had been prodigious because, for all the British willingness to revise the treaty, it never was revised, though some parts were never implemented either, and reparations were steadily reduced in their scale and their impact. Failure to revise the treaty in respect of war guilt and boundaries arose from Britain's increasingly difficult relations with France, where opinion towards Germany remained unforgiving. Occupation of the Rhineland, noted a British official in 1919, could be justified 'only on the assumption that Germany will remain a strong, vigorous and aggressive military power, but that France will remain peaceful and unambitious; this is an assumption that will be difficult to justify'. While Britain did not stick to the fiction that Germany had freely consented to the 1919 treaty, France did, thereby justifying strong-arm tactics to enforce it. In 1920 Lloyd George offered France renewed alliance in return for flexibility towards Germany, but he was unwilling to provide France with sufficiently solid assurances to persuade her to give up her 'rights', and discussions failed. The difference in approach was huge, as Britain's Berlin chargé d'affaires noted in 1923: 'we don't want Germany to be a carcass. France does not mind very much if she becomes one, and decomposition supervenes.' On a visit to the Rhineland that year, Violet Bonham Carter was confidentially asked by a British officer if she was 'pro-French'; when she whispered that she was not, he explained that it was all too easy to be thought 'pro-Hun', but 'the Germans have been awfully amenable and easy to deal with, and one can't help liking them and feeling sorry for them'. German diplomats carefully watched this process, seeking benefits from the falling out of former enemies: the German leaders, thought Harold Nicolson in 1928, 'will hesitate to do anything for us unless we can offer them in return something more remunerative and more concrete than polite appreciation'. Britain therefore drifted away from the alliance with France that had seen her through the Great War, without ever finding a focus to replace it: Leo Amery noted in 1923 a cabinet meeting in which the Foreign Secretary had offered 'elaborate recapitulations' of events in the Ruhr, 'without any sort of indication of a policy'. As Neville Chamberlain put it with irritation in the same year, 'although France wants the money which can only be got out of a strong Germany, she always shrinks from any course which would help Germany to pay'. British policy was by the time of the 1925 Locarno Treaty almost neutral between France and Germany, and more sympathetic to German aspirations than to French negativism. Locarno, wrote D'Abernon, brought to an end the 'war entente against Germany'. He thought 'one cannot repeat too often that the German view is largely what Allied action makes it; recognise goodwill, show appreciation of German action, and you have a different Germany from that produced by unjustified suspicion and unrestrained criticism'. To an extent, this approach worked: 'The Germans', reported Sir Horace Rumbold when he arrived in Berlin as ambassador in 1928, were 'remarkably friendly to Englishmen both official and unofficial. We are asked to go places to which Frenchmen would certainly not be asked.' Dedicated as he was to improving relations, he too soon lamented that there were not 'sufficient Frenchmen in authority broadminded enough to realise that some sacrifice may be needed to remove this cause of unrest'. If, he wrote in December 1931, the French continued both to refuse to disarm and to let Germany have arms, there would be a 'Dämmerung of the world'. When Hitler announced German conscription in 1935, 'Chips' Channon on the Tory backbenches thought it meant 'the end of the Treaty of Versailles. I think France, as usual, is to blame.'[19]

During Germany's Weimar Republic, the great question in British minds was: just how secure was German democracy – how well had the Germans taken to a novel situation? Gustav Stresemann, German Foreign Minister between 1923 and his death in 1929, sent his son to Cambridge but was horrified to learn that his undergraduate friends mainly wanted to know when the Kaiser would return. More often, the British blamed themselves, the French and the 1919 treaty for the relative weakness of German democracy. That generation still thought of the Great War as the product of an undemocratic Junker regime: 'If Germany remains or becomes really democratic,' thought Austen Chamberlain in July 1919, 'they cannot repeat the policy of Frederick the Great & Bismarck & his late followers. No democracy can or will make aggressive war its year long study & business.' This was not simply a matter of passive observation, for after watching the Ruhr's civilian leaders opposing French occupation in 1923, Violet Bonham Carter told the National Liberal Federation that in Germany 'a new and unsteady Democracy is struggling onto its feet, and we've got to keep it there'. British diplomats in Germany were constantly reminding the government that it should help Germany establish its democracy, but this is exactly what ran into the sands because of French indifference. Diplomats also anxiously scanned the legislature and the streets for evidence of the health of democracy, noting the easy suppression of the Kapp and Munich putsch attempts in 1923. On the other hand, proposals to make Tirpitz President in 1925, and the actual presidency of Hindenburg, were seen as evidence that the old regime still had supporters. Even the relative stability of the later 1920s did not satisfy everybody, a British consul reporting that 'the renascence of Germany is, in view of the German character, not to be contemplated without a certain anxiety'. Rumbold was struck though by the great difference since his previous posting to Berlin in 1913–14: militarism was in 1928 hardly visible in areas dominated by uniforms before the war, and 'the noisy self-assertiveness and bumptiousness' of Wilhelmine Berlin had been replaced by an altogether quieter mood. The dilemma was eloquently expressed by Keynes in 1920: either the Germans had learned their lesson from defeat in 1918, or they were as a nation irretrievably wicked, in which case 'Europe is finished, and the mantle of civilisation will once more sweep onto other shoulders'.[20]

Until about 1930 the prognosis seemed hopeful, with the return of economic growth and with Stresemann establishing the continuity of a reasonable German foreign policy. Gooch thought in 1926 that 'no one would dare to maintain that finality has been reached, either in the political or economic sphere', but he took an optimistic view. He thought the most remarkable thing about contemporary Germany was 'the disappearance of the army' as a political and social force, though he regretted the survival of the Junkers' social base in 'Eastelbia'. British observers, over-anxious about communism, tended to understate that threat to democracy from the Right, tacitly condoning violence and illegality more in one direction than the other. The Nazis' first experience of power in Thuringia in 1930 seemed distinctly unthreatening: the record, thought the *Manchester Guardian*, showed that Nazis were 'ordinary politicians when in office'. In November 1928 the British Embassy in Berlin reported that democratic forces remained stronger than extremists, and that a 'march on Berlin', equivalent to what had happened in Italy, need not be feared, for 'so long as Germany remains economically, socially and politically as sound as she is today, there is no chance of any such Putsch being successful'. Unfortunately, this was exactly the moment when Stresemann's death and the world slump began the slide towards Nazi dictatorship. 'Poor old Germany', thought Christopher Isherwood by 1932, 'She's not much of an Etat to coup'.[21]

Yet before 1933 an enthusiastically positive image of Germany had developed alongside these doubts and hesitations, a Germany free, exciting and modern, especially in Berlin's 'golden twenties'. That alternative cultural Germany for the young was known to British readers in the 1930s through visitors and expatriates – especially Isherwood and his friends W. H. Auden and Stephen Spender, who claimed it as personal literary territory – and remained influential, though not always in a positive sense. Isherwood, who lived in the German capital for three years before the Nazis took over, published in *Mr Norris Changes Trains* (1935) and *Goodbye to Berlin* (1938) classic accounts of Weimar Berlin in English, accounts that were indirectly influential as the sources of *I Am a Camera* and *Cabaret*. When published and since, these short stories have generally been treated as contemporary reportage, but they were actually historical works, written with the crucial hindsight afforded by knowing that the Nazis took power. Though Isherwood writes eloquently about Berlin's

Communists as well as the Nazis, and certainly did see it all at first hand, he has virtually nothing to say about the democratic parties that dominated Berlin when he arrived, if not when he left; the mood throughout is of the tendency towards disaster, dancing and making love while the ship of democracy sinks. As a result, his 'Berlin stories' and works derived from them have over the years suggested to millions that Germans were just not very good at democracy, all too ready to take things to brutal extremes or to ignore warning signs, and paid the 'inevitable' price for this in the Third Reich. Interviewed in Los Angeles in 1976, Isherwood thought that 'the rise of Nazi power is still a great mystery', but suggested only that disunity among German artists had contributed to the disaster, an extraordinarily feeble conclusion from one who had been there and seen it all for himself. Britain had 'a continuing fascination with Weimar Berlin', wrote Lisa Appignanesi in the *Guardian* in 2004, because it showed so tellingly how freedom of all kinds could lead 'inevitably to an apocalypse'.[22]

Spender recalled much later that Isherwood spoke of Germany as 'the country where all the obstructions and complexities of this life were cut through'. He too, when visiting Hamburg, 'felt a tremendous sense of relief . . . I seemed to be moving in a trance of sensuous freedom, where everything was possible and plausible and easy.' In sharp contrast to Britain, where censorship was tight, 1920s 'Germany seemed a paradise where there was no censorship and young Germans enjoyed extraordinary freedom'. All this naturally appealed to Isherwood, whose first essay at Cambridge had been a defence of the proposition, 'Better England Free than England Sober'.[23] In 1928–9 merely choosing to live and work in Germany was provocative enough, for Britain remained very insular; when Terence Prittie was at Stowe, German was taught only to 'a tiny minority' by a man who knew hardly any German himself, while the majority were 'taught next to nothing about Germany'. Christopher Hollis, recalling Oxford in the 1920s, thought only Anthony Powell, Cyril Connolly and Kenneth Clark among his contemporaries appreciated European culture; 'the rest of us were ignorant'. Spender later recalled that friends 'deplored my spending so much time in Germany and wished I went more often to France', but they were thinking more of Proust than of the Popular

Front; he might have added that France was a recent British ally, and Paris more resorted to for heterosexual than homosexual encounters. All this, however, was positive as well as negative, affection for Germany accompanying rejection of Britain. Isherwood recalled that when he crossed the German frontier to reside in Berlin, and was asked the purpose of his trip, he 'could have truthfully replied "I'm looking for my homeland and I've come to find out if this is it"'. He soon knew that it was, and when seeking other places to live after 1933 was insistent that German must be spoken there, while at the end of his life he demanded Wagner's music for his funeral. Auden, who had 'loved all things Germanic' ever since visiting Austria in 1925, was not able to make such a decisive choice, having to return to schoolmastering in England, but he was soon 'homesick for Germany', which he revisited whenever he could. As a character in Spender's *The Temple* observes, Germany seemed in the 1920s to be discovering 'something marvellous – an understanding of the values of living, nothing but living, life for its own sake, life, like a new world, like the new architecture, not materialistic'. Also typical of their opinions was Spender's own hymn to the sun and its worshippers; in *World within Worlds* he describes swimming with friends.

> To these young Germans, who had little money and who spent what they had immediately, the life of the sense was a sunlit garden from which sin was excluded. Perhaps they thought that their generation had been purged of the bourgeois ideal of accumulated property by the great inflation of 1923. Now their aims were to live from day to day, and to enjoy to the utmost everything that was free: sun, water, friendship, their bodies. The sun – symbol of the great wealth of nature within the poverty of man – was a primary social force in this Germany.

The aesthete Brian Howard also found 'a religion of life values, of living according to the rhythms of the earth'. If freedom from convention was one impression noticed by visitors to Weimar Germany, far outside expectations from the German past, then modernity was another and less surprising. Modernist approaches associated with the flowering of Weimar culture had their roots in the Edwardian period, but it took the relaxation from restraint brought by revolution in 1919 to set them free.[24]

Such a world deeply impressed self-exiled artists. For Spender, free Germans' lives 'flowed easily into the movements of art, literature and painting . . . There were buildings, with broad clean vertical lines crossed by strong horizontals, which drove into the sky like railroads. There were experiments in the theatre and opera, all in a style which expressed with facility the fusion of naked liberation with a kind of bitter pathos, which was characteristic of this Germany.' What impressed them even more was the extent to which artistic modernism seemed a 'popular mass-movement', like the democracy of sun worship; the first nudist film was made in Germany in 1925, and when nude sunbathing eventually came to Britain it was thought a German custom, one of the first nudist beaches being called a *spielplatz*. In Germany, as Spender put it, 'it was easy to be advanced. You had only to take off your clothes' – just what he could not do either literally or metaphorically in Britain. That idea of Germany being freer than Britain was astonishingly new.[25] Exiles and tourists came from all over the world, not least the British, for whom during the 1920s Berlin replaced Paris as the most desirable overseas destination, especially for those mixing sex with tourism. When Berlin was denied to them after 1933 many of these rootless exiles never easily settled again, and became, in Valentine Cunningham's phrase, 'bright young Baedekers'. Sefton Delmer, born in Imperial Berlin and back there reporting for the *Daily Express*, remembered later 'a ferment of ultra-modernism and get-rich-quick hysteria. The exhilarating avant-garde intellectualism of painters, musicians and theatrical producers exploring new aesthetic worlds vied with sordid bucket-shop swindles, corruption scandals . . . and teenage vice clubs whose orgies ended in murder and suicide.' Here was *Cabaret*'s world, German life becoming, as Sally Bowles sings, 'a cabaret, old chum'.[26]

It was a vintage era in literature, marked by the fame of Thomas Mann, whose 1929 Nobel Prize was a milestone in Germany's recovery from the pariah status of 1914–18, the emergence of Kafka and Rilke, and the re-canonisation of iconic figures: the centenary of Goethe's death was celebrated with huge enthusiasm in 1932.[27] Theatre flourished, too: fine writing from Ernst Toller and Bertholt Brecht, acting by Elizabeth Bergner and Marlene Dietrich, and historically important production styles introduced by Erwin Piscator and Max Reinhardt. Isherwood admired the political theatre of Brecht and Piscator, but also loved Reinhardt's elaborately traditional productions, and his sometime flatmate Jean Ross (the model for Sally Bowles) appeared in one of Reinhardt's shows. Reinhardt's *A Midsummer Night's Dream* toured England and played in the open air in Oxford. Most visitors attended performances of Brecht's *Threepenny Opera*, a different type of political theatre which delighted the whole of Germany. *The Times*, somewhat missing the point when lamenting in March 1928 Germans' 'chronic incapacity to produce drawing room comedies', reported the vigour and originality of Berlin's political theatre. A few months later, though not happy that *The Threepenny Opera* was 'one of those combinations of drama, cinema, jazz, and discord with which the name of the Communistic Herr Piscator is associated', the paper recognised it as a great piece of drama which would sweep Europe as it was sweeping Germany. For those who were more in love with novelty than was *The Times*, this was not only new but extremely exciting.[28] Music and opera also flourished. Otto Klemperer was presenting new operas in Berlin, Carl Hindemith offering new music at the Baden-Baden Festival, and there was a general welcome for innovation: German radio was among the first to take microphones into opera houses to bring culture to the masses, and was soon staging specially commissioned operas of its own. The BBC duly followed suit, in its mission to educate the British public, and learned much too about broadcasting techniques from Germany.[29]

Germany's 'golden twenties' bear comparison to the Italian Renaissance in the sudden flowering of all art forms, but film and architecture made the greatest impact on Britain. A 1973 British anthology of *Masterworks of the German Cinema* contained nothing but films from the 1920s. *The Cabinet of Dr Caligari* (1920), claimed Peter Gay, 'continues to embody the Weimar spirit to posterity as palpably as Gropius' buildings, Kandinsky's abstractions, Grosz's cartoons, and Marlene Dietrich's legs' (the last known to Britain through another Weimar film, *The Blue Angel*). Though several such masterpieces – like *Dr Mabuse* and *Nosferatu* (1922), *The Golem* (1925) and *The Student of Prague* (1926) – were Gothic tales from the German past which prefigured Hitler's appeal to the irrational, there were also assertions of the modernity of German cities, notably Walter Ruttmann's *Berlin, the Symphony of a Great City*, and Fritz Lang's *Metropolis* (both 1927). By 1929 such films as *Nosferatu* were already 'legendary cinema'. That last point is certainly demonstrated by the films chosen for the private, uncensored screenings by the Film Society when it started in Britain in 1925. One of the first shown was *Caligari*, then members worked their way through all these 'master-works', so that by the early 1930s many classic German Expressionist films were back on the programme for a second time. Of the films shown in the 1931–2 season, thirteen were from Germany; the next largest group were nine American films, with just five each from Britain and France.[30]

By then, Alfred Hitchcock, who had learned his trade as a director in Ufa's Berlin studios and made the Expressionist thriller *The Lodger* (1927) after returning to Britain, was integrating Expressionism into the mainstream culture of British and American films. The personal experience of the Catholic, sexually timid and virginal Hitchcock could, though, hardly have been more different from that of Isherwood and his friends. He met the seven-foot-tall, flamboyantly homosexual director F. W. Murnau but seems barely to have noticed his orientation, and when taken in Munich to see a live sex show repeatedly declined invitations to join in. Hitch enjoyed that face of Weimar Germany more when retelling the story in interviews many years later than he had at the time.[31]

The new German architecture, mainly associated with Walter Gropius and his fellow-workers in the Bauhaus school, was, thought the French philosopher Aristide Maillol, part of a new German world view, equally to be seen in the 'unabashed nudity' of swimmers at the bathing places and the buildings of Frankfurt. Particularly after the Bauhaus moved from Weimar to Dessau, its broad aims embraced the design and interior decoration of buildings, furniture, fittings and lamps, posters and even typefaces, in a quest for conceptual wholeness that incorporated architects, sculptors and painters, artists, craftsmen and manufacturers. There was a quick impact on Britain, for the Bauhaus union of artist and craftsman matched an indigenous tradition going back to William Morris. German influences were ardently championed by Frank Pick, who tried to sign up Gropius himself as an adviser. From the radical new stations and poster designs that Pick commissioned for the London Underground, modernist concepts spread to other corporations, Shell-Mex, the Post Office and Cunard. In the 1930s German émigrés designed influential British buildings: the penguin pool and gorilla house at London Zoo, the de la Warr Pavilion at Bexhill, Impington Village College in Cambridgeshire. Such uninhibited modernism was never fully accepted until the Attlee government commissioned another German to design the Royal Festival Hall for 1951. In 1929 *The Times* hailed recent buildings in Berlin as marking a decisive 'change in style'. It noted three years later that 'Germany has been a pioneer of the newer architectural styles', but thought there were also excesses that were easily explained 'by the play of recent events on well-known traits of the German character . . . That much of the architecture that the traveller sees has been the expression of another *Stürm under Drang* need not be laboured.' Such German excesses had though been toned down when applied abroad, the paper adding complacently that the best examples of *moderated* modernism were in London. Opening an exhibition on Gropius in 1934, the publisher Sir Stanley Unwin made a similar distinction between Germans who 'take up a theory readily and follow it devotedly' and the pragmatic British who were 'naturally suspicious . . . and afraid of ridicule', if they showed any awareness of theory at all. Others were more ready to give credit where it was due, the painter Paul Nash noting in 1932 how many lamps were brought back by tourists from Germany because they were more interesting than anything yet available in Britain. Under continental influence, British designers were catching up, however, led by progressive firms like Ambrose Heal's London furniture shop; in 1933 Nash founded his own collective of architects, painters and sculptors along Bauhaus lines. For Dorothy Todd and Raymond Mortimer, too, explanations lay in political history, for 'in Germany and Austria the catastrophe of the war and post-war periods have shaken people out of a blind following of old habits, and audacious experiments have been attempted'. When choosing in 1929 examples of 'objects characteristic of our time', two of their four images were recent German buildings.[32]

Auden called in one of his early poems for 'new styles of architecture, a change of heart', endorsing the German concept that modern architecture involved a changed world-view. For Norman Page, that line of verse also 'expresses the mood of a whole generation for whom Berlin seemed to offer the promise of social and artistic tolerance'. Time and again in Isherwood's writings there is reference to modernism in buildings and design, not expressed propagandistically, merely describing the way in which civilised Berliners now lived, habits the British still had to learn. When 'William' goes to visit Baron von Pregnitz, his villa in Mecklenburg is fitted with the most modern objects; later he visits Herr Bernstein, whose house had been ordered 'from a popular *avant-garde* architect', looks like a power station, and is full of modernist lamps and fittings. It is much the same in Spender's *The Temple*, where Joachim has 'ordered from the Bauhaus from Dessau all the furnishings of [his] room'. Joachim's beautiful, modernist apartment is later smashed up by Nazi thugs, an event clearly representing the fragility of Weimar democracy's hold on the future.[33]

Berlin was not Germany, and 'Red Berlin' could be sharply contrasted with conservative, right-wing Bavaria; one British diplomat remarked in 1920 that arriving in Munich from Berlin was 'like entering what Germany must have been in the middle of the last century'. Bavarians hated Prussians, he reported, and saw Berlin as 'a cesspool of atheism and vice, a sordid market where culture is at a discount and only the money-grubber flourishes, a town without a soul'. Nor was all of Germany committed to either modernism or libertarianism: a British guidebook of 1934 reminded its readers that rural Germany was a land of 'primitive conservatism'. In Saxon villages the locals still sang Easter carols in traditional costume, and Easter promenades continued just as they had been dramatised in Goethe's *Faust* – exactly the *volkisch* tradition the Nazis were then busily reinventing. Berlin was also perceived as different from the other great world cities. Reflecting on 'the charm of Berlin' in 1932, Harold Nicolson thought London was by comparison a 'lady in black lace . . . who guards her secrets with dignity', Paris 'a woman in the prime of life to whom one would only tell those secrets that one desires to have repeated'. Berlin was 'a girl in a pullover, not much powder on her face, Hölderlein in her pocket, thighs like those of Atalanta, an undigested education, a heart that is almost too ready to sympathise, and a breadth of view that charms one's repressions from their poisons and shames one's correctitude'. This was a long way from the better-remembered Third Reich capital city.[34]

Hitler becoming Chancellor in January 1933 rang immediate warning bells. The head of the Foreign Office, Sir Robert Vansittart, predicted just three months later that 'the present regime in Germany will, on past and present form, loose off another European war just as soon as it feels strong enough'. Fascism in Italy was too far away to threaten British interests, and Soviet Russia too inefficient to be an immediate threat, but 'Germany is an exceedingly competent country, and she is being visibly prepared for external aggression.' He drew ministers' attention to Hitler's *Mein Kampf*, explaining that the only English edition excluded the worst parts and toned down the rest. Labour's reaction was to hold mass movements of protest, demanding boycotts of German goods and international sanctions. Its pacifist wing still pressed the government to make concessions to Germany, but the tough-minded, like Bevin, were consistently hostile to Nazism. The *Manchester Guardian* determined to tell the terrible truth about the Nazis, not least for readers of its weekly edition in Germany, now denied free papers of their own; its German correspondent thought the Third Reich a 'third realm', utterly surreal. Violet Bonham Carter, too, horrified by early examples of anti-Jewish persecution, felt 'quite ill with shame and rage', and even 'foolish at having been so steadfast a pro-German ever since they became underdogs'. Neville Chamberlain took a similar view: Hitler's regime reminded him of the former Reich, 'instigating, suggesting, encouraging bloodshed and assassination, for her old selfish aggrandisement and pride'. Maybe he had been reading the *National Review*, which revisited in 1933 its pre-1914 view of Germans: 'it makes not a tattle of difference to us what sort of Germans are in power. Whoever they are . . . they will be the consistent enemies of peace and good European order.' There were also books arguing this case, like Dorothy Woodman's *Hitler Rearms* (1933), which traced Hitlerism back to 1914 and beyond. The Liberal *News Chronicle* and the Tory *Daily Mail* were united in deciding that the Prussian military trappings displayed with Hitler and Hindenburg at Potsdam in April 1933 showed old threats in new clothes. There was in 1933–4, then, initial fear of the Nazi regime, and unease about the persecution it unleashed. When the Canadian Fred Ney, successful impresario of

earlier international youth rallies, tried to mount a British Empire pilgrimage to Oberammergau in 1934, his plans came a cropper, for
neither education authorities nor parents wanted their children in
Nazi Germany; asked to write an anthem for the pilgrimage, Kipling
politely declined, and the Archbishop of Canterbury was equally
unobliging when asked for a prayer. Of the five thousand planned for
the trip, only six hundred went, and little money was raised to pay for
scholarships; uniquely for Ney's schemes, there was no commemora-
tive book this time.[35]

Yet there was neither then nor later an understanding of the Nazi
movement, and little attempt to reach one. Benny Morris points out
that although there were literally thousands of articles on Germany
in the British weekly press in the 1930s, 'no more than 25 (!) specifically set out to define, explain or analyse Nazi ideology. Most of the
editors apparently regarded that ideology as ridiculous, irrelevant or
simply intellectually uninteresting.' One noted Germanophile,
Evelyn Wrench of the *Spectator*, could not understand why Hitler
'embarked on an anti-Jew policy', failing to see that anti-Semitism
was a core Nazi belief. Nor did such blinkered observers understand
that Nazism must be expansionist, and could not be just 'a sadist
nationalism' that would be 'satisfied at home', as the *New Statesman*
anticipated in 1934. Nazism was thought a 'normal' nationalism,
generated by resentment against Versailles: even the anti-appeasement campaigner Vernon Bartlett was initially fooled in just this
way. Almost all Britons, explained the Foreign Office's Ivone
Kirkpatrick, thought Hitler 'a more excitable and dangerous politician perhaps, but of the same species' as themselves; it was thought
that once the heady excitement of the Nazi revolution had passed,
Germany would settle down. The press reported the flag-waving
stage-management of Nuremberg rallies more than the speeches,
and when the speeches were reported it was as a one-day wonder
rather than a consistent ideology: as late as 1939, the *Daily Telegraph*
reported a Hitler tirade as 'polemical in tone . . . but allowance has
to be made for Herr Hitler's temperamental tendency to be polemical'. Newspapers routinely underplayed the *Führerprinzip* in
Nazism, and failed to recognise that its reckless dynamism was
unlike anything in the democratic world. Reporters and commentators therefore often ignored Hitler's words and tried to analyse his

motivation from deeds, as if he were an empirical British politician compelled to say disagreeable things to maintain his popularity. It was easy to assume that as the Nazis became more numerous between 1930 and 1933, they must also have become more pragmatic in winning moderate votes: Nazis must become less anti-Semitic, since most Germans simply could not hate all Jews. The truth was exactly the opposite: dynamic Nazism radicalised moderate Germans rather than itself becoming diluted. Hitler was even viewed as a brake on Nazi extremists, a tendency reinforced by his 1934 purge of Brownshirts, in alliance with the army. The War Office thought in 1935 that the German army had 'escaped the danger of political infection' and become instead an important force for stability. If Hitler failed to rant against Jews in a couple of speeches, he was thought to have dropped anti-Semitism. British observers did not see him as a revolutionary, for 'revolution' came from the Left, while the Right went in for 'reaction', which in Germany's case meant reverting to Prussian militarism. The British defence community did at least now stop preparing for naval war against the USA or air war against France, as they had been doing in the later 1920s, naming Germany 'the ultimate enemy' against whom rearmament should be planned, but wider opinion barely grasped the predicament that the country faced. Vansittart wrote, 'it is conceivable that Germany may make a turn for the better, when the dust, the shouting and the parading subside; that the fever may pass, instead of being endemic as most good judges of Germany suspect', but such scepticism was exceptionally rare.[36]

Hence Hitler becoming Chancellor did not end calls to right German grievances; in fact his assumption of power probably reinforced such ideas, since resentment about Versailles was thought to explain Nazi popularity. An Anglo-German group was formed in the winter of 1933–4, working for revision of the treaty, filled with high-minded people like Walter Layton of *The Economist* and the former pacifist Clifford Allen, rather than pro-Nazi fellow-travellers. Hitler, reported Rumbold from Berlin in 1930, was saying nothing about Germany's grievances 'that has not often been said before', and such nationalist politicians expressed only 'what all Germans feel'. Lord Lothian told a Nottingham meeting in November 1933 that 'in part, at any rate', the German regime 'is the product of our own conduct in trying to exact impossible reparations and in requiring her to disarm while her neighbours were armed to the teeth for fifteen years'. In 1938 he wrote to *The Times* to welcome the Austro-German *Anschluss*, since it 'at long last' ended 'the disastrous period' in which the German people had been driven 'to accept a totalitarian regime as the one method by which they could secure their national unity and their natural rights'. Alec Cadogan, at the Foreign Office, felt that Germany could not be tied down to 'the vindictive clauses of a Peace Treaty which was really more in the nature of an armistice', while Harold Macmillan, who built his later career around the fact that he had been an 'anti-appeaser', argued in March 1938 that German breaches of the treaty were not yet, 'in principle, of a kind to which real objection could be made'. The arch-opponent of German expansionism, Vansittart, argued in 1936 for restoring to Germany colonies confiscated in 1919, while in 1938 Lord Tweedsmuir (formerly John Buchan) thought when accepting the *Anschluss* that 'surely the Versailles agreement was the most half-witted thing every perpetrated?' When the Munich crisis began to discredit appeasement in autumn 1938, some of its supporters remained unrepentant, as was Barrington Ward of *The Times*: 'I am one of those who campaigned against the Treaty of Versailles from February 1919 onwards. No reasoning that has yet come my way can convince me that what was inexpedient and immoral then . . . has suddenly become both moral and expedient merely because we have brought the Nazis to power in Germany.' *The Times* was also able to point out that fifteen years earlier, in *The World Crisis*, even Churchill had written about the folly of including so many Germans within Czechoslovakia, as an 'affront to the principle of self-determination'. The *Daily Express* brutally noted that 'whatever the Germans are doing now, they had a rough ride at the peace conference which set up Czechoslovakia, and carved up Germany, and, however the Czechs are treated now, twenty years ago they did some of the rough riding'. Benny Morris may be right to say that such arguments were sometimes just excuses for those who wanted to appease Nazi Germany anyway, but there were certainly others for whom it seemed illogical to deny Hitler what they had always wanted to offer to Stresemann.[37]

With the benefit of hindsight, and especially because Churchill's *War Memoirs* presented it that way, Hitler's remilitarisation of the Rhineland in 1936 has generally been seen as the key moment in appeasement, the missed opportunity to stop Nazi expansion in its tracks. At the time, hardly anyone in Britain saw it as anything other than Germany redressing for itself a generally acknowledged grievance from 1919; if there was regret about her unilateral action, there was understanding that she would not wait for ever. For all its hostility to Hitler, the Labour Party was unready for decisive action: Dalton frankly conceded that public opinion would simply not have stood for strong action which risked war, 'in order to put German troops out of the German Rhineland'; the *New Statesman* acquiesced because 'we all have bad consciences about Germany's treatment since the war'. The League of Nations Union was told by one speaker that the British people held such strong opinions about Germans' grievances that they would not notice Hitler's breach of international law. They may, though, have held no views at all: when George Orwell rushed into a pub in Barnsley, shouting, 'The German army has crossed the Rhine,' the only reaction was one man murmuring, 'Parley-voo', while the rest stared into their beer. A conversation with workingmen in Leeds convinced him that they were 'with two exceptions pro-German'. When Kirkpatrick demanded retaliatory action, politicians warily told him that 'the country would never have stood for the threat of force against a Germany that was not doing any harm to anyone, but merely exercising its sovereign rights in its own territory'. J. L. Garvin urged in the *Observer* the need to distinguish between 'right and wrong. The Rhineland is German territory . . . To give Germany a legitimate grievance might be a fatal disservice to Europe.' Harold Nicolson noted that the mood of the Commons was dominated by fear: 'the House is terribly "pro-German"; which means afraid of war'. The Foreign Secretary asked his press bureau, 'What will the press say tomorrow?' and received a prophetic reply: 'I think they will say that Germany is on her own territory.' In so far as anyone was to blame, it was the French, for provoking Hitler by their pact with Soviet Russia, which many Conservatives regarded (in Austen Chamberlain's words) as 'almost a betrayal of Western Civilisation' – within which Germany, on the other hand, remained. There was indeed a swing of mood in the Commons away from France and towards Germany. Nicolson noted on 10 March that 'on all sides one hears sympathy for the Germans. It is all very tragic and sad.' There was even talk of a German alliance, and Tom Jones

thought 'our PM is not indisposed to attempt this'. In spring 1937
Robert Bruce Lockhart detected even in the Foreign Office 'a new
wave of pro-Germanism, idea being to pal up with Germany and put
Italy in its place'. He was told later in the year that there was 'quite a
strong pro-German feeling among certain Conservatives', and that
the 'Duke and Duchess of Kent are strong in German camp'. An
opinion poll found at this time that when British people were asked
to name the foreign country they liked most, Germany came third,
after only the USA and France, an amazing turnaround since 1918.[38]

Thus occurred 'the Olympic pause', the period in 1936–7 (including Berlin's Olympic Games) during which British views of Hitler's
Germany relaxed. The international youth camp linked with the
games was a success, and Fred Ney duly played his part in organising
the British Empire contingent. There was no boycott as there had
been in 1934; the problem now was that British boys upset their
hosts by refusing to get up for pre-breakfast physical exercises, and by
singing 'What Shall We Do with the Drunken Sailor' after German
boys had rendered the '*Horst Wessel* Song' (it being thought just too
embarrassing to sing 'Land of Hope and Glory' abroad). These camps
were an important propaganda success for Germany: one headmaster
noted that 'the adolescent at Charterhouse seldom goes abroad again',
so his 'whole impression of Europe is derived from that trip to
Germany . . . which was neatly arranged for him by Herr Goebbels'.
To achieve a substantial public relations success with the Olympics,
the Nazis soft-pedalled for a time their repressive policies, and pulled
out all the stops to impress visitors. Most who visited and were
impressed were no doubt sympathetic to Germany already, like Chips
Channon (delighted to be given his own car and stormtrooper
driver), while the most hostile stayed away. Cabarets reopened, and it
seemed that Berlin's golden twenties might yet resume their course,
while parties held by Göring and Ribbentrop suggested that even
Nazis could let their hair down. This was what Richard Griffiths
sees as 'the heyday' for 'fellow travellers of the right'. It was also the
time when the press was most effectively managed to avoid upsetting
the Germans: 'I spend my nights', wrote Geoffrey Dawson, editor of
The Times, 'taking out anything which I think will hurt their susceptibilities, and in dropping in little things which are intended to
soothe them.'[39]

It went wider than media management, as the involvement of the mass-membership British Legion demonstrates. The Legion was keen to establish international relations, hoping that the brotherhood of old soldiers would foster an atmosphere of peace. When it first joined the international veterans' federation in 1921, German organisations remained barred from membership, and it was largely British pressure that enabled the Germans to join in 1926, though the whole thing then went wrong when German delegates promised only to 'recognise existing treaties' rather than 'respect' them. Bilateral meetings proved more successful, however, and it was through such links that the Legion secured the symbolic return of the colours of the Gordon Highlanders, lost during the Great War but now handed back by President Hindenburg in person. Reciprocal visits were discussed, and given extra impetus when the Legion's president, the Prince of Wales, called for veterans' visits to be arranged: the Prince asked for 'the hand of friendship to be offered to the Germans' by 'we ex-servicemen, who fought them and have now forgotten all about it, in the Great War'. Though Edward was reprimanded by George V for failing to consult the Foreign Office, the visits went ahead. One British delegation met Hitler, and Legion branches entertained visiting Germans until 1938, when German veterans laid a wreath in London as the Munich crisis brought the two countries close to war. Arnold Toynbee in *The Economist* thought that Hitler's support for contact between war veterans showed 'all the marks of sincerity of "the ex-service man" who has seen war and its aftermath at close quarters'. (As the magazine's founding editor Walter Bagehot once put it, 'in the faculty of writing nonsense, stupidity is no match for genius'.) Ironically, the new Legion president, Sir Brunel Cohen, was Jewish, and declined to visit Nazi Germany himself, but he did not obstruct the wishes of his members and helped welcome Germans to Britain. He was nevertheless relieved to say 'good-bye and not *auf wiedersehn*' when the last Germans, eight hundred strong and Nazi to a man, left London in 1938. There was naivety here, typical of British views of Nazi Germany, for the Legion never understood that the Nazis had absorbed groups like old-soldier clubs, integrated them into the party, and manipulated them at will for propaganda purposes. As a veteran of the trenches himself, Hitler could talk the talk on such occasions, just as he could mimic the language of democracy when entertaining visitors like Lloyd George. In neither case did the visitors even get near to understanding what made him tick. While legionaries who visited Munich were allowed to see the Dachau concentration camp (explained to them personally by Himmler at 'a quiet family supper'), they had no idea that the 'prisoners' describing the 'very reasonable' conditions there were SS men in disguise. The spirit of these exchanges is also to be seen in the Legion's offer to provide international policemen to patrol the Sudetenland during the Munich crisis, a task for which seventeen thousand British veterans volunteered. The offer was fraternally welcomed by the German government and then brusquely dismissed once it had served its propaganda purpose.[40]

Many Anglo-German contacts in the mid-to-late 1930s were orchestrated in a similar manner, and conducted with naivety by the British. There were some pro-Nazis in high places in Britain: Bruce Lockhart met one at Lady Cunard's house in 1934, outraged that the British government had not been officially represented at the recent Nuremberg rally. There were, though, never more than a handful of such people, and the myth of the 'Cliveden set' of highly placed people secretly determining British policy at weekend parties was exactly that – a myth. Others met Nazis socially in the hope of understanding them, even perhaps influencing them with a show of British resolve, as did Austen Chamberlain when Hitler came to power; having recognised the sheer evil of the Nazi regime, Chamberlain would have nothing more to do with it, refusing to set foot in Germany even during the Olympics. When G. M. Trevelyan's life of Sir Edward Grey came out just before Chamberlain's death, he urged his sister to read it, for 'it's a lesson in German ways'. Likewise, though Duff and Diana Cooper had visited Germany soon after Hitler became Chancellor, they were by 1936 determinedly hostile: looking forward to his trip to the Olympics, Chips Channon found that 'Harold Nicolson and Lady Colefax disapprove of our journey, and so . . . do the truculent Coopers'. Examples of British naivety were legion. Tom Jones thought it really significant when in 1936 Hitler promised to make English the first foreign language learned in German schools. Later in the year he helped stage-manage Lloyd George's disastrous visit to Hitler, the former British war leader laying wreaths with the Führer at a war memorial. As they moved on to

Stuttgart, Lloyd George was excitedly 'ruminating . . . on what effect
their talk at Berchtesgaden would have on Hitler's speeches at the
Party meetings in Nuremberg' – the answer, of course, was none
whatsoever.[41]

Keynes was never deceived. Though later historians have detected
in Hitler's economic policies neo-Keynesian deficit financing to
reduce unemployment, Keynes knew that Hitler's public works
schemes were about rearmament not economics, the new autobahns
proving extremely useful when the Nazis mobilised their army.
'Germany', he wrote soon after Hitler took over, 'is at the mercy of
unchained irresponsibles', adding soon afterwards that they sought
'escape in a return backwards to the modes and manners of the
Middle Ages, if not of Odin'. When a German friend objected to
him using 'barbarism' to describe Nazi methods, assuring him that
they were 'an expression of the general will' of Germans, Keynes
responded that this would make the situation 'ten times more
horrible'. The Hamburg banker Carl Melchiot, with whom he had
struck up a friendship in 1919, and with whom he had collaborated in
the 1920s on attempts to sort out reparations, died in December
1933. When the Mayor invited Keynes to revisit his city in the
following year, the 'pro-German' Keynes replied that 'there is nothing
left that could attract me to Hamburg'. Though many in the liberal
circles in which Keynes moved were now uncertain about both armaments and foreign policy, he himself was tough-minded and
consistent: there could be no agreement with the 'brigand powers',
unless dictated by Britain from a position of strength. His view,
regularly aired in letters to the press, was that 'it is better to have a
policy of strong forces and no clear-cut foreign policy' than the other
way round, which was what most of the Left seemed to prefer.[42]

In addition to tourism and social and professional contacts, there
were organisations whose purpose was the improvement of Anglo-
German relations, just as before 1914; historians have somewhat
inconsistently assumed that in the Edwardian period their British
organisers were well intentioned while the 1930s equivalents were
either malevolent or utterly naive. There was an Anglo-German
Society formed in 1935 by businesses like Dunlop and Unilever, dedicated to protecting their interests in Anglo-German trade, but used
by the Nazis to promote economic appeasement. The Anglo-German

Fellowship was more obviously political, its British leader Lord Mount Temple having audiences with Hitler. If its admiration was more for German culture than Nazi ideology, its pronouncements nevertheless helped Goebbels: Mount Temple announced in 1936 that Germany's 'strength and determination have liberated Europe from a real danger', communism, and argued when launching the Fellowship that Germany had fought fair in the 1914–18 war – a view that would have been hard to express at the time; 'next time' the two countries should be allies. An Anglo-German Association had existed since 1929, augmented by an Anglo-German Group since 1933, with elite political involvement still as much from the Left as the Right. Such networks, lubricated by Nazi gold, helped promote reciprocal visits and placed sympathetic newspaper articles and books in the shops. As before 1914, the Churches tried to maintain peace, too, with the Bishop of Gloucester taking the lead, and an Anglo-German Brotherhood provided the platform. Bishop Headlam thought socialism 'the creed of the German Jew', from which admiration for Hitler followed logically enough. Sympathetic visitors were impressed with what they saw during arranged visits to Germany, for this seemed an open society where reporters were welcomed (unlike Stalin's Russia), while in practice they saw only what Nazi hosts showed them, and many British reporters were expelled for writing hostile stories. A Blackpool councillor enthused in 1936, in a letter to his local press, 'there was no trace of the oppression and suppression of individuality one had heard of'. The *Anglo-German Review* promoted such opinions among twelve thousand subscribers, though it is unlikely that it sold to anyone except those who already believed. Such contacts did not greatly influence official British policy, though they may have impressed Sir Nevile Henderson, sent to Berlin as ambassador in 1937 with a specific brief to improve relations. The Link was the only genuinely pro-Nazi Anglo-German organisation of the time, and though its membership increased as war approached, it never reached five thousand; and even some of these were more naive than ideologically opposed to democracy.[43]

All efforts to maintain Anglo-German friendship were disrupted by Nazi words and deeds in 1938–9. The Austro-German *Anschluss* of March 1938 and the Czech crisis in the summer could both be seen to fall within the idea of allowing the same self-determination to

Germans as was allowed to others in 1919, but there was already an air of the final acceptable instalments about these revisions of the treaty. British feebleness in the face of Hitler's demands now owed more to fear than to morality. Changed Nazi rhetoric towards Britain at the end of 1938 nevertheless came as a shock, as Hitler abandoned *Mein Kampf*'s claim of an Anglo-German racial affinity for the more familiar pan-German claim, *circa* 1910, that the British Empire was Germany's natural enemy. Tom Jones noted with incomprehension in January 1939 that German radio 'attacks us daily', while Cadogan thought it a reaction against Britain's success in restraining Hitler at Munich, limited though that success had been. Since it was now understood that there was no free press in Germany, hostility being intensively 'worked up' in the German papers could only mean, as *Time and Tide* put it, that Britain had become 'the supreme objective' of Germany's 'imperialist and revolutionary campaign'. The German announcement of accelerated submarine-building had a similar impact; it could be aimed only at a maritime power like Britain. Anti-Nazi Germans meanwhile passed on rumours that Hitler planned a 'bolt from the blue' air assault on Britain. For those who feared the effects of bombing (almost everyone), remembered Germany's 1914 invasion of Belgium, and had read William Le Queux (everyone over forty), such thoughts were deeply worrying. It was hard to miss the point when Hitler screamed even at Nevile Henderson that 'England was determined to destroy and exterminate Germany'.[44]

These fears were given added impetus by Nazi actions that were far from theoretical: *Kristallnacht* in November 1938 and the occupation of Bohemia and Moravia the following March. The first destroyed lingering hopes that the Nazi revolution would burn itself out, while the second wrecked residual belief that Hitler aimed only to reunite Germans denied their rights since 1919. Brutal attacks on Jewish property during *Kristallnacht* produced instant condemnation, from the future BBC director-general Hugh Carleton Greene, for example, in the *Daily Telegraph*:

Mob law ruled in Berlin throughout the afternoon and evening and hordes of hooligans indulged in an orgy of destruction. I have seen several anti-Jewish outbreaks in Germany during the last five years, but never anything as nauseating as this. Racial hatred and hysteria seemed to have taken hold of otherwise decent people. I saw fashionably dressed women clapping their hands and screaming with glee, while respectable middle-class mothers held up their babies to see the 'fun'.

The *Manchester Guardian* accepted that the German government had not ordered the attacks: 'No, but the government's faithful servants carried them out, while others, equally acquainted with its mind, looked on.' The *Daily Mail*'s Collin Brooks found that even in that bastion of pro-German sympathies, 'the Jewish pogrom in Germany is arousing great indignation'; *Picture Post* wrote of the beginning of 'a new dark age in Europe'. Mount Temple resigned the leadership of the Anglo-German Fellowship in protest, and though few members followed him out it was henceforth of even less significance. A Tory MP not previously an anti-appeaser told his constituents that recent Jewish persecutions 'should be a lesson to others not to allow themselves to be underdogs of the Germans'. Another decided that 'it really looks as if these mad creatures who are in charge of Germany mean to have war'.[45]

The German march into Prague in March 1939 reinforced these conclusions, and was anyway a direct slap in the face to Britain, which had forced Czechs to accept the Munich deal. Away from the Foreign Office while Prague fell, Kirkpatrick returned to find 'the whole picture had changed'. Nevile Henderson's final dispatch as British ambassador in Berlin concluded that until March 1939 Germany had 'flown the German national flag. On those Ides of March its captain defiantly hoisted the skull and crossbones of the pirate.' The British Legion, though reaffirming respect for German veterans, now withdrew from any international bodies on which they were represented 'for an indefinite period'. *The Times*, another former appeaser, thundered that Prague 'gave notice to the world that German policy no longer seeks the protection of a moral cause'. There were now few apologists for either Hitler or Germany; one who had been 'a lifelong lover of Germany', Evelyn Wrench, thought this 'a shattering experience'. Chips Channon wrote that *Kristallnacht* showed 'Hitler never helps', for although 'no-one ever accused me of being anti-German ... I really cannot cope with the present regime . . . Are they mad?' He now decided that 'no balder, bolder departure from the written bond has ever been committed in history', and was outraged by Hitler's insult to Neville Chamberlain, for which 'I can never forgive him'. Chamberlain was incensed too: according to Sir Horace Wilson, when Hitler occupied Prague the Prime Minister said to himself, 'you don't do that to me'. A Gallup poll now found that 54 per cent of the British people thought that Germany was 'the foreign country you like least', compared to a mere 5 per cent who hated Russia, while only 3 per cent thought Germans their favourite foreigners. That revolution in feeling is explicable only as the re-emergence of convictions dating back to before 1918; Kipling would have said that the English were re-learning to hate.[46]

In condemning the occupation of Prague, *The Times* argued that if Germans wished to live under 'a revolting system, unworthy of a civilised state', that was fine, but they must not impose it on others. British opinion during the thirties was uncertain as to how far the German people chose Nazi rule, how much they supported Hitler. Censorship and repression made it impossible to measure public opinion with any pretence of accuracy, but as a result British observers gradually moved towards pessimism. Tom Jones knew in 1933 that he had 'no inside information of any value. Friends of mine', recently at Dachau, 'learned nothing, as though free to move about there were spies everywhere and the prisoners said nothing'. Austen Chamberlain wondered in 1936 whether Nazi censorship was 'silly or dangerous'; although he initially inclined to the view that it was foolish, he had by then decided that 'if you can ride . . . a people in blinkers, they will be your tools for any purpose for which you need them'. Newspaper columnists continuously debated how far Hitler needed popular support, though there was general recognition that easy successes until 1938 had bolstered his position. Even a hardliner like Vansittart could use the argument that to give way further was 'sounding the death knell of the German moderates'. He was, though, in sympathy with Neville Chamberlain when the Prime Minister 'drily' but pertinently asked, when told of the German opposition, 'What can these people offer us?' The *News Chronicle*'s Vernon Bartlett, so opposed to appease-ment as to get himself banned from Germany, had no belief that the army would overthrow Hitler. He was highly displeased when his paper printed such stories, and strongly advised the editor not to believe them.[47]

Though historians later devoted a good deal of attention to the German resistance to Hitler, and the possibility that strong action by the democracies in 1936 or 1938 would have prompted the overthrow of the regime, few informed observers gave this more credence than Bartlett at the time. British intelligence and military planners attributed little weight to the German opposition, and too much to Germany's economic problems, which, they predicted, would prevent her from fighting a prolonged war. Oliver Harvey at the Foreign Office concluded after *Kristallnacht* that 'the German people, or the better part . . . are probably in their heart of hearts opposed to the Nazi regime, particularly its worst excesses, and want peace – but they are passive, they will not oppose Hitler, and they will march – though without great heart, if required to do so'. His boss Alec Cadogan had decided 'that Hitler's orders would be carried out' in a war, and that 'no revolt can be anticipated at all events during the initial stages'. This was largely the view of the press, too, regrettable though it might be that a people known as 'truth-seekers' were now regimented 'killers of truth', as the *Manchester Guardian* put it. The *Mail*'s sources convinced it that, however much the German people disliked inflation, and however much they lived on 'jokes and ribald songs' in the absence of a free press, 'they are behind the Administration'. There were anyway those who, like the Conservative MP Arnold White, visited Germany and wrote about the extent to which Germans were excited by the rebuilding of their country, and diehards like Lord Winterton who warned when war began that Germans backed Hitler with a 'fanatical devotion comparable only to the followers of Genghis Khan or the prophet Mohammed'.[48]

Against widespread acknowledgement of mass German acquiescence in Nazism, if not actual support, there was again readiness to think in terms of two Germanies – Nazis on the one hand, decent Germans on the other – not least because so many of the 'good Germans' had fled to Britain. Hitler's appointment as Chancellor, reported the British ambassador, was an 'arbitrary decision' by Hindenburg, thus placing a political minority 'in supreme control'; against them were ranged 'the entire intelligentsia of the country, its scientists, writers, artists, the Bar, the Churches', industry and the trades unions. The rapid departure of so many opinion formers then created 'a kind of vacuum' within which the Nazis and the army became the only sources of authority. A former German diplomat told Bruce Lockhart in 1938 that there was 'not an intellectual German in Berlin who did not believe the Führer was mad', but intellectuals were powerless against the anti-intellectual forces Hitler had mobilised. Belief in a better Germany could be based more on faith than evidence: Ernest Bevin declined altogether to believe in an immutable 'German national character', since, if that were true, 'the only hope for the world would be to crush Germany, and, as she rises, to crush her again, which gives one a very pessimistic outlook'; he had changed his mind by 1945. Others determined to be optimistic, too, recognising that many Germans had opposed Hitler and come to a sticky end in the process. Harold Nicolson, told by a Nazi apologist that he should visit the new Germany, which he would find remarkably changed, responded that he would indeed, for he would find all his German friends in prison. Debating with Chips Channon soon afterwards, he rejected the argument that what Hitler did within Germany was his own affair, for 'I hate to see all that is best in the German character being exploited by all that is worst'. There were British admirers of dissenters like Karl Goerdeler, the Mayor of Leipzig who resigned when the Nazis removed the statue of Mendelssohn from his city, just as the Jewish composer's music had been banned. It was with such people in mind that *The Times* responded to criticisms of its 'pro-Nazi' stance in 1938, its editor protesting that the paper hoped only for 'a genuine friendship with the German PEOPLE'.[49]

Karl Goerdeler stayed in Germany to resist and eventually died at Nazi hands, but other Germans were both more visible in their resistance and able to keep going longer by leaving the country. This allowed a clear distinction to be made between 1914 and 1939: Kenneth Clark, the art historian then working on British propaganda, asserted in 1941 that 'in the last war all the best elements of German culture and science were still in Germany and were supporting the German cause, whereas now they are outside Germany and supporting us'. Unlike the last great influx of European refugees into Britain in the late nineteenth century (poor and often uneducated émigrés from Tsarist Russia), refugees from Hitler were frequently high-ranking professionals, wealthy and educated. They could therefore move into elite circles, and have a highly visible impact on their new country: among the first to arrive were Walter Gropius, the architectural historian Nikolaus Pevsner, and the musicians Carl Ebert and Fritz Busch (who within a year ran the Glyndebourne Opera Festival). The Warburg Library, all sixty thousand volumes, was moved from Hamburg to London and began a new life within London's world of cultural history. Academics supported their German peers, an Academic Assistance Council being set up in 1933, led by William Beveridge of the LSE. If there was a self-interest in this – Churchill's chief scientific adviser, Professor Lindemann, made a 'shopping trip' through Germany to load his trolley with fellow-professors who would strengthen Oxford science – there was also genuine goodwill. For all his advocacy of better relations with Germany, Tom Jones was horrified to learn that all but one of Göttingen's Mathematical Faculty had been dismissed. Maths was to be a subject much influenced by such refugees as Hermann Bondi and John von Neumann. Although he thought 'what rubbish his theory is', Keynes welcomed to Cambridge Friedrich von Hayek when the LSE was evacuated from wartime London, and nominated him for a fellowship of the British Academy; the rest of the century was a duel between their rival approaches to economics, with Keynes eventually the loser. In much the same way, Albert Einstein was welcomed in Oxford, lamenting that 'I shall never see the land of my birth again'. The overall impact on British learning was staggering: Daniel Snowman shows that by 1992 the émigrés and their children had collected sixteen Nobel Prizes and eighteen knighthoods; seventy-four had become fellows of the Royal Society and thirty-four fellows of the British Academy. It is impossible to imagine post-war British intellectual life without Ernst Gombrich and Jacob Bronowski in cultural history, Geoffrey Elton among political historians, Claus Moser in arts administration, George Weidenfeld in publishing, Hans Keller among musicologists – not to mention Gerard Hoffnung. A similar list could be made for practically every discipline. Germans in early post-war Britain were frequently people of high visibility and even higher levels of achievement.[50]

Of course, not all émigrés were eminent, at least not yet: the future Amadeus String Quartet met during wartime internment, and if Sigmund Freud did not live long in exile, his grandsons Clement and Lucian each achieved eminence some years later. There were around seventy thousand refugees from Germany, some of whom moved on to America or Palestine, but about 55,000 remained British residents. The German community in Britain in 1939 was therefore larger than it had been in 1914 and much larger than it was in 1919. Once it was understood that the Nazi regime would not quickly disappear but drive more and more Jews into exile, the British government adopted a discriminatory policy, refusing automatic entry to all who applied and giving priority to 'distinguished persons', defined as 'those of international repute in the field of science, medicine, research or art', and 'industrialists with a well-established business'. One consequence was to condemn thousands of poorer Jews to the gas chambers – though without anyone ever being aware of making decisions in those terms – but the policy also ensured that many émigrés would be highly valued.[51]

Kenneth Clark's claim that all that was best of Germany was in 1941 living abroad and working for Hitler's defeat thus seemed plausible. Robert Bruce Lockhart recalled Germans living in London in their thousands, as they 'waited only for the day when the retribution of war would overtake the Nazi devil'. As a result of this, despite bruising debates on the subject during the Second World War, the idea that all Germans were ancestrally guilty could never pass unchallenged – among the British elite, though, in circles where names like Bondi and Gombrich meant nothing, all this probably made little difference. Nobody articulated the new situation better than Keynes. In a speech during a Cambridge charity fundraising performance in December 1939, he welcomed both the fact that there were now a thousand refugees in the city, and the ballet company (led by a German refugee) giving the entertainment:

> The truth is that there are now two Germanies. The presence here of Germany in exile is one more symptom of what has been called the queerness of this war. It is a sign that this is a war not between nationalities and imperialism, but between two opposed ways of life and over what we are to mean by civilisation. Our object in this mad,

unavoidable struggle is not to conquer Germany, but to convert her, and bring her back within the historic fold of Western civilisation.

Much the same was proclaimed by British liberals in 1914, but such generous war aims had been swept away into the vengefulness of 1919. Could they survive a second war, when *undoubted* atrocities were committed by Germans, far worse than anything alleged about 1914–18?[52]

5

'Don't let's be beastly to the Germans': War and post-war the second time around

Noel Coward had a disappointing Second World War. In entertainment, where he excelled, things went well, and during the war years he reached his pinnacle of fame and popularity. 'London Pride' was a patriotic hit (the tune partly stolen from 'Deutschland über Alles'), *In Which We Serve* (1942) was one of the most popular films and was followed by *This Happy Breed* (1944) and *Brief Encounter* (1945). The *New Yorker* reported in May 1943 that Coward's plays had been 'rapturously received by his public and very nearly as handsomely by the critics, who invited him to step right up into the distinguished playwrights' gallery between Mr Congreve and Mr Wilde'. His singing to troops and war-workers was tireless, taking him around North America, the Middle East, Australia, New Zealand, Singapore and India, and even to Burma. Two days before VE Day in 1945 he dined with Churchill, and the *Daily Mail* published Coward's article about the victory alongside speeches by the King and the Prime Minister. When Nazi archives were captured, Coward's name was on the list marked down for liquidation had a German invasion succeeded.[1] However, none of this satisfied him, for Coward had had only an inglorious army career when conscripted in 1918. He loathed the loss of individuality in barrack-room life (where neither his surname nor his orientation can have helped), suffered fainting fits and was invalided out after spending most of his army life in hospital. By 1939, he had a strongly patriotic persona, displayed in *Cavalcade* (1931), when he had assured the first-night audience that it was 'pretty exciting to be English'; he wrote these same words privately in his diary during the 1941 Blitz. War reinforced that patriotic tendency, and in May 1940, in a hotel room in New York, he realised that despite his 'cynical detachment', he had a passionate love for 'England', and hated its enemies: 'There was no escape, no getting round it, that was my personal truth, and facing up to it, once and for all, I experienced a strong relief [and was] at peace until the end of the war'. Just as well, he admitted ruefully in his autobiography, for in 'the months and years to come', the war 'handed me a few unpleasant surprises'.[2]

The unpleasantness had actually begun in 1939, for Coward could not persuade anyone to value his potential contribution to the war effort. There was a homophobic element here, but also a refusal to take him seriously. He was himself responsible for this: as 'Roland Maule' tells the 'Coward' character in *Present Laughter* (1939), 'you are frivolous and without the slightest intellectual significance . . . All you do with your talent is wear dressing gowns and make witty remarks.' When vetoing a 'stupidity proposal' to employ Coward in America in 1941, Hugh Dalton thought him 'an indiscreet stinker, off his proper beat . . . utterly unreliable and attracts publicity everywhere . . . a roaring pansy'. Consulted confidentially, Winston Churchill declared grandiloquently that Coward must 'sing to them when the guns are firing – that's your job!' Reflecting that the outlook must be terrible if the Royal Navy needed regular doses of 'Mad Dogs and Englishmen', Coward thanked Churchill 'and went sadly away'. Within days he was given a job in Paris, liaising with the French on propaganda, but his advice was rarely heeded, and he was wholly out of sympathy with the methods of the Phoney War. Deploring the RAF dropping leaflets rather than bombs, he thought distributing Chamberlain speeches meant the Allies' plan must be to bore Germans to death, but doubted if there was time. George Orwell believed in 1941 that the British people welcomed leaflet drops, and would have done even 'if we had known at the time what drivel these leaflets were': they proved to Germans that Britain had a quarrel only with the Nazis. Chamberlain said this in his first wartime broadcast, and the leaflets reiterated it, though Orwell thought that their not being explosives would really make the point. Coward's alternative suggestion that the RAF should drop millions of self-adhesive Union

Jacks, which would then affix themselves to roofs all over Germany, was turned down as just silly. Eventually he secured a transfer to the United States, where, as in Paris, he already had extensive contacts, and hence was in New York at the war's crisis point in May 1940. Though hoping Churchill's assumption of power would bring a real job, he was dismissed back to America for undercover work that Dalton cancelled before it even began. From then on he sang for victory, and to general applause. Expectation of success contributed to the 'Noel Coward manner' that others resented, for, as he put it himself, 'I behaved through most of the war with gallantry tinged, I suspect, with a strong urge to show off.' That manner explains the *Sunday Express*'s dismissal of Coward as 'a wandering minstrel', and a vicious attack on him by the *Daily Mirror*: he represented 'cocktails, countesses and caviare', the Britain that had disappeared with the 'People's War'.[3]

In 1940–1 a steady newspaper battering began, and continued for the duration. Coward had received the Royal Navy's hospitality during the 1930s and been offered honorary officer rank (which he refused) after setting up a company to publicise the navy in films; the *Daily Telegraph* nevertheless reported him 'sauntering along the Rue Royale in naval uniform', while the *Sunday Pictorial* put him top of the list of eight civilians 'masquerading' in uniform. This brought a 'flood' of hate mail, and when he went to America to propagandise he was said to have 'gone with the wind up'. Things became really nasty with *In Which We Serve*, though it had support from Lord Mountbatten, the captain of the destroyer whose sinking provided the plot. Mountbatten was, like Coward, atoning in 1939–45 for the family's record in 1914–18, when his 'pro-German' father had been driven out of the Admiralty; he brought his manoeuvre off with aplomb where Coward largely failed. Newspapers were outraged that a 'playboy' should act on screen as a war hero, but even while the film was in production they found a heavier stick with which to beat him when Coward was prosecuted for non-compliance with currency regulations. He was inevitably convicted (although only for obscure, technical offences), and was widely thought to have placed personal gain ahead of the national need. When he set off to sing to the troops, the Ministry of Information insisted he submit in advance the lyrics of songs in his programmes, so worried were civil servants about his 'unreliability'. That trip was the subject of his *Middle East Diary* (1944), which indulged in a big way in his usual name-dropping, presenting what had been an exhausting tour as if he had spent the time sipping cocktails by sunny North African pools. Readers were shocked by his description of a naval rating aboard HMS *Charybdis*, 'who is really magnificent. He is about six foot, youngish, and dressed in an abbreviated pair of faded blue shorts.' The further error of identifying a weeping soldier in hospital ensured that American papers joined in the assault, furious at an effete Limey's attack on New Yorkers. Detecting covert anti-Semitism in Coward's sentimental reference to 'mournful little Brooklyn boys lying there in tears amidst the alien corn', the Mayor of Brooklyn launched a society for the 'Prevention of Noel Coward re-entering America'. By then, his knighthood, gratefully arranged by Mountbatten, had disappeared just before the New Year's Honour's List was published.[4]

As he left for Gibraltar in 1943, Coward stirred up another hornet's nest with 'a little satirical song' which hit a raw nerve. He first publicly sang 'Don't Let's Be Beastly to the Germans' during a BBC broadcast just before he sailed. As Robert Greacen puts it, Coward's best songs contain 'just a little acid'. In this case, acid was the entire taste of the song, if taste can be found there at all. The lyrics incorporated every German stereotype – lack of humour, over-sensitivity, British pro-Germans ('Let's be free with them, and share the BBC with them') – and the idea of two Germanies ('It was just those nasty Nazis who persuaded them to fight / And their Beethoven and Bach are really far worse than their bite'). There was ironic insistence on historic German characteristics ('We must send them steel and oil and coal and everything they need / For their peaceable intentions can be always guaranteed'), current Nazi evils, and British self-interest:

> Let's help the filthy swine again
> To fortify the Rhine again,
> But don't let's be beastly to the Hun.

This was an outspoken if quirkily humorous attack on those who were by 1943 suggesting a generous peace with Germany. Churchill demanded three encores when Coward sang it to him, but the radio public were less enthusiastic, mainly because many thought Coward himself advocated being nice to Germans. The consequence was sacks of hate mail and polemical attacks in the press, notably by the *Daily Herald*, which detected 'appalling taste and mischievous disregard of public feeling'. The BBC did not allow the song on air again in case it was misrepresented by Goebbels, and HMV suppressed its recording. In the USA, on the other hand, not only did President Roosevelt like the song as much as Churchill, but Treasury Secretary Henry Morgenthau personally invited Coward to sing it on American radio to encourage Americans to buy war bonds. Nor is there evidence that the ordinary British objected once they understood it, for Coward found that it was 'pretty sure fire' at concerts for servicemen.[5]

The 1943–4 row over Coward's song and diary was one moment in a debate that ran on throughout the war. A second conflict – to British thinking, unequivocally the fault of 'Germany' – raised the tricky question of whether Germans were naturally bad or just badly led – in this case by the Nazis, whom everyone agreed were historically evil. Were the Nazis an aberration from German history or its natural outcome, albeit in extreme form? On the answer would hang British policy towards post-war Germany and Anglo-German relations for generations. The debate was slow to ignite, for during the Phoney War there was little disposition to stir things up, and in summer 1940 people had more urgent things on their minds. During the 1930s the government had planned a Ministry of Information, sensing that in any conflict with the Nazis it would be necessary to rebut Joseph Goebbels. Alongside administrative preparations, designated officials outlined as propaganda themes the celebration of Britishness, to encourage mass patriotism. This approach, rooted in suspicion of ordinary people's reliability, contributed to the ministry's poor performance in its first year, for its core assumption proved wide of the mark. At the end of September 1939, an opinion poll found that 89 per cent of the British public already intended to fight until Hitlerism disappeared, while over three-quarters opposed holding peace talks. It was difficult to maintain that momentum during six months of Phoney War, and no propaganda campaign could have achieved such a feat, but the exciting events of 1940 quickly renewed popular determination to win, though the avoidance of defeat was the most that then made any practical sense as a 'war aim'. Churchill told the Commons when appointed Prime Minister that the only objective of his government was 'victory', and soon afterwards he advised President Roosevelt that his 'We shall fight them on the beaches' speech was directed mainly at Hitler and Mussolini; all that the dictators learned from his speech was a restatement of determination neither to surrender nor negotiate, nothing about Germans' fate should Britain defeat them.[6]

Churchill remained for the rest of the war an opponent of stating British aims, and even when victory became a probability he was reluctant to tell Germans what would happen to them when they lost. He dismissed plans to make such an announcement with the crushing observation that 'precise aims would be compromising whereas vague principles would disappoint'. When he met Roosevelt in August 1941, he urged that nothing be said in detail, but that nobody should plan for a peace that would be vindictive or economically ruinous; post-war Germany should be 'fat but impotent'. That reluctance to state war aims owed something to memories of the difficult relationship between war aims and peacemaking in 1919, but more to his innate resistance to commitment to *any* policy far in advance. As Prime Minister in 1940–5 he obstructed his own party's policy-planning for a post-war election until it was too late, and would have done the same as Leader of the Opposition in 1945–51 had the Conservative Party itself not rebelled against such restrictions. As a result, however, the Ministry of Information never set up a German section and the BBC was repeatedly refused permission to offer anti-Nazi Germans a 'hope clause' to encourage resistance to Nazism. So determined was he to prevent others from filling the gap created by his saying nothing that, when the junior information minister Harold Nicolson made off-the-record remarks to a private meeting which leaked to the press, Churchill sent 'a stinking note' to Nicolson's boss that left the errant junior 'shattered'. At their next meeting, the worried Nicolson observed that Churchill was 'not as genial as usual'.[7]

When Russia entered the war, and Churchill proclaimed that all anti-Nazis were friends while 'any man or state who marches with Hitler is our foe', he still refused to allow the BBC to say that anti-Nazi Germans came into the first category rather than the second. About this time, the head of the BBC German service, Robert Bruce

Lockhart, met the South African Prime Minister Jan Smuts, one of Churchill's closest friends. Smuts was convinced that ordinary Germans must be given something to hope for from an Allied victory, and assured Bruce Lockhart that Churchill was 'perfectly sound', knowing it was 'pure folly' to exploit wartime hatred. With recent experience of Churchill, and real difficulty making German broadcasts effective, Bruce Lockhart begged to differ as to whether Smuts 'had interpreted correctly Mr Churchill's present attitude towards a people who had twice within twenty-five years plunged the world into war'. His pessimism was confirmed when Churchill negotiated the Atlantic Charter but refused to allow propagandists to say that the human rights promised to all enslaved peoples would necessarily apply to anti-Nazi Germans. When a 'V for victory' campaign was launched, encouraging opponents of Nazi rule to demonstrate resistance by adopting the 'V' symbol, it was aimed at Britain and occupied Europe, not at Germany. When Germans learned of it from foreign radio stations and painted a series of 'V's across German towns – so much so that Goebbels had to claim that it was his own campaign celebrating German victory – it owed nothing to British policy.[8]

Judging from his speeches and his warmaking, Churchill was himself unsure whether all Germans were responsible for the war and should therefore be punished. Historians often argue that neither he nor the British people displayed between 1939 and 1945 the anti-German hysteria prevalent in 1914–18; that, while the First World War had been a battle of peoples, the Second was a contest between ideologies. As the novelist E. M. Forster argued in a 1940 broadcast, 'In the Kaiser's war, Germany was just a hostile country. She and England were enemies, but they both belonged to the same civilisation. In Hitler's war, Germany is not a hostile people, she is a hostile principle.' Hence, Forster reminded listeners that Nazis had already made war on Germans, mentioning Einstein, Freud and other refugees as proof of the fact. At a more popular level, Germans who were 'Huns' in the Great War were more homely 'Jerries' this time – 'Jerry' having merely a mildly rude double meaning. In Richmal Crompton's *Just William* books, British schoolboys referred even to 'ole 'Itler', in tones which fall far short of hatred. George Orwell regularly reassured foreign readers of *Partisan Review*, and repeated in diary entries, that 'there has been none of the nonsensical racialism that there was last time – no pretence that all Germans have faces like pigs, for instance', no looting of 'German' shops. All this can be overemphasised, though, not least with respect to Churchill. His remarks were as likely to be anti-German as anti-Nazi, and he denounced 'Prussian militarism' (in effect, the German army) as often as he excoriated 'Narzies'. 'You may take it as absolutely certain', he argued in one broadcast, 'that either all that Britain and France stand for in the modern world will go down, or that Hitler, the Nazi regime, and the recurring German or Prussian menace to Europe will be broken and destroyed.' Moreover, fighting the war until Germans had *seen* they were defeated meant that anti-Nazis as well as Nazis had to suffer. 'Hitler and his Nazi gang have sowed the wind, let them reap the whirlwind,' he declared, a useful biblical justification for bombing; if the Nazis sowed but *all* Germans reaped, the morality was less clear. When at Tehran Stalin coolly suggested that the Allies should shoot the top fifty thousand Germans when the war ended, Churchill angrily rejected such 'cold-blooded murder'. (Stalin quickly explained that he'd been joking, though, knowing the fate of thousands of Poles at Katyn, we now may think otherwise.) Churchill was equally hostile at first to Henry Morgenthau's plan to turn Germany into a pastoral country, denouncing it as 'un-Christian' (an odd reaction when Morgenthau was Jewish). However, he eventually came round to Morgenthau's idea, though the State Department and the Foreign Office had rubbished it, and toyed with such ideas even after the war. He also made blood-curdling proposals of his own, as when suggesting that all German males should be castrated, which would have ended the German problem – and the Germans – even more effectively than either Stalin's plan or Morgenthau's. This was of course said in exasperation during the London Blitz, not as a considered opinion. Churchill did though frequently talk about the need to 'abolish' Germany, by which he meant neither saturation bombing nor mass mutilation of German manhood, but the reversal of Bismarck's unification of Germans into one state; this also remained in his mind after 1945. When the Buchenwald concentration camp was found by Allied troops, he was horrified, writing to Clementine Churchill about 'the horrible revelation of German cruelty'. When victory came, Churchill proposed in carefully crafted and rehearsed words that the Commons adjourn to St Margaret's church, 'to give humble and reverent thanks to Almighty God for our deliverance from the threat of German domination'. No mention of Nazis; only Germans. His 1941 version had been equally undiscriminating: then he had told the Commons that there were 'less than seventy million malignant Huns, some of whom are curable, and the rest killable'.[9]

With no definite war aims coming from the Prime Minister and his government, public debate ranged far and wide, the running made by those who wanted a tougher peace even than Versailles. As the *New Yorker*'s correspondent reported early in December 1940, the Commons had recently discussed the issue and 'there emerged from the debate a strong feeling that Britain's war aims ought to be given a good deal more coherence than they have been, if they are to compete with the German alternative of a new European order'. Two years later she reported a general view that 'lots of Germans . . . are anxious to hear just what is in store for them – whether they are going to live in a partitioned Germany, or be led wholesale to the executioner, or be policed for the rest of their lives'. The real debate started in December 1940, when the BBC broadcast overseas talks by the government's chief diplomatic adviser, Sir Robert Vansittart. Word of these broadcasts spread, edited extracts appeared in the *Sunday Times*, and parliamentary questions were asked: was Vansittart speaking for the government? In January 1941 expanded texts appeared commercially as *Black Record: Germans Past and Present*, a sixpenny pamphlet; by 1 March it had sold two hundred thousand copies, and by July (despite wartime paper shortages) it had run through ten reprints. By the end of the year, a critic estimated that it had secured half a million sales and around three million readers.[10]

For Vansittart, fear and loathing were personal, having experienced at first hand Germans' anti-British sentiment during the Boer War, when he had even been challenged to a duel after winning at tennis; his autobiography recalled 'no escape from the gibes in the house, press, theatre, street', for Germany was 'alive with malice'. As a diplomat he observed the drift to war in 1914 and the amateurish peacemaking efforts of Lloyd George in 1919; as head of the Foreign Office he had vainly urged quicker rearmament, deploring the equally amateur diplomacy of Neville Chamberlain – 'if at first you can't concede, fly, fly again', was a Foreign Office joke attributed to 'Van'. So vehement was his criticism of ministers that Chamberlain made him chief diplomatic adviser, and then neither asked nor heeded his advice. Vansittart therefore combined personal hostility to Germany, the diplomatic professional's commitment to balance of power policies, and wounded feelings after the unsatisfactory termination of his career. Parliamentary debates about *Black Record* centred on the constitutional issue: what was a civil servant doing in such controversial territory? But the consequence was that Vansittart retired with a peerage, becoming better placed for campaigning and with a public platform. There were plenty of people ready to enter the fray on the other side, mainly leftist internationalists like Michael Foot, but Vansittart was no easy antagonist, for he had formidable intellectual powers, a knowledge of German history and literature that far exceeded their own, and quite a gift in the writing of English; during 1940 the press not only reported his official activities but printed his poetry and announced the production in the West End of a play he had written.[11]

Black Record's message was simple: the German nation – he rarely discussed 'race' – had exhibited aggressive tendencies over two thousand years, especially since the establishment of the Prussian military tradition in the seventeenth and eighteenth centuries; there was much to admire in German culture but nothing to outweigh the threat from inherent aggressiveness. 'There have been bright, ineffectual angels in Germany: but those who have suffered from Germans through the years know only that they have always been ineffectual, and so we must consider them.' Germany must be totally defeated, disarmed and occupied, and Germans re-educated, so that a completely new course could be set for her people. For 'the Germans have made five wars in the past seventy-five years, besides four "near misses". If the Germans had had their way, there would have been a war every eight years for the last three-quarters of a century.' He disclaimed belief in any theory or philosophy – 'I have merely said that Germans have continually and copiously killed their neighbours, and how, and why' – but was certain that Nazi atrocities, like 'the open return to literal slavery in Europe', did not comprise an 'accidental and ephemeral outcrop. They are a reversion to something much further back than the Kaiser, or Bismarck or Frederick the

Great, to the doings of a thousand, and two thousand, years ago.' The extreme longevity of that claim relied on accounts by Tacitus of Germanic tribes confronting the Romans. When critics pointed out that the English had, through Anglo-Saxons, the same racial inheritance, Van replied that the English had risen above barbarism during centuries of progress, while Germans' dark side remained dominant.[12]

Vansittart wrote with clarity and force, making effective use of imagery and example: Germans are from the outset the 'butcher-bird', and a 'bird of prey is no sudden apparition. It is a species. Hitler is no accident.' The dominant characteristics of the German psyche were 'envy, self-pity and cruelty', a claim illustrated with examples from historical and recent wars. There is also in *Black Record* a ready recourse to the language of polemic, the Germans being 'a race of hooligans which is a curse to the world'. Frederick the Great, worshipped by Germans as 'old Fritz', was 'a Prussian pervert with a bent for killing and dominating people', while German leaders throughout history were 'a procession of mirthless braggarts ruling over dreary robots'. Selectively quoting from Goethe and Hölderlein, Van was able to show that Germans too had accepted that their country remained in modern times a barbarous place, though it had been left to Hitler to state that 'We want to be barbarians'. No problem, responds Van: 'Germans, you don't have to want. You are.'[13]

Van was scathing about those who failed to understand this truth, 'the School of Advanced Flying in the Face of Experience': 'Oh dear', such people as Keynes had said in 1919, it was really too harsh to blame the German people for the errors of the Kaiser, and reparations were 'too big to make sense'; yet those 'huge' sums were dwarfed by Nazi demands on France in 1940. A change in *British* thinking was required because of 'the hallucination that there is in Germany an effective element of kindly and learned old gentlemen, and sweet pig-tailed maidens'. The key word here was 'effective': Van need not show that all Germans were bad, merely that good ones tended to 'vanish on the day of battle'. Germans were a race of 'homicidal maniacs', and the British had for too long deluded themselves with 'a lot of saccharine, like the play *Old Heidelberg*'. 'England, always England' had been historically 'in the German way, and must be destroyed', but the current war allowed Britain to settle the problem once and for all, in her own – and Europe's – favour. This was not though an entirely bleak message, for 'the soul of a people *can* be changed'; Germany's tragedy was that she had 'never tried'. It must be done after the war, 'largely self-administered', but under 'drastic' tutelage from the Allies, and it would take 'at least a generation'. Viewed with sixty years of hindsight, *Black Record* can thus seem an insightful prophecy, whatever view is taken of Van's perversion of history. He can also be credited with consistency, for in a memorandum in August 1933 he had argued along similar lines, suggesting the inevitability of war, since 'the true German nature has never changed'. Baldwin told Tom Jones in 1934 that 'Van hates the Germans', and Ribbentrop thought there could be no friendship between Britain and Germany as long as Vansittart retained any influence. His successor as permanent secretary thought in February 1939 that 'Van . . . out-Cassandras Cassandra in a kind of spirit of pantomime', but a month later was forced to admit that 'it is turning out – at present – as Van predicted and as I never believed'.[14]

Though leading from the front, Vansittart was not alone, for the 'Vansittartism' that his critics opposed went wider. It was no accident that *Black Record* was serialised in the *Sunday Times*, for the paper backed Vansittartite views throughout the war, as did the *Daily Express*: 'Why all this bosh about being gentle with the Germans after we have beaten them,' demanded the *Express* in 1942, 'when ALL GERMANS ARE GUILTY?' 'The German mentality' was 'a bog of mental evil'. Hutchinson's was notable for the 'hate-Germany' books on its list, while Dennis Wheatley took time off from working in black propaganda to write such books as *V is for Vengeance* (rather than 'victory'). Those broadcasting to Germany were under constant observation by Van's allies, on the hunt for pro-German moles within the British government. He himself did not stop with *Black Record* and letters to *The Times*, for two further wartime books followed, *Roots of the Trouble* (1941) and *Lessons of My Life* (1943). He refuted critics as their own accounts appeared, and there was a steady flow of introductory essays when supporters entered the fray. He also sparred regularly in the Lords with supporters of a generous peace, notably the Bishop of Chichester, George Bell. When two enterprising editors put together a huge anthology of German quotations to support the

Vansittart case, he was on hand to provide the preface, assuring readers that Hitler was the inevitable descendant of Clausewitz. This
provided an opportunity for another swipe at his critics, who had
claimed that he favoured exterminating the German race altogether:
'They then proceed to found their own arguments on what it might
have suited them had I said it. That is not controversy but cheating.'
The new anthology demonstrated that Hitler and the Nazis were
the products of German history and culture. 'For the present, we
must never lose sight of the fact that the German nation was solidly
behind the Kaiser in the last war – while it went well – and is solidly
behind Hitler in this one so far; for Nazism is a people's movement,
just as this war, like the last, of which it is a continuation, is a people's
war.' Vansittart argued that he was no racialist; he had merely said,
and 'will say again, that the German nation needs the most drastic
cure in history, and that, if it is not applied, the world will die of the
German disease'.[15]

Vansittartism was assailed mainly from the Left and the Churches,
though it was only with difficulty that their voices were heard. A correspondent to *The Times* pointed out that it was all very well for the
paper to say that the critics' best course was to debate his views, but
the BBC would not let them near a microphone, and few newspapers
gave them space either. The Left therefore relied on its own publishing outlets while church critics used their foothold in the legislature
(since the press could hardly ignore parliamentary debates). H. N.
Brailsford, supported by the Fabian Society and the progressive publisher Penguin, published in 1944 *Our Settlement with Germany*. For
critics on the Left, Hitler was even in 1944 mainly a tool of 'Big
Business' and his 'New European Order' an updated, capitalist
Mitteleuropa from Kaiser Wilhelm's day. The Nazi regime would have
been socially progressive, but for the murder of Ernst Röhm in 1934,
when Hitler sold out to the army and capitalism. Such an argument
sat unconvincingly alongside the Left's entirely justified insistence
that German socialists had opposed the Nazis and many socialist
leaders been murdered as a result, but often before these events of
1934. Germany needed a real socialist revolution, not the halfway revolution of 1919 whose limited success allowed the army and business
to reclaim their dominance. Like the French in the 1790s, Allied
armies should sweep across Europe with socialism in their knapsacks,

though Brailsford reminded readers that Frenchmen had first 'deposed their feudal class at home. Armies which fight to preserve "traditional England" and "the American way of life" cannot do it.' These were pleas as much for revolution at home as for changes abroad, almost suggesting that one would not succeed without the other. Brailsford had great faith in the Red Army, pointing out that Stalin, unlike Britain's government, promised revenge only on Nazis, and thought it 'reasonably certain' that Russia 'has had no thought of promoting a communistic revolution'. He was on surer ground when arguing that, for all his apparent logic, Vansittart was too emotional to be rational about Germany.[16]

Douglas Brown assailed Vansittart on behalf of the Independent Labour Party and 'common sense'. To Brown, Vansittartism was 'a mass of prejudice, scientific untruth, and historical distortion . . . the ideological expression of the economic policy which the British ruling class will endeavour to pursue in the post-war years'. The fact that a major backer of 'Win the War' was the Austrian émigré banker Walter Loeb was for Brown a key fact in understanding economic Vansittartism, as was Van himself being an old Etonian and therefore 'so prejudiced that he is incapable of an objective approach'. Vansittart's call for the re-education of Germans cloaked a policy which demanded not only the smashing of Germany but perpetual control of the German economy by British capitalists. Germans had not deserved such treatment, for the Nazis had never won an election and there had been no socialist quislings – German socialists had died for their beliefs and those beliefs should be respected once the war ended. The only route to peace lay through world socialist revolution, awakening the German people as the foundation on which all else would rest.[17]

Victor Gollancz had no great difficulty propagating his views, for he had been through the Left Book Club chief purveyor of leftist opinions for years. His 'reply to Lord Vansittart on the German Problem' – *Shall Our Children Live or Die?* – appeared in 1942. Vansittartism surrendered the moral high ground, a failure that 'robs our war-effort of a dynamic as powerful for good as the Nazis' is for evil, as surely as it plays in the hands of Dr Goebbels and so weakens the growing movement of German revolt'. Germany was deterred from revolt against Hitler only by fear of Allied reprisals, and that fear reflected their awareness of Vansittart's refusal to distinguish between contemporary Nazis and German guilt over centuries. Like Brailsford, Gollancz knew this was an imperialist war on all sides (except the Russian, naturally, as the Red Army was merely defending its homeland). 'World capitalism' was the root cause, not any one nationality, and war could be avoided only by eradicating *this* threat: 'if we concentrate our minds on the special German responsibility and the special German problem, we are failing to see the wood for the trees'. He too wanted to fight the same battles at home as abroad, doubting the practical possibility of socialism in one country; on the other hand, 'a socialist bloc, stretching from Vladivostok to Brest, would transform the situation' (America being beyond hope, even for such an incurable optimist). He tried to establish that most Germans did not support Hitler, and was driven onto some unsafe ground when doing so. The Russians had explained that most German prisoners taken in 1941 had been staunchly anti-Nazi; actually Russians took very few POWs as they retreated in 1941, but it is hardly surprising that those few claimed not to be Nazis when interrogated. Naivety about Soviet Russia was the corrosive weakness of anti-Vansittartism on the Left. It was not much more helpful to refer to the numbers of oppositionists that the Gestapo had executed, for while this proved that not all Germans supported Hitler, it also demonstrated their ineffectiveness as an opposition, exactly what Van claimed. Gollancz ridiculed the idea that the British could 're-educate' the Germans, for British leaders were responsible 'for conditions in the Indian Empire which we acquired by conquest and for commercial gain'. His was an idealistic message: the end of capitalism and nationalism would constitute 'our freedom from selfishness and egoism'. A civilised person must be able to hate a crime without hating the criminal, and so the paramount factor must be to prevent Vansittartism inflaming the British people, so constraining their political leaders when peacemaking, as in 1919.[18]

Idealism was also found among Christian critics of Vansittartism, for here there was insistence on separating hatred for sin from compassion for the sinner; one over-the-top critic identified Vansittart as 'one of the big guns of the enemy of humankind', called for love to rule the world, supported Gollancz and commended Stalin as 'no Vansittartite'. Where newspapers identified the Allied armies as

'God's force for vengeance', Christians thought this blasphemy, for vengeance must be the Lord's. Love and humanity were *not* 'pro-Germanism'. At a rather higher level both of rationality and the Anglican hierarchy, Bishop Bell of Chichester argued a similar case in the Lords. Bell had enjoyed international Christian friendships before the war and sought after 1939 to maintain contact with German Christians like Dietrich Bonhoeffer through neutrals; he cannot have been impressed by Van's assertion that Martin Luther was 'the lineal forefather of Nazism'. Even before summer 1940 he was defending the belief that 'Germany and National Socialism are *not* the same thing', and bravely denounced a speech made on St George's Day 1940 by Duff Cooper, standing in for Churchill. It was, argued Cooper, 'wishful thinking and dangerous thinking to believe that we could drive a wedge between the German Government and the German people'. The speech was not disowned by Churchill, who soon afterwards made Cooper Minister of Information, in which role he authorised Vansittart's broadcasts. Years later, Cooper recalled this as 'the most successful speech I ever made'; at the end 'the whole audience' – which had begun disconsolately since it was missing a Churchill oration – 'rose spontaneously to their feet, clapping and cheering.'[19]

Bell responded to *Black Record* with letters to the press and questions to ministers, and when Vansittart joined him in the Lords they began a series of personal jousts on the war. Bell was tireless in campaigning against warfare by retaliation, criticising British bombing of German civilians even in 1941, when the RAF had little capacity to bomb anything much at all. In May 1942 Bell became the conduit through which German Christians tried (via a Swedish pastor) to persuade the British government to make a conciliatory announcement about anti-Nazi Germans, to mobilise resistance to Hitler. During these discussions, he learned the names of German resistance leaders and passed the intelligence to the government, whose response was the discouraging reiteration of what Anthony Eden as Foreign Secretary had already said: 'if any section of the German people really wants to see a return to a German State which is based on respect for law and for the rights of the individual, they must understand that no one will believe them until they have taken active steps to rid themselves of their present regime'. German pastors were powerless to do this, but for the British government the German army was the practical meaning of the 'Prussian militarism' that Churchill was still denouncing as often as Nazism. When the generals named by Bell failed in their July 1944 plot, their inability to seize power even when the war was clearly lost seemed to prove Vansittart's point – the German opposition was irrelevant to Britain's war effort. Churchill's response to the July plot was to tell the Commons that he was not very excited about 'the highest personalities in the German Reich murdering one another'. On the Tory backbenches, Cuthbert Headlam thought that 'everyone seems pleased that the Generals should try and murder Hitler, but they are accused of doing so only to save the *Junkers* and the military caste . . . Germany is certain to make another war later if she is given an opportunity, whatever the Generals do now.' Bell argued that the German opposition would be stronger if encouraged, Vansittart that there was no evidence to support such a claim, and these debates continued among historians after 1945, neither side able to prove its case. The most that Bell could wring from Eden was an endorsement of Stalin's view: although 'the Hitlerite state' must be destroyed, that did not mean that 'the whole German people is . . . thereby doomed to destruction'. The dramatic irony involved in an Anglican bishop enlisting the aid of an atheist butcher to make his moral point was curious, though that irony depends on a lavish application of hindsight.[20]

As British bombing built to a crescendo in 1943–4, and as claims that only military targets were bombed became increasingly threadbare, Bell was subjected to a shrill campaign against him in the press. He attacked even the Dambusters' raid of 1943 because of collateral damage done to civilians by flooding, and sharply criticised the firebombing of Hamburg and the destruction of Dresden. Responding to such attacks, the *Daily Mail's* cartoonist depicted two bishops carrying placards, one reading, '*Let's* not be nasty to the Germans'. Coward's song went, 'Let's send them out some bishops as a form of lease and lend', but Bell himself wrote lines that better described his own position:

> NOBODY more completely hated
> The Nazi system – vile – ill-fated!
> But NOBODY loved me when I found
> A better Germany underground.

When a vacancy occurred at Canterbury in 1944, Bell was a candidate for Anglicanism's top job, but he was passed over for the Bishop of London, Geoffrey Fisher, and with the vacancy in London he again missed out on promotion. Churchill, into whose hands such patronage fell, was unlikely to promote one of his most effective critics, but there is little evidence that Bell was strongly backed in church circles either. He had been effectively banned by the Dean from preaching in his own cathedral on Battle of Britain Sunday 1943, since his message would not promote 'amity and concord'. Bell was admired for his courage, but nevertheless put up the backs of fellow-bishops, even more so other members of the Lords. More fundamentally, while he believed that war was generally wrong, he was not a pacifist and did not therefore oppose war against the Nazis; having willed the end, he seemed mired in illogical reluctance to support the means necessary to achieve that end, while at the same time adopting a tone of moral superiority. Kenneth Slack, whose adulatory biography of Bell called him 'one of the most significant Christian figures of the Twentieth Century', also recorded from personal experience that he had been 'a speaker of almost overpowering dullness', with 'the fatal inability to make righteousness interesting'; few Anglicans were at the time surprised that he had not assumed the leadership of their Church. His failure to become Archbishop of Canterbury later seemed a personal sacrifice, willingly accepted in a moral cause, and this tended to obscure his lack of effectiveness.[21]

A major problem for both types of critics was that they were not able to speak even on behalf of the group to which they belonged. Douglas Brown paused from attacking Vansittart to denounce with equal fervour decisions made at the 1943 Labour Party conference, which had 'diverged' from socialist internationalism in favour of 'the ideas favoured by Lord Vansittart'. The miners' leader Will Lawther, moving the relevant resolution, had been 'amazed by the suggestion that there were two Germanies'. It was vital, argued Brown, that the 'minority' of Labour leaders who felt like this be forced to see the error of their ways. Gollancz too hinted darkly that 'a high official of the Labour Party is a perfervid adherent of the Vansittart School . . . engaged in working out the practical measures which, in his view, should be adopted at the end of the war as the logical conclusion of

Lord Vansittart's analysis'. He was referring to William Gillies, head of Labour's international department and always ready to remind people that German rearmament began while the Social Democrats were running the Weimar Republic; he worked with Vansittart in 'Fight for Freedom', spreading their views among trades unionists. Gillies wore his opinions on his sleeve and was consequently a controversial figure within the Labour Party, but when the Left sought to get the National Executive Committee's international sub-committee to disown his view of German socialists, it received a stinging rebuff: the resolution passed, later endorsed by the full NEC, stated that 'the document of Mr Gillies is true in all essentials'. When similar views were endorsed by the party conference in 1943, the frontbencher James Chuter Ede chortled that the Left, which normally preached observance of conference decisions, 'are now announcing an agitation to upset Conference decisions'. Two years later, when a leftist Labour MP urged an end to the unnecessary 'slaughter of Germans', Chuter Ede demanded, 'who started the bloody war?' Though Gillies overplayed his hand, it was Attlee, as party leader, who ensured that he kept his job, and personally prevented any German socialist from fraternally addressing a wartime Labour conference. Partly because the internationalists who saw German socialists as comrades were also pushing for a popular front at home, and contained fellow-travellers among them, party and trades union leaders marginalised both them and their opinion of Germany.[22]

Gollancz might equally have included Hugh Dalton in his strictures. Dalton was Labour's chief pre-war expert on foreign policy and dominated the international sub-committee. To those who argued that 'there are no victors in wars', he responded sharply that 'they would have learned otherwise from a German conqueror. If they were Poles or Czechs today, they would begin to understand the distinction.' Dalton had been a German-hater since his experiences as a soldier in the Great War, and wrote in spring 1940 that 'now again, as twenty-five years before, German hands had pulled the levers that had launched the Death Ship'. He told the Society of Labour Candidates in 1941 that they were all on a list in Himmler's office and would all be shot if the Germans won the war. Dalton was determined as a minister to secure an economic settlement that would 'weaken Germany so much that she will be industrially unable to repeat her crimes in future'. During 1944, he had little difficulty in manoeuvring the NEC towards these views, set out in the policy statement *The International Post-war Settlement*, which called for the revision inwards of Germany's frontiers. Though at the December 1944 party conference there were attacks on proposals for the 'dismemberment' of Germany as Vansittartism, the policy statement was approved with what Dalton thought 'a very easy passage'. A relatively harsh view of Germany was held by almost all the key Labour leaders, not Douglas Brown's 'minority'. Arthur Greenwood, who as Leader of the Opposition after most Labour frontbenchers joined Churchill's government was not constrained by ministerial responsibility, took a very tough line indeed, and in 1942 stood in for the indisposed Vansittart at a Fight for Freedom rally. Ernest Bevin argued in the *Daily Herald* in 1941 that 'even if they get rid of Hitler, Göring and the others, that would not solve the German problem. It is Prussian militarism . . . that has to be got rid of from Europe for all time.'[23]

'Major' Attlee's own sympathies were not far from Dalton's, for he too had had anti-German sentiments since 1914–18. As chairman of the cabinet sub-committee devising plans for an occupied Germany, he resisted the Foreign Office proposal that 'normality' be restored as soon as possible, since, for Attlee, German 'normality was 'Prussian militarism'; he refused to allow a German police force to remain after surrender, and insisted that, when trying war criminals, army leaders as well as Nazis be included on the hit lists. When told that Britain would be taking dangerous responsibility for German civilians, including the necessity of preventing their starvation, he observed that whatever happened to them would be just retribution, since they had enslaved millions. For him, preferable to 'normality' was the alternative: 'that Germany will feel the full impact of military defeat, including loss of territory, influx of transferred populations, political and economic turmoil and so on . . . Even if one does not take an extreme view of the responsibility of the German people for our trials, one can still argue that everything that brings home to the Germans the completeness and irrevocability of their defeat is worthwhile in the end.' His argument won the day, Eden and the Foreign Office were forced into retreat, and the Attlee plan for a dismembered Germany occupied by Allied armies became the British government's, and in due course the Allies', policy. Even long after retirement, when

Germany had become a NATO ally, Attlee told Francis Williams that the London Blitz proved 'the Germans never understand psychology'; he remained utterly unconvinced that insistence on unconditional surrender had weakened the German resistance, for 'it was pretty hopeless to expect much from them. A futile lot, lacking in will and lacking in execution. How they failed to bump off Hitler with the opportunities they had I don't know.' These were brutal words, but then, as Trevor Burridge puts it, 'the non-realisation of the hope of a rising within Germany [was] perhaps the greatest blow to the left during the whole war'.[24]

Important as he had been in the 1930s, Victor Gollancz did not now speak for the Left, but the same can be said of Bishop Bell within Anglicanism, admired only in retrospect, for what is striking was his singularity within the hierarchy. If no bishop preached hatred of Germans as the Bishop of London had done twenty years earlier, none came near to endorsing Bell's campaigns either. At the outset Anglicans were led by Archbishop Cosmo Lang, who dissociated himself from Bell's belief that there were good as well as bad Germans and urged the country in 1939–40 to 'pray for victory'. When Bell asked leave to call for peace talks during a convocation debate, Lang thought this would suggest British fear of Germany, and that 'things would be said that would be undesirable . . . I fear all this means is that . . . you are an optimist and I am a realist'. Instead, Bell proposed a motion praising the fortitude of British victims of bombing, Lang himself condemned reprisals, but then in his speech Bell supported peace talks anyway, greatly annoying brother-bishops. Archbishop Fisher at the war's end was also a hardliner, perhaps stiffened in his views when his diocese took the brunt of the Luftwaffe bombing, including the loss of historic churches which were certainly not military targets. As the war developed, Fisher came to believe that suffering inflicted on Germans might be necessary if they were ever to 'hate and abjure that militarism which for so long they have idolised and idealised', a very Vansittartite view. Despite his conviction that 'our governing purpose must be the reconciliation of our enemies and the redemption of evil-doers', this would be a matter for the peacemakers, not a limitation on waging war. Fisher's belated statement (in May 1945) that 'there are good Germans', the basis for his proposal that VE Day services should concentrate on forgiveness, produced stinging criticism, one vicar denouncing his archbishop as neither manly nor British: Fisher offered services with 'the tone of the whining mendicant, the general trend is "Let us be kind to the Germans"' (echoes of Coward again here). In practice few incumbents held services as suggested by Fisher, while huge numbers attended victory celebrations (so many at St Paul's Cathedral that services continued all day to accommodate the 35,000 people trying to get in), and only one senior cleric refused a triumphalist celebration. Though sometimes critical of Britain's methods of waging war, Archbishop Garbett of York was tough-minded on the main point, and unwilling to offer Bell support: the left-wing *Tribune* newspaper thought Garbett would have made a good primate around the time of the Boer War. When there was opposition to the idea of prayers for a British victory – as opposed to prayers for victory if that happened to be God's will – he responded robustly that 'unless we thought it was God's Will that we should war against the Nazis, we ought to have opposed the war; if it is His Will, then we must pray for victory'. Garbett was not a man for the grand gesture, but on one occasion he let himself go in the Lords about German atrocities in Poland, noting in his diary that 'I was trembling with anger and I am afraid that my language was violent. I felt so deeply that I hardly dared trust myself to speak. The House was clearly moved, and cheered repeatedly.' He asked that 'the Government state repeatedly and solemnly that when the hour of deliverance came retribution would be dealt out, not only to the cold-blooded and cowardly brutes who ordered the massacres but to the thousands of underlings who appeared to be joyfully carrying out the cruelties.' For the government, Lord Cranborne had the unusual task of inviting an archbishop to calm down, but assured the House, 'the government felt as keenly as anyone about the shocking events in Poland'.[25]

More surprisingly, something similar was true of the brief, dramatic tenure of Canterbury by William Temple, archbishop between Lang and Fisher. If Lang, Fisher and Garbett all seemed conservative men of the old school, Temple was young, charismatic and modern, a figurehead of the generalised shift towards equality and fairness that characterised wartime Britain. He was quick to point out in 1939 that it was not for man to judge other men, and that 'a nation

must not be personified. It consisted of a multitude of individuals.'
He thus supported Bell's campaign for the release from internment of
anti-Nazi refugees and braved with Bell accusations from the *Church
Times* of being 'pro-Nazi'. On the need to fight the war to a finish,
Temple was though pretty much alongside Fisher and Lang. He told
a correspondent in 1943 that the alternative to fighting the war was to
let the Nazis rule England. He had no doubt, therefore, that 'the
bombing of the Ruhr dams was a perfectly legitimate act of war'. His
concluding remarks offered greater clarity than George Bell managed:
'There is a great deal to be said for refusing to fight, though I think
myself that in this case it would be the shirking of duty. There is still
more I think to be said for fighting in support of freedom and justice,
but there is nothing whatever to be said for fighting ineffectively.'
Temple opposed deliberate reprisals against Germany, and mustered
withering rebukes for clergymen who demanded them, but did not
deny the necessity of German suffering if the war was to be won. He
was therefore a willing victim of the government's deliberate obfus-
cation of its bombing policy, claiming to be going after military
targets when in practice whole cities were being set alight, this smoke-
screen being specifically laid down by the Air Ministry in case church
leaders' condemnation of the policy damaged the morale of bomber
crews. Hence, when Bishop Bell asked him in July 1943 to campaign
against British bombing of Germany, Temple responded briskly, 'I am
not at all disposed to be the mouthpiece of the concern which I
know exists, because I do not share it.' This was not the national
Church's trumpet sounding with an uncertain voice and its flock
therefore being unready for the battle; rather it was that the trumpet
just did not play George Bell's tune. We have reviewed here only the
established Church, but a wider perspective would not vary the picture much. Some nonconformists, especially Quakers, were near to
Bell's standpoint, but Cardinal Hinsley and the Chief Rabbi were
nearer to Vansittart's.[26]

One claim common to all critics was that for Vansittart to brand
all Germans as culpable reduced the chance of 'good' Germans rising
up against the Nazis, a claim apparently borne out when the Nazis
placarded German cities with extracts from *Black Record*. Goebbels
thought this of real significance in the propaganda war, noting in his
diary that 'after the war' (which Germany would win), 'a monument

ought to be erected to Vansittart somewhere in Germany with the inscription "To the Englishman who rendered the greatest service to the German cause during the war"'. Meanwhile, the Germans exiles who now worked for the BBC were furious about *Black Record*, and contemplated putting out a counter-manifesto (which was stopped by their political masters). Vansittartites like Dalton conceded that *Black Record* could 'be criticised as being hysterical and venomous in tone, even though it is true in substance', but its popularity was such that critics like Brailsford were by 1944 agreeing that there must be wholesale changes to Germany's education system to promote democratic values. On the Right, Vansittart's message was almost universally accepted, as when the retired Conservative MP Sir George Cockerell argued the absolute necessity to 'eradicate', by the 'de-education' of Germany, 'deep-rooted traditions that glorify physical force, assert a claim to racial superiority, justify territorial aggrandisement, and challenge all the liberties for which democracies are fighting'. In support of his views, Cockerell cited the recent 'significant study of the German national character' by the historian Lewis Namier, concluding that 'a sense of moral responsibility' among Germans 'may come', but that, 'until it does, there can be no place in a sane world for German untutored independence'. Hardly any British people did not believe in the need to defeat Germany, and if Orwell exaggerated when arguing that 'hundreds of thousands of Russians, Poles, Czechs and whatnot were fighting for the Germans . . . but no British or Americans at all', this was nearly true: the number of POWs who joined Germany's 'British *Freikorps*' was less than forty, all criminals, social misfits or pre-war fascists who became an oddball group that gave the German army such a disciplinary problem, by deserting and fighting among themselves, that they were never used in combat.[27]

Van's BBC critics succeeded in putting out one broadcast after he left the Foreign Office in which it was explained that he was 'an ordinary private citizen with whose views the Government were not in sympathy at all'. Vansittart, though, was never disowned by the government, and he had a powerful ally in Churchill. The Prime Minister was not likely to find uncongenial a man who had helped feed him information for anti-appeasement campaigning in the 1930s and been placed under surveillance (like Churchill himself) because of his unhelpful views on Germany. When later overseas broadcasts by Van were banned as likely to prove too controversial, the ban was overruled by Churchill when he was appealed to personally; Van explained that he would speak in French, and Churchill approved, since in that case no member of the House of Lords would understand them. It is hard to gauge the strength of such Vansittartite groups as Never Again and Fight for Freedom, which had patchy existences and depended locally on dedicated individuals, but Win the Peace claimed ten thousand supporters in Bristol alone. His rallies were well attended and had generally supportive audiences, voluntary groups from Rotary Clubs to the Oxford Union let him address their members, correspondence columns were full of supporters' letters, and there was a flood of subsidiary literature.[28]

An administrative policy that clearly indicated what the government thought about Germans was the internment of those resident in the United Kingdom. Since most were anti-Nazi refugees, the Chamberlain government quickly screened them and released most back into the community. In summer 1940, however, with an imminent invasion feared, a brisk Churchillian instruction went out to 'collar the lot', and the number of imprisoned 'enemy aliens' rose from two thousand to twenty-seven thousand. The immediate cause was Italy's declaration of war, for while recent German refugees were already known to the police, the political views of the older Italian community were largely unrecorded. Jews were terrified that if a German invasion took place, the British would have rounded up in advance Germans that the Gestapo most wanted to murder. But the contribution of fifth columnists and quislings to German successes abroad dictated erring well on the side of caution, and neither in Parliament nor in the press was there much criticism of internment. The consequence was that Germans deeply hostile to Nazism spent months in internment camps, mainly on the Isle of Man; thousands were deported to Canada or Australia and hundreds drowned when a submarine sank a refugee ship in transit. A policy with international implications was administered by the Home Office and the army, with virtually no input from diplomats or propagandists, and there was little urgency. By February 1941, eleven thousand remained in the camps, while half the released had been elderly or ill; by November, only 2765 were still in detention, but another five thousand languished overseas. The brilliant mathematician Hermann Bondi was shipped off to Canada; it took months to reverse the decision and get him on an eastbound ship, but once returned he wasted another month in camp before proceeding to Cambridge, where research on radar awaited him. A few émigrés managed, like Bondi, to do useful work in the war effort; some, like Ernst Gombrich, even remained with the BBC (though monitoring German propaganda rather than contributing to the British version). Refugees found it hard to accept Britain's alliance with Russia in 1941, not finding it quite as easy as the British to ally with one anti-Semitic dictatorship to resist another. Most émigrés were eventually released, with those who could find a respected name to vouch for them getting out first: Ralph Vaughan Williams helped musicians back into useful work, including the conductor Walter Goehr, who had the pleasure of conducting in 1944 the premiere of Michael Tippett's *A Child of Our Time*, inspired by *Kristallnacht*. For most, it was a slower process, followed by employment that made little use of their skills. At best, the story demonstrates careless disregard by the British state for vulnerable people admitted as refugees; at worst, it shows continuing suspicion of 'good Germans', even those who had sacrificed everything to leave Germany. In a 1946 Lords debate Lord Swinton, who had much to do with managing wartime detentions, recalled that, 'as for the scum, quite rightly, we put lots of them inside at the critical time, but a great many of them did not really matter very much'.[29]

As the war continued, many remained convinced that not all Germans were responsible for Hitler: 'every possible view exists on this subject', noted a BBC official in 1941, 'and the average of them all is just about zero'. There was some portrayal of German resistance as well as of evil Nazis in early wartime British films, notably in *Pastor Hall* (1940), *49th Parallel*, *Pimpernel Smith* and *Freedom Radio* (all 1941). Yet after 1941 *The Life and Death of Colonel Blimp* (1943) was one of very few to argue that case, and tellingly presented its anti-Nazi German as out of touch with modern German realities, while his sons have become Nazis. More typical of the second half of the war was *Went the Day Well* (1942), assuming generic German duplicity. Propagandists did try to drive a wedge between Hitler and the German people, for example tape-recording such speeches as his 1941 claim that the war in the East was as good as won, and then playing it back on overseas broadcasts in 1943–4; even for this they were sometimes accused of being pro-German, and when refugees working for the BBC were interned, the *Daily Herald* headlined its story, 'Country Saved from the Fifth Column Scab'. The head of broadcasting to Germany felt later that most of his efforts had been wasted, and that resources would have been better used in occupied rather than enemy countries. The research done into German documents captured in 1945 suggested however that German-language broadcasts, 22 per cent of the BBC's wartime foreign output, had been much listened to, and were making an impact, until the Allied proclamation that Germany must surrender unconditionally.[30]

Churchill agreed to 'unconditional surrender' rather casually, when Roosevelt suggested it at Casablanca in January 1943, claiming not even to have realised he had agreed until he read the conference minutes on returning home. Having anticipated no such discussion, Churchill had taken neither Eden nor Cadogan with him, and the Foreign Office was far from pleased to learn what had been agreed in their absence. 'Unconditional surrender' had several advantages as a statement of war aims: it dealt with the criticism that Britain had not said what she was fighting for; it was so sweeping as to disallow most supplementary questions about its meaning; and it offered the paranoid Stalin a guarantee that the West would not make a separate peace. The demand for nothing less than unconditional surrender nevertheless played into Goebbels' hands, as John Mander has pointed out. Henceforth German propaganda asserted that

the door was bolted, the German people must fight to the bitter end. Wagner had long been the Nazis' favourite composer, now Siegfried's funeral march and Brunnhilde's ride into the flames resounded from the studios of Berlin Radio night after night. Goebbels was celebrating the orgies of Nihilism; for the German people it would be total victory or total oblivion, *das Nichts*.

Goebbels, writing in his diary rather than as propaganda, thought 'unconditional surrender' proved that defeat would mean 'all our history would be declared null and void', *exactly* what Vansittartism demanded. Alec Cadogan had never accepted Vansittart's view 'that all Germans are equally wicked', and even if it were 'a true reflection, then it is not a helpful one, because it leads nowhere', since massacring all Germans or compulsory sterilisation as not 'practical politics'. It was also 'not very clever' propaganda; although, since he too had little belief that the German resistance would ever achieve anything, it is not clear what he expected that propaganda might otherwise achieve.[31]

In both theory and practice 'unconditional surrender' was susceptible of different meanings, as became clear when Italy was allowed to surrender – in effect switch to the Allied side – without being totally defeated and with most of its hierarchy remaining in post. Churchill had difficulty explaining this in the Commons, leaning across to the opposition front bench and asking if it was 'all right', at which they 'grinned back affectionately', according to Harold Nicolson. The circle was partly squared by assuming that, as a BBC staffer put it, 'Fascism does not hang as naturally on Italian shoulders as Nazism hangs on German shoulders'. Requests for clarification of 'unconditional surrender' continued to be made, and Churchill's explanations often rested on similar racial assumptions. In November 1944 he asserted that the Germans were not afraid of British or American reprisals: 'what they are afraid of is a Russian occupation, and a large proportion of their people being taken off to toil to death in Russia or Siberia' (which he knew to be what 'Uncle Joe' intended). The implication of repeated claims that unconditional surrender was a fair policy because the Anglo-Americans could be trusted to be merciful and constructive was that Germans could not claim the same inborn right to trust, any more than Russians. As an army educational lecturer told bored recruits in 1941, 'that was the difference between them and us, we wouldn't kill innocent people'. The same distinction was made in a popular wartime board game, the rules of which required that Germany always move first; only Germany could invade neighbouring countries. A home intelligence report in 1943 found though that many Britons hoped that the Russians got to Berlin first, 'since they're more ruthless', a wonderful example of eating your cake as well as dieting on principle.[32]

It is hard to gauge how widespread Vansittartism became in the popular mind, how much hatred existed. A fairly typical establishment reaction was that of the *Times Literary Supplement*. In 1941 it welcomed *Black Record*'s 'terrible indictment' of Germans, as telling 'truths that will be unpalatable to a generous and optimistic people like the British and which may well chill the hopes of those who look beyond the present conflict to a reconciled and unified humanity'. It had been necessary to face such unpalatable 'facts'; the paper's only reservation was in carrying the argument back to Roman times, when 'all were barbarous', but 'from Frederick, called the Great, onwards, Sir Robert is not unfair in tracing a continuous current of savage aggression'. After *The Roots of the Matter* appeared, Vansittart's views were again endorsed, for 'Hitlerism is just German militarism conducted on a lower and more popular plane'. When a Liberal reader protested against such racist views, the editor responded that 'Sir Robert is not the only writer to conclude that the "nihilism" of National Socialist Germany does in fact represent the dominant temper of the German nation as it has been for generations before the advent of Hitler'. The correspondent's claim that a responsible journal should rather encourage 'the other Germany' was not deemed worthy of comment.[33]

Apart from desperate moments in summer 1940 and early 1942, official propagandists did not attempt actually to create hatred. Even at critical times, hate campaigns were of dubious effectiveness: the decision to make an official film about a German invasion that almost succeeded had seemed timely when taken shortly after three German warships steamed unmolested through the Straits of Dover, but by the time *Went the Day Well* hit the cinemas in autumn 1942 its message was out of date, and the public seemed at best sceptical. However, though Churchill did not tell his radio listeners to hate Germans, he did regularly say that Germans had *made themselves hated* all over Europe, and hence legitimated hatred for those who wanted to practise it. He was also quick to intervene when the press credited Germans with chivalry in the Desert War, even though he himself contributed by praising Rommel: it was important to remember, he lectured Harold Macmillan in 1943, that 'these beastly Huns are murdering people wholesale in Europe and have committed the most frightful atrocities in Russia'. But Orwell was right to say that hysterical anti-Germanism was less common than in 1914–18. There were few calls for the BBC to stop playing German music, and a theme from Beethoven's Fifth Symphony became the 'victory anthem', the aural equivalent of Churchill's V sign, when it was noticed that the first four notes were rhythmically the Morse signal for 'V'. A British film carried this beyond its logical conclusion as *Battle for Music*, celebrating the survival of the London Philharmonic Orchestra, abandoned by its creator Sir Thomas Beecham but rescued by its players and provincial wartime audiences. The climax comes when an air raid interrupts a concert, but the conductor breezily announces that they will finish the performance; nobody leaves for the shelters and the LPO launches headlong into the finale of Beethoven's 'Victory' Symphony. Playing Mendelssohn, a Jewish composer banned by the Nazis, had different implications, especially during a 1941 Prom concert in which performers and audience alike were stranded in the Queen's Hall when bombing made it too dangerous to go home: to keep everyone occupied until 3 a.m. the band played on, one instalment being Mendelssohn's Violin Concerto played entirely from memory, no music being to hand. Nor was Hitler's favourite composer neglected: on another occasion, as an American correspondent reported, 'a Wagner concert ran to greater length than *Götterdammerung*, while the immortal Richard's compatriots droned somewhere in the vicinity'; the eventual all-clear was mistaken for Siegfried's horn-call, according to *The Times*. Gramophones also played German music, a complete rendition of *The Magic Flute* proving so popular in one London shelter that it had to be encored the following night. Not everyone was happy with this situation, but critics had to concede their minority status: a Bristolian wrote in 1943 to complain that the BBC had broadcast over 120 pieces of German music in six weeks, but in concerts received with 'clamorous expressions of applause'.[34]

However, as Richard Weight puts it, 'no amount of Christianity, classical music and casual sex [with German POWs] could overcome the popular belief that once again Britain had been forced to sort out the mess in which the Germans had left Europe, and that it had suffered greatly in the process'. At least in the aftermath of the 1940–1 Blitz and during the indiscriminate V1 raids of 1944, hostility to Germans was widely expressed, and the horrors of the concentration camps when overrun by Allied troops in 1945 reinforced such feelings as the war ended. It was often those who had not personally experienced the war's worst who took the hardest line, actual victims of the bombing showing that 'Britain could take it' more philosophically, as did bombed-out victims in Birmingham. Clara Milburn, a church-going Leamington housewife yet to experience bombing in her own town, wrote during the London Blitz that 'the wickedness of this enemy is beyond words and tears. One hopes they will lose all they possess and be made vassals of the other nations – not vindictively, but with a cold, hard feeling such as one feels for the destroyers of human life and sacred, holy things.' When Cologne was the subject of the first thousand-bomber raid, she noted that 'the Germans are having a great wail over the damage to Cologne Cathedral . . . They were very glad when [Coventry] Cathedral was burnt, and not sorry about the damage to Exeter, Bristol and Canterbury Cathedrals. Nemesis!' When in 1945 she heard Ed Murrow broadcasting about Buchenwald, she exploded, 'Oh these evil Germans!' Noticing that just outside the camp's fences had been prosperous farms and 'well-fed Germans', she asked, 'how can one forgive such horrible deeds – or even forget them! We must *not* forget. This would have been happening here if the Germans had invaded and conquered England.' Confronted with news of fires started in Holland by the German army to delay the Allied advance in 1944, Cuthbert Headlam thought 'it is too damnable. The brutes are beat to the world – and they know it – and yet they do these things – one feels there is no punishment too harsh for them. They should be made the Helots of Europe for 100 years.'[35]

Conversely, there was little criticism of British bombing of Germany outside the Left and the Churches, while real pleasure was evinced by news that Britain could make Germans suffer as London had done. Opinion surveys in 1941 showed exasperation with assertions that 'Britain could take it', and increasing demands that Britain should give 'it' back with interest, and 'stop playing cricket' with the Germans: the Special Operations Executive would deliver 'body-line bowling at the Hun', according to one of its founders. By August 1944, over 80 per cent of Britons thought a harsh peace would be more likely to last. Broadcasting overseas in August 1942, Orwell scoffed that 'the Germans cry out against these raids', apparently forgetting that a year earlier they were 'openly boasting of the slaughter they were achieving among the civilian population'. In his diary around the same time he jubilantly noted that the 'pinks' who now said bombing was never effective were the people who had most panicked when London was bombed. Two weeks later he told overseas listeners that Britain was dumping on places like Hamburg 'a far greater weight of bombs than has ever been dropped on Britain, even including the terrible raid that almost wiped out the city of Coventry'; there was grim satisfaction in his remark that British people's experience enabled them to 'get some impression of what is now happening to various German industrial towns'. Nor were such messages only for abroad: when the BBC reported a raid on Hamburg in November 1940, the newsreader explained that it was 'the best news of the war in the air – particularly for the people of Coventry [and] very satisfactory to the Royal Air Force men who carried it out'. Half the people surveyed by Mass-Observation in Portsmouth said that they would feel better to know that Germany was also suffering. As Mollie Panter-Downes told Americans in June 1943, recent German raids on south coast towns had been limited, but 'nasty enough to justify their citizens feeling better, whatever the bishops say, when they hear the [Flying] Fortresses roaring out over the Channel some of these bright mornings'. Early in 1944 six out of ten Londoners gave 'unqualified verbal approval' to the strategic bombing offensive, two had qualms, and only one thought it should be stopped. After the German invasion of Russia, Churchill promised to 'make the German people taste and gulp each month a sharper dose of the miseries they have showered on mankind'. Privately he wondered if carpet bombing was not as barbarous as anything the Nazis had done, and as the war ended discreditably shifted responsibility on to the RAF and then largely ignored Bomber Command in his memoirs. But his public statements were unapologetic; all that German civilians had to do to escape destruction, he argued in 1942, was 'to leave the cities where munitions work is being carried on – abandon their work, and go out into the fields, and watch the home fires burning from a distance'.[36]

Evidence of atrocities reignited hatred, especially that from concentration camps. Earlier in the war British propaganda made little of the camps, but in 1944–5 both film and personal testimony confirmed the worst. Alec Cadogan, who as head of the diplomatic service was hardly uninformed, was nevertheless shattered by visiting a Belgian camp late in 1944: he confided to his diary that '*Everyone*

ought to see it and know how the Germans behaved (which I could-
n't possibly write down)'. Cecil Beaton, photographing the same
month pathetic farewell messages scrawled on the cell walls of
Gestapo headquarters in Paris, saw 'a writing on the wall for all the
world. They ought to be preserved so that future generations read
them in order to realise that Germans are capable of perpetrating
such brutality.' Hardly anyone reacted by blaming only Nazis, and
the Political Warfare Executive formally decided that 'the moral
responsibility for these crimes should be laid wholly and solely on the
German nation . . . Had any considerable number of protesting
voices been heard, these bestial practices would not have been possible.' Although Churchill refused to endorse an MP's claim that
Belsen proved Vansittart's case, he sent a delegation of parliamentarians to visit the camp before the clear-up operation, to gain 'ocular
proof' of its horrors. One of that delegation, the moderate
Conservative Mavis Tate, described what she had seen for the
Spectator. Tate, already horrified by 'hard-faced women' she met *outside* the camps, reported that 'their land has been cultivated to the last
inch with the help of slave labour, and they look well-fed, truculent
and aggressive . . . The Hun ambition may be foiled, but the Hun
spirit still lives.' On her return, she decided that 'there is indubitably
a deep streak of evil and sadism in the German race', so that 'only
with extreme firmness shall we eradicate the beast from the German
Heart'. On the other side, the future Labour Foreign Minister Patrick
Gordon Walker had visited Belsen as a radio propagandist. Gordon
Walker had for years helped to tell the world that Germany was
making war bestially, but he was now deeply distressed, and set down
in his diary 'reflections on Belsen'. He had no doubt from talking to
Germans in the area that there had been widespread awareness 'that
unspeakable things were being done on German soil'. What really
upset him was that the camps had been such a 'coldly calculated and
coolly executed' *system* of murder, and although he understood that
Germans had also been camp victims, he decided that the only hope
would be 'if the German people admits and recognises, both openly
and in its heart, that these 12 years have been the blackest in the
whole of Europe's history. If this becomes part of the German conscience and tradition, there is some hope. If not, none.' Britain must
contribute to the 'purging of the German soul . . . German shame at

Hitler's regime must appear, indelibly and beyond doubt, in German schools, in German history, in literature, in sermons, in cinemas, in conversation, beyond chance of reversal. Till then we will not be safe again.' Further to the left, the socialist novelist Naomi Mitchinson had in 1941 lost her temper with her mother's Vansittartite views, and maintained her detachment even when atrocities were committed against the Highland Division, which made Campbelltown locals 'crying mad', determined to 'destroy Germany'. Yet she now worried about what was 'wrong with the German soul', while Scots gathered to give blood for the war effort surprised her in the vehemence of their opinions, 'for the concentration camps . . . really seem to have got under the skin of even Carradale'. The Liberal philanthropist Violet Markham took a similar view: although Germany must rejoin the community of nations, she had 'come home with little patience with the people who want to be kind to the Germans', preferring to believe that 'there has got to be very stern treatment until they show some signs of repentance and horror for the enormities that have been committed in their name'. Neither Tate, Gordon Walker, Mitchinson nor Markham mentioned Vansittart, and none had supported him in the past, but each was a 'Vansittartite' in 1945.[37]

Back in suburban Buckinghamshire that spring, 'William Brown' sternly tells Violet Elizabeth Bott that the Germans in the village's VE Day pageant must march last, and 'gotter be sorry for all the wrong [they've] done'. Plans for the pageant falter when no village children will agree to play the Germans, though eventually a conscripted juvenile 'German' wearing a coal-scuttle as helmet proclaims that, 'I am ole Germany, Beat in the War. / A goothe that won't go goothe-thtepping any more.' The last major wartime propaganda film, *The True Glory*, tracing the campaign from D-Day to the German surrender, culminates with footage of Belsen and of destroyed German cities. The narrator intones Drake's prayer: 'O Lord God, when Thou givest to Thy servants to endeavour any great matter, grant us also to know that it is not the beginning, but the continuing of the same, until it be thoroughly finished, which yieldeth the true glory.' The true glory was yet to come; or, as Berlin graffiti put it just before the Red Army arrived, Germans should enjoy the war, for peace would not be much fun. Gallup polls now found that 90 per cent of Britons blamed Germans rather than Nazis for the war, while Mass-Observation found that a third wanted Germany to pay reparations like those of 1919, with another third supporting the case for Germany being permanently neutered as a political and economic entity. By 1945 there was every intention in the British mind of being 'beastly to the Germans' for years to come.[38]

Yet such hatred had never been deep seated this time round, and in some areas did not last long after 1945, either – certainly less than the loathing of Japan occasioned by atrocities in the Far East. As Stephen Taylor, a leading British propagandist, put it, looking back thirty years later, the British people in 1945 'were not interested in vengeance. They were interested in *no repetition*.' In his *Middle East Diary* Noel Coward records how Harold Macmillan, minister resident in North Africa, explained to him in Algiers the reception of his broadcast 'Don't Let's Be Beastly to the Germans'. Coward affected to regret only that the *Daily Herald*'s 'tirade' was by Spike Hughes, who had collaborated with him on *Words and Music*: it was 'over-personal, and far, far too long. If I have time when I return I shall get hold of him and we will re-do it together in a more adroit and concentrated form, and he can re-print it with much more deadly effect.' This response was thought unconvincingly flippant when the diary was published, but it barely matched the wounded entry Coward wrote when he read 'with astonishment' his mail: 'a number of them were just plain abusive; the rest were bewildered and proved that their writers had obviously missed the point of the "Germans" song altogether'. His main feeling was 'extreme irritation that people could be so absolutely idiotic [for] the satire of "Don't Let's Be Beastly to the Germans" was surely not all that subtle'. What Coward really felt about Germans emerged from other parts of his *Middle East Diary*, especially his visit to a POW camp, 'an interesting experience and at the same time irritating'. He watched 'rows and rows of the much vaunted "Master Race", springing to attention with such overdone discipline that I was surprised that they didn't break their necks', but was unimpressed with them as physical specimens. Acknowledging that these young men were indoctrinated by the Nazis, he nevertheless dismissed sentimentalists who believed this expiated their guilt, asking, 'Who trained them?' Nazis were themselves more a product of Germany than vice versa, there having been no 'wicked Nazis' in 1870 and 1914, merely 'wicked Prussians'. Coward felt no admiration

The German Elector Palatine and his British wife, ancestors of the royal family. *(Mary Evans Picture Library)*

Wellington meets Blücher at the battle of Waterloo, 1815, in an illustration after a painting by Daniel Maclise. *(Mary Evans Picture Library)*

Queen Victoria among the serried ranks of Anglo-German royalty; Kaiser Wilhelm seems appropriately semi-detached. *(Ullstein bild/akg-images)*

Jerome K. Jerome at the time of his first encounter with Germany. *(TopFoto)*

William Le Queux,
proudly wearing his
medals.

Le Queux leaps
aboard the atrocities
bandwagon in 1914.
(Private Collection)

Ready Now.   TWOPENCE.

GERMAN ATROCITIES

A Record of Shameless Deeds.

By

WILLIAM LE QUEUX.

THE HUNS OF ATTILA.

The Kaiser, we read, has exhorted his soldiers to make themselves as much dreaded as the Huns of Attila. It is worth while to recall the methods of this savage, for he was nothing better. In one expedition across Greece and in another across Italy he reduced seventy of the finest cities to smoking ruins and to shambles. The inhabitants were either slaughtered on the spot or marched away in chains to end their lives as slaves. Men, women, children, babies—all came alike to this black demon of outrage and destruction. Briefly, the Monarch of the Huns may be best described as the worthy leader of one vast gang of Jack-the-Rippers.

And this is the bloodguilty ruffian whom the Kaiser now holds up as his examplar! Judging by Louvain, he is no unworthy follower of his Master.

WHAT THE KAISER SAID:—

"When you meet the foe you will smash him. No quarter will be given, no prisoners will be taken. Let all who fall into your hands be at your mercy. GAIN THE REPUTATION OF THE HUNS OF ATTILA."

(Address to his Troops on their departure for Pekin, July 27th, 1900.)

Secure your copy early. Over One Million copies have been ordered by the trade. The demand is sensational.

2^{D.}

OBTAINABLE EVERYWHERE.

J. M. Keynes, whose *Economic Consequences of the Peace* aroused sympathy for Germans in 1919. *(TopFoto)*

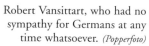

Robert Vansittart, who had no sympathy for Germans at any time whatsoever. *(Popperfoto)*

Ernest Bevin with Clement Attlee: Bevin said of the Germans, 'I tries 'ard but I 'ates 'em.'
(Corbis)

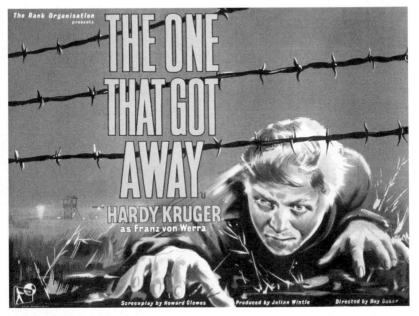

Hardy Kruger gets away from both prison camp and British prejudice in 1957. *(bfi)*

English soccer players give the Nazi salute in Berlin, 1938. *(Popperfoto)*

Bert Trautmann, with broken neck, receives a cup-winner's medal from 'your Queen', 1956.
(Ullstein Bld/akg-images)

The classic nightmare image of the Nazi invasion that succeeded, from *It Happened Here*, 1966. *(Photoplay)*

Michael Caine, Bobby Moore and Mike Summerbee *Escape to Victory*, 1981.
(Lorimar/Paramount/Kobal Collection)

The Empire strikes back, 2001.
(Rex Features)

for 'a race, however cultured, sensitive and civilised, that willingly allows itself time and again to be stampeded into the same state of neurotic bestiality'. If this time it was against its will, then so much the worse, for 'if its will is so weak and malleable, I can't feel that, as a race, it is much good anyway'. He expected few converts among 'our amiable sentimentalists, sodden with nostalgia for those dear dead summers in Bavaria and the beer gardens of Heidelberg', for they would never 'face the unpalatable fact that sadistic tendencies and an unregenerate passion for world dominance have been inherent in the German people since the beginning'. They had of course 'contributed magnificently to world literature, music and science', but it was 'equally undeniable' that they had 'contributed more agony, misery, destruction and despair to modern civilisation than any other race'. Or, as his song put it, 'They gave us culture, science, art, and music – to excess; / They also gave us two world wars and Mr Rudolf Hess.' The camp commandant told him that German POWs were 'very uppish and difficult to handle and never stopped complaining of their treatment, which I need hardly say, was far more kindly and lenient than they deserved'. Vansittartite views like Coward's had been popular enough in 1940–1, and for lack of plausible alternatives dominated British planning for the post-war treatment of Germany, but the Vansittartite tone was not a comfortable one even in 1943. 'Don't Let's Be Beastly to the Germans' was a song that nobody other than Coward ever wanted to sing, which he himself rarely sang after 1945, and of which unexpurgated recordings remain hard to find. The *Daily Express* proclaimed on VE Day, 'ALL GERMANS ARE GUILTY', in an edition that also contained Coward's article explaining recent events: 'It is certainly victory over the Nazis . . . It remains to be seen whether or not we have really conquered the Germans.'[39]

6

'Putting poor Germany on its feet again'[1]: Re-educating the Germans and the British after 1945

Winston Churchill's Second World War memoirs proclaimed the moral 'in war resolution . . . in victory magnanimity, in peace goodwill'. He had disappointing sales of the German translation, so few Germans read these words of comfort to defeated enemies, but Churchill was a keen defender of a magnanimous policy towards Germany. He could not be written off as 'pro-German', and few even pointed out his inconsistencies. Late in 1945 in Brussels Churchill reminded Belgians that Hitler had never been elected by Germans, something he had distinctly failed to mention before; he even claimed that 'the sane elements' in Germany would have overthrown the 'maniacal dictatorship' if the Allies had given the lead, again hard to square with his views at the time, though it matched what his memoirs would argue about 1936–8 (though not about 1944). He called for the early re-establishment of German local government, to give 'trustworthy' Germans the chance, 'under Allied supervision', to behave responsibly. At the Alamein reunion in August 1945, he had appealed to veterans to help 'those misguided and now terribly smitten people' through the winter. In the Commons he deplored the 'expulsion and exodus of Germans from the New Poland' as a 'tragedy on a prodigious scale'. Back in 1941, confronted by Duncan Sandys' bloodthirsty opinions, Churchill had insisted that he 'did not believe in pariah nations, and saw no alternative to the acceptance of Germany as part of the family of Europe'. At

Zurich in September 1946 he advocated a 'united states of Europe' in which Germany would be a partner. 'Where are the Germans?' he demanded of astonished Council of Europe delegates in 1949; 'Where are the Germans?' Visiting Berlin in July 1945, he was surprised to be cheered by Germans in the streets, and so moved by the devastation that 'my hate had died with their surrender'. Reiterating in September of that year his wartime pledges that, since 'indescribable crimes have been committed by Germans under Nazi rule, justice must take its course [and] the guilty must be punished', he nevertheless concluded, 'I fall back on Edmund Burke: I cannot frame an indictment against an entire people.' Churchill feared the threat from Russia and needed a re-emergent Germany as a Cold War ally, but he also felt real personal magnanimity and was disappointed by other Britons' failure to accept either the pragmatic or the generous case for closing the German account. Even during wartime, he had regretted the hostility aroused by any proposal of 'putting poor Germany on its feet again'. The Allies would 're-educate' Germany, but it was much harder to re-educate the British.[2]

Churchill's resistance to announcing war aims inhibited detailed planning for the way in which Germany would be run after victory. Britain was thus less ready for its responsibilities as an occupying power than Russia or America. The Prime Minister would not even read papers on the subject; although, as Attlee complained, that did not prevent him from holding forth in cabinet – so he privately bracketed 'Atler' with 'Hitlee' as equally objectionable. His secretary Jock Colville, noting in September 1944 the risk of the Prime Minister going unbriefed into summit meetings, read aloud a paper on zones of occupation while Churchill had his bath, 'but the difficulties were accentuated by his inclination to submerge himself entirely from time to time and thus become deaf to certain passages'. Churchill remained averse to 'making plans for a country which we do not yet occupy', arguing that passions should cool before drafting plans 'on little pieces of paper'. Occasionally he meditated that his advisers might think ahead about the peace, even suggesting that a great 'Book of Transition' be prepared, but the job was never done, and the idea that there would be a transition between war and peace was anyway an illusion. Churchill was not the only offender: Anthony Eden's secretary noted in November 1944, 'neither AE nor the PM have yet given serious thought even to the future of Germany. Bad enough in the PM but worse in the Foreign Secretary.' Sir Vaughan Berry, British Governor of Hamburg, later admitted ('though it's absolute heresy to say so') that 'the British government during the war had no policy beyond unconditional surrender. What they were to *do* with the unconditional surrender when they had got it – I really don't think they'd thought about it.' As Richard Crossman put it, unconditional surrender was mainly 'a formula to avoid discussing the future of Germany'. Lord Strang, political adviser to British army HQ in Germany in summer 1945, claimed plans for the German surrender were 'completed' in November 1944, but were amended and added to until the following September – four months *after* that surrender occurred. One improvisation involved Strang himself stealing senior staff from other departments which had prepared but which did not now have the personnel to implement their plans. Montgomery himself, according to his memoirs, was in July 1945 'pondering deeply' over the problem of Germany and deciding 'there must be a plan for this', though he had by then already governed the British zone for three months. Many difficulties and much of the bewilderment faced by Germans in 1945–6, confusion that led them to form a poor impression of British government, were due to that failure to think ahead.[3]

There had been more coherent thinking about 're-education', and, as a result of Vansittart's campaigns, there was agreement that Germans needed their collective mindset changed. While the Right required this for national security, the Left wanted Germany to become a social democracy much as Labour was building in post-war Britain, while humanitarians were desperate to prevent reversion to the bestialities practised by the Nazis. That wide consensus demanded something like 'the four Ds' agreed at the July 1945 Potsdam conference: the denazification, decentralisation, demilitarisation and democratisation of Germany. If detailed plans did not exist for any of these areas, there had been thinking ahead, not least because Britain had from 1941 German POWs on its hands and no initial idea what to do with them. The past quarter century had promoted the idea that beliefs could be changed by propaganda, a theory that George Orwell would shortly carry to its horrifying conclusion in *1984*. British ideas about 're-education' were a foal bred out of Vansittartism by propaganda theory, POW camps its first paddock. It was here that British re-educators developed the idea that Germans could be usefully classified as 'white' ('good Germans'), 'grey' (the easily led) or 'black' (incorrigible Nazis), a process applied to POWs and only later to German civilians. But what to do with those classified was another matter on which too little work had been done, and as a result the few who had practical experience in successful camps had real influence. Among these was Captain Henry Faulk, the Scottish teacher who shaped the treatment of POWs, wrote about his experiences, and received the signal honour of being invited to write the appropriate volume of the German official war history.[4]

The first relevant report on POWs appeared in 1940, though at that stage there were so few prisoners that the issue evoked little interest. Even when the number of POWs increased, there was no British initiative comparable to the 'Free Germany' movement launched by Russians among their prisoners; the British authorities wondered what techniques the Russians might have used to persuade battle-hardened Nazi generals to change sides, but soon decided that British opinion would never sanction such methods. In Britain ideas revolved around the need to make POWs understand democracy, and a key influence was Heinz Koeppler, a German-born medieval historian who had been in Britain since 1933. Following the adoption of his proposals in 1943, Koeppler devised courses for POWs, 'to project the British way of life, to provide an impartial view of German social and political developments during the last 80 years, and to bring into proper perspective the relations between individuals and state'. His first courses began when a special camp, Wilton Park, opened in January 1946, but by then there were 400,000 POWs in Britain (and in summer 1945 there had been four times as many in Germany), so the effect of a short course for a few dozen volunteers would be minimal. In the meantime British policy was dominated by security (many POWs, like civilian internees, being shipped overseas) and the economy: in January 1944 a thousand German prisoners were assisting the British war effort on farms. Italian POWs could not be used as labourers once Italy was an ally, though farmers preferred Germans anyway, as they appeared to work harder. This led to growing dependence on German POWs to keep a key industry going, even to re-importing POWs from North America to maintain manpower

when the Italians went home. POWs used were those classified
'white', while Luftwaffe personnel, paratroops and submariners, all
groups dominated by Nazi ideology, were not put to work. POWs'
treatment was relatively generous, for fear of reprisals against British
prisoners in Germany, at least until the system was overwhelmed by
the influx of prisoners in 1944–5. German POWs received the same
ration as British soldiers stationed at home, as the Geneva
Convention required, which meant they were better fed than British
civilians. A press outcry against this late in 1944 caused the POW
ration to be reduced to civilian levels, but when civilian rations were
reduced further during post-war austerity these cuts were not applied
to POWs. Prisoners attributed the 1944 ration cut to British anger
about concentration camps, but the cut also led some British civilians
to offer food parcels (illegally) to POWs. By 1945, the pattern was set:
dependence on German labour that would retard repatriation, official
determination to treat POWs fairly and growing civilian sympathy
for the men behind the wire.[5]

Three further areas of wartime thinking need to be explored: the
dismemberment of Germany, that country's economic future, and
war criminals. Shortly before his death in 1942, Nevile Henderson
urged flexibility about future borders. There could be, he thought,
'no greater folly' than to hand over three million Germans to seven
million vengeful Czechs; he recommended that Sudeten Germans,
Rhinelanders, Silesians and Austrians should each have the right of
self-determination, so that Germany's boundaries would match the
aspirations of those who lived near to them. When these views were
published in July 1945, they could hardly have been further from the
realities developing on Germany's borders, but they do indicate
awareness among diplomats that the problems of the 1930s would not
just go away. The European Advisory Group of diplomats wrestled
with such issues, without much political direction. Agreement
between the Allies was reached only on zones of occupation after hostilities ceased, but this would be merely temporary. The permanent
secretary Alec Cadogan speculated in December 1941 whether
Germany should be split into three or four separate states, and in
1944 Churchill reminded him that piecemeal summit decisions, such
as Stalin's requirement that four million Germans help rebuild the
USSR 'for an indefinite period', added up to 'German ruin and

indefinite prevention of their rising again as an armed Power'. What piecemeal decisions had not done was produce a British blueprint for the future, let alone one her allies might support, for, as Churchill also reported, 'both President Roosevelt and Marshal Stalin at Tehran wished to cut Germany into smaller pieces than I had in mind' (whatever that was, he did not say).[6]

The future German economy was an aspect of the same problem. Keynes protested against the decision to divide Germany into even temporary occupation zones, since this would inhibit economic progress, while hardliners like Dalton wanted a German economy so depressed as to encourage Austrians and Rhinelanders to form states of their own. The focus was the 'Morgenthau plan', whereby Germany would be stripped not only of munitions industries but of all industry that could contribute to warmaking (in practice nearly all manufacturing); under such a scheme Germany would become, as Orwell put it, 'a sort of overcrowded rural slum'. Despite his hard-nosed defence of the British war effort, Orwell was no supporter of a vindictive peace. In December 1943 he quoted in *Tribune* an American author's *Tunis Diary*, which recorded the British socialist John Strachey asking in horror, 'You surely don't want a Carthaginian peace, do you?' and being flattened by the reply, 'I don't recollect we've had much trouble with the Carthaginians since.' Orwell, pointing out how much trouble Europe had with the Romans once they had destroyed Carthage, argued that while it might be feasible to wipe out an ancient city of five thousand people, this was hardly viable for a country of seventy million: 'what is the best way of killing off seventy million Germans? Rat poison?' Within the Foreign Office a civil servant was lamenting that 'there are still going to be too many Germans in the world as this century draws to a close'. He hoped that it would not 'seem too shocking' to propose means to limit the Germans' post-war birth-rate; a colleague thought this 'a kind of thing the Russians might tackle more effectively than ourselves', so Britain could encourage Stalin to demand more German slave labour, including women. Further options included the repeal of family legislation designed by the Nazis to raise the birth-rate, though it was agreed that all this must be kept secret, for 'if the Germans become aware we are deliberately seeking to depress their birth-rate, they will probably breed all the more to spite us' (which may lead us to conclude that the exchanges were a bad joke, though they probably were not). Over at Number Ten, Jock Colville was wondering whether it might be necessary to corral Germans under eight and force-feed them democratic principles, somewhere far from Prussia, but he was unsure how practical this was. Short of unacceptable measures (such as, the same diplomats sadly concluded, the legalisation of abortion in post-war Germany), the only course would be to work for an economically viable Germany which would help produce prosperity for herself and for Europe. Not many were yet prepared to follow Keynes and Orwell down that line.[7]

One who certainly was not was Dalton, who noted in August 1942 a discussion at the Soviet Embassy when it was agreed 'that it was an unhealthy condition in Europe where Germany was very highly industrialised while the countries to the east of her were largely restricted to agriculture and extractive industries. All these countries should have their share of European industry' through confiscations from Germany, while the Ruhr could be 'internationalised' and then supply 'peace products' to the whole of Europe. Dalton's only concern was that Germany might then become so weak as to be absorbed by Russia, though characteristically that nightmare was actually a dread of 'the Germans running Russia as well as Germany'. These were the fantasies not of a man on the political fringe but of Churchill's Minister of Economic Warfare; from 1945 he was Chancellor of the Exchequer, responsible for financing the British occupation. Even for diplomats, as Cadogan noted in September 1944, the alternatives seemed to lie between destroying the Ruhr industries altogether, destroying the entire German steel industry, or internationalising them, which Cadogan found 'attractive, but I don't know how practical it is'. Churchill was attracted to these crazy notions largely because his scientific adviser, 'Prof' Cherwell, assured him they would allow Britain to take over German export markets. As Colville noted, Cherwell argued in February 1945 that 'Germany must not be allowed to export but must live on an autarchic system and accept a low standard of living. I know nothing of economics, but instinctively I feel the Prof's views to be both immoral and unsound.' Knowing plenty about economics, the Foreign Office responded that Cherwell said 'nothing about the difficulties of administering a desert traversed by swarms of unemployed nomads', and economists like

Keynes were yet more scathing. Once news of the Morgenthau plan leaked (and incidentally provided Goebbels with an even bigger free hit than had 'unconditional surrender'), the British financial press was damning. This was not, *The Economist* explained, about being 'kind to Germans': 'Let it be conceded for the purpose of the argument that all Germans are thoroughly and irredeemably bad . . . Let us all agree to hate them for ever. But let us, for heaven's sake, leave all such emotions out of the very serious business of peacemaking, which is a matter for cold calculation, not for emotions of either hate or love.' When this attitude came under attack, the editor responded that he was not in favour of a weak peace, but of the strongest peace that would be permanently enforced, for 'it is only the moderate that will be enforced – not now, but in fifteen or twenty years' time when the fat and lazy habits of peace have returned'. This was not 'a matter of German psychology', but of British psychology, given the country's tendency to be pragmatic in the medium term. With the battle raging inconclusively, official pronouncements remained generous; several times from 1941 onwards, Churchill and Eden repeated that there would be no 'economic discrimination' against post-war Germany. To that extent, Keynes won the battle, and if Britain was poorly prepared in 1945, then this was at least better than anything definite that the government might have decided – as trying to implement the industrial demolitions agreed by the Allies at Potsdam clearly indicated.[8]

An area in which planning might have been uncontroversial was the treatment of war criminals, but here too policy had to be improvised in 1945. In October 1942 Churchill announced that 'retribution for these crimes must henceforth take its place among the major purposes of the war', and in July 1944 described the Holocaust as 'probably the greatest and most horrible crime ever committed in the whole history of the world . . . It is quite clear that all concerned in this crime who may fall into our hands, including the people who only obeyed orders by carrying out the butcheries, should be put to death after their association with the murders has been proved.' As the war ended, though, Churchill recognised the divisiveness within Germany of hunts for atrocity-merchants and favoured summarily shooting star offenders when captured but drawing a veil over lesser figures as soon as was decently possible. In this he was overborne by Russian and American demands for public trials. There was no great debate during Britain's 1945 election about war crimes (as there had been in 1918), though the Attorney-General told his constituents what 'he' was going to do to Hermann Göring once the Conservatives had won. When they didn't, David Maxwell Fyfe had his chance anyway as chief British prosecutor at Nuremberg. Britain's leaders underestimated both the thirst for vengeance in France and Russia, and Americans' desire for public proof that the Allies had been the good guys. Eden confirmed only in May 1945 Britain's agreement to trials, but even then the commitment was unconvincing: Colville noted the same month Churchill's regular 'diatribe against those who wish to treat all leading Germans as war criminals and leave none with authority to administer that battered and disordered land'. Few preparations were thus made, and only after the discovery of Belsen did the army set up special units – three teams of just four men each – to collect evidence; but twelve men were not likely to make much headway in an occupation zone containing eighty-one camps, and when the complete disintegration of order allowed many to slip off into obscurity. As Lord Chancellor Simon had argued, an international tribunal was all very well, but judges could get nowhere without effective police forces to collect evidence first. Tom Bower compares the lack of effort put into that process with the large teams – a headquarters staff of 230 – scouring Germany for scientists with secrets or transferable skills: 'In contrast to "Project Paperclip" [searching for scientists] the operation to hunt down the murderers of twelve million people did not even boast a code-name. It had no trained staff, no headquarters, no plans and no priority.'[9]

With so little effort put into collecting material – or defendants – the Nuremberg trials of major Nazis relied heavily on captured German archives. It was useful to confound Keitel and Ribbentrop with their own documents, and helped in defending the process against claims that the trials were 'victors' vengeance', but the same archives proved ineffective when used against lesser defendants, many of whom were acquitted because witnesses had not been identified in spring 1945. Even the trial of the major offenders disturbed British observers: Harold Nicolson could not refuse to report such a historic event, but he dreaded watching men 'caught like rats in a trap', when everyone knew they would hang. Even Ribbentrop, whom he loathed, aroused sympathy. Members of the Foreign Office shared this revulsion when it came to prosecuting businessmen and bankers, and the FO's initial trial list did not include a single figure from the Nazi economy, while the army deprecated trials of senior military officers. The first British list contained only ten names, while the Americans suggested at least fifty. Each occupying power was also free to try more war criminals in its own zone – and here again the Americans and Russians went for a deeper cut than Britain: the British zone, in which most German industry lay, was the only one where no industrialist was tried. To senior Nazis in the dock were added, again mainly against British advice, organisations like the SS, the Nazi Party and the General Staff, so that documentary proof would show that there had been systematic criminality, as well as individual criminals. This generalised attack sometimes sat uncomfortably alongside efforts to make defendants personally culpable, as when Maxwell Fyfe ripped into Keitel as unfit for the uniform once worn by Blücher, von Moltke and Gneisenau (all historic leaders of the General Staff). The court decided more cautiously that Keitel 'disgraced the honourable profession of arms', without going into its German antecedents. Inevitably, most personal defendants were found guilty and sentenced to hang or to heavy prison sentences, though the prosecuted organisations were mainly acquitted for want of proof to sustain the charge of conspiracy. Most of the condemned went to their deaths unrepentant, though there were helpful confessions from Baldur von Schirach (who escaped the gallows) and Hans Frank, especially the latter's assertion that 'a thousand years will pass and the moral guilt of Germany will not be assuaged'.[10]

There was pride in the actual proceedings, presided over by a British judge, with British lawyers doing well compared to their international counterparts and excelling at cross-examination, though since the trials were conducted mainly by English legal procedure (and Stalin's lawyers at least had little experience of asking questions without already knowing the answers), this is hardly surprising. It was British insistence on procedural rules that gave the trials some appearance of fair play, though the point was undermined when the Bar Council accepted the Attorney-General's proposal that no British barrister must defend at Nuremberg (it being thought that this would be misunderstood by Germans). The key figure was the British alternate judge Norman Birkett, broker of compromises on issues where judges disagreed and draftsman of many key judgements. Birkett had, as a Liberal candidate in 1917, deplored those who spoke of 'crushing Germany', and in wartime broadcasts had stretched to the limit the propaganda line on Germany, since he was convinced that many Germans were not Hitler's willing accomplices. Now he concluded that there were two trials going on, 'the trial of the Defendants in the dock and the greater trial of a whole nation and its way of thought'. Nevertheless, he sympathised with the defendants, for 'while the Master Race on trial sounds dramatic enough, the Master Race in the dock seems singularly like the dregs of humanity'. Yet Birkett noted the danger when Göring dominated his American prosecutor and delighted when Maxwell Fyfe skewered him, for the crucial audience was the German people, who must be left with no excuse to believe in the Nazis. For the same reason, the press must see the condemned men hang, so that no myth would allege that they had somehow survived. However, in his assumption that Germans were agog for news from Nuremberg, Birkett was surely wrong, for in 1945–6 they had more urgent concerns, staying alive being uppermost: one British visitor noticed in Recklinghausen in 1947 identical signs pointing to 'War Crimes Trials' and 'Sausage Factory'. For some Germans, British newspapers argued, the Nazis' crime was not to have started the war but to have lost it; while for others anything done by the victors lacked impartiality, as Cardinal Frings of Cologne asserted. There were contradictions between the court's judgement, that 'contemporary German militarism flourished briefly with its recent ally, National Socialism, as well as or better than it had in the generations of the past', and the 150,000 Germans who even now volunteered evidence for the SS. Similar avalanches of affidavits supported other prosecuted organisations, though this process was helped by the fact that convicting the SA of 'war crimes' would have rendered four million Germans open to individual prosecution.[11]

Reluctance to prosecute mass-member organisations set the tone for denazification generally, characterised by reluctance and elitism. The Americans tried 169,282 for war crimes: Britain, 22,296 in a zone with a larger population. The British were the first to demand an end to the process, the Americans keenest to continue; in 1948 the British view prevailed. Raymond Ebsworth, working for the Control Commission for Germany (CCG), observed the ineffectiveness of the

British hunt for ex-Nazis, centred on a unit in the Public Safety branch, 'staffed by policemen from England' who had 'little or no experience of German or even continental politics and ways of life'; inevitably, they arrived not knowing the language. Army-run trials were not much better, and when in 1954 lawyers reviewed the cases of those still in jail, it proved 'a humiliating experience' (as the tribunal's chairman expressed it), for of eighty-five convictions under review only two dozen seemed 'safe', according to the recorded evidence; there had often been disproportionately harsh sentences for minor crimes. The tribunal did not review the cases of Germans hanged in 1946–8 after trial in the same courts. Responsibility for this, which Ivone Kirkpatrick thought 'a disgrace to this country . . . a miserable chapter in our otherwise creditable judicial history', lay with the Judge Advocate-General, Lord Russell of Liverpool, who later wrote *The Scourge of the Swastika*, as unforgiving a book about Germany as any by a British author. A decision to proceed like the Russians, as zealots urged, would have generated more convictions but, since trials of East Germans averaged twenty minutes per case, hardly better justice. With hindsight, it has been argued that – as Tom Bower puts it – British laxity turned *A Blind Eye to Murder*, but there was another side to the argument. Many responsible Britons like Churchill deplored the process throughout and gradually swayed opinion towards bringing it to an early end. Lord Beveridge argued as early as January 1946 that Britain was pursuing policies 'fit only for a totalitarian state', for it was not possible 'to teach democracy by repression'. Hindsight merchants have the supreme advantage of knowing that a working democracy did emerge in Germany, and can thus assume that this would have happened even if more Germans had been executed and jailed by the Allies, but this was horribly unclear at the time. It is equally easy to forget difficulties the authorities confronted, since they too were eventually overcome; in early 1946 the danger of Germans freezing to death for lack of coal led to the suspension of denazification among mining engineers, but not until a mine disaster when no qualified engineer was on duty had killed 402 miners. Much was done: the authorities had by 1947 screened two million Germans and removed a third of a million from their posts because of Nazi activities. Yet the eventual curtailment of denazification had a lasting consequence, suspicion remaining that Hitler's minions were still at large. This would under-pin British views of Germany for decades.[12]

As has been said, alongside failing to prepare or to persist with the process, there was timidity in removing from office and/or prosecution of military and business leaders. The CCG report of October 1945, claiming that the administration, police and financial institutions had now been 'purged', was probably, as Bower puts it, 'an outright lie', but attitudes emerged clearly enough when the army suggested releasing all six thousand officer-POWs, arguing persuasively that this would save the taxpayer a million pounds a year. The proposal was agreed by the Foreign Office before being dropped: it would be hard for a Labour government to defend favouritism for officers. The Attorney-General, Hartley Shawcross, thought the Nuremberg acquittal of the banker Schacht and the aristocratic von Papen reflected similar elitism in judicial circles, and his memoirs describe his unavailing efforts to promote more egalitarian principles in trials from 1946 onwards. Even when backed by the Prime Minister and Foreign Secretary, Shawcross could not bring to symbolic trial even five hundred of the ten thousand senior figures in custody. There was a huge row in 1947 when Field Marshal von Kesselring was sentenced to death, Churchill thundering that 'the process of killing the leaders of the defeated enemy has now exhausted any usefulness it may have had'. Kesselring's sentence was commuted to life imprisonment, but he was released in 1952 and by 1955 was telling the BBC that the Waffen SS had been 'the finest blood of the race . . . true soldiers born'. The Kesselring affair led to prolonged discussions about trying other generals, discussions in which well-intentioned Labour ministers – 'We've tried the corporals, now the generals must be tried too' – ran into entrenched army opposition. Senior officers gave the game away when they entertained Field Marshal von Rundstedt to an elaborate mess dinner as he traversed the British zone on his way to American interrogation; Rundstedt well recognised differing approaches, observing when returned to his Welsh prison that he would be happy to accept imprisonment for ever, provided he was never sent back to the Americans. Eventually, ministerial pressure ensured that four senior generals were chosen, though one died before trial and two others (including Rundstedt) were declared too old and unfit, so that only

Erich von Manstein was eventually tried (and with extreme difficulty, since by then the Russians refused to provide witnesses, while
much of Manstein's service had been in the East). This was a pyrrhic
victory, for the charming Manstein evoked great sympathy from
people as diverse as Bishop Bell and Lord Hankey, Churchill subscribed to his defence fund (which raised two thousand pounds),
and the Labour MP Reginald Paget declined to accept any fee as
defence counsel. Manstein was convicted and sent back to prison,
though released once the West German government had the bargaining power to demand it; the publicity ensured that his 1958
memoirs were a best-seller, unapologetically entitled *Lost Victories*. By
1948 British leaders shared Churchill's view that 'retributive persecution is of all policies the most pernicious', and that it was time to
draw a line under the past. There had never been much inclination to
prosecute businessmen and administrators, so the most that could be
achieved, as Ebsworth noted, was 'keeping them out of influential
positions in the new state'. To an extent this succeeded, so that when
Kirkpatrick returned to Germany as high commissioner in 1950, he
noticed that leaders of the democracy were almost all new men. But
he also encountered 'the ghosts of Hitler's Reich, men who had occupied positions in the administration, in industry or the society of the
day. They were either living in retirement, or were taking jobs in
banks, commerce or industry.' It was thus appropriate that a 1953
survey should find that, while only 30 per cent of Germans identified
with members of their own class in other countries, for Britain the
proportion was twice as large.[13]

The German past hung as heavily over Nuremberg as did the
future, for many remembered that atrocity stories of 1914–18 had
turned out to be false, and there was absolute determination that the
atrocities of 1939–45 should never be deniable. Nuremberg was, as
the novelist Rebecca West argued in the *Daily Telegraph*, 'a sort of
legalistic prayer that the Kingdom of Heaven should be with us'. By
1946, the dropping of the atom bomb had compromised the Allies'
self-righteousness, to say nothing of such 'war crimes' as the devastation of German cities by bombing, to which Cardinal Frings drew
attention when he asked why only Germans were being tried.
Among the more sensitive, many shared the guilt that Nuremberg
exemplified, and for these the re-education of Germany was itself an

expiation. As the educationalist Robert Birley suggested, explaining to a Christian audience in 1947 'the German Problem and the Responsibilities of Britain', the British had failed as much as the Germans, by not responding adequately to pre-war challenges which 'quite candidly rejected the moral order which we had come to accept as almost part of nature'. That failure implied a British obligation to accept responsibility now, after the 'break which has occurred in the history of civilisation'. Or, as Rebecca West put it, the Nuremberg prosecutors did not forget their own methods of warmaking; 'they wished not only that Germany might not do again what it had done, but that they need not do again what they had had to do in self-defence against the Germans'. Stephen Spender thought Germany in 1945 'one vast monument or tomb of lost freedom [since] the Germans had deprived first themselves and then Europe of freedom and now they had made for themselves a prison and a ruin, and we were the gaolers'. Perceptions of 'the Responsibilities of Britain' were heavily coloured by the concentration camps, especially Belsen, liberated by British troops. The war correspondent Alan Moorhead, whose reports helped to publicise Belsen, wondered if it had served a deep psychological purpose. The wave of collective indignation enabled Britons to forget that they had ignored stories about Dachau in the 1930s, and now focused on Belsen more than even grislier camp stories emerging from Poland: 'since Germany was manifestly beaten, people wanted to have a justification for their fight, proof that they were engaged against evil'. Though he was sure from what he saw that 'the Junkers and the Wehrmacht power-through-class' faction were 'utterly compromised', and that Germans deserved the lion's share of blame for the catastrophe, to some extent all of mankind was responsible. He reported without comment the brutality of British soldiers guarding Belsen's SS guards, as they beat the life out of the camp doctor and ignored his pleas for a quick death; another reporter, Leonard Mosley, reported the army making ex-guards carry typhus victims to their graves, and hence contract the disease from which many of them died. Moorhead decided that German soldiers had carried out cruelties in a more organised manner because they were better disciplined, but what he saw of British behaviour without organisation or premeditation left him feeling shaky about the moral borderlines. The more he saw devastated cities, the more refugees crowding the roads, 'the less one had the sense of victory'.[14]

Less deep-thinking Britons viewed Belsen as proof of what they had been told but never quite believed about Germany: this was what Moorhead called 'a journey to some Dantesque pit, unreal, leprous and frightening' – and Germany's responsibility. It was hard to equate beatings carried out under the influence of outrage with the fact that eight hundred *deliberately* starved inmates died even on the day Belsen was liberated. As the Mayor and leading citizens of nearby Celle were compulsorily toured around the camp, they were harangued from a loudspeaker, in language that had little to do with shared guilt:

> What you see here is the final and utter condemnation of the Nazi Party. It justifies every measure which the United Nations will take to exterminate that party. What you see here is such a disgrace to the German people that their name must be erased from the list of civilised nations. You stand here judged by what you see in this camp. It is your lot to begin the hard task of restoring the name of the German people to the list of civilised nations. But this cannot be done until you have reared a new generation amongst whom it is impossible to find people prepared to commit such crimes.

In the heat of the moment violent language and behaviour were understandable, but POWs in a camp in Derbyshire were treated brutally that month by guards who merely read about Belsen in newspapers or saw it in newsreels. Even Britons who later tried to enlist sympathy for Germans facing starvation had difficulty retaining their own moral compass. Bertrand Russell, watching refugees arriving at Berlin stations in August 1945, where their few remaining goods were stolen by Russian soldiers and their womenfolk raped, saw 'Belsen over again', while, faced with terrible scenes in German cities in 1946, Victor Gollancz had to 'restore [his] sense of proportion by remembering that Belsen and Auschwitz were far, almost infinitely wickeder'. When conditions in British prison camps deteriorated, or when interrogated POWs replied that 'concentration camps' had been a British invention during the Boer War, the authorities took refuge in an equivalent moral relativity: bureaucratic incompetence or overreaction while angry was not on the same moral plane as organised, industrialised murder.[15]

At first, there was no disposition to ram home lessons from the camps – Richard Dimbleby had to insist before the BBC would broadcast his Belsen report – but this soon changed. The message was graphically carried by newsreels, each company producing special editions, and there can have been few British adults who did not see at least one such film. Mavis Tate added the commentary to Pathé's special report, while Movietone hired Vansittart. Pathé explained that 'the responsibility for these terrible crimes falls squarely on the German people'; British Gaumont suggested that the camps were 'a perpetual reminder of a dark age in the history of the German race, a race which does not know the meaning of humanity'. British Paramount titled its report 'Proof Positive'.[16]

Germans being forced to walk among ruined humanity in the camps was occupation policy, and photographed for British newspapers. It was often the case, as *Picture Post* showed, that German civilians refused to look. Such reports thus linked with widespread German denial of personal culpability, evidencing the need to re-educate Germans to 'face the facts'. Hence there was a concerted effort by occupation authorities to get ordinary Germans to watch an explicit film about the camps, *The Mills of Death*. The British media reported this process too, showing Germans queuing to see evidence of 'their' crimes. *Pathé Gazette*, noting that this was part of re-education, added gratuitously, 'Time alone will show whether in fact Germans can be re-educated.' Unsurprisingly, it was hard to get German civilians to go to the cinema to watch atrocity films, or to discuss them afterwards; more generally, indeed, cinema audiences voted with their feet against any film which was not escapist and cheerful. With POWs, though, the British government literally had a captive audience, to whom a special film about the camps was shown, footage more explicit than that shown to civilians. Guarded by armed soldiers as they watched, the prisoners knew they were being force-fed a political message, and reactions were mixed: a Catholic priest who had served in Hitler's army even complained that 'what we couldn't understand was why we were all more guilty than the British, who after all had liberated us much too late from Hitler'. In some POW camps remorse predominated: prisoners in a dozen camps signed manifestos expressing shame for the Nazi regime, and four made collections for camp victims. The message got through, for even in camps dominated by 'black' (Nazi) POWs two in five thought the film genuine, while among 'whites' and 'greys' (comprising nine-tenths of all POWs) the film was overwhelmingly accepted as true. When asked if concentration camps had been necessary, more than half even of 'black' POWs said 'no', and only one in five said 'yes'; nine-tenths of 'greys' and 'whites' said 'no'. This brutal part of re-education apparently worked, and there is no reason to think that German civilians responded differently from soldiers. Yet concentration of attention on concentration camps and war criminals in 1945–6 did little to soften British attitudes.[17]

Post-war 'Germany' was in few ways the successor state to the Third Reich, and for historic British attitudes the discontinuities mattered. To begin with geography, even with the Soviet zone included (which made little sense before 1990), 'Germany' was only two-thirds the size of Hitler's Reich in 1939, and 'West Germany' of 1949–90 half the size. The area known for forty years as 'East Germany' was central Germany to previous generations, eastern provinces having vanished into Poland. Since those lost provinces included the Junker heartland of East and West Prussia, and part of Mecklenburg and Silesia, the social base and landed wealth of the offi-cer corps were utterly broken. If Britain had been fighting both the Nazis and 'Prussian militarism', as Churchill asserted, then the second enemy was irreversibly wrecked by the Red Army and Stalin's foreign policy. Defeat in 1945 had a limited lasting impact on Germany's business elite, but it made a huge difference to the army-orientated service class. The ruthless mass expulsion of Germans from districts now within neighbouring countries wrecked pan-Germans' historic *Mitteleuropa*, and liquidated German communities whose grievances Hitler had ventilated in 1938–9. Here was achieved, with Britain doing nothing except protesting against the methods by which expul-sions happened, a cardinal principle of Vansittartism. That beneficial consequence to Britain of the failure of British policy to restrain Stalin, the Czechs and the Poles was reinforced by deliberate deci-sions. 'Prussia' was formally abolished as a political unit in 1947, and the parts of old Prussia within the British zone distributed into three of the four *Länder* which became the lower tier of West Germany. For

Prussia, history came to a full stop, and since British fear of Germans had been summed up by 'Prussia', this was highly significant. The popular German rumour that Britain would not only reverse the German unification of the 1860s but reclaim Hanover for the British Empire was though a total myth; the occupation authorities were embarrassed when 'Old Hanoverians' briefly campaigned for that programme. There was more satisfaction when von Rundstedt, the epitome of the Prussian military tradition, was buried after a civilian funeral in 1953: no firing party, no uniformed escort, not a drum tolling the death-knell of everything he represented.[18]

The 1945 expulsions refocused British opinion, since they showed Germans among war's victims. Once again journalists and photographers ensured that readers recognised the problem, the 'good picture' beloved of editors so often being one of dispossessed civilians: a photographic essay in *Illustrated* magazine showed in September 1945 scenes at Berlin's Anhalter Station, 'where refugees arrive, depart, live, die'. This was, as accompanying text explained, 'a Gallery of misery: blind, mutilated soldiers, homeless boys, grannies, starving, verminous mothers, infants'. Reminders that the refugees' brutal treatment by gangs of Polish youths was a consequence of Germany's ravaging of Poland did not undercut sympathy for their personal plight. The *Daily Mail* and *News Chronicle* carried similar reports, and the issue was raised with ministers by the Churches and by MPs. The government could only respond that at Potsdam the Allies had agreed that movements of population should be orderly and humane, but it had no ability whatsoever to mitigate the greatest-ever European case of what would later be known as 'ethnic cleansing'. In 1945 British people were aware of this catastrophe, during which two million Germans were murdered or driven to their deaths, while ten million were dispossessed and driven out of lands where their ancestors had long dwelt. Here is the selectivity of collective memory, for hardly any Britons now have the slightest awareness of the episode, while the Holocaust remains fixed in their minds. At the time, Violet Bonham Carter left meetings with German refugees 'feeling that in subscribing at Yalta & Potsdam to the Partition of Poland we had connived at one of the greatest crimes in history'.[19]

Awareness of German refugees was reinforced by growing knowledge of the physical state of Germany. Arriving in Nuremberg for the trials, British lawyers were astonished by what they saw: Elwyn Jones saw a 'tormented city . . . the city of Albrecht Dürer, Viet Stoss and the Mastersingers', reduced to rubble; Hartley Shawcross remembered seeing bombers flying out over his Sussex home, but had 'never fully visualised the destruction they would inflict'. George Bell was equally shattered by the reality, which was 'unbelievable unless you see it with your own eyes'. Richard Rumbold, the ex-ambassador's son and so familiar with 1930s Berlin, reported to Harold Nicolson in May 1945 that 'the destruction is inconceivable; the desolation complete; the despair unutterable', and Nicolson rightly anticipated that 'the mood of hatred induced by Buchenwald will be succeeded by a wave of pity'. Rumbold was reporting for the *News of the World,* one of many papers to rub its readers' noses in images of destruction. A photograph of pretty young women carrying buckets of water through the ruins had been precisely the image offered to readers during the London Blitz, photogenic civilians smiling for the camera as they somehow kept going. Darmstadt, a British scientist wrote in his diary, was 'a city of the dead – literally and figuratively. Not a soul in its alleyways between red rubble that were once streets. Long vistas of gaunt ruins – most only shoulder high.' Stephen Spender decided that the ruin of Cologne was 'reflected in the internal ruin of its inhabitants who, instead of being lives that can form a scar over the city's wounds, are parasites sucking at a dead carcase, digging among the ruins for hidden food, doing business at their black market near the Cathedral – the commerce of destruction instead of production'. This was a timely reminder, as Rebecca West put it, 'that the war had been worse for the Germans than for us', a discovery that took Britons by surprise. Ivone Kirkpatrick was struck by the contrast between himself and a German he met one day in the Rhineland, a bank manager returning from Chiemsee to Paderborn by walking the five hundred miles pushing a pram full of suitcases, there being no other way home. Kirkpatrick drove on to Frankfurt, where he lodged in comfort with Air Marshal Tedder, who enjoyed 'an idyllic existence' away from 'the turmoil of war'. Inescapable evidence that even the professional classes endured primeval suffering had a profound effect on Kirkpatrick, who so deeply believed in 'the inner circle' that he chose that title for his autobiography.[20]

Awareness of German victimhood caused moral confusion, as the

correspondence of Leo Schnitter indicates. Schnitter was a POW
befriended by the Rev. Michael Smith in his Norfolk parish where
Schnitter was sent to help on the farm. Smith tried unavailingly to
get the British government to allow Schnitter to remain in Britain
rather than being repatriated – a relentless campaign of letter-writing
that met only bureaucratic apathy. The German was deported to the
Sudetenland, where his family had lived for generations, but was
then expelled by the Czechs into the Russian zone of Germany, where
he eventually found his family, but from which they could not
depart. Despite this lamentable personal narrative, when confronted
with Schnitter's complaint that he now was forced by the Allies to live
in a land where even Germans thought him a foreigner, Smith felt
obliged in 1947 to lecture him on collective guilt: 'You have to
remember that the Sudeten Germans behaved abominably to the
Czechs, and shouted and screamed about that madman Hitler . . .
The Nazi Sudetens brought the trouble entirely upon themselves
and innocent people like you and yours have to suffer for their sins.
But we do not hate you all, thank God!' The story had a happy, if
long-delayed, ending, for Leo Schnitter was one of many 'East
Germans' who managed to escape to the West, after which from
1950 he corresponded again with Smith.[21]

Leo Schnitter's story typifies the long transition from war to peace
for individuals caught in the machinery. Technically, war with
Germany did not end in 1945, for there was by May of that year no
government left to surrender on behalf of the German people. This
was in part accidental, the consequence of Hitler's determination to
take Germany down with him, but the British army arrested Admiral
Karl Dönitz's Flensburg 'government' before it could establish legitimacy as Hitler's heirs. The Allied armies therefore occupied
Germany by conquest, as their declarations insisted, not as in 1919 by
consent; any future German government would be the Allies' creation. This created real legal difficulties, for how could Britain remain
at war with a country she herself administered? How could the King
be at war with himself, asked Foreign Office lawyers, when a court
asked if it could refuse rights of habeas corpus to 'enemy' aliens.
Undeterred by this legal minefield, and possibly reassured by the
official who complained that this was just the sort of objection which
would be raised 'by the type of mind that sees difficulties', the Foreign

Secretary assured British courts that 'no treaty of peace or declaration by the Allied Powers having been made terminating the state of war with Germany, His Majesty is still in a state of war with Germany, although, as provided in the declaration of surrender, all active hostilities have ceased'. The value of this was that, as long as 'war' continued, the Geneva Convention allowed Britain to keep her POWs, which was vital to the economy; a member of the Foreign Office minuted confidentially that 'they will really be forced labourers, but I can see no need to say so'. The Foreign Secretary eventually ruled that war against Germany ended at 4 p.m. on 9 July 1951, by which time West Germany was a British ally: the reason given was that it was now 'psychologically and politically embarrassing' to maintain the fiction of war, but it was also long after the German POWs had gone home. It was, thought Churchill, 'a tragic fact' that it had taken six years before the word 'peace' could be uttered 'between two great branches of the human family'.[22]

For German POWs in Britain, length of captivity was their main grievance, and for those still held after the winter of 1947–8 it was an obsession that negated 're-education'. It was one thing to be held prisoner while the countries fought, or kept until machinery for release was developed, something quite different to be 'slave labour' for two years after the fighting stopped. The prisoners most outraged were those ferried back from America to 'Europe', only to discover that work in Britain was their destination, when they had destitute families needing their help. Germans captured in Italy, returned to Germany but then shipped to Britain to become mine-clearance companies because they had technical skills had even better ground for complaint, for so employing POWs was outlawed by the Geneva Convention. Some Britons were outraged too: Harold Nicolson, after watching Germans 'slouching' along Cotswold roads in 1947, concluded that 'we have no right to use this slave labour and I feel ashamed'. Churchmen were equally unhappy, but there were plenty of farmers who were happy to retain low-paid labour, and few who ate their produce in a time of scarcity asked how it was produced. As Prime Minister, Attlee bravely referred to this as 'German' reparation for war damage, and Churchill had POWs working for two years restoring his grounds at Chartwell. Once German newspapers circulated again in 1946–7, this was a popular grievance; Albert Speer had pleaded guilty at Nuremberg to using forced labour for the Nazi economy, and his imprisonment demonstrated it to be a 'war crime'. Captain Faulk noted though that Britons and Germans implied different meanings by 'slavery': for Germans, it was enforced detention; for the British, inadequate pay, and hence could be uneasily justified as 'reparations'. It says much about the British view of Germans that so few initially shared Nicolson's anger, while there were hardly any who understood that 'German' POWs included many other nationalities, conscripted into German armies in 1939–43; in some cases these were men who were neither ethnic Germans nor able to speak the language, while at Toft Camp near Knutsford in 1947 the inmates claimed to be of thirty-eight different nationalities (though the camp authorities recognised *only* twenty-six). Since there was an acute shortage of Britons who spoke German, much screening of POWs was delegated to Dutch, Czech and Norwegian interrogators, some of whom notably lacked sympathy for their recent occupiers, though the category into which a prisoner was placed determined both his treatment and his date of release. Not that British personnel were always notable for Churchillian magnanimity: an army report on POW camps in Germany in April 1947 concluded that the British really needed to be screened, not the Germans. Some methods employed – formal notes of interviews neither available to the prisoner nor agreed by him; neither witnesses nor defence counsel required (the army regarding these as 'merely a time-wasting device'); and no requirement for review boards to be bound by 'the technical rules of evidence' – were practices not sanctioned again by the British state until the onset of the 'war on terrorism'. There is also a depressingly contemporary feel to the requirement that POWs sign an undertaking before release, promising not to talk to the press about their imprisonment, on pain of rearrest.[23]

Eventually, a surge of conscience accelerated the process of release and repatriation; but only in summer 1947, when economic circumstances began to seem less dire, did opinion awaken to the moral issues. A 'Save Europe Now' petition in August was signed by 118 MPs, 55 bishops and 76 fellows of the Royal Society. Soon afterwards POW repatriation by December 1948 was agreed by the Western Allies, with Britain completing the process in August of that year. By that stage, the fact that the POW camps were costing the taxpayer

£90,000 a day may have been a contributory factor, for once it was decided to close them down, there was little point in delaying the process, whereas in 1946 a quarter of the agricultural workforce had been German. As the *Manchester Guardian* suggested, 'the story of their long captivity in these islands does not do us any particular credit', but the main charge against the government was that it allowed its economic and labour departments to determine policy towards foreign nationals, and refused to say anything definite about its intentions to the POWs themselves – largely because it had little idea from month to month what its policy would be. As one ex-POW wrote twenty years later, 'there was nothing of the legendary British fairness about it and . . . many prisoners . . . were convinced that the British too acted on the dictum that the victor is always right'.[24]

It is unclear how far 're-education' worked, but the way in which it was conducted did tend to educate both sides. Destruction in total war surely had more effect on changing German ideas about warfare than any education programme could have achieved. POW camps until the end of the war could be brutal environments, dominated by Nazis on whom commandants failed to impress their authority; guards were powerless to stop four thousand POWs singing the '*Horst Wessel Lied*' in camp at Bury, loud enough to be heard two miles away, and could not even prevent occasional killings of anti-Nazis by other POWs. These, though, were wartime incidents, and once the toughest Nazis were segregated from the rest, behaviour markedly improved and re-education began to make some progress. The British gradually recognised that when POWs insisted that the world was blind to 'the good side' of National Socialism, they were referring to such things as the eradication of unemployment, which carried no weight in Britain, but mattered a great deal to Germans who had experienced the deprivations of 1930–3. The final survey of camp opinion, in March 1948, found that over half of the POWs still thought that National Socialism had been 'a good idea, badly carried out'. That alarming figure may reflect the fact that 'white' Germans had by then gone home, while those who remained were growing hostile to Britain because of continued detention, but it is not far from the proportion who answered the question similarly among civilians in the British zone throughout the occupation period. However, the

British gradually grasped that their saying this did not mean that half of Germans wanted the Nazis back: the same survey found that only 7 per cent even of remaining POWs still 'believed in National Socialism'. Faulk recognised that a refusal to *admit* to having been re-educated was a way for a POW to retain his self-respect, so the only proof of the pudding could be how they behaved after release. This was certainly true of Wolfgang Schmidt, a POW in the custody of the Americans, whose autobiography claims to be 'not an account of re-education and related magic but in spite of it'. Yet Schmidt worked for the American army and migrated to America, which hardly suggests he remained unaffected by his experiences. Twenty years after the war one ex-POW wrote to a former captor of his 'luck' to have been in a British POW camp, 'because the intellectual and political perspective of the men from Britain is deeper', while those from Russian captivity showed themselves 'less patient and tolerant'.[25]

The atmosphere was affected by the way in which British authorities approached the task, for planning delays meant that re-education began only after the war ended, when it was easier to agree to encourage prisoners to re-educate themselves, rather than impose new standards from the outside. Several former inmates of Wilton Park praised the fact that it encouraged discussion rather than suggested answers, with only a relaxed hand on the tiller from British tutors. Heinz Koeppler, like Henry Faulk, hated 're-education', thinking it a word 'born of arrogance out of ignorance'. The British were convinced that they were non-ideological in re-education, whereas Russians and Americans had openly ideological objectives, but this defined 'ideology' too narrowly. When the former dean of Wilton Park recalled that 'we were only trying to conduct a dialogue on an equal basis', he added that 'the only basic theme was democracy. I am an Englishman, and therefore the ideal form for me personally is parliamentary democracy. Naturally, this was the basis for our discussion.' If inmates did not perceive a restricted debate, so much the better, but restrictions were certainly there. Wilton Park sought originally a cross-section of all POWs, but rapidly recognised that it should bias its intake towards the more intelligent, and may even have gone too far in that direction, since the inmates demanded that British other ranks do the camp's menial work, leaving campers freer for reading and discussion. It must though have been a rare attraction for bored but intelligent prisoners when they could debate Germany's future with Richard Crossman, George Bell or A. J. P. Taylor. Witnessing Denis Healey and Julian Amery debating hammer and tongs but laughing together in the bar afterwards must also have been educational for anyone brought up under a dictatorship. Koeppler vigorously denied that he was creating a German elite imbued with British attitudes, for these 'Wiltonians' were meant to influence other POWs, and once released they were given no special facilities in civilian life. Nevertheless, the original prohibition on those 4500 POWs who attended Wilton Park calling themselves 'Old Wiltonians' was unenforceable, especially once they were released, and several German cities had in the 1950s 'Wilton Clubs' of former 'students'. Parallel with this, and in tribute to the enlightened work of the émigré Herbert Sulzbach among POWs at Featherstone Park Camp, annual dinners of old-boys were held for several years in Düsseldorf; Sulzbach received more than three thousand letters of thanks from ex-POWs and was even invited to reunions.[26]

German civilians formed an even poorer impression of Britain from its occupation forces than did POWs. Political direction was haphazard, for the CCG, planned by the Foreign Office, was transferred to the War Office in 1945 then shunted back to the FO in 1947. Soldiers despised the CCG, claiming its initials stood for 'Complete Chaos Guaranteed'. Its minister – John Hynd – had only low status, was perceived as pro-German and exerted little influence on overall policy; his office was dubbed the 'Hyndquarters'. Although things marginally improved when Lord Pakenham took over in 1947, *Spiegel* still thought him 'the great, slightly clumsy zonal lord' (though it was impressed when such a 'pious man' worked right through Whitsuntide). Lack of preparation meant the CCG was staffed by a motley but large crew: while the USA managed its zone with five thousand staff, the British employed five times as many; in 1950, when well on the way out, the CCG still employed six thousand Britons supervising (often duplicating the work of) seventy thousand Germans. German civilians, experienced with an intrusive bureaucracy, nevertheless thought the Commission's obsession with detailed control highly inefficient. A joke about CCG screening was that the final question (out of 133) was 'Did you play with toy soldiers as a child? If so, what regiment?' The top echelon of staff were capable, even justifying Strang's complacent conclusion that they exemplified Britain's 'traditional aptitude for government', but lower down it was very different. Able civil servants avoided the CCG, for while in 1947 the Foreign Office expected it to exist for another twenty years, there was still no decent pension scheme and no proper contracts. A parliamentary select committee reported that the Commission had squadrons of harassed bureaucrats walled off from German realities behind ramparts of files. The Foreign Office thought government more effectively carried out by fewer people in the Russian zone, because 'the Russians have never bothered to import a highly-paid army of retired drain-inspectors, unsuccessful businessmen and idle ex-policemen'. Evaluating his own experience after visiting the British zone in 1946, Victor Gollancz paid tribute to senior CCG staff, but decided they were 'frustrated by the uncoordinated working of a bureaucratic machine, by the growing divorce between Berlin and the zone, and above all by the absence of a policy in London'.[27]

The administration of stricken Germany clearly had a low priority in London, but high-handed attitudes towards Germans indicate something deeper. British occupation, argued Douglas Botting, 'was like a new Raj – colonial, exploitative, but in part paternalistic and well-intentioned'. The leader of the German Social Democrats welcomed Britain giving independence to India in 1947, but hoped that yet more ex-colonial administrators would not come to Germany; one, transferred from Nigeria to what Gollancz called 'darkest Germany', began by demanding separate staff lists of Europeans and non-Europeans. Much like India, Berlin had a Winston Club for officers (it was the Victory Club in Hamburg) while the NAAFI looked after other ranks. Gollancz in 1946 published menus for five-course meals served in officers' and CCG messes, luxury he had not seen since visiting Singapore decades earlier, but flourishing alongside shortages in Britain and starvation in Germany. It was not against the rules to bring a German into the mess – no more than Indians could not join the club at Poona – but in six weeks Gollancz never saw one. Concerts and cinema showings were at first segregated, in a manner common in the American South, with no Germans allowed inside while their conquerors were entertained. What went for food and entertainment was equally true of living space, for while the average German had 3.2 square metres of accommodation, Gollancz as a British visitor had a bedroom of 80 square metres, hot and cold running water, central heating and servants. It was equally embarrassing for 'Red Robert' Birley. Though a full member of the old-boy network and future headmaster of Eton, Birley had a well-developed conscience and was deeply embarrassed by the magnificent (and probably stolen) Lagonda in which he travelled as CCG educational adviser. Universal rank surprised visitors, for all important civilians acquired an equivalent military rank, to impress Germans and so that bureaucrats would know the exact extent of their privileges; Bishop Bell, of all people, was made an honorary major general, and 'chatted tolerantly to a mere Major of Gunners with seven ribbons on his tunic!' In these circumstances Germans found it easiest to salute everyone not speaking German, to be on the safe side. Gollancz doubted whether 'the best way to "re-educate" people cursed by a *Herrenvolk* tradition is to behave like the *Herrenvolk* – if in the main very kind and decent *Herrenvolk* – yourselves', while German liberals claimed it was hard to persuade young people that Nazi militarism had been so terrible 'when British militarism is just as bad'. Konrad Adenauer later recalled that he was sacked as Mayor of Cologne by both the Nazis and the 'liberators', implying a similar moral equivalence. He was alienated not by dismissal – which allowed him to become Chancellor of West Germany instead of Mayor of Cologne – but by the attitude displayed; Adenauer's ambassador in London thought him 'irritated by the inherent self-confidence of the British political class'. Here indeed was the hauteur of the Raj, deployed to equally self-defeating effect.[28]

Encouraged to believe in their innate superiority and segregated from Germans, standards of behaviour were often ungenerous. Gollancz told the *Manchester Guardian* that although 'the general standard of honour, devotion to duty and even ability in the Control Commission is higher than rumour had led me to believe', which was not saying much, 'the number of people I met who behaved in a civilised fashion to the Germans – who mixed freely with them, and treated them quite naturally as equal human beings – was inconsiderable'. He noted that, even though he had set aside half of his cubicles for British customers, a Hamburg hairdresser was nevertheless obliged to move German customers over whenever additional British women entered his shop. Strang, who thought that the British had such genius for government, recounts in his memoirs meeting the Mayor of Hamburg (an anti-Nazi the British had installed in office, though you would hardly grasp this from his account). Dr Peterson, 'whom I took to be a "good German", if there were any such', represented the recent past as folly rather than 'guilt' and hoped for a constructive partnership since otherwise Germans might turn communist. Strang 'interrupted this exercise in self-pity and covert blackmail' to remind Peterson of collective German shame, the Anglo-Russian alliance and the need to crush militarism; the occupation's purposes were 'not to promote Anglo-German friendship or to bring about the economic revival of Germany'. When a career diplomat took pride in such incidents, it was open season for others. The Military Governor ordered in October 1946 that, while it was now unnecessary for Germans always to step off pavements to give 'the right of way to British personnel', they must still not obstruct British pedestrians. In Düsseldorf a young officer, forced to wait ten minutes to meet with a senior official of the city administration (delayed by the transport problems in the ruined city), exploded that if he was late again he would go to prison. This German at least had the last word, replying that, having spent some time in a Nazi jail, he did not expect to find a British one any worse. The Deputy Military Governor told his commissioner in Cologne that if he needed to consult Cardinal Frings he should call him in, if necessary sending the police to make sure that he came, conduct even Hitler would have thought twice about.[29]

Nor were ethical standards high, a factor reinforced by young soldiers' relief at having survived and by contempt for a defeated enemy. Bill Deedes found that since his seniors could not agree, Montgomery having 'distinctly old-fashioned views about the entitlement of victorious soldiers to booty', while Corps Commander Horrocks 'held stricter views', a company officer had to determine his own morality: his riflemen took goods for use but not to defile or loot, though 'if you found wine in the cellar or geese in the orchard, you did not consult higher command'. Others were less careful: after watching a local youth being slapped about by a major in the Green Howards, one subaltern reflected that

> none of us could have cared a bit for that little boy . . . They had been
> public enemy number one. So now we commandeered their horses,
> commandeered their Mercedes, commandeered their women. I would
> reckon 60 or 70 per cent of young Englishmen in Germany thought
> that way. Most of us were for having a bloody good time and believed
> we could get away with anything.

Since the authorities 'commandeered' everything they needed, such as
furniture, young soldiers naturally behaved the same way. In Bonn
Stephen Spender was told by soldiers how they had rescued German
girls attacked by German men 'for fraternising with our men'; after a
fist-fight they 'escorted them home as well'. The overriding attitude
was exemplified by the 'Hamburg Project', whereby the CCG planned
a kind of German New Delhi as a monument to British authority, dis-
placing six thousand civilians to house 340 British officers, taking over
altogether one of the few quarters not ruined, and erecting a 'canton-
ment' for British administrators and their families. This monster of
civil engineering monopolised labour and building resources in the
entire British zone, being quietly abandoned only when complaints
in Parliament and the press became irresistible (the abandonment was
quiet in case it diminished the sahibs' prestige). 'Requisitions' were
even more onerous when army wives moved into Germany in 1947,
the army routinely providing at German civilians' expense married
quarters far superior to Aldershot. Such requisitioning easily carried
over into theft, as in silverware, tapestries, jewellery and paintings
looted from the Krupps' Villa Hügel. Following *Daily Mail* investigations, Scotland Yard interrogated senior British officers, including
an air vice marshal who had vanished to his next posting with a great
deal of private property, and there was suspicion that the early retirement of the Military Governor was linked to the scandal. Nobody
was prosecuted.[30]

British police were further involved in investigating the black
market which flourished in the ruins of German cities, a taskforce of
forty detectives being required, while in 1948 the CCG chief of internal affairs resigned: he could not improve staff behaviour, so refused
further responsibility. Occupation policy, combined with the determination of young men to have a good time, almost guaranteed
illicit activity. In 1946 all CCG staff received two hundred cigarettes

a week, plus an allowance of soap, matches and chocolate, while German civilians could buy only seven cigarettes a week and had a tiny allowance of very poor soap. These articles all became an effective currency of which the occupiers had plenty to spare, and this remained the case until a new German mark was launched in June 1948. In the meantime the British lived the life of Riley and bought anything they wanted with cigarettes, so that many soldiers were able to send home regular cash sums, and some rarely bothered even to draw their pay. Nor was this a matter only of squaddies subjected to temptation, for *The Times* reported in March 1947 a scam involving a brigadier and two colonels. If Germany was 'the cesspool of Europe', as British and German churchmen complained, this was due to occupation as well as war.[31]

Cigarettes bought women as well as goods, which really upset the bishops; it upset generals too, though mainly because venereal disease reached epidemic proportions among their troops. At first British soldiers were forbidden to fraternise with civilians, to bring home to Germans that they were untouchable, but these rules were eased before the end of 1945. In his memoirs Montgomery argued that this was a planned policy of moving towards relaxation after a tough start when guerrilla warfare by fanatical Nazis was expected: as Britons crossed the Dutch–German border, they passed a sign warning, 'YOU ARE ENTERING ENEMY TERRITORY: BE ON YOUR GUARD!' But the army really relaxed restrictions because they were not being obeyed; the only rules that then remained were prohibitions on soldiers living with German families or marrying German women. Propaganda might tell soldiers that every child was a member of the Hitler Youth who would assassinate them in some dark alley, but nothing prevented soldiers making friends with children; and it was a short step from befriending toddlers to becoming intimate with their mothers. Aware that this was all rather daring, GIs called German women 'frats', while going out with them was 'going fratting'. 'Fraternisation', recalled William Deedes forty years on, was mainly 'a euphemism for fornication'. Under immense pressure to keep their families together during desperate times, with their husbands still imprisoned, many women went in for casual prostitution or found a 'protector' in the occupying forces; a snack became a 'frat sandwich'. Appalled by evidence of moral decline, military police put a new slant on the 'good and bad Germans' idea, wondering despairingly if there were any 'good girls' left. Some couples stayed together, though few cases were as remarkable as Derek Sington, the first Allied officer to enter Belsen: he met there a German girl who became his interpreter and secretary, and after three years' working together chasing war criminals they moved to London where they married. Even less representative was Josef Gaertner (born in Brighton as Joseph Gardner). He was a Guards sergeant who married a German wife during the Rhineland occupation of 1919, remained in a small town near Bonn throughout the Nazi period (and suffered no reprisals), only to be installed as Burgermeister by the Americans in 1945, and eventually elected to the post by his German fellow-citizens. It was partly horror that mixed marriages might become common that led the army to install wives in Germany, with negative effects on Anglo-German relationships (much as the memsahibs 'lost India' for the British). The army was reluctant to acknowledge the offspring of casual unions between soldiers and Germans, the Foreign Office concurring that paternity suits must never be admitted in either British or German courts, since they could 'have a most damaging effect on British prestige'. Nevertheless, there must still be fifty-somethings all over the former British zone who are not only Lower Saxons but Anglo-Saxons.[32]

The government's nutritional adviser Sir Jack Drummond concluded that 'venereal disease amongst the Occupation troops follows closely on the development of hunger amongst the population'. It was not necessary to draw attention to hunger, however, for widespread campaigning took place in Britain to publicise the problem itself. Here critics who were marginalised in wartime came into their own, and both Gollancz and Bell played big parts in awakening British concern. Some believed at first, like Strang, that 'Germans of the British zone did not bear the appearance of a broken people', since at least rural Germans had lived for years with slave labour to produce agricultural plenty and had had 'the material resources of Europe' at their disposal; the *Daily Mirror* ran in May 1945 the headline 'Huns in Clover!' But this was a temporary impression. In the cities destruction included shops, warehouses and food-distribution systems, while even on farms lack of labour and poor harvests in 1945–6 brought catastrophe; by spring 1946 calorie consumption was little over half the level deemed 'indispensable' for Britain, while later that year it barely exceeded what had been provided for prisoners in Belsen, despite the diversion to Germany of a million tons of wheat destined for Britain. Newspapers and newsreels shrilly reported the problem; Gollancz's 1946 reports on German malnutrition were carried by half a dozen papers, from the Labour-supporting *Daily Herald*, through the liberal *News Chronicle* to the *Observer* and *The Times*. By October Ernest Bevin was appealing to the country 'not to indulge in sloppy sentimentality' in respect of Germany. But all the press publicised *In Darkest Germany*, many of them borrowing one of Gollancz's photographs of malnourished children, and there was barely a hint of 'serve them right' in the coverage. No paper would though print his report from Jülich, which described his 'affection' for its people; it was one thing to pity Germans, quite different to express liking. Gollancz argued uncompromisingly that malnutrition was Britain's responsibility, and so Britain must deal with it; heretofore 'we have conspicuously failed'. His claim was robustly supported by calorie-consumption figures and statistics proving that suffering had worsened since the British arrived. German shortages were remorsely contrasted with the bonuses the Ministry of Food allowed the British for Christmas 1946, the implication being that Germans starved so that the British could have turkeys. Germans were now so listless, he reported, that they wandered aimlessly across the streets, so 'you are always in danger of running them down if you are in a car – as, being a Britisher, you almost invariably are'. Lord Beveridge, at the height of his fame, chipped in with an 'urgent message from Germany' delivered in broadcasts, press articles and a pamphlet, the gist of which was that 'by allowing misery to continue we are generating hate'. Breadth of concern was shown in the million food parcels sent to German families by ordinary Britons between December 1946 and May 1949, despite government restrictions on anyone sending out more than one parcel a month.[33]

Not only was the will to go on being sapped, and morality collapsing, but in places like Hamburg there were mass demonstrations that threatened public order, challenging the army with the unpleasant thought that it might soon need to shoot civilians to maintain order. Starvation also undermined the fostering of democratic attitudes, for as Raymond Ebsworth puts it, by 1947, 'for most of the population democracy had so far meant shortages of food, fuel and the comforts of life'. A combination of humanitarianism and growing awareness of the contradictions in government policies produced a change of mood early in 1947, when ministers realised a more generous policy had become politically acceptable. Strang now advised that it 'would not be practical politics to leave British soldiers and civilians in Germany among a starving population. We must therefore either pay to feed them for a necessary period or get out [but] getting out now would be letting the Russians in.' Churchill chimed in, urging that 'we cannot afford . . . to let chaos and misery continue indefinitely in our Zones of Occupation. The idea of keeping millions of people hanging about in a sub-human state between earth and hell' threatened to make them all communists. His alternative was 'Let Germany Live!' Reduced British rations were introduced to close the gap between German and British consumption.[34]

Debates over food shortages induced reluctant Britons to concede by 1947 that Germans were fellow-human beings, albeit within the developing Cold War. Public support for feeding Berlin through the 1948–9 airlift, when the Soviet Union blockaded the city, showed just how far the trend had by then gone. The press recycled clichés of the London Blitz to celebrate Berliners' heroism, Germany's 'finest hour' and one that restored a degree of moral equality. For some Britons in the occupation zone this was nothing new, for although the overall tone had been detachment there were always individuals who made friendships. While the CCG and military mainly insisted on formality, the education and cultural branches behaved more flexibly. As early as summer 1945 Spender had interacted normally with German civilians when inspecting libraries in the British zone, and the book of his travels, *European Witness*, carried the message to British readers. Robert Birley both made German friends while working for the CCG and ensured that the British knew about it through his speeches and broadcasts, as well as inviting MPs to take part in debates with democratic Germans. His Anglo-German socialising included a Shakespeare-reading circle which managed an uncut *Hamlet*, but he also brought theatre and music groups to Germany, to see and be seen. Birley would be a lifelong supporter of Wilton Park when it expanded its educational activities from POWs to German civilians, and of the Königswinter conferences. The Governor of Hamburg, Sir Vaughan Berry, was another who invited Germans into his home when the occasion arose; one such was the future Chancellor Helmut Schmidt, who also went to Wilton Park. Hugh Carleton Greene, who had been expelled from Hitler's Germany, telling his friends that he would return one day as *gauleiter*, now took charge of radio in the zone, but although he used his authority to promote a politically neutral broadcasting model on British lines, he co-existed with German staff and allowed satirists even to lampoon the occupation authorities. It was harder work to change attitudes among the military, but the experience of Ian Warner of the Hampshires was probably typical: he recalled that 'as the months progressed, things slowly got better and the anti-German feeling among the troops became tempered with a lighter vein of humour and tolerance – the British soldier is, in the main, a friendly, helpful sort of chap, not given to bearing grudges or hate for long'. The army command though retarded, and in 1947 tried to prevent, further fraternisation; it insisted on defining what was a 'German', so that discipline could be maintained, and expressed horror that fraternisation might lead to the men marrying Germans and acquiring divided loyalties. Security operatives who assumed that the *Manchester Guardian*'s Terence Prittie must be a communist because he tried to make German friends were equally obtuse, but such people were by now unable to hold back the tide, for as the memory of Belsen faded and Cold War urgencies quickened, even army wives began to socialise, often after their children had made local friends. Some noticed and admired the homemaking skills that German mothers demonstrated under such adverse circumstances. At least one wife was effectively forced to integrate when her infant blurted out, 'Those aren't Germans, are they? I thought Germans were animals.' The ubiquity of German nannies among CCG families meant that many young Britons uttered their first words in German, but the choice of Germans as godparents was a conscious act.[35]

If never more than a small proportion of British soldiers brought German wives home when their national service ended (wives often unwelcome to their in-laws, it must be said), there was nevertheless a continuing minority who did just that throughout the forty-year life of the British Army of the Rhine (BAOR). The extension of peacetime conscription until 1960, and increasing manpower requirements in the 1950s, when the BAOR rose from two divisions in Germany to four, meant that for fifteen years a significant proportion of young British males spent months of their lives in Germany – as they had never done before and have not done since. Since this occurred in the final generation that was not otherwise familiar with overseas travel, service in the BAOR had extra impact, for it was the conscripts' only experience of 'abroad'. While they spent time mainly with their mates, even that included bars, sporting fixtures and clubs in nearby towns, and weekend leave visits further afield; almost all visited Berlin, and many availed themselves of ski-holiday facilities at the Winterburg 'winter warfare' school. No doubt few conscripts learned to appreciate the worlds of Goethe and Kant which had long fascinated the most educated Britons, and only a minority appreciated the post-war cultural recovery epitomised by Beethoven performances conducted by Hans Schmidt-Isserstedt on British-controlled Hamburg Radio. There were though thousands who noticed that the north-west German countryside was not unlike Britain, and that once barriers of misunderstanding and language came down, Germans did not seem very unlike the British. There were occasional clashes, as at Minden where the Cameronians earned the nickname 'the poison-dwarfs', but there were also parades that German crowds turned out to watch (even if they were not often impressed by British drill). More commonly, soldiers gradually appreciated such diverse aspects of German life as Christmas markets and an efficient transport system, and Britain seemed grey and charmless when they returned home. Even linguistic barriers would be recalled affectionately. German POWs wondered why the English said, 'How do you do?' when they did not expect an answer, but 'How are you doing?' when they did, while British soldiers could find the phonetic similarity of German words for turkey and dog challenging in restaurants. Few can have been as flummoxed as Birley was when a female administrator assured him that Pforzheim would never recover until the British supplied 'a couple of buggers'; she was not requesting Foreign Office assistance, merely under the impression that this was the British

word for 'Bagger' (a bulldozer). A conscript army involved the whole
nation in the 'German experience' of the BAOR and its RAF counterpart, a fact brought out by huge domestic radio audiences clocked
up by *Two-Way Family Favourites*, a record request show broadcast
by the British Forces Network. One interesting aspect was the way
in which soldiers and airmen in Germany and their families in
Britain followed a single human-interest story, as Cliff Michelmore
and Jean Metcalfe (anchoring the show in Hamburg and London,
respectively) exchanged greetings between servicemen and their girl-
friends each week – but eventually got married themselves.[36]

A mirror image of that BAOR voyage of collective discovery was
experienced in Britain, as POWs gradually made contacts among
the host community. Here, too, children could be a bridge between
mutually suspicious adults, for once allowed out of the camps many
POWs made toys to distribute locally, selling them to buy basic comforts for their families. Initially, only the most trusted POWs were
allowed out of camp, generally only in work parties under guard, but
some were billeted directly with farmers to facilitate working at unso-
cial hours, and gradually restrictions on movement and fraternisation
were lifted. POWs were always allowed out of camp for church services (where some were amazed to find that the British sang, 'Glorious
things of Thee are spoken' to Germany's national anthem), but it was
illegal to enter a British home. Where wider contact developed, it
could still produce the wrong results: the Musicians' Union complained about non-union labour in a POW orchestra fundraising for
a British charity, while in Cheshire a POW band working for 'Save
Europe Now' was banned by a local authority disapproving of 'military music'. In December 1946, however, following vociferous
demands for greater flexibility, general fraternisation was authorised
in time for Christmas; on Christmas Day, queues formed outside
many camps, each Briton collecting 'one live body' (for which the
army made them sign) to take home for lunch; in a Kentish village
where there had previously been petitions against having a camp at
all, there were two hundred invitations to unknown POWs to share
Christmas Day with a family. In the first half of 1947 identifying
marks were removed from POWs' clothes, and they were allowed use
of British money and the postal system; they could also marry British
women (a provision implying that socialising was already wide-

spread), and from Christmas 1947 could leave the camps for weekends and travel about more or less at will. The security risks were not high, for only around one in two hundred tried to escape, it being difficult to get off an island without official papers. Some Britons were initially surprised by POWs they met, finding them rather normal people; if they did not have 'white' status this was especially puzzling, for how could such men be Nazis? As George Bell pointed out in the Lords, this demonstrated the crudity of putting every POW into one of the three groups in the first place, but it did prompt people to ask helpful questions.[37]

Some camps were run by men with limited imaginations, concerned only with security, and here inmates must have found that nineteen-month period of peacetime non-fraternisation interminable, but there were also enlightened commandants who assisted re-education by themselves providing positive role models to teenagers who had previously known nothing but dictatorial authority. One repatriated POW wrote to the education officer Charles Stambrook (Karl Starnberg when fleeing pre-war Vienna) to lay stress on 'the ease of human relations' in his camp: 'It was important that Mr Stambrook and the Commandant were no feared "Authority"', allowing POWs to discover that 'Jews and Britishers are *also* human beings' – as surprising to recipients of Goebbels' propaganda as the British discovery of the ordinariness of individual Germans. POWs in Scottish camps initially believed that special editions of the *Scotsman* were produced, to give them false news about German defeats. The presence of anti-Nazi Germans, especially Jews, among their 're-educators' could itself be a re-education. The British, it hardly needs saying, were less sure, wondering even whether the enlightened Heinz Koeppler was 'too German', and thus 'too domineering', to make a success of re-education.[38]

George Bell was not alone in pressing such issues on behalf of the Churches, for Christian leaders were the most determined advocates of the normalisation of Anglo-German relations, especially once German Protestant leaders acknowledged collective shame for the Nazi period in the October 1945 Stuttgart declaration inspired by the anti-Nazi theologian Martin Niemöller. At the international level, Britain helped to ensure that German Churches were invited to rejoin the World Council of Churches from early 1946, long before other international bodies took such initiatives, and as individuals bishops and Free Church leaders campaigned on POWs' rights and food supplies to Germany (for which Anglicans alone subscribed over a million pounds). They agreed with Birley's assertion that the Churches must tell the British people that Germans were their 'neighbours', in the sense of the Good Samaritan, and welcomed evidence of a religious revival in Germany and among POWs. Here the work had to be done locally, as by Martin Smith in Norfolk, who corresponded with Leo Schnitter and several other former POW-parishioners long after they had returned home.[39]

What could be achieved by enlightened leadership is indicated by the mining community of Ripley in Derbyshire, where the Baptist minister Len Addicott had military experience as an army chaplain. When refused admittance to one local POW camp, he found another where the commandant was more welcoming and the Lutheran pastor happy to try ecumenism. Things began slowly, for few POWs spoke English and no Ripley Baptists spoke German, but communication through music proved easier, the camp's brass band playing for services and a pre-war opera singer POW proving a real find. Church families gave supper to POWs before they returned to camp, illegally at first but with local shops providing equally illegal food; the pastor noticed that more and more Baptist homes displayed a POW's photograph on the mantelpiece. Some locals prophesied disaster, but church attendance increased, the experience of practical Christianity having a bracing effect, and both Bell and Niemöller offered encouragement by letter. When a local cinema or a bus conductor refused POWs admittance, usually by claiming to be already full, the camp commandant helped Addicott shame their superiors into a more liberal policy, while the police confirmed that Riptonians who insulted Germans in the street were already known to them for rough behaviour. Once fraternisation was allowed, POWs joined carol-singing parties, went out with local girls and generally joined the community; some stayed on when their internment ended and a few married locals (at least a thousand POWs nationally, but no doubt thousands more once surveillance of former POWs ended, since recording their marriages then ended too). Many remained friends with their host families, exchanging letters and visits for decades. There can have been few post-war reconciliations that went as well as in Ripley, but less visibly there were thousands of German POWs who experienced hospitable British homes from Christmas 1946 onwards, regular social contact that exceeded anything before or since, and the direct consequence was growing British sympathy for Germans as individuals. Prisoners joked that they were assisted just as the British succoured stray cats, but for men starved of affection and family life the motive hardly mattered, and the consequence was the same. One POW later recalled how his sense of belonging provided revenge against the British occupation forces: overhearing in a Gateshead café a British soldier on leave, boasting that he could always get a *Fräulein* for a couple of cigarettes, he produced a packet of Players, explained that 'in *this* country you get a packet of cigarettes as a present' and gave them to the soldier for free. More common was the dazed recollection of another POW that 'it could only be in Britain' that, when a couple of POWs waited at the head of a queue in the rain, they were the only ones to board the bus when it arrived with room for just two passengers.[40]

Despite the fate of Leo Schnitter, it soon became possible for POWs to delay their repatriation, and from June 1947 to stay in Britain for good, albeit initially only as agricultural workers. Ten per cent of POWs asked permission to stay, mainly those who should have returned to the Russian zone or to areas now outside Germany; with no idea where their families were, unattached young men had not much reason to return, and those attached by then to British girl-friends had every reason to stay. In the end 6 per cent of POWs remained when the camps closed, just over twenty-five thousand Germans to be added to Britain's German community (except that few ex-POWs ever joined a 'community'), about as many as the entire German population in Britain in the 1920s. Through the next two generations almost every farming region of Britain had its share of hard-working Germans, rarely drawing attention to themselves but confounding stereotypes by their ordinariness in churches, pubs and village shops. When the agricultural workforce declined, many moved on to industry, where their presence was further diluted, though any effect on the British would have been equally positive. As the POW generation retired in the 1970s and 1980s, it was increasingly common for ex-POWs from Germany to revisit the scenes of their youthful detention, as the ex-High Court judge Martin Baring did when visiting Lancashire in 1977, thirty years after he had helped to dedicate a 'German Window' in a church in Widnes.[41]

Twenty-five thousand ex-POWs were not much fewer than the 'Hitler émigrés', most of whom also elected to stay in the UK in 1945, to similarly positive effect in eliminating harmful stereotypes, though by the 1950s that community also had its favourite restaurant (Schmidt's, in Charlotte Street), and enough speciality shops in Swiss Cottage for locals to refer to 'Finchleystrasse'. It was during the post-war years that refugees came into their own. Having helped launch Glyndebourne, Rudolph Byng was the administrator who started the Edinburgh Festival in 1947, the opening performances given by the Vienna Philharmonic Orchestra, which went on to London to join a tour by the Vienna State Opera (no actual German company was seen in London until the Bavarians toured in 1953, shortly before theatre audiences also saw performances by Brecht's Berliner Ensemble). The Royal Opera House, Covent Garden, reopened with a German, Karl Rankl, as musical director, proclaiming to the cultured that Germans were welcome back. According to Sir Claus Moser (who ought to know since he became chairman of the board), émigrés provided the backbone of early post-war audiences for opera and had a similar significance at other London arts venues, a fact that says as much about their incomes as their taste. In other cultural worlds, Nikolaus Pevsner, allowed to do little more than clear up bomb debris in wartime, now embarked on his massive evaluation of 'the buildings of England'. It was also now that André Deutsch and George Weidenfeld exerted real influence as publishers, as did another émigré, the 'bouncing Czech' Robert Maxwell. Over in Fleet Street, the *Observer* had an editorial team conspicuous for the number of Germans. The British cultural establishment had thus taken dozens of Germans to its bosom, just when British soldiers in Germany, football crowds in Manchester (as we shall see) and Baptists in Derbyshire were all discovering that Germans were really not too bad. It seemed when the 1950s began that for the first time since 1895 something like normal relations could develop. Belatedly, the British apparently grasped, as Churchill argued in the Commons in 1947, 'that some consideration ought to be given to ordinary people. Everyone is not a Pastor Niemöller or a martyr, and when ordinary people are hurled this way and that, when the cruel hands of tyrants are laid upon them and vile systems of regimentation are imposed and enforced by espionage and other forms of cruelty, there are great numbers of people who succumb.' Perhaps 80 per cent had 'succumbed' and 10 per cent had resisted, if the screening of British POWs was any guide. Even more generously, Churchill added, 'I thank God that in this island home of ours, we have never been put to the test.'[42]

7

'I tries 'ard, Brian, but I 'ates 'em'[1]: Normalising relations in the 1950s and 1960s

Donald Cameron Watt anticipated in 1964 that the forthcoming state visit by the Queen to West Germany offered British people the opportunity of 'examining their own sentiments towards Germany'. The 'need for such a re-examination' was 'acute', since public opinion and government policy were dangerously out of step: 'The state of public opinion has always acted as a brake and a limitation on the freedom of action of the British Government, and as a discouragement to the development of any more cordial and closer relations than the immediate needs of British policy seemed to prescribe.' While formal relations demonstrated 'the traditional realism of Britain's political and professional diplomatic leadership', below stairs there were 'emotional attitudes of hostility'. The *Tagesspiegel* thought in 1965 that while 'individual Englishmen were moved by hardship in Germany after 1945 and tried to help, and their government became involved in the political and economic reconstruction of West Germany, for the English people a barrier remained'. Watt was ideally placed to comment on Anglo-German relations, having begun his career with the Control Commission in Austria, proceeding to three years in the Foreign Office, before beginning at the London School of Economics in 1954 half a century as the pre-eminent British diplomatic historian of his generation. Though his *Britain Looks to Germany* provided evidence that things had been difficult between the two countries, and that below elite levels the British had not stopped thinking about past wars, he mainly described normalising relations over two decades, with realism overcoming emotion. He also warned that Britain and Germany needed each other's friendship more than ever. Recent evidence suggested that the press at least was slowly accepting that fact, allowing a modestly optimistic conclusion. Parallel chapters follow here on the cultural worlds of cinema and soccer but first we shall consider the context of official relationships in the quarter century after 1945. With more access to the private thinking of the elite than was available forty years ago, we can see that its Germanophobia was, if not another brake on the machine, then at least a speed limit. Britain did eventually accept a more normal relationship with Germany, but it was slow going.[2]

It is surprising that Britain should have had difficult relations with a state which she had helped to shape in the first place, for while there was no rush to praise Germans, there was plenty of writing about the wisdom of British policy in Germany: the graceless tendency was to claim credit when German democracy seemed to be working and to blame Germans when it did not. If few argued that all that was best in German democracy derived from the British input, this was nevertheless an inference easily drawn: Robert Birley welcomed Raymond Ebsworth's *Restoring Democracy in Germany* (1960) as the story of 'a stimulating and exciting time', when re-educators had done 'a piece of work of which our country can afford to be proud'. Some such claims had limited justification, for while few democratic structures in West Germany followed directly the re-educators' models, many bore an imprint of decisions taken before Germans recovered self-government. Once policy-makers understood that a Germany under a single government, as the Russians demanded, would pose political dangers far outweighing its economic benefits, Britain pressed instead for economic integration (and in due course political union) of the Western occupation zones; first 'bizonia' when the British and American zones were merged economically, then France joined to avoid the disproportionate economic burden of going it alone; the 1948 'Westmark' that provided the cement for economic union also sealed 'East Germany' into Russia's East European empire. The eventual constitutional arrangements were also most to the British taste: torn between desire for centralisation for economic reasons and decentralisation for political ones, the British model of a federalised state became the natural compromise on which the Western Allies converged. By mid-1947, elected *Land* governments had limited internal authority before any central government was restored, though the occupiers remained free to veto their decisions; only then did a West German federal government emerge. In this, the occupiers had not bargained for the reassertion of German traditions once they were free to make their own decisions, nor for the effect of Konrad Adenauer's forceful personality over his long chancellorship in influencing the implementation of such theories.[3]

In detail, too, Britain left behind influences after she had handed back power. The electoral system for the British zone was in due course adopted for all of West Germany (and from 1990 also in East Germany). Britain demanded a 'first past the post' system to ensure parliamentary majorities and strong government rather than the weak coalitions of 1919–33 (which most Germans were equally determined not to revisit), but had to compromise with Germans' own preference for greater proportionality between votes and seats than Britain herself has ever enjoyed. There was arrogance here, the belief that Britons understood democratic elections and Germans did not; a CCG directive reminded staff that British democracy was 'the most robust in the world. It is on British soil that it flourishes best, but we do export it, and, tended carefully, it grows and flourishes in diverse lands, even if it takes a long time to acclimatise itself.' Hence, occupation authorities insisted that ballot boxes must be collected into one place before counting, a British practice dropped in the 1950s; Germans joked that the British also prescribed the length of pieces of string connecting pencils to voting booths. The eventual hybrid system was only semi-proportional representation, but from about 1970 it was often proposed for Britain itself, Germany by then having become a mature democracy rather than an infant expected to learn from its elders. In local government structures, too, there were residual British influences, for three of the four zonal *Länder* retained structures the British set up; Germans visiting Britain later could not understand why the British, having insisted on local autonomy, spent the next half century demolishing the independence of their own local authorities. In developing political parties the British thought these should emerge from below, and preferred a small number of large parties rather than the Weimar Republic's rainbow of fragments; what emerged were three major parties not unlike Britain's own. British authorities banned parties of the extreme Right, as when the Deutsche Reichspartei briefly won control of Wolfsburg in 1948, but this stance was supported by German political leaders, while the 1951 ban on the Sozialistische Reichspartei was jointly imposed by Adenauer's federal government and the occupiers. In broadcasting the British approach remained in restrictions on the influence of political parties. *Die Welt*, first published in the British zone in 1946, was modelled on *The Times* and also attempted detachment from the party fray. Efforts to depoliticise Germany's civil service were unsuccessful, the vested interests of those in post proving an effective barrier. There was also only partial success in limiting political management of the police – another area where Britain would not in future practise what she was then preaching. Even such failures were triumphs from another perspective, though, for the success of German democracy since 1945 owes something to the fact that the Allies did not impose a model of their own, teaching a lesson in respect for other people's views that worked best when they did not get their way. They welcomed the Basic Law, effectively West Germany's constitution when occupation ended in 1949, as 'happily' combining 'German democratic tradition' with broader concepts of representative government – which by inference had been imported from somewhere else, but adopted by German choice.[4]

Education also showed mixed results, though since re-education was a prime objective, more might have been hoped for. Those who worked in education had a good basis for their work, for they were bound to take what Watt called 'an optimistic idealistic view of the amenability of human nature to improvement through correction'. A few suffered from the CCG's 'Raj' mentality: one felt for 'his' university 'the same paternal regard as a District Commissioner would feel for his native tribes, or an officer of a Gurkha regiment for his men'. German education was traditionally more egalitarian than Britain's, there being no influential private sector, and educational historians have lamented a lost chance to reform German schools as comprehensives during the occupation, but this was hardly likely with re-educators who were themselves products of British public schools, notably Robert Birley, temping in Germany between heading Charterhouse and Eton. For Birley, the main problem was that Bismarck had obstructed the development of political education in Germany, so the country had remained politically immature; what mattered now was not the schools 'but *what* [was] taught in them and how it [was] taught'. Structures remained intact and education policy consisted mainly of the reinstatement of Germany's pre-Nazi liberal heritage, encouraged by visits to schools abroad and short training courses in Germany, to remind teachers what free education looked like. Few guidelines were available, and one CCG educator in charge of the ancient university of Göttingen, when he asked what the job would entail, was told, 'For Christ's sake man, find out when you get there.' Such advice was not as silly as it sounds, for dealing with sheer physical destruction through improvisation was the most urgent requirement: Kiel University reopened only by using ships in the harbour as teaching space, while only a tenth of Cologne's schools were habitable. There was though an inescapable curriculum problem, for Nazi education incorporated every subject into its ideology: Douglas Botting cites an arithmetic question asking pupils, 'If it takes 50,000 members of the Wehrmacht three days to conquer Holland [area given], how long will it take 80,000 men to conquer England [area given]?' Such biases were easy to remove once teachers had been denazified, but there remained real difficulty in subjects like history: a crash programme to print 'democratic' textbooks was undermined by their failure to allow for teaching German history, since the Allies – never mind the Germans – could not agree on what facts to include, let alone the lessons to be drawn from them. Something similar occurred when an international team wrestled with producing books 'without bias' for German children, a worthy enterprise which showed that even Copernicus remained controversial (since both Germans and Poles now claimed him). British officials advised that Frederick the Great might be emphasised less than had been traditional, and that colonial expansion (British as well as German) was best avoided altogether, though the Napoleonic Wars were encouraged as subject-matter – Britain and Germany having then been on the same side. Both teachers and pupils relished freedom after years of crushing control, it being noted how stimulating it was to rediscover Jerome K. Jerome. By contrast, an English reader used during East Germany's educational reconstruction included Dickens extracts as if they typified contemporary Britain; bullying scenes from *Tom Brown's Schooldays* were also prominently featured.[5]

In broader terms, educationalists took the indirect approach even more subtly than the CCG as a whole, and were so keen not to force British methods on reluctant Germans that they encouraged teachers to visit Swiss and Scandinavian schools as well as British ones. Likewise, although Ernest Bevin in 1947 called on British universities to make 'a great missionary effort' to help their German counterparts, and vice-chancellors sponsored visits, delegations and committee reports, the recovery of German universities was substantially achieved by Germans, once purged of their Nazi masters. As education adviser, Birley kept a close eye on the job, but was careful to limit his interventions, so that practical self-government would be learned: speaking in 1947, and citing in support of his views Max Weber, he strongly opposed the imposition of 'intensive education' in Germany as human engineering, which would over-standardise exactly as the Nazis had done. Since education was one of the first services handed back to Germans when *Land* governments reappeared, the education branch then concerned itself with cultural affairs. Eventually renamed the 'Cultural Branch', it established 'British Centres' in German cities which remained as information offices when occupation ended, suggestively named *die Brücken* – bridges.[6]

Another bridge emerged from the educational programme, when reciprocal visits of British and German teenagers began in 1950, the first boat bringing pupils from Arnsberg to the West Riding of Yorkshire; in 1952 these exchanges involved about ten thousand annual visits. Twinning arrangements already existed between British and German local authorities, as between Bristol and Hanover, but regional exchanges now added conferences that involved groups of towns on both sides: Leeds and Dortmund, Sheffield and Bochum, Wakefield and Herne; outside Yorkshire, Oxford and Bonn. Such educational connections were still being developed nearly thirty years after the war, when York twinned with Münster in 1974, and did not only involve the former British zone; by then, regional programmes linked Scotland with Bavaria and the English south-west with Lower Saxony. By the 1990s, there were four hundred local twinning arrangements and eight hundred school pairings; twenty thousand German children each year came to Britain; but only half as many British teenagers went to Germany.[7]

Helping to reconstruct post-war Germany was a commentary on British assumptions about Germans and about themselves. It was repeatedly denied as being about imposing anything on the defeated enemy, *The Times* reminding its readers on the day of the German army's surrender that Germany had a humanist tradition of her own. But Germans were constantly suspicious of the importation of 'the British way of life', and some émigrés returning to Germany did have this aim. Re-education was informed by 'a vague feeling', as Henry Faulk put it, 'that it was necessary to make the Germans more like the British'. Democracy, of which the British thought themselves the special guardians, was installed on the foundation of this assumption, which had developed out of the belief that Germans were naturally authoritarian, unlike 'us'. It certainly seemed this way to many Germans: a cartoon in the *Kasseler Zeitung* in January 1951 depicted the High Commissioner lecturing a German, 'You must not see things through German spectacles. Copy the English!' 'How do the English see things?' 'Through English spectacles.' Attempts to encourage Westphalians to play cricket were no more successful than American efforts to launch baseball in Bavaria, but both campaigns tell us much about the re-educators. Unsurprisingly, re-educators were delighted that one in five POWs in Britain learned English. Faulk thought this 'a vital factor' in the encouragement of civilian contacts; as an ex-schoolmaster, he presumably had little hope that the British might ever learn German, but then this would not have been quite the same thing anyway, since it was assumed that learning must be a one-way process. Camp authorities took equal pleasure when POWs put on English as well as German plays, though goodness knows what image of Britain was conveyed to POW audiences by the plays most frequently chosen: *Pygmalion*, *Charley's Aunt* and *Troilus and Cressida*. Similarly, a Northumbrian camp, once dubbed *Deutschland am Tyne*, helped change minds by staging *As You Like It*, though locals probably had no idea that educated Germans had long known Shakespeare. Those POWs in a Scottish camp who called their commandant 'Irene' because he wore a kilt had clearly not learned to appreciate Britishness to quite the same extent.[8]

How deep any of this went is questionable, for neither the British nor the Germans found the other especially attractive in the mass. When surveyed by UNESCO in 1953, only 1 per cent of Germans thought Britain a country in which they would like to live (though nearly half preferred Switzerland or America to Germany); even fewer Britons reported any desire to live in Germany, though once again about half ideally wanted to live somewhere else (mainly America or the white Commonwealth). Self-attributes measured by the survey again suggest that a huge gulf still existed.

Do you associate the following words with your own country or other countries (% Yes)?

Attribute	British self-image	German self-image	German view of British
Hardworking	57	90	13
Intelligent	62	64	34
Practical	47	53	20
Conceited	11	15	23
Generous	48	11	14
Brave	59	63	8
Self-controlled	44	12	24
Progressive	31	39	17
Peace-loving	77	37	15

As this table suggests, Germans could be self-critical, but they still had a lower opinion of the British. The British, on the other hand, where the survey did not even ask respondents their opinion of foreigners, seemed blind to their own faults (if less so than Americans, 96 per cent of whom thought America the only place to live). In the context of re-education, 59 per cent of Germans believed that national characteristics 'are born in us', though half also said that such characteristics could be changed over time (a view held by under a third of the British, who were supposed to believe in re-education). Britain just did not register with Germans asked to rank their most and least favourite countries, but Germany was the second-least popular country among the British, though mentioned by only half as many as cited Soviet Russia, so far had the Cold War already taken over the national psyche. Underlining Watt's identification of a gap between the elite and the rest, those Britons most hostile to Germany (apart from the old, who had after all experienced two world wars), were the working class; those least unfavourable to Germany were the professional classes and the rich. Bridges were needed, but would British workers cross them?[9]

In fact bridges existed mainly at the elite level, and although they were enthusiastically supported, they would make little impact on the main problems, differences of opinion within Britain and the one-sidedness of the process. Although German local authorities provided funds to keep British information offices open, there were no such German centres in British cities, and at first no awareness by the German government that it needed to woo British opinion. By the end of the 1950s this had become a major preoccupation of German ambassadors in London; Watt thought that by 1964 they had already done valuable work, though once again overwhelmingly among the metropolitan elite. It could be heavy going, for the slightest slip brought the press crashing down on them. The *Daily Express* had a great time reporting in 1957 a German diplomat's demand for reinstatement after being sacked, the ostensible cause being his wife saying during a reception that 'England is enemy territory'. His defence, that she merely meant German diplomats in Britain had 'a difficult job to do', did not much help. Wilton Park did not enjoy universal British admiration either: the British army refused to assist parties of civilians travelling to courses there, it being 'highly undesirable that Germans should be accommodated in a transit camp with Service personnel, from a disciplinary, security and morale point of view'. On their way home, one party had the food parcels given by British sympathisers confiscated by Customs at Harwich, since they were not allowed even to export goods permitted to returning POWs. Reporting this in *Tribune*, George Orwell remarked that the newspaper carrying the story had added, 'without apparent irony', that the Germans had been in Britain 'on a six-weeks course in democracy'. After that sticky start, conditions improved, and the decision to keep Wilton Park open when the POWs left, henceforth for German civilians, was a key moment, since it meant, as Ebsworth put it, that 'year after year, there came to courses German politicians, journalists, teachers, trades unionists, to see and discuss British democratic practices, but also the burning questions of the day such as European Unity, the Cold War, disarmament and post-war economic reconstruction'. Though courses were in German, to be accessible to the widest cross-section of German civilians, social-ising was done with visiting speakers in English too. Many students ultimately became leaders of their country, and Willy Brandt later declared that 'almost a whole generation of German politicians defined their concept of and attitude towards Britain and the British on the basis of impressions they received at Wilton Park'; Helmut Schmidt thought it 'a most significant chapter in Anglo-German relations'. Such was its popularity that when in 1956 the Foreign Office tried to close it down to save money, Wilton Park was rescued by German funds, much as Germany had already paid for its own re-education and for the British Army of the Rhine. 'Wilton Park' moved to Sussex and reopened as a European Centre rather than an Anglo-German one, thereby surviving but losing its special mission. This was all understandable within the general illusion of the time, that Britain's problem with Germans would wither away in a common European future: 'the only possible ideal is a federal Germany in a federal Europe', thought Harold Nicolson, as early as 1946.[10]

Other mechanisms – generally more informal and less intensive – existed alongside Wilton Park. Nicolson attended the dinner in London in October 1952 at which an Anglo-German Association was launched, with around two hundred members. He thought that Foreign Secretary Eden made 'a good speech', and the German chargé d'affaires 'an honourable one'. Required to reply, Nicolson found it hard, 'in front of so distinguished an audience'; it cannot have helped when his wife insisted that such contacts amounted to 'shaking hands with blood-stained murderers, who would start it all up again if they had the chance'. Eight years later the Duke of Edinburgh addressed another dinner, urging no more 'stoking up the fires of hatred and suspicion', though newspapers commented on the time he himself spent in Germany among rela-tions. The most significant initiative was the establishment of the

Königswinter conferences of the Anglo-German Association, begun in a Rhineland town in 1949, the brainchild of a local enthusiast, Lilo Milchsack, and enthusiastically backed by Robert Birley; the conferences have continued annually, with the award of an exalted title to Milchsack as Dame Lilo showing how highly they are valued in British government circles. Violet Bonham Carter never missed a Königswinter conference; she felt such 'loyalty' that she went even when feeling hardly fit for extended travelling. Meetings could be useful as lightning conductors, as when Anglophile Germans needed reassurance that not all Britons had gone mad during the Suez crisis ('they had written off the French, but they believed in us', noted Lady Violet). Hugh Gaitskell had a similarly surreal experience, reassuring German Social Democratic Party (SPD) members who demanded to know 'how people in the Twentieth Century at this date could think in terms like the Suez group of the Tory Party'. In North Rhine–Westphalia the SPD was at the time in coalition with Free Democrats whom Gaitskell thought 'neo-Nazis' – until Milchsack arranged for him to meet their younger leaders. Early meetings also conveyed lessons to Germans in the seamier side of democracy, as squabbling Labour delegates practised procedures learned in smoke-filled rooms at Blackpool – packing committees, nobbling rapporteurs, and ensuring that someone sensible spoke after Richard Crossman, to repair the damage. Gaitskell was by 1956 sufficiently impressed by Königswinter to suggest that similar Anglo-Russian meetings could be run, 'but it would be no good if the whole idea was to put across Soviet propaganda rather than to have a genuine exchange of views'.[11]

With a view to the future, there were also 'Young Königswinter' meetings of an Anglo-German youth scheme, and such events specific to individual professions as the Vale lectures on 'German Educational Reconstruction' for teachers, visiting talks funded initially by an English couple who had been influenced by German refugees living with them in 1942. It is surely significant that by 1957 this mechanism for the exchange of views by private citizens had three hundred German corresponding members but only fifty in Britain, and that after successful fundraising in 1946–50 its finances and its activities then steadily declined; the society was dissolved in 1958.[12]

The effect of continuous pressure for better relations can be seen in conversions from former antagonism among warriors, re-educators and diplomats. Field Marshal Earl Alexander had decided by May 1952 that although 'war was a tradition among men' (a view he nevertheless attributed to Clausewitz, and to Prussian traditions), atomic bombs could mean 'the end of war, by making war impossible'. In the meantime, he thought, 'now was the time to show an imaginative policy to Germany: we should lose all if we niggled'. Raymond Ebsworth concluded in 1959 that 'even when one reads . . . of some session of the Bundestag reminiscent of the worst days of the Weimar Republic, one can, I think, console oneself with the thought that this is a passing phenomenon. After all, the base is sound.' A positive view was taken even by Robert Vansittart, who accordingly wrote to *The Times* in May 1954: after endorsing a recent editorial's view that 'steadfast support' for European union in Germany had been 'the most encouraging feature of post-war Europe', he added: 'My lifelong antipathy to Germany is known, yet for once in all the blue moons of existence I acknowledge a German Government and tendency which might perhaps be turned to the account of Christian civilisation.' For Van, it just did not get more generous than that.[13]

Despite growing support for friendship and understanding, unreconstructed attitudes persisted on the bridge of the British ship of state, as well as below decks. There were narrow parameters to the acceptance of Germany, limits present and future as well as deriving from the past: when Bishop Bell proposed in May 1957 to talk on BBC Radio about German resistance to Hitler, a lecture he had given to great acclaim in Germany, the offer was refused because the BBC felt 'an official voice ought to put the opposite point of view' (presumably that there had been no effective resistance), but no official was prepared to offer one. Books on German resistance were usually reviewed as being much ado about nothing, while accounts of the Holocaust mainly ignored Hitler's Gentile victims. Small wonder that when Bell died in the following year, just hours before President Heuss was to announce a German decoration for him, he was mourned as one of Germany's best friends abroad, and commemorated in a 'Bell Room' in Berlin-Schoenfeld's Church Centre. Within the Attlee cabinet of 1945–51 there were few men with a good word to say for Germans; Attlee himself once remarked that he'd never met a good German, except possibly when his wife had one as a housemaid. Dalton remained to his dying day obsessively anti-German: meeting Callaghan, Jenkins and Jay in June 1952 he 'told them that Germans were murderers, individuals excepted. They'd killed all my friends in the First World War etc. *Deutschland über Alles* was their song and they meant it.' Churchill scoffed at such views in 1950, pointing out that the German anthem was no more offensive to foreigners than 'Rule Britannia'. Ernest Bevin did not harbour grudges as deeply as Dalton, but was uncomfortable in Germans' company, did not visit Germany more than was strictly necessary, and did not measure his words when there. His private secretary later recalled that 'though Ernie accepted that there was a convincing case for bringing . . . the Germans' into the international community, 'he did not really relish the prospect'. Germans certainly thought him hostile. The *Rheinische Post* considered in 1950, when Bevin rejected Churchill's suggestion to accelerate Germany's reacceptance internationally, that he could 'not forget what the Germans had done in two wars'; National Socialism was for him 'characteristic of the German mentality'. In 1947 Bevin himself had told the British Military Governor in Germany, General Sir Brian Robertson (and Robertson enjoyed quoting this to others), 'I tries 'ard Brian, but I 'ates 'em'.[14]

When Bevin was briefly succeeded at the Foreign Office by Herbert Morrison, that viewpoint acquired cockney rather than Bristolian vowels but otherwise changed little, and when Anthony Eden took over he added mainly aspirates and an Oxonian polish. Back in 1919, Eden had written that Louvain, where he had just seen the destruction wrought by the German army, 'stamps the Germans for ever as entirely lacking in love of the beautiful and as a brutish monster beneath a veneer of civilisation'. From 1940 to 1963, all four British prime ministers were veterans of the Western Front of 1914–18, surrounded in cabinet by men of the same vintage. Those with military experience in the Second World War – Crosland, Healey and Jenkins, Heath, Maudling and Whitelaw – took a less deterministic view of Germans, but their generation had in 1945 two decades to wait for real power. They applauded in 1953 when Churchill preached reconciliation after leftist MPs criticised a visit by Rommel's chief of staff. He somewhat generously praised Rommel as an anti-Nazi, and received thanks from the Afrika Korps veterans' club. If the Labour

Left's line were pursued, Churchill argued, 'there would be no peace possible between those two great branches of the human family. Such keeping alive of hatred was one of the worst injuries that could be done to the peace of the world.' Nor was this only a debating point for public occasions: in 1954 he told his doctor that 'if millions of people in one country learn to hate millions in another, trouble is bound to come. This fellow Aneurin Bevan is deliberately stirring up anger and passion by bringing up Germany's aims in the war. It is very wrong.' No doubt, but he himself gained little popularity from preaching harmony, for many Conservatives also doubted whether Germans had changed – or even could change – their ways. That was certainly true of diehards like Lords Swinton and Chandos, while Churchill himself counted virulent anti-Germans like Lord Beaverbrook and Brendan Bracken among his cronies. He could not himself resist the type of witticisms that have so bedevilled better understanding: the trouble with Germans, he once said, was that they were always either at your feet or at your throat. He resisted several Adenauer invitations to visit Germany as Prime Minister (something even Attlee had managed), and evaded an act of public reconciliation when the Chancellor suggested a meeting attended by their grandchildren for exactly that purpose. Having been surprised by Berliners' cheers in 1945, Churchill was relieved not to be booed when he collected his Charlemagne Prize ten years later. Rather than his usual message of reconciliation, he told the Aachen audience that demands for reunion with the German East must be put aside, for this could be only 'a unity of ashes and death'. This was a brutal reminder of 1945 and utterly out of keeping with the occasion. Even among younger men in Churchill's cabinet, anti-Germanism was rampant: both Peter Thorneycroft and David Eccles went public with their views, in 1956–7, seeing in West Germany's economic recovery the renewal of an older threat. Harold Macmillan, Prime Minister between 1957 and 1963, retained a vision of Germany much like the one acquired through a trench periscope in 1916. Speculating in 1956 on whether the Messina conference which pressed towards European integration would 'come off', he feared that a success would mean 'Western Europe dominated in fact by Germany and used as an instrument for the revival of German power through economic means. It is really giving them on a plate what we fought two world wars to prevent.' Even at Adenauer's funeral in 1967, noticing 'the guard of honour, those coal-scuttle helmets', Macmillan decided, 'they haven't changed'. Maybe they had and maybe they hadn't, but he hadn't.[15]

Stereotypes blowing in the wind long after the storm has passed are notoriously hard to pin down, but the flavour of assumptions about Germany within post-1945 Britain was nicely evoked by the Anglo-Irish poet D. J. Enright. Since he worked so long in the Far East, his main 'post-war' preoccupation was with the Japanese, but he was troubled enough by an academic year at the Free University in Berlin to write suggestively about Germany. Enright did not like Berlin, where the only choice lay between 'boredom and factitious excitement', and although he had been previously disgusted by 'the bad public behaviour of the Japanese', 'the good public behaviour of the Germans, compared to whom the British are a rabble of hysterical dagoes', alarmed him even more: 'Disorder along with charm is feasible' (he was part Irish) and 'order accompanied by politeness is highly acceptable' (and part English), but 'order accompanied by a stupid uncouthness is intolerable'. That blast in his 1969 memoir is supported by an anecdote about the terrible consequence of standing in the wrong place to queue for a postage stamp, so that he could 'not have any official existence among the customers of the post office'. Enright demonstrated positive feelings for German literature, and in his essay 'Aimez-vous Goethe?' persuasively explained British resistance: they found it 'wordy, philosophical, humourless, both highly abstract and crammed with details', yet resistance to the literature was really resistance to Germans.[16]

Some Men Are Brothers (1962) includes 'Am Steinplatz', an evocation of the Berlin square near Enright's apartment in Charlottenburg, where twin memorials to the victims of Hitler and Stalin demanded the citizen's attention and sympathy. Yet the memory of war was passing by 1956, the park's memorials bearing only 'the fading ribbons of the fading wreaths', while Berliners got on with their lives, heeding everything but the memorials' injunction to remember: 'They have forgotten. As they must. / Remember those who live. Yes they are right. They must.' A dog's antics seem like 'a game of war', though it was a 'nice doggie: never killed a Jew, or Gentile'. 'No Offence' has a mood straight out of Jerome but mixed with memories of

Auschwitz: 'In no country, are the disposal services more efficient'. Dustbins are efficiently emptied, 'You could dispose of a corpse like this / Without giving the least offence.' And on he goes, through public lavatories, where 'your sins are washed away', with 'a roar like distant Wagner'; ambulances that arrive, 'before the police, the bystanders and the neighbouring shopkeepers have finished lecturing you'; and 'burial facilities' which are the best in the world. All this, we discover, goes through his mind:

> As I am sorted out, dressed down, lined up,
> Shepherded through the door,
> Marshalled across the smooth-faced asphalt,
> And fed into the mouth of a large cylinder,
> Labelled 'Lufthansa'.

In *Addictions* (1965) Enright reacts in 'Apocalypse' to reading in a Berlin tourist brochure how difficult it had been for musicians in 1945; but soon, even 'while the town still reeked of smoke, charred buildings and the stench of corpses', the Berlin Philharmonic 'bestowed the everlasting and imperishable joy which music never fails to give'. He begins with a savage verse on the morality of such recollections:

> It soothes the savage doubts.
> One Bach outweighs ten Belsens. If 200,000 people
> Were remaindered at Hiroshima, the sales of So-and-So's
> New novel reached a higher figure in as short a time.

So 'All, in a sense, goes on. All is in order.' An insect may be crushed by a reed warbler as it sings, 'Still, the everlasting and imperishable joy / Which music never fails to give is being given.' Which, of course, is not a lot of help to the insect; all this is not only about Germans, but about other countries uncertainly rehabilitating Germany.[17]

The reading public during the Cold War would have acquired greater familiarity with Germany through spy thrillers, notably from John Le Carré and Len Deighton, in whose espionage novels Berlin is both the battleground and an excuse to discuss the Germans. Since the Cold War was against the Russians, it is extraordinary how often the villains of such books are Germanic, if not actually Germans: Blofeld and Goldfinger, Karfeld and 'Karla', Mundt and Stinnes. James Bond's opponents do not really belong on that list, for Ian Fleming turned away from Cold War backgrounds just when Le Carré and Deighton arrived; henceforth his locations were increasingly exotic, and the enemy shifted from communist SMERSH to the international crooks of SPECTRE, though three ex-Gestapo men did retain their places in the latter's first team.[18]

With John Le Carré there was no retreat from Germany, always central in his thought-world; he taught German at Eton before joining the diplomatic service, has deep knowledge of German culture, and served as a diplomat in Bonn while writing his earliest novels. His philosophy is thought to derive from Schiller, while the hero of *The Naïve and Sentimental Lover* (1971) is himself a Schiller scholar, as the title implies. Germany is ever present in Le Carré's spy novels and within the characters' inner lives; it seems natural that British agents use the satirical journal *Simplicissimus* as a codebook in *A Perfect Spy* (1986), though for British readers he has to explain what the book actually was. George Smiley, Le Carré's recurrent hero, originally joined 'the Circus' in the 1930s to oppose Germany (not Nazis); he speaks German like a native, taught literature at 'an obscure German university', and occasionally withdraws from the Circus to dabble in seventeenth-century German love lyrics. All Le Carré's characters have secrets from the Second World War, and in *The Looking Glass War* (1965) the 1940s seem more real to his characters than the sixties; the novel offers a perspective on Britain's inability to come to terms with contemporary, prosperous Germany, while hinting that a neo-Nazi undercurrent links the past with the Federal Republic. The neo-Nazi Karfeld makes that link:

> Germany was rich . . . Richer than England he added casually, but we must not be rude to the English for the English won the war after all, and were a people of uncommon gifts. His voice remained wonderfully reasonable as he recited all the English gifts: their mini skirts, their pop singers, their Empire that was falling apart, their national deficit . . . Without these gifts, Europe would surely fail.

Karfeld's irony can be compared with an outburst by the British policeman Mendel in *Call for the Dead* (1961): 'Krauts. Huns. Jerries. Bloody Germans. Wouldn't give you sixpence for the lot of them. Carnivorous ruddy sheep. Kicking Jews about again. Us all over. Knock 'em down, set 'em up. Forgive and forget. *Why* bloody well forget, I'd like to know? Why forget murder and rape just because millions committed it?' Concern about post-war German democracy also arises in *A Small Town in Germany* (1968), where the narrator thinks Bonn 'a stained and secret capital village', a 'state within a village', populated by men hiding Nazi pasts while planning a neo-Nazi future.[19]

As Le Carré's spy novels developed, their geographical focus moved back towards London, where members of the Circus play intricate games of spy-catching among themselves, though continually referring back to earlier days and German connections. In the 1960s Le Carré's fiction was firmly anchored in West Germany; his first novel, *Call for the Dead*, is set there, and the best-seller that made his name, *The Spy Who Came in from the Cold* (1963), both begins and ends at the Berlin Wall, with other scenes set in East Germany. The film was a big enough production to entice Richard Burton into the main role, and reinforced the impact of the novel, as did later television adaptations of the Smiley books. The villain in *The Spy Who Came in from the Cold*, Hans-Dieter Mundt, is a blond former Gestapo man, 'ex-Hitler Youth and all that kind of thing', as is the woman jailer, delighted that 'Comrade Mundt knows what to do with Jews'. The East German prosecutor is 'a very tough man. Looks like a country doctor, small and benevolent. Used to be at Buchenwald.' The anti-heroic hero, Alec Leamas, worked in Berlin for the BBC and hence is usefully bilingual, rendering help from Germans superfluous. If East Germans are involved in the Cold War as practitioners, West Germans are onlookers treated with little respect by the British: 'If the allies weren't here, the wall would be gone by now,' mutters a Berlin policeman. 'So would Berlin,' they reply. When interrogated about the Circus, and asked if he discusses its philosophy with colleagues, Leamas laughingly replies, 'No, we're not Germans.' Mundt, though, thinks Germans 'too introspective to make good agents', while his deputy confesses that 'as a nation we tend to over-organise'. Here is Germany with Nazism alive and well, albeit living in the East, while democratic West Germans are merely spectators.[20]

If Le Carré moved towards London-centred plots, Len Deighton's novels went the other way. Divided Berlin and the possibility of German reunification are constant themes, while the nature of Germans becomes increasingly a preoccupation: a character in *Spy Story* (1974) remarks that the Foreign Office had once fed all the data on a united Germany into its computer 'and didn't like the scenario one little bit'. Deighton exhibits, as Edward Milward Oliver puts it, a 'fascination with the complicated soul of the Twentieth-Century German', even in stories written between 1962 and 1966 and especially in the three 'Bernard Samson' trilogies written between 1983 and 1996. In *The Ipcress File* (1962) 'Jay' is a Pole who worked for Nazi Germany, the hero is bilingual in German and English, his boss previously worked in Munich, and 'Grenade' was first active in the French resistance in 1940; none of these references is central to the plot but cumulatively they remind us that the characters have a history in fighting or assisting Nazi Germany. In *Funeral in Berlin* (1964) the war is more central: marketing presented the novel as 'a game in which the bloodstained legacy of Nazi Germany is enmeshed in the intricate moves of cold war espionage'. Opening and closing scenes are set in London, but each time there is a newspaper announcing, 'Berlin: new crisis?' while much of the action in between is set in Germany, where Nazi survivors remain at large; Berlin is 'sitting at attention upon Brandenburg', and physical reminders of Bismarck and Hitler are ever present. West German intelligence represents both 'the new prosperous Germany' and 'something much older', just as East German organisations employ former Nazis; offered unlimited help by the West German authorities, the hero quips that he cannot decide between 'having Dover encircled and Stalingrad subjugated'. The plot revolves around a wartime murder in a concentration camp and money stolen from murdered Jews. A Russian, pondering German efficiency, muses, 'I sometimes wonder how we managed to beat them.' When his colleague asks, 'The Nazis?' he responds, 'Oh, we still haven't beaten them. The Germans I mean.' The climax comes with a re-enactment of the war during a Guy Fawkes party, the hero hurling fireworks as if they were grenades and immolating the villain with a flamethrower. In nobody's mind is the war yet over, and for no one has Germany made a clean break with the past. Unsurprisingly, Deighton also wrote novels set in wartime and non-fiction about the war.[21]

Professional historians exhibited a similar fascination with Germany, often as 'the German problem'. The experience of defeat and occupation in 1940 or 1944–5 made recent events too painful for most post-war European historians; British historians, though, conscious of being counted among the sheep rather than the goats, devoted great effort to understanding the dramatic events through which they had just lived. Like many professions, history-writing was in the 1950s dominated by conservative elders, who (as Donald Watt feelingly wrote in 1964) 'were drawn from the patriotic chauvinist right', men like Sir John Wheeler-Bennett, whose specialism had in any case been modern international history. Wheeler-Bennett's books on the Munich crisis (1948) and the German army (1953) were classics, doubting neither Germany's guilt nor that Nazism derived from the longer tides of German history. Alongside these conservatives was a clutch of leftists taking a remarkably similar view of German history: E. H. Carr, Geoffrey Barraclough and A. L. Rowse. Together, through books and reviews, this ill-assorted bunch ensured, as Watt put it, 'that the dominant passions of the war gave way to a deep and enduring antipathy to Germany and all things German, from which only a handful of the intellectual elite escaped'. A few straws bear witness to that wind. When the liberal musicologist Alec Robertson wrote on the Czech composer Dvořák, he incorporated unnecessary paragraphs on the history of Czechs and Germans to make his Vansittartite point: discussing migrations into medieval Bohemia, he thought 'there is a familiar sound about German merchants settling, like a swarm of ants, around Prague Castle between 1061 and 1092', eight centuries before Dvořák himself arrived. Though Bohemian Germans improved art, industry and agriculture, 'of course they only did so at the price of retarding Czech progress and self-determination'. Later chapters record Germans' remorseless efforts to retard Dvořák's growing fame, underplaying Brahms as his greatest champion abroad. Angus Wilson's novel *Anglo-Saxon Attitudes* (1956) has a similarly distant focus, a historian's investigation into whether a distinguished predecessor faked evidence about the conversion of Britain from paganism, but he manages to work in the collaboration of German historians with the Nazis. There is a rival historian, Pforzheim, who is, thinks the president of the Medievalists' Association, 'a nice Hun, if there was such a thing'. Francis Carsten's scholarly *The Rise of Prussia*, which stopped well short of modern times, nevertheless prompted the *Times Literary Supplement*'s reviewer to detect 'the fatal alliance' of the Junkers and the throne, which would soon have such terrible effects. His fellow *TLS* reviewer thought even Wheeler-Bennett's book on the German army did not go far enough in condemning the July 1944 conspirators ('that feeble and ill-starred plot . . . which has been so much over-exploited in the interests of the myth of German resistance') or the alliance of the army with industry ('The rehabilitation of Herr Krupp may yet be seen as an important date in history'). A few years later, reviewing Terence Prittie's *Germany Divided*, and regretting that West Germany was 'blatantly materialistic', the *TLS* sulkily agreed that 'one would rather have its citizens making money than guns'. When Karl Jaspers' *The Idea of the University* was translated into English in 1960, its editor reminisced at length about those 'who had forsaken the books of Kant for the loudspeakers of Goebbels'.[22]

The most influential historian with the reading public was A. J. P. Taylor, neither a man of the establishment nor a conventional socialist. Taylor wrote for the intellectual *New Statesman*, the labour movement's *Daily Herald* and the empire-worshipping *Sunday Express*; in 1957 he seized his chance to become Britain's first 'telly don' with virtuoso lectures delivered to huge audiences. He rarely resisted a puckish viewpoint, such as his claim that the Great War's outbreak was due to railway timetables, but there is no doubt about his view of Germany. During the thirties, he recognised the threat to Britain as being a 'German' not a fascist one, and his research was mainly into the historical roots of that problem. The Germans, Taylor argued in wartime, were 'numerous, rich and assertive, possessed of the potential to master Europe and the urge to try'. Hitler was thus the 'contemporary return of a longstanding problem'; there were 'too many Germans, and Germany is too strong, too well organised, too well equipped with industrial resources'. Hence, early Taylor books on *The Habsburg Monarchy* (1941), *The Course of German History* (1946) and *Bismarck* (1955), all best-sellers that were read by generations of students, prefigured 'the Taylor thesis' in his *Origins of the*

Second World War (1961): that Hitler was but an extreme version of what any German leader would have done if given the chance; his racial persecutions followed logically from 'racial doctrines in which most Germans vaguely believed'; 'in international affairs, there was nothing wrong with Hitler except that he was a German'. Taylor's books provided chapter and verse for these views, or convinced readers that he himself knew the documents, while his journalism consistently argued against the reunification of Germany. As he expressed it to the *New Statesman*'s editor: 'anyone who is in favour of a united Germany is led by an inevitable and fatal logic to desire first a peaceful and then a warlike German mastery of Europe'. His first article for the *Sunday Express*, 'Why Must We Soft-Soap the Germans?', went further, arguing that 'whoever commits himself to the reunification of Germany commits himself to the Munich settlement and to the demands that Hitler made on Poland in August 1939'. Taylor could go too far for good taste: his 1973 Creighton Lecture, claiming that gas chambers 'represented Germany as truly as Gothic cathedrals represented the civilisation of the Middle Ages', caused a ruckus in the University of London, and 'Germany' became 'National Socialism' in the published lecture. For Taylor, as Gordon Martel has it, 'modern international history is the story in the main of Germany's attempt to dominate Europe and the efforts of others to prevent it from succeeding'. That view was relentlessly expounded by easily the most widely read historian since the war; when in 1977 Chris Wrigley asked sixty-two history undergraduates to name historians they already knew at the start of their course, thirty-nine named Taylor and only a handful mentioned anyone else.[23]

The Origins of the Second World War sold well: reviews varied from the ecstatic to the deeply hostile, and the controversy added to its readership. Even before publication in German, it was badly received in Germany, in part reflecting incomprehension among stuffier German professors that an Oxford fellow could so conflate the roles of public educator and popular entertainer. But they also worried that Taylor's book could impede Germany's reacceptance internationally. The consensus, espoused as much by Wheeler-Bennett as by his German equivalents, was that Nuremberg proved that specific people and organisations were at fault, and Hitler was most responsible for the Second World War. On this 'Nuremberg thesis', the dead Hitler took the shame and blame with him to the grave, and Germans could move on. Taylor stood the argument on its head, and asserted, 'it was no more of a mistake for the German people to end up with Hitler than it is an accident when a river flows into the sea, though the process is, I daresay, unpleasant for the fresh water'. Taylor was, wrote Golo Mann, '*Hitler's britischer Advocat*', who 'seeks to disconcert by expressing wicked thoughts that other people are ashamed to express openly, as, for example, that Germany's division into two is the greatest luck for England'. In all this Taylor, as Donald Watt remarked, at least showed consistency, with his pieces for the *Sunday Express* arguing the same case. 'Why This Picture Alarms Me' (April 1958) regretted that the Queen must shake Adenauer's hand; 'Should the Queen Go to Germany?' (October 1958) argued that 'we cannot be friendly with all Germans until the generation which served Hitler has passed away'; in March 1959 he called for a free, possibly united but certainly disarmed, Germany, and in May he denounced the EEC as 'working out in practice as a device for bringing all Continental Europe under German control'.[24]

Given persistently prejudicial perceptions of Germany in high places and in broad culture, Europe's Cold War cannot be overstressed as the factor facilitating reconciliation. In this context it is not surprising that it was the Labour Left (which also rejected East–West conflict) and the Beaverbrook press (which emphasised non-European parts of the British Empire) that constituted the 'Bevanbrook' axis against a kiss-and-make-up attitude to Germany – lineal ancestor of the Foot–Powell front which in 1975 opposed British membership of 'Europe'. For others, as Ernest Bevin's private secretary put it, at the outset the 'ostensible aim had been to prevent the revival of German aggressive tendencies', but priority was 'soon given to dealing with the aggressive policies of the Russians in Germany'. Former critics quickly became allies of British policy, George Bell among them: returning from Berlin when the Russian blockade was beginning, he urged ministers that 'from every point of view it was our duty to be absolutely clear and firm in our reply to the Russian demands, and to stand unyieldingly in Berlin'. The Health Minister, Aneurin Bevan, soon Labour's leading advocate of slowing down German readmission to the Western club, was equally staunch, urging that a military convey advance and challenge the Russians to fire first. It was not only that West and East were contesting *in* Germany, but that they were contesting *for* Germany. For those with a good memory, there was fear of 'another Rapallo', whereby Russia and defeated Germany might ally as they had done in 1921. Here, with hindsight, is politicians' invariable determination to avoid last time's mistakes; as they deterred defeated Germany from realigning with Russia, British leaders barely noticed that she had the alternative option of aligning with (defeated) France, a much better analogy with 1921, which duly occurred and frustrated Britain's European policy for the rest of the century. 'The danger of Russia', Bevin briefed colleagues as early as May 1946, 'has become as great as, and possibly even greater than that of a revived Germany.' A year later, with Western occupation zones integrated and a West German government on the way, British leaders realised that it behoved them to behave better towards Germans, if 'Rapallo' were to be avoided. It was now that army wives and administrators were instructed to be friendlier, and that the occupiers' greed and black-marketeering were reined in, though in shifting towards charm the British were months behind the Russians: 'We are dignified and insulting,' claimed Churchill. 'The Russians are boon companions and enslavers.' British commissioners ordered in May 1947 that 'we should behave towards the Germans as the people of one Christian and civilised race towards another whose interests in many ways converge with our own and for whom we have no longer any ill-will'.[25]

The fortitude of Berliners through the Berlin airlift of 1948–9 accelerated that process, and gave Britain the chance to stop dismantling industrial plant, which had been faithfully carried out under the Potsdam agreements, to the irritation of Germans and British sympathisers who saw this as wantonly creating destitution. German heavy industry was henceforth viewed as a Western asset rather than an odorous bequest from Hitler. West Germany was incorporated into the Marshall Plan for European Economic Recovery, which tied her ever closer to Western Europe, while Russia's refusal to let East Germany join meant that the economic division of Germany became political and lasting: the Federal Republic of 'West Germany' with its own government was functioning by 1950. When the Korean War began, it was easy to see how Russian communists might walk across German zone borders just as Asian communists had done in Korea; Donald Watt recalled of his army days in Austria 'a deep underlying fear which was part of general everyday life at the time', fear that the Red Army might one day just appear in unstoppable force. Korea became a second crisis reinforcing the policy impact of Berlin. When Ivone Kirkpatrick returned as high commissioner in 1950, he was instructed to terminate occupation as smoothly as possible, and 'eliminate all causes of Anglo-German friction', which at the time still included demilitarisation and restrictions on travel. Though denying that he was 'pandering to agitation', he and the Foreign Office were 'anxious not to allow our exceptional post-war measures to drag on . . . we should place our relations with Germany on a normal footing as soon as possible'. The consequence, as Watt put it, was that 'the Western allies found themselves forced increasingly to choose between bullying, bribing or supplicating to obtain their way, where before a hint or an order was enough'. At the height of dismantling German industry, a CCG official loftily dismissed local complaints, since 'what the Germans think about it does not matter very much'. It did now, and before the end of 1948 Bevin decided that 'the fate of German industry ought to be settled by a freely elected West German Government'. Although Kirkpatrick sometimes upbraided German leaders, urging them not to criticise so often the efforts of their allies, he now needed German help at least as much as Germans needed his. Substituting for Churchill and choking down his own opinions, Macmillan demanded Germany's admission to the Council of Europe ('Bring on the Germans!') though in language which remained guarded: if outside in the cold, 'Germany, now cast down, despised, shunned like an unclean thing, will once again be courted by each of the two groups [East and West], and from a starving outcast she will become the pampered courtesan of Europe, selling her favours to the highest bidder'. More than twenty years later, a cartoon in both the *Sunday Express* and *Spiegel* expressed the same fear during Willy Brandt's chancellorship: Brandt is Marlene Dietrich, receiving flowers from a kneeling Brezhnev, but his boudoir displays love-letters from de Gaulle, Heath and Nixon – and an Iron Cross.[26]

One consequence of Germany's enhanced bargaining power, especially after the Federal Republic became fully independent, and of the Cold War being fought over Germany's future, was that Britain had

to aim at reunifying East and West Germany. Though to some
Britons it still appeared that a divided Germany suited British interests very well, this loose end from the war demanded a tidy knot, lest
tension along the Elbe (and from 1961 along the Berlin Wall) should
explode into nuclear war. German leaders seemed to British diplomats hypersensitive about any statement implying recognition of
'East Germany' or any reduced commitment to German reunion.
Hence, the British talked continually about reunification, but without meaning it very sincerely or believing much in its practicality.
The success of the Federal Republic during the 1950s, politically and
economically, ensured that when the West demanded free elections
for Germany as a whole they were making an offer that the Russians
would never accept, since a government elected freely by both halves
of Germany could only be an anti-communist one within NATO. In
December 1953 Churchill warned Eden that this stance guaranteed a
dangerous stand-off with Russia, whereas the West ought to seek
détente: he wanted references to German reunification left out of the
Bermuda conference's final communiqué, 'on the ground that you
couldn't confront the Russians at Berlin with both our determination
that Western Germany should be an armed member of the E[uro-
pean] D[efence] C[ommunity] *and* a demand that Eastern Germany
should be united to it'. Yet the official British view, as Macmillan
reiterated it soon after becoming Prime Minister in 1957, was that 'all
Western proposals for European security are contingent on a unified
Germany with a freely elected all-German government free to choose
its own foreign policy'. Struck by the irony here, Michael Foot
observed in 1973 that 'not many years before, that apparition had
been the cause of most of Europe's problems'. Recalling that he had
pressed for German unification, Macmillan himself conceded many
years later that 'we always had to talk about it to strengthen
Adenauer . . . and it was an issue which had to be put forward . . . but
it was something of a fraud'. Not that Adenauer as a Rhinelander was
all that keen on unification himself, especially if it returned Prussia to
Germany before democracy was strong, but he too could hardly say
so. He could though express himself forcibly whenever the possibility emerged that a deal might be done over the Germans' heads. In
May 1959 a foreign ministers' summit took place with two German
delegations forced to sit apart, two inches away from the top table

where Britain, France, America and Russia deliberated. Britain seemed unaware of sensitivities outraged on these occasions, which was one of the openings exploited by France once de Gaulle determined to court Adenauer. As long as Adenauer's Christian Democrats remained in office, reunification was a potential bone of contention with Britain, and only with Willy Brandt's search for a flexible *Ostpolitik* did the problem diminish; it was to explode again when reunification occurred after the Cold War.[27]

German independence and reunion were inherently tied up with German rearmament (and hence with memories of German militarism), for as Eden pointed out in 1954, all options required external policing: 'Is Germany to be neutral and disarmed? If so who will keep Germany disarmed? Or is Germany to be neutral and armed? If so, who will keep Germany neutral?' The British government was cornered into supporting a rearmed Germany as the price of permanent American forces in Europe. The Anglo-American 'special relationship' guaranteeing British security was Britain's overriding aim internationally, so there was never a doubt she would pay that price. Most newspapers, and according to opinion polls most of the public, gradually accommodated themselves to this, but the Labour Party was divided for years. Although their reasoning was different – Bevan opposing the economics of German rearmament, Dalton wanting to deny guns to Germans – the alliance of Dalton with the Bevanite Left allowed opponents of German rearmament to capture the party, but not for long and only when Labour was in opposition. Bevan declared that 'we must never have Germans in uniform', while Dalton told Labour's 'young men' that 'as soon as Germany is armed again . . . they'll be getting the Death Ship into position for launching'. The *Manchester Guardian* more sedately concluded that 'There may be strategic advantages for us . . . but they are not worth the loss of confidence involved.' All this when Germany had not even asked for an army, and its Chancellor was not sure he wanted one: in 1955 Harold Nicolson was told by friends that nine out of ten Germans would vote against an army if given the chance – 'and I do not blame them'. Two of the high commissioner's staff were so moved by the novelty of Britain forcing even a limited army on Germany that they offered a new Christmas carol:

Hark! The Foreign Ministers sing
A German army in the spring.
Peace on earth and goosestep mild
Sturmbannführers reconciled.

Yet their third verse had darker tones:

Just in case the Bundesmensch
Might turn round to fight the French,
We will keep your units small,
So they'll be no good at all.

Less humorously, the *Express* enquired, 'if we do allow Germany to have the guns, who can be sure which way they will point them?' Such suspicions explain why the Bundeswehr (definitely not a Wehrmacht) demonstrated by its structure, recruitment, uniforms, drill, and 'the complete absence of pomp and pageantry', that Prussianism had not returned. It would only be in East Germany that British visitors would see goose-stepping soldiers in uniforms like Nazis in war films, but few Britons went there anyway. East Germany was in other ways too the successor state to the Third Reich, taking over intact parts of its terror apparatus, including the Sachsenhausen and Buchenwald camps. Though, as Raymond Ebsworth recalled, loyal CCG staffers noticed that 'Germans of every political shade except the extreme right wanted to leave the militaristic side of the German character to decay' for longer before acquiring armed forces, they now had to argue that Germans should be ashamed of not helping with their own defence. Adenauer's government used the fact that NATO now needed German soldiers to get war criminals out of jail; after all, he needed as Christian Democrat voters millions of Germans who had once voted for Hitler, and it was hard to recruit for a new army when heroes of the last one remained behind bars. The consequent programme of early releases in turn played into the hands of those who wanted to believe 'they've not changed'.[28]

Nor did such debates fade away when in 1955 – ten years to the day after VE Day – German armed forces were accepted within NATO and the Federal Republic became a sovereign state. As American political scientists found when interviewing West German leaders in

1958, the Hitlerian 'excess of nationalism' ensured that German ministers obsessively denied any aspiration to greater regional influence just because they had armed forces: a senior Foreign Ministry official explained that the aim was to underplay the Federal Republic's strength, 'to make our strength bearable to our neighbours and acceptable to them. Everything begins from there.' Large tracts of Germany were dedicated training areas for the British army, but whenever elements of Germany's new army went abroad to train, there were predictable flouts and sneers in the British press. A training programme in Spain raised enough hackles, since visiting troops would be hosted by one of the few remaining fascist dictators, but 'Panzers in the Valleys' was directly provocative in 1961. Even allowing German armed forces storage space in Britain had produced barbed comments the previous year, and there were ongoing complaints that 'tight-fisted Germans' were refusing to share their 'Rhinegold' to pay for the BAOR, now a serious drain of foreign exchange as Britain's economy weakened. But the news that German troops would train at a Welsh army camp gave papers like the *Express* an opportunity to bash both governments, just when Macmillan launched Britain's first bid to join the European Economic Community with German support. The *Daily Herald* and elements of the labour movement joined the Beaverbrook press in encouraging protest. Defying the platform, the TUC passed a 'Panzers Go Home' motion: welcoming German soldiers to Wales would betray 'all those who fought, suffered and died in two world wars'. The ensuing demonstration was actually small – the *Express* would hardly have understated the numbers when claiming two thousand as present – but feelings were inflamed and the story ran for several weeks, sometimes even interestingly: a British officer met a German he had captured in 1944 (but they got along fine); even while a demonstrator carrying a 'bomb' was arrested outside the wire, soldiers inside were playing Wales–Germany soccer matches. Proposals to unite NATO's nuclear and non-nuclear powers into a 'Multilateral Force' (MLF) provoked in the mid-1960s hysterical questions as to whether German fingers would reach the nuclear button.[29]

Arguments about financing the BAOR and control of the MLF were signs that the pendulum had by the early 1960s swung heavily against Britain, both diplomatically and economically; West

Germany's 'economic miracle' was by then evoking both admiration and fear, much as a similar surge of growth had done in 1890–1910, except that this time there were worries that blood sacrifices of 1939–45 would have been in vain if Germany ruled Europe through the Community. Even those who thought like this faced a dilemma: should Britain contest the trend from inside, joining European integration in order to limit German influence, or obstruct integration processes from the outside, relying on her Commonwealth (a declining asset), on North America (an uncertain one) and on countries on the outer rim of Europe (a fragmented one). In the first place the dilemma emerged from the triangular relations of Britain, France and Germany. Britain needed Germany to be friendly with France, and Churchill had urged normal Franco-German relations within a 'united states of Europe', but if Germany became *too* friendly with France then Britain would be correspondingly isolated. Poorly chosen diplomatic options in 1955–8 antagonised both Paris and Bonn, just when the emergent EEC gave them a market place within which to trade German money for five recent enemies accepting Germany's friendship. Irrespective of whether Britain 'missed the European boat' in 1955–8, as is often alleged, she certainly missed developing a relationship of friendly normality with democratic Germany, as France was doing. French opinion was at first even less supportive of friendship with Germany than the British, yet in France responsible leadership carried the day, while in Britain there was doubt, hesitation and pain. However prickly Britain's leaders thought Adenauer, he did regularly warn about the danger of self-isolation. In 1950 he replied to Churchill's assurance that Britain would stand by Europe, saying, 'I am a little disappointed. England is a part of Europe.' Churchill and Macmillan preferred to keep a free hand and an open line to Washington, never grasping that for Adenauer Franco-German rapprochement and European integration were higher priorities even than reunification – and much more achievable. Macmillan thought rather in apocalyptic terms, worrying in 1952 about 'a boastful, powerful "Empire of Charlemagne" – now under French but later bound to come under German control'. British efforts to use Germany to 'break up' the six countries which in 1957 formed the EEC were doomed to failure, since Bonn would always plump for Paris rather than London. Britain gave inadequate attention to the fact that many post-war Germans favoured the partial surrender of nationality as insurance against a Nazi resurgence. Adenauer, as Sir Christopher Steel (British ambassador in Bonn) later put it, aimed at 'a Europe in which Germany could sublimate all the things that he regretted about her past'. Sailing with Macmillan on a Rhine riverboat in 1958, Adenauer assured the Prime Minister that he hated uniforms and militarism, 'the curse of Germany', and that no foreigner understood 'the harm that Nazism has done to the German soul', which was 'why I yearn so for European unity and (in view of France's weakness) for British participation'. Such prophecies fell on deaf ears, and as a result, as Sabine Lee puts it, 'Anglo-German relations never really took off after the war', as did British relations with America and Germany's with France. Even while Adenauer and Macmillan got on personally, short-term cooling was attributed by Macmillan to Adenauer's 'trickiness' rather than to German interests, while Macmillan's 1959 mission to Moscow persuaded Adenauer that British policy had become 'unreliable and anti-German'. Such opinions were naturally reinforced by Macmillan's 'bullying' Adenauer (his own word) with threats to bring the BAOR home, though these were unconvincing threats, since the army's watch on the Rhine was more for Britain's security than for Germany's.[30]

The long saga of Britain applying three times between 1961 and 1973, before membership of the European Economic Community was achieved, ensured that mutual suspicion was often repeated; an *Evening Standard* columnist, noticing that 'Adenauer's old and trusted crony' Walter Hallstein was the president of the European Commission, thought in 1962 that 'where Hitler failed in war, Hallstein expects to succeed in peace . . . to bring about . . . German-controlled political domination of Europe'. In 1961–2 the British strategy was to negotiate details, leaving on the table as little as possible to justify a French veto, but the expectation was that the other five members would follow a German lead in forcing de Gaulle to back down. Britain's negotiator, Edward Heath, told parliamentarians early in 1961 that 'Germany is friendly and welcoming' and was helping negotiations along in many areas. However, with a Franco-German friendship treaty, to which he had devoted years of his life, due for signature when de Gaulle delivered his veto on British membership, Adenauer made no fight for British acceptance. The humiliation of this setback occasioned a good deal of indiscriminate chauvinism in Britain, but much was directed at Germany, for while French opposition had been anticipated, lack of German support had not. Even the Anglo-Germans at the Königswinter conference became acrimonious: Crossman thanked the Germans for keeping Britain out, while Lady Violet thought this all wrong, 'after we had been trying to instil a sense of responsibility into the Germans!' The Germans could hardly win, for Germany was now blamed for stopping Britain getting in, yet when it seemed that Britain might join, the EEC had been denounced by Beaverbrook as 'an American device to put us alongside Germany', and by Montgomery as bound to lead to British soldiers serving under German generals. Germany, claimed Monty, had 'disturbed the peace of the world twice during the past 48 years, in 1914 and 1940 (*sic*, so much for Poland in 1939). Are we to put up with all this again? Never!' Even while talks went on, and he was desperate that they should succeed, Macmillan confided to Prince Philip that 'the Huns are always the same. When they are down they crawl under your feet, and when they are up they use their feet to stamp on your face.' He was though outraged when people he despised did not act as Britain's Brussels marionettes.[31]

Relations improved once the dust settled after the first round of EEC negotiations, especially after Adenauer retired and was replaced by Ludwig Erhard, who was both more pro-British and more admired in Britain; *Die Welt* thought when he came to London in 1964 that 'Great Britain places its hopes on the German card.' Anglo-German relations in the next decade were mainly characterised by the two countries having little substantial to talk about, and so little about which to disagree, though always with the potential that a new British EEC application would ruffle feathers. Carrying that application process to its successful conclusion in 1973, the 'German' aspect of Britain's European negotiations gradually reduced. Chancellor Kiesinger argued strongly for Britain's admission to the EEC in 1967–8, but made it clear throughout that he would not jeopardise German relations with France to achieve it; having lower expectations, there was less excuse for Britain to blame Germany when talks again failed. Even so, Harold Wilson's decision to tell the German government what de Gaulle had said confidentially to him about Britain, Germany and France becoming the directorate of an enlarged EEC did more harm in Paris than good in Bonn. Wilson's achievement in signing an Anglo-German declaration on the future of Europe was thus rendered nugatory. All this ensured that when the third application began, Heath had drawn the right conclusion – that a deal with France was crucial and would not antagonise the other members, since like Germany they wanted Britain to join. If the road to Brussels lay through Paris, then there would be no collision with Bonn, but German lobbying in Paris anyway earned goodwill in London. Heath had a good relationship with Brandt, to which the Chancellor later attested: 'I never felt Edward Heath's reputed lack of personal warmth. Uncomplicated and characterised by mutual trust, our talks might almost have been described, without triteness, as friendly.' In Heath's own memory though Brandt was 'one of the most perplexing personalities with whom I have ever had to deal . . . in some respects the least Germanic of men', but he paid tribute to Brandt's support for British entry. As John Campbell points out, relationships with Heath were never warmer than this. When Wilson's Labour government was in 1974 renegotiating the terms of entry to which Heath had signed up, the personalities had changed again. Germany in the shape of Helmut Schmidt presided at the EEC's Council of Ministers, and the Foreign Secretary was Jim Callaghan. Schmidt and Callaghan respected each other, neither wanting a politically integrated Europe, and this allowed Labour to achieve enough to commend the new terms to the people in a referendum; in his memoirs Wilson speaks of Schmidt making 'some very generous proposals'. Schmidt even turned up at a Labour Party conference, addressing delegates in English and using Shakespearean quotations to appeal fraternally to comrades to support their own government; he did it far more tactfully than Labour's Eurosceptics had hoped when they threatened to stage a walk-out in protest at a foreigner dictating to Britain. In the 1975 referendum campaign in which the 'No' side delivered its appeal in chauvinistic tones, anti-German rhetoric was mainly noticeable by its absence, 'dictation from Brussels' being the Eurosceptic scare rather than collaboration with Germans.[32]

Personal relations could make real differences at governmental levels, but personal appearances also provided chances to review the relationship as a whole. Adenauer's visits to London, whatever their success or failure as diplomacy, tended not to have wider positive effects, for the British press never warmed to him and he made few attempts to win friends: even sympathetic journalists like the *Manchester Guardian*'s Terence Prittie were frozen out by Adenauer after critical stories appeared. Newspapers described Adenauer's ambiguities during the Nazi period, his appeals to ex-Nazi voters and support for the release of war criminals, poisoning the wells before each appearance in London. When in 1951 Adenauer arrived as Federal Chancellor, he convened the first official gathering of Germans in London since Ribbentrop was the host, so papers solicitously enquired whether he too would serve champagne to guests: 'a clink of glasses, a click of heels'? During that visit he went to Oxford, Westminster Abbey, the National Gallery and the Palace (George VI's thoughts imaginatively reconstructed by journalists out of no actual information). Readers were told the costs of accommodating him at the Ritz and of his Claridge's reception. When he flew home, 'to his garden, his collection of antique clocks, his children . . . and the problems of a divided Germany', the *Express* offered a rancorous editorial: Germans 'must not expect us to forget the past – or to pretend that it is forgotten. A bad memory cannot be the basis of a good policy.' Six years later, little had changed, except that moves towards European free trade had further antagonised old-fashioned imperialists. Though the *Express* reported a generous speech by Adenauer, which somehow celebrated Britons as 'good Europeans', an editorial the same day urged that Macmillan 'pause a moment from his continental preoccupations' on Empire Day and recall the British Empire's casualties in two world wars.[33]

It was hard for an active politician to be an effective goodwill ambassador, having both a past to live down and present policies to justify, but both governments recognised that something needed to be done to improve British perceptions of Germany, hence the state visit of President Theodor Heuss in October 1957, the first such visit since 1907. Heuss had been attacked in Britain for congratulating Konstantin von Neurath after release from Spandau, on the end of his 'martyrdom' – which is not quite how Britons viewed those convicted at Nuremberg – but had lately made himself into a good-will ambassador, and had already visited Greece, Canada and America. Now in London he appeared warm-hearted where Adenauer seemed icy, and the visit was a great success. There was widespread praise for the decision not to attempt a 'don't mention the war' approach, and planners of the visit seemed rather to have gone out of their way to exorcise the memory. Heuss delivered funds collected by German Christians towards the rebuilding of Coventry Cathedral, foreshadowing the reconciliation staged at the new cathedral's dedication in 1962, with Benjamin Britten's *War Requiem* performed by English, German and Russian soloists. He privately visited the Wiener Library's collection of works on the Nazi period, and laid a wreath at the tomb of the unknown warrior, 'a silent memory of the slaughter of two world wars'. At a reception he sought out anti-Nazi refugees among the guests and in Oxford announced a scholarship scheme to finance postgraduate study in Germany. The Queen put on a special show of pictures at Buckingham Palace, so he saw Holbeins that represented an earlier period of cultural free trade. The real meaning of the visit was captured in a *Spiegel* cartoon, showing a shirt-sleeved Heuss wearily clearing bomb-damage in London, with the bomb of 'Distrust' still to be defused. Some German papers more openly resented the limitations on Heuss's reception, and *Tagesspiegel* mused that 'at best the English will tolerate our President as a man who, thank God, is not typically German, who actually deserved to have been born English'. It was happy that 'the Queen, too, has not ignored the armed enmity of two World Wars, but referred to it where it belonged, as history'. Yet, 'in this respect a large part of the English press did not follow her lead, but used the opportunity to enumerate our sins, so that many among us will recently have told themselves that all courtship of the English was in vain. After all, as Bismarck once said: "They do not want to let themselves be loved!"'[34]

Heuss's visit climaxed when the President welcomed the Queen to a 'diamonds and mink reception for 450' at the German Embassy, which no monarch had visited since 1913 (all such precedents being meticulously chronicled). 'With swift German efficiency', the embassy had been 'furnished and decorated to meet the occasion'. The Queen entertained the President at the Palace, where she referred

to her German blood (which no monarch had cared to mention since 1915), and drew the appropriate moral: 'There were occasions in the past when our two countries were closely allied', but the 'tragic events of the last half century in the relations between our two countries' were also now 'part of history', and there was a need to move on. The recent past should be remembered mainly as a warning of the dangers to which democracy was everywhere subject, and as an incentive to be vigilant in its defence. Heuss responded appropriately, reminding listeners of past collaborations like Waterloo, as did the Lord Mayor when giving Heuss lunch at London's Guildhall. On that occasion, Heuss referred to 'the terrible things that were done in the last war', and explained that Germany was 'aware too of the duty to make amends for the wrong that was done'. On each occasion, the German national anthem was played as well as the British, but the tune was still a provocation; it was noticed that some Guildhall guests were unable to drink the toast to West Germany, not out of disrespect but as 'an involuntary action'. Reports indicated that while crowds on the streets were respectful, they did not cheer much, exactly as

Aachen had received Churchill two years earlier. *The Times* referred to London buildings having been 'dutifully beflagged'. Harold Nicolson was one of several Britons invested with German decorations during Heuss's visit – 'an enamelled dingle-dangle and a brass star [and] an excellent, indeed super, *Moselwein*' – though, had she been there, his wife 'would have turned on the gramophone record about, "I can't understand how you can possibly accept Orders from those horrible people who tried to destroy us".' In the circumstances the response to Heuss's invitation to the Queen to make an early return visit to Germany raised difficulties, though she agreed to do it 'some time'. It was considered necessary that at least two more years elapse, British opinion not yet being ready for such reciprocal relations: for Germany to offer the hand of friendship seemed right and just, but for Britain to respond in kind – as 'a top-level Whitehall view' quoted in several newspapers put it – 'would stir up controversy and worsen Anglo-German relations'. Though some papers, notably the *Daily Mirror*, had been unhelpful, the *Telegraph* concluded that reconciliation must come, but would be the duty of the next generation; the present generation had 'a duty not to make unnecessary difficulties for them'. Though it had reported the visit generously, the *Express* correctly concluded that 'Germany is not QUITE back in the fold'. Anglo-German difficulties over Berlin and the EEC then intervened, but as the dust of those arguments settled in 1963–4 a royal visit to Germany resurfaced and was agreed for 1965 during Sir Alec Douglas-Home's brief premiership. As Watt remarked in 1964, the very fact that 'her advisers feel it safe for her to go is an immense step forward'.[35]

That 1965 state visit to Germany restaged in the mirror the Heuss visit of seven years earlier, except that German crowds were enthusiastic; to such an extent indeed that the Queen is said to have found their relentless chanting of 'EL-IZ-A-BET!' unnerving (according to the Foreign Secretary, reminiscent of the period of German history not now mentionable). The British press, basking as always in the popular glow of British celebrities cheered by foreigners – Elizabeth was on German television for *fifty* hours – reported the visit as an unqualified success and a milestone in Anglo-German relations. British newspapers enjoyed references in the official speeches to Anglo-German cooperation at Waterloo, especially when *Le Figaro* demanded that everyone should stop talking about long-forgotten battles, and *Paris Presse* accused the Queen of 'monumental tactlessness'. 'Baedeker' guides to the cities she visited were offered to British readers, telling them more about Bonn than they can ever have wanted to know; when she was taken to *Der Rosenkavalier*, readers were even given a summary of the plot. Every day they read accounts of what was worn, eaten and drunk, and how large were the crowds. Though *Express* editorials had carped – it had been 'a wrong decision' to send her and 'manoeuvred her' into a false position – the headline 'The Queen Dazzles Them' typified its enthusiastic coverage. Tabloids speculated whether Prince Charles might now 'marry a *Fräulein*' like most of his ancestors, and all reported as conclusive evidence of the changed mood the hundred thousand cheering Germans who came out to see the Queen sail home from Hamburg. German papers noticed that Elizabeth attracted bigger crowds than either de Gaulle or Kennedy, but some hinted that enthusiasm had been less than on those occasions. The visit included sites highlighting shared history, as when the Queen visited the state archives in Hanover and saw the letter which had invited George I to become British King, all such human-interest stuff duly reported as the successful building of an international partnership. The Queen's six hours in Berlin, thought the *Süddeutsche Zeitung*, 'measured against the expectations that a German or British citizen could have had only ten years ago . . . almost seem like a political miracle', but this was true of the entire trip. Sir Frank Roberts, British ambassador to the Federal Republic, 1963–8, and used to despairing of Fleet Street's negative attitudes, recently claimed that 'all this changed really with the Queen's visit to Germany in 1965'.[36]

It was not quite that simple, as depictions even of the Queen indicated: *Private Eye* produced a 'Special Issue, Anglo-German Relations', the cover of which showed Her Majesty inspecting a German guard of honour, saying, 'Hello Uncle Otto, Cousin Karl, Auntie Eva . . .' (Twenty-seven years later, another state visit produced an atmosphere almost like a family reunion: the *Evening Standard*'s cartoon showed Elizabeth with Chancellor Kohl greeting old Prussian military men and their wives, with spiked helmets, bath-chairs and Zimmer frames.) Nevertheless, the 1965 state visit did provide an opportunity for the growing harmonisation to become a fixed point in popular perceptions. As Donald Watt had tentatively concluded the previous year, the trend in the 1960s was setting in a positive direction. In part this reflected a belated recognition that West Germany had indeed changed since 1945, in part because of the arrival of a generation of politicians in both Britain and the Federal Republic whose opinions and previous careers needed less living down. The former British Minister for Germany John Hynd overstated the case when he declared in 1960 that 'there is absolutely no anti-German feeling in England', merely a few anti-German articles by the same journalists, but this was nearer to the truth by 1965. More responsible newspapers came off the fence and populist dailies began to pull their punches. The shift in tone adopted by the left-leaning *Herald* and *Mirror* was especially helpful, reflecting the fact that the Social Democratic Party now had leaders whom British socialists could admire, and with whom they could work in harmony. The growing readiness of SDP leaders to begin dialogue with Eastern Europe, culminating in Brandt's *Ostpolitik*, was ammunition for those arguing that another *Drang nach Osten* need not be feared. German diplomats in London had played their part, banishing the illusion that Germany's envoys were invariably caricatures of Franz von Papen, wearing monocles and lying through their teeth. It was though unfortunate that in the next generation German ambassadors to London included a Moltke and a Richthofen, men whose names obliged even supportive newspapers to refer constantly to military ancestors; sometimes they printed 'then and now' photographs, as did *The Times* when Ambassador von Moltke departed in 1999. Nobody did more effective work than Herbert Sulzbach, a German-Jewish war-hero émigré who later served in the British army, helped to re-educate POWs, and in 1951 joined the West German Embassy in London. He remained there for thirty years; when well over eighty, he retired with German decorations from the First World War, British medals from the Second, post-war honours from West Germany, the OBE, and unstinting praise from the *Daily Mail*. Most of all, European developments had enforced collaboration and would do so even more once Britain joined the EEC. Reaching back beyond the current century for his analogy, as supporters of closer relations so often did, Watt asserted that 'Britain needs Germany as Marlborough needed Prince Eugene of Savoy and Castlereagh . . . needed Metternich.' There might at last be a positive lead given to British opinion after the Queen's successful tour; the Foreign Secretary argued in a cabinet paper that 'two world wars and the horrors of Nazism have left such a legacy of bitterness that we cannot be sure that Anglo-German reconciliation will last unless we for our part make it do so'. The cabinet agreed an extensive programme of ministerial contacts, technical collaboration, and cultural and youth exchanges, 'to encourage the British people to think of contemporary Germany in a more friendly way'. As Richard Weight points out, when agreeing that programme Wilson's cabinet could hardly be blamed for not foreseeing the negative effects of the two countries' contests on the football field which began at Wembley in the following year.[37]

Watt had nevertheless already concluded that so far, below the elite level, 'lacking any positive leadership, British opinion has remained fixed in the stereotypes established in two world wars'. Even among the most sympathetic, nagging doubts had remained throughout these years of reconciliation. Nobody loved Germans more than Harold Nicolson, yet when in 1949 T. S. Eliot asked him what line to adopt during a lecture tour of West Germany, he advised the poet 'to treat them as ordinary members of cultured society, much as one would treat a dypsomaniac' (a condition from which it is notoriously difficult permanently to recover). Nobody was more sympathetic than Violet Bonham Carter, yet in 1964 she had 'a very agreeable talk' about Germany with Sir Harold Caccia, a career diplomat: they agreed about 'the curiously (superficial) friendly amenities that we establish with the Germans – so *much* more easily than we do with the French for instance – and yet the strange hang-over of national prejudice which has remained so much more deeply rooted here than in Europe – even in the countries being occupied'. As so often, Lady Violet put her finger on the real paradox: why did the British, who had less reason than most Europeans to resent Germans for the events of 1939–45, seem the most determined never to forget? When in 1965 British Overseas Airways launched an advertising campaign for its flights, it used Marlene Dietrich 'and her famous legs' as the central figure on posters in most countries, but had to replace her in Germany with a young male figure, since research indicated that the anti-Nazi Dietrich was thought a traitor by Germans. Several news-papers offered thoughts on which male it should be: the *Daily Mail*'s cartoonist Emmwood showed advertising agents offering BOAC (Germany) a seductive drawing of Adolf Hitler; a model Stuka swoops over the managing director's desk.[38]

'How iss dot, for a nice, nostalgic compromise, Herr Direktor?!?'

8

'Hardy comes through':
Germans in British war films

In 1957 the Rank Organisation assigned Roy Ward Baker to direct *The One That Got Away*, a film about a German struggling for freedom from the British during the recent war. Since it would be based on the 1956 best-seller, Rank expected a film with good commercial prospects – including the lucrative German market. Baker nevertheless had a major problem before he could even begin filming, for the dominant figure in Rank, John Davis, was 'adamant he would not play a German actor in the part', suggesting rather that Baker use Dirk Bogarde. This would compromise the film's chances of realism, for Bogarde was known for playing British rather than German heroes, and Baker wanted to be more creative. He had though to offer the lead to Kenneth More, who helpfully turned it down, thinking himself not credible as a German so soon after playing Douglas Bader in *Reach for the Sky*.[1] More's refusal to play Oberleutnant Franz von Werra enabled Baker to make the film as he had envisaged it. As his memoirs recall:

> I have never been the sort of director who deliberately makes films with a message, but I came close to it with *The One That Got Away* . . . I became more and more irritated by the depiction of Germans as homosexual Prussians, Gestapo torturers or beer-swilling Bavarians, all presented in ridiculously hammy performances. I had no doubt at all that these characteristics could be proved to exist in

Germans – and possibly other nations – but in my opinion these cartoon caricatures were dangerously misleading. Just the sort of thing to get the filmmakers a bad name and give the audiences a wrong impression.

Baker was not alone in facing resistance to the idea of casting a German actor in a lead role: when making *Ill Met by Moonlight* in 1956, Michael Powell wanted Curt Jurgens as Major General Kreipe, but Rank flatly rejected the idea. The furthest they would go was Anton Walbrook, an Austrian who had fled the Nazis before the war. Jurgens was not only German, but too expensive, so Powell cast Marius Goring, whose German name belied a very English accent and style.[2]

Baker did eventually get permission to use a German actor, and the publisher of *Stern* magazine suggested Hardy Kruger. In Hamburg the director met Kruger and quickly signed him as von Werra. This was Kruger's eighteenth film, but his first credited role outside Germany. He had tried to work internationally but had recently returned home after six months vainly seeking employment in Britain and France (being once thrown out of a taxi when the Parisian driver discovered he was German). It was inspired casting, for Kruger was young enough to convince as a 1940 fighter pilot but experienced enough in acting to carry the film. He himself had been captured in 1945 but escaped, and during his final period of liberty had lived rough for a week. 'The realism was there all right,' he later recalled. 'I relived all too many moments of my personal experiences in the war.' He was also not unusual for that generation in having lost his father in the war. His lonely isolation in the main role was enhanced by Baker having him move always across the screen from left to right – towards Germany on our subconscious European map – while British characters move from right to left, hemming him in.[3]

Being so young – he was born only in 1928 but started his adult film career in 1949 – Kruger had been too young to fight in the real war, and so had no Nazi past; except, that is, attendance at an Adolf-Hitler-Nazi-Elite school and membership of the Hitler Youth. He always accepted that as a young teenager 'I was a Nazi then', coming from a family that had Hitler's bust on the piano (though he recalls his father's support for the party having more to do with their rescuing him from unemployment than with ideology). His reluctance to write a candid autobiography of his war experiences, so as not to have to name contemporaries who collaborated with the Nazis, meant that neither admirers nor critics knew then of his involvement from 1943 in the anti-Nazi resistance, carrying messages for a network that smuggled German Jews into Switzerland.[4]

Kruger was not only young but blond, and had charm, presence and talent, an international star ready for his chance. By 1980, he had made thirty-five further films in seven different countries and in all the major European languages. The umlaut in his name disappeared from international film credits after *The One That Got Away*, though he continued to be the West's favourite casting for wartime Germans, one of his last roles being Rommel in the 1990 television mini-series *War and Remembrance*. He recently recalled refusing 'at least twenty or thirty German parts in international movies. Those cliché charac-ters, wasted by for example Otto Preminger in *Stalag 17*, were something I never wanted to imitate.'[5] In the starring parts he did play, though, he helped normalise cultural relations between Britain and Germany (and with other former enemies of Germany). As a 1958 British newspaper headline put it, 'Now Mr Kruger Leads the German Invasion . . . (This Time They're Welcome!)'. It began more problematically, for when Rank held a press conference to introduce Kruger, it turned into a public relations disaster. The first questioner asked him if he had been a Nazi; when he conceded that he had, there was a pregnant silence. Why, he asked, should that be a sensi-ble question to ask? Well, responded a film journalist, Kruger should 'look in the mirror' (where he would see a tall, blond German). Kruger haltingly explained that he understood why Germans had much to apologise for, and could see why Jews in particular might never forgive them, which brought his interlocutor to his feet with, 'Why should you think I am a Jew?' to which Kruger unwisely riposted, 'Look in the mirror.' The press conference ended at once and media journalists boycotted reporting the film's production. Meanwhile, Rank executives tried to cancel the film, and it took Roy Baker's threatened resignation to stop them. Other actors treated Kruger professionally, but few at Pinewood Studios at first socialised with the outcast. In due course a newsworthy stunt dreamed up by Rank's press office compelled newspapers to end their boycott, the film was released to general acclaim, and reviews were positive. The film was successful in Britain, acceptable in France, and extremely popular in Germany. Kruger recalls from personal appearances both the pleasure that German film-goers took in a foreign film that showed a wartime German as a real person, and his own mixed feelings when conservative German politicians congratulated him on what he had done for his country. Hardy Kruger had, despite the initial press conference, 'come through'. However, the impact that he made in 1957 can be understood only through awareness of films that went before.[6]

British war films softened the images used in portraying Germans in wartime films.[7] Germans sometimes figured as major characters, forcing film-makers into decisions as to how they were portrayed and how other characters reacted to them. *Frieda* (1947) was, wrote Roger Manvell, 'a timely reminder to the British that they must decide their attitude to the German people . . . to the possible survival of Nazism . . . the innocence of many Germans of direct involvement in Hitler's regime'.[8] The first point about 1950s British war films is how rarely Germans had on-screen significance; scarcely any British films directly confronted German complicity in Nazi crimes. Manvell listed in 1974 twenty-three films made between 1954 and 1965 in which the Third Reich had been analysed, but only one of them was British. There was no British equivalent of the French *Nuit et Brouillard* (1955), the Swedish *Mein Kampf* (1960), the West German *So Macht man Kanzler* (1961), or the American *Verboten* (1958).[9] Reviewing *Judgement at Nuremberg* in December 1961, Dilys Powell found its 'single-minded ferocity of condemnation . . . a bit repellent', but thought its analysis of the 'ethical and intellectual problems' of justice in wartime and during the Cold War to be gripping. She cited it as evidence that the cinema was maturing, 'readier than it was to assume in its audience the power of reasoning', but the patriotic Miss Powell did not point out that it was not often so in British films.[10]

In the 1950s, when cinema remained the dominant medium of mass communication, films were bound to stray into political issues. Film-makers were conscious both of their own role in fostering wartime hatred and of the possibility of now repairing some of the damage. *The Way to the Stars* was consciously made in 1945, recalled

John Mills, to cement good relations between Britain and the USA, while the actress Kathleen Byron thought that Powell and Pressburger's *A Matter of Life and Death* (1946) was 'trying to do a United Nations thing'.[11] Reviewing Humphrey Jennings' documentary *A Defeated People* in 1946, Manvell saw it both as an accurate picture of 'the new Germany of democratic control' and an answer 'to those who say "leave the Germans alone; let them suffer and die"'. Though there was 'no attempt to work up pity for the Germans', the film would change people's view. While making *A Defeated People*, Jennings himself was more equivocal. He wrote to Cecily Jennings from Düsseldorf that German people

> certainly don't behave guilty or beaten . . . They have their fatalism to fall back on: 'Kaput' says the housewife finding the street water pipe not working . . . 'Kaput . . . alles ist kaput.' Everything is smashed . . . how right – but absolutely no suggestion that it might be their fault – her fault. 'Why?' asks another woman fetching water, 'why do you not help us?' 'You' being us. At the same time nothing is clearer straight away than that we cannot – must not – leave them to stew in their own juice.[12]

That final line was to be included in the film's commentary, which, far from working up pity for Germans, stressed that reconstructing Germany was in British self-interest, since it was impossible to live safely near a 'diseased' neighbour.[13]

So many POW films were made that reviewers begged for escape from a genre which dominated both the book market and the cinemas. Bryan Forbes calculated that he spent almost two years of the 1950s 'behind fake barbed wire' as a 'prisoner', acting in successive British films. Others remarked wearily that the endless repetition of moral fables about innate British superiority to Germans made them wonder how Germany had almost won the war. In post-war prison-camp films British POWs are superior intellectually, their cunning, adaptability and ingenuity invariably deceiving Germans who are hampered by lack of imagination and sheer stupidity. However, the film plots' authenticity blunted attacks on them, deriving as they generally did from well-researched books and the memoirs of escapees.[14]

The cycle began with *The Wooden Horse* (1950). Eric Williams' book barely bothered to characterise Germans, and since Williams wrote the screenplay the film followed suit. The first time we meet the book's camp commandant, he is 'tall and immaculately uniformed . . . mincing across the square' to meet the senior British officer; he is given no name, and this is the film's policy too.[15] Germans, described by prisoners as 'goons', are not humans; they 'yelp', 'bark' and utter 'typically bullying shouts' in the book, and actors do this in the film, though one, called 'Dopey' by the prisoners, is individualised enough to take bribes. There is one half-hearted attempt at balance, when a POW refuses to believe that a German airman intended to machine-gun a pilot escaping his burning plane, since the war 'wasn't anyone's fault. You can't blame a whole nation.' But you can, for others ask: 'Why do you always stand up for the Hun?' The incident precedes the introduction of another POW who has made 'Goon hatred into a sort of religion'. However, even this minimally balanced scene does not survive the transition from book to film script. The hero's reminiscence of a camp with 'kindly, tolerant guards with families at home and their fear of the Gestapo and the Russian front', and of a bullying sergeant who could just as easily have been English, was another episode dropped for the film version.[16] Reviewers accepted without demur that it could all be stereotypes: *Variety* thought 'the German officers . . . are played by a competent cast' but did not name either an actor or a character. The *Motion Picture Herald* welcomed the fact that 'the Germans aren't brutal villains', but added that they were 'soldiers doing a job they enjoy'. Many reviewers noted the audacious escaping 'under the very noses of the Germans', as *Today's Cinema* put it. Caroline Lejeune in the *Observer* produced a stereotype of her own, noting that the 'age-old trick' of the wooden horse, for the knowledge of which she thanked a British classical education, worked 'mainly through a nice calculation of the psychology of the people it was meant to deceive'. If she meant that prison guards, rather than Germans, were stolid and unimaginative, she did not say so.[17]

With *Albert RN* (1953), the situation was more complex, but the production derived from media used to more depth – this was 'the film of the play of the television programme'. Once again a factual story disarmed critics, and *Today's Cinema* reported that 'Frederick

Valk and Anton Diffring respectively portray the tolerable and intolerable types of German Commander'. Valk was praised as the senior officer, but Diffring was dismissed as just 'the typical ruthless Nazi type'. Diffring had been playing Nazis on screen for years, but here he excelled himself. He not only strutted and sneered but murdered a surrendering escapee. Unlike many who played Germans in films, he had not been a pre-war refugee from the Gestapo. Born in 1918, he was Flemish but trained in Berlin, and was on his way to Hollywood when interned in Canada on the outbreak of war. After 1945 he appeared on North American stages in Shakespeare, Goethe and Coward, and was a villainous success in the melodrama *Gaslight*. He came to Britain only in 1950 but eventually took British citizenship. Icy blond features and piercing blue eyes meant he was invariably cast either as a sadistic Nazi or the alien villain in science fiction. When he died in 1989, the *Guardian* headed its obituary 'Typecast', while the *Sun* headlined, 'Nasty Film Nazi Anton Dies at 70'. In revenge for Diffring's Nazi pitilessness, the hero of *Albert RN* has the chance to settle accounts with this 'typical Nazi' when escaping.[18]

With *The Colditz Story* (1954), the characterisation of Germans was added for the film, rather than taken from the book by P. R. Reid. When the prisoners arrive in this Gothic pile from which no escape is thought possible, they are addressed by the commandant – Frederick Valk again – who tells them 'with Teutonic seriousness' that anyone trying to escape will be shot, generating hysterical laughter from the British.[19] Again the cast includes Anton Diffring, limbering up to repeat his usual performance when he inexplicably disappears from the film altogether, replaced by another overbearing SS officer from the same mould. What marks the advance since *Albert RN* is the presence of a third German, Hauptmann Priem, overweight and jolly (and so expected to be incompetent, like all Göring lookalikes). Priem though turns out to be the most effective officer British POWs ever encounter. He is shrewd, has a sense of humour and enjoys rapport with the prisoners, at one point going specially to tell the senior British officer (SBO) that a wounded escapee has recovered. It is Priem who foils escape attempts, and he is aware that something is going on when an escape eventually succeeds, but just cannot work out what. He settles in to enjoy the prisoners' concert party, but when in the next scene he is bawled out, it is hard not to feel sympathetic.

If Priem undermines assumptions about Germans, the commandant develops over ninety minutes into a likeable personality. Once again he has a sense of humour (which no German was supposed to have, as Priem points out). When an SS underling asks for volunteers for the German war effort, and a French prisoner says he would rather work for eight Germans than one Frenchman, but then discloses that he is an undertaker, the commandant laughs out loud. In the following scene, Pat Reid (John Mills) remarks, 'See the commandant laugh? Bad for my morale!' The commandant then agrees to a British request to transfer a Polish informer to save his life, and the SBO comments, 'The Old Man's really quite amiable. All the same, I wouldn't spread it around.' By the end, the commandant can ask the SBO to quieten his men, 'if you please', to avoid bloodshed. He goes to the camp concert and laughs at jokes about himself. What has happened is convergence, each side respecting the other, and more rounded characterisations emerge. This owes a good deal to the commandant's declaration that he was a POW himself, so understands the other side of the wire. There was even some justification for the Borstal governor who in 1957 had to explain to a judge why he had showed the film to his charges (so prompting a mass break-out): 'the escape was only incidental to the film story. The idea was to portray how men got on with each other when they were in prison.'[20]

Almost every reviewer praised Valk's performance. The *Monthly Film Bulletin* thought that the role of the commandant was acted with 'irony but with little malice [as] an old soldier, stern but not without a sense of humour'.[21] Valk had been born into a German-Jewish family, and had success as a classical actor specialising in Shakespearean roles. With the Nazis in power, he moved to Prague, taking Czech nationality in 1938; when the Nazis arrived there too, he escaped through Germany, acting his way out. In London he joined the BBC (re-broadcasting Churchill speeches in German), and so perfected his English as to play Shylock at the Old Vic. He claimed indeed that his life experience enhanced his acting in Shakespeare, whose heroes were 'born in hell, and an actor who dares to play them must make a trip to hell. But most of the actors who play him don't go down to hell. Either they don't know the way or they don't want to go at all.'[22]

Valk was ambivalent about Germany, not only because of his

Jewishness. He was in 1918 'a conscript in the Kaiser's army', an 'unhappy warrior' who as that war ended 'demobilised himself' on 'the best day of my military career'. In 1947 in Hamburg, 'my first impression was, pack your bag and leave this country by the next train. In Hamburg you see bad faces, without a smile, and with dangerous eyes. "Why do they stare at me?" I asked . . . "They don't stare at you because you look Jewish. They stare at you because you look healthy and well-fed."' If this suggests guilt at missing Germany's years of austerity, time did not lend enchantment. When he acted in Bavaria in 1954, he remained downbeat: 'I have gone away from Germany. I don't feel at home here any more. The people? What they say and do, it doesn't touch me. They are strangers.'[23] The 'German' playing Colditz's humane commandant was legally a Czech and a person who felt a foreigner among Germans. Valk probably worked harder being the 'Teutonic authoritarian' at the film's start than the humane figure later.

Not everyone was positive about this film, for it was, as the *Manchester Guardian* put it, showing 'truthfulness and good taste' when portraying Germans. The director Guy Hamilton had considerable difficulty with Alexander Korda, whose London Films distributed it, for 'Korda said we couldn't have nice Germans in the film, because in his opinion all Germans were pigs'. Many reviewers were equally reluctant to give up stereotypes. *Reynold's News* thought 'only the Germans, with their heavy-handed sense of humour, could have had the idea of putting all the prisoners who escaped from other camps into one big burglar-proof castle. From here of course they all tried to escape.'[24] Yet if the Germans are characterised, the French and Polish POWs seem to have escaped from cartoons. Nevertheless, the short journey from *The Wooden Horse* to *Colditz* marked a relaxation of hatred, and made some viewers uncomfortable in the process. Nothing brings the change out more than when Douglas Bader is shot down in *Reach for the Sky* (1956) and a German does *not* fire at him as he parachutes to safety; the German fighter screams in as he dangles helplessly but then passes by with a saluting wave from its pilot. Bader winds up eventually in Colditz, but finds there polite and personable guards as well as bullies. When he himself escapes, he is rounded up by Anton Diffring playing a perfect gentleman, a far cry from the time when he was every film-maker's 'nasty Nazi'.

In such films Germans were merely secondary characters, and any depth was limited by their small time on screen. Films in which Germans were major characters carried these 1953–4 developments much further. The first, *The Battle of the River Plate* (1956), was a high-profile production by a famous director–writer team (Michael Powell and Emeric Pressburger), in colour and widescreen format, selected for a Royal Film Performance. The idea derived from Pressburger's chum Gunther von Stapenhorst, who fought at the Battle of Jutland, and Pressburger probably conceived the character of Captain Langsdorff as a tribute to this veteran of the Kaiser's navy. But stumbling on British Merchant Captain Dove's narrative of his imprisonment on the *Graf Spee* gave Powell and Pressburger their handle on the events, so presenting the battle as a personal story. This enabled them to avoid the amorous sub-plot that ruins so many war films, though since Dove practically hero-worshipped Langsdorff, and acted as adviser to the production, it was a love story of sorts anyway. Dove becomes the audience's viewpoint on the German captain.[25]

This tendency was underscored by casting and by a linguistic trick. Getting Peter Finch as Langsdorff guaranteed a charismatic 'German' presence. Powell later recalled Finch explaining that 'he felt that he knew more about the way that this man felt than Langsdorff himself. This was a real gift of the gods, for Peter had that magical thing, star quality.'[26] With Finch in the role, Langsdorff effortlessly controls the German side of the narrative, and is later contrasted with a Nazi bully, the German Minister in Montevideo. A clue to what Powell tried to do can be found in his book of the film. Arguing that Langsdorff and the *Graf Spee* had been victims of the Nazis' insistence on never showing weakness, he added a reflection on national rather than political characteristics. 'When well-led, there is no better human material than a German, but what is one to make of a nation which inevitably chooses madmen for its leaders?' 'Inevitably', in the present tense, does not suggest confidence that this had ended in 1945. Germans are portrayed throughout the book as committed to the *führerprinzip*, and the best that Powell can say is that they can be induced to follow good (Langsdorff) as well as bad (Hitler) leaders.[27] By comparison with this absolute concentration on Langsdorff among the Germans, there are many British officers sharing less limelight. Try as they might, John Gregson, Anthony Quayle and the others could not make real people out of wooden lines.

It was decided that realism would be improved by having the Germans speak to each other in German, but this was then kept to a minimum, so that audiences were not alienated. Langsdorff speaks English with a faint accent, but the effect is that he only speaks words we need to understand when talking to Dove. We never hear Langsdorff discussing the situation with other Germans, and we never get any idea of what he is like, merely eavesdropping on what he says to a sympathetic British officer. This guarantees that *The Battle of the River Plate* foregrounds a German and plays him for sympathy. He wears no Nazi armband, never mentions Hitler, and shows himself urbane and cultured. While this is supported by investigations of the real Langsdorff – and Powell certainly did his research – it also over-simplifies the situation. In Hitler's navy senior officers did not have to be fanatical Nazis, but nor were capital ships entrusted to the regime's opponents.

We see how Langsdorff charms Dove (who had initially called his captors 'Pirates!'), but we also hear how he hates the necessity to wage war against civilians. Dove is then joined by another British POW who demands, 'How's the captain?' 'Fine, fine. He's a gentleman.' This is confirmed by Langsdorff's present of Christmas decorations for his prisoners, while sailors sing '*Stille Nacht*'. Langsdorff then practically disappears, since we see no fighting from the German side – it being impossible to stage plausible conversations with Dove in English while shells fall. He does though have final scenes with Dove. In one of them the British captain says, 'I'd like to say thanks for everything. You've done your best for us, and I can only wish you the best for yourself.' Dove's final words are to tell Langsdorff that everyone has learned to respect him; close to reality, but nevertheless a surprising last word on the enemy in a British war film. By then, Langsdorff has inexplicably lost the 'German' chin-beard sported earlier and only the most vestigial accent remains. Having become a 'good chap' and a 'gentleman', he almost ceases to be visibly or audibly foreign. This is the last word on Langsdorff mainly because the film never explains what happens next, and reviewers who knew the story were critical of this. Powell misses the chance to deepen his psychological study of Langsdorff and bring the film to a yet more downbeat end than scuttling the *Graf Spee* by showing him committing suicide, wrapped not in a swastika but in a German naval flag of the Great War.[28] Instead of suicide, the final images are of the burning *Graf Spee*, while the British ambassador intones, 'Exactly at sunset – the Twilight of the Gods', and the soundtrack plays the final pages of *Götterdammerung*. This surely points to Berlin in 1945, whereas Langsdorff's suicide would have emphasised the earlier failure of the 'good' German.[29]

Not all reviewers were generous, for many disliked a film in which, as the *Daily Herald* put it, 'the Germans get all the glory'. Its critic thought that the Queen would get a shock when she saw the film, adding, 'I don't think this kind of whitewash is fitting, especially at a Royal Film performance'. The *Daily Sketch* too viewed it as 'an odd film for a Queen', while *Reynold's News* thought it 'carrying fairness too far'. The *News Chronicle* noted sourly that Langsdorff was that 'rarity of rarities, a Nazi gentleman', and the *Manchester Guardian* reckoned it was, 'if anything, over-scrupulous in its justice to the enemy'. Such critics would have been far from reassured to read that senior German diplomats attended a premiere (though not on the same evening as the royal family). Rank's executives were happy to entertain German journalists too, one asserting that 'We are delighted that the two countries are getting together over this film. The war is over now.' Critics would have been even less impressed when the film did good business in Germany, the first British war film after 1945 to do so. The story that it was West Germany's top-grossing import that year was unhelpfully headlined by *Variety*, 'British *Graf Spee* B[ox] O[ffice] Wow in Reich'.[30]

German critics had little doubt that the *Panzerschiff Graf Spee* broke new ground. For the *Süddeutsche Zeitung*, 'it [was] an English movie with a German hero, the sea captain Hans Langsdorff – that gives the movie its chivalrous trait.' It was 'as fair as a war movie can be. The English guns . . . also fire a salute to the enemy of yesterday. One watches this deep respect for the enemy with deep respect.' The German premiere was in the *Graf Spee*'s home port, Kiel, patronised by former Grand Admiral Raeder (recently released from Spandau), and invitations went to surviving members of Langsdorff's crew. *Der Spiegel*, perceptively noting that in British films 'only the courageous leader counts, one who loves his fatherland alone, not also a blond super-siren', as in Hollywood, explained this through English audiences' 'tendency to be generally fascinated by a show of all-male activities'. It also quoted Michael Powell, saying that 'we have tried to make the film in a supra-national spirit'.[31]

With their next effort, *Ill Met by Moonlight*, the film made while awaiting their royal premiere, Powell and Pressburger missed both commercial and critical success. They had thought for years of making a film about the audacious exploit of British officers who in 1943 kidnapped General Kreipe, spirited him over the mountains and carried him off to captivity in Cairo. It was a mad exploit, intended only to damage German prestige and raise the morale of the Cretan resistance.[32] This could all have been an unqualified disaster for British and Cretans alike, but the idea seized their imaginations, so that neither Powell nor Pressburger realised how flaccid was their script. Later Powell was not proud of this picture, writing that 'the performances of the principals were atrocious. Marius Goring as General Kreipe wouldn't have scared a rabbit; David Oxley as Captain Stanley Moss *was* the rabbit; while as for Dirk Bogarde's performance as Major Patrick Leigh-Fermor . . . it's a wonder that Paddy didn't sue both Dirk and me.' Amid this breast-beating you would hardly know that Powell was at least as responsible for their shortcomings as the actors. Nor did he recall that portraying a Nazi general as harmless, however damaging to the drama, was something new. There was no danger whatsoever of being sued, for when the film appeared, Leigh-Fermor explained how gratifying it was to be played on screen by Dirk Bogarde, apparently not noticing how badly Bogarde did it.[33]

First the South of France and then Corsica became 'Crete', while Powell disappeared for days in the search for locations and the rest of the team got bored. It is not surprising that the only actor taking it seriously comes through as the dominating figure, General Kreipe.[34] Marius Goring was a veteran of playing sympathetic Germans on film, his character demonstrating dignity, readiness to cooperate with his captors and resourcefulness in leaving clues to his whereabouts for the pursuing Germans. On the final embarkation beach, he discovers with amazement that his gentlemanly captors do not know the Morse code they must use to signal the boat waiting offshore. Powell later thought this scene one of the best in an unexciting screenplay, the dramatic equivalent of similar moments of premature triumphalism by Nazi characters in such earlier Powell and Pressburger successes as *One of Our Aircraft is Missing*.[35] In *Ill Met by Moonlight*, though, the episode is the peg on which hangs a generous declaration by the Nazi: when given back the articles he left behind as clues, which we had no idea his captors were collecting, Kreipe declares them not amateurs at all, but professionals like himself. *Ill Met by Moonlight* is, like *The Battle of the River Plate*, a story of convergence; the two films are indeed twins in the subversion of wartime stereotypes. Captain Langsdorff is told that he is a gentleman, the highest accolade in a British film, while Kreipe's kidnappers are awarded the badge of German efficiency.

Again, not all liked it. The original event was celebrated by British reviewers, and most were impressed by Goring, recognising him as a real person in a German uniform. Josh Billings wrote, 'Marius Goring impresses as the smug, arrogant, typically Teutonic, though by no means humourless Kreipe [who] good-humouredly accepts the inevitable'. *The Times* thought Kreipe 'not quite so stainless as Captain Langsdorff' and that 'bias towards enemy rather than friend is less apparent', but welcomed a truthful and interesting portrayal.[36] One positive review of Goring's acting rather ruined the effect by calling him 'Krupp', revealing stereotyping by sub-editors. A more hostile view from the *Daily Worker* was that this was 'the Rank Organisation's calculated effort to clean up on the Continent – especially Germany [so] every aspect of Nazi brutality, and the wholesale revenge wreaked on the Cretan villages by the Germans after the kidnapping is soft-pedalled, and not allowed to ruffle the surface of Byronic adventure'. It was, in short, a 'pantomime by public schoolboys'. From this perspective, Goring played 'the Nazi General with an Oxford accent and all the natural qualifications of a public school prefect'. However, even so hostile a review indicates just how far the image of Germans had changed from Anton Diffring's roles. Put more positively, but in effect saying the same thing, the *Daily Telegraph* reported Kreipe accepting defeat 'like a sportsman'.[37]

It was into this world of believable Germans on screen that Roy Baker ventured with *The One That Got Away*. The book by Kendal

Burt and James Leasor was a researched account of the 1940–1 activities of Luftwaffe Oberleutnant Franz von Werra, who was free several times in Britain before recapture, but escaped from Canada, crossing the frozen St Lawrence River to the neutral USA. He got home to Germany via Mexico and Spain, later visiting POW camps to advise on security, but was finally shot down on the Eastern Front and this time did not 'get away'. Such a book was property invariably made into a film. When reissued to coincide with the picture, a review quoted on the cover was the *People*'s view of 'a heartening tribute to the skill and resourcefulness of the Britons who guarded' POWs, which somewhat missed the point. Though the authors had access to the typescript of von Werra's incomplete autobiography, they 'preferred to rely on the British sources who had been contacted already [with] their more objective, if less colourful, reminiscences'. The dubious assumption that the British view of von Werra's escape was more reliable than his own coloured both book and film, certainly nullifying the *Evening Standard*'s claim of 'a fine piece of objective reporting'. Quite what the difference would have been is impossible now to say – except that the typescript would have included the inconvenient fact that von Werra was Swiss; the authors reported that two projected German wartime films of his escape had to be cancelled on security grounds (though it is hard to see what these could have been, given that only British security would be breached), partly because von Werra's account was thought too pro-British. The von Werra of the book was a shallow figure, if even more dedicated to escaping, since he had run away from home as an adolescent, boarded a ship in Hamburg and had only been recaptured in New Orleans after working his passage as a cabin boy. He joined the Luftwaffe soon after the Nazis seized power and achieved pilot-officer rank in 1938, partly through widely discussed daredevil exploits. The authors thought 'political indoctrination fostered rather than cured his adolescent romanticism'.[38]

The film employs several strategies to limit the damage to British prestige from a story bound to end in defeat. Hardy Kruger is six feet tall, but von Werra was short, so the framing of the actor makes him seem von Werra's height. We are shown the efficiency of British interrogators, who have a file on von Werra before he is even shot down. Like von Werra, we are initially deceived by bumbling British characters, but this hides a subtlety that deceives him. We see an unrelenting pursuit whenever he escapes. Most crucially, the film undermines von Werra himself, who at first looks a born Aryan Nazi. 'Same old claptrap,' observes the secretary typing up his interrogation, but the interrogator already knows this is untrue, reporting that von Werra uses the usual jargon, but doesn't believe a word of it: 'The only thing von Werra believes in is von Werra.' Shortly afterwards, he demolishes the hero's confidence by proving he has claimed kills of fighters that did not take place, cheating for the Iron Cross he conspicuously wears. The Nazi *Übermensch* is neither a Nazi nor an authentic hero, though he self-righteously refuses to reveal military information. 'You have a unique code of ethics, Oberleutnant,' remarks the interrogator.

That moment is von Werra's low point, but, just as in the wartime *Forty-ninth Parallel*, concentrating the plot on an enemy's escape enlists sympathy for him, striving to be free. In the long run Hardy Kruger engenders such sympathy for von Werra that we cannot help but want him to succeed in the final reel. One reviewer thought the director had 'let Kruger play the part in a breezy and affable style that wins the audience from the start', and Baker did indeed encourage Kruger to act that way, using boyish cheek and his experience in comedy to rally the audience to his side, when they were expected to be hostile. Kruger recalls that, when he attended early British showings to make personal appearances, the atmosphere was 'ice-cold', but then gradually warmed, and at the end he was invariably cheered.[39]

Once he has escaped, we see his interrogator receiving von Werra's triumphant postcard from Berlin, claiming the packet of cigarettes they had wagered; though he conscientiously adds it to the file, he seems happy enough that one has got away (but only one, of course). The film's von Werra was, thought the *Motion Picture Herald*, 'a daring and ingenious fellow, more to be respected than censured for his obsession to break out'. Overall, the picture showed British filmmakers had 'a broad-minded outlook that admire[d] determination and resourcefulness, regardless of nationality'. That sense that it denoted convergence between Britain and Germany was emphasised when the premiere was attended not only by von Werra's widow, and by Hardy Kruger with his 'young wife and daughter', but by members of the RAF Escaping Society. These veterans had graced the premieres of earlier POW films and did not intend to miss one just because the escaper was German. This too was a long way from the chauvinistic premiere of *The Wooden Horse*.[40]

Reactions were rather mixed. *Variety*, reflecting Hollywood's greater resistance to rehabilitating Germans, queried whether it had been 'worth devoting a complete feature film to the exploits of a German making fools of the British army, airforce and intelligence corps'. Audience sympathies would be 'entirely with the Nazi officer, which may well be considered carrying "fair play" too far'. Nevertheless, even this reviewer had to admit Kruger was admirable in 'showing insolence and bravado . . . but, on the whole, he comes out of the adventure as quite a nice fellow'. British reviewers were generally defensive. Josh Billings emphasised that von Werra was the *only* one to get away, but that it was a 'real life adventure'. A few weeks later, once it was established in cinemas and had been doing excellent business, he summarised the plot as 'one Jerry against the British and proves we are good losers'. After six weeks, the film had 'never faltered' after its 'flying start', and even later was 'an exciting, as well as an unusual' war film. At the end of the year, it was not on Billings' shortlist of 1957's box-office winners, but it did feature among the near misses.[41] Some were yet more sceptical of the idea behind the film. The *Daily Film Renter*, while noticing the film's stratagems for belittling von Werra's achievement, still thought it had achieved the opposite, for he 'comes through as a man of boyish charm hiding an invincible will to be free; while the British are defeated at every turn!'[42]

The idea of convergence can also be found in films where the very idea of British relations with Germans was foregrounded in the present: *Frieda* (1947) and the romantic comedy *Bachelor of Hearts* (1958). *Frieda* was a stage play by Ronald Millar, written as the war drew to a close. The author summarised it as the tale of 'a young British air force officer who marries a German nurse who has helped him to escape from the prison camp in which he was interned, and brings her home with him to wartime England, to the dismay of his family and in defiance of a scandalised public to whom "fraternisation" with the enemy (if one can "fraternise" with one's wife) is akin to treason'.[43] Re-establishing relations with Germany is dramatised through a 'reasonably comfortable but by no means prosperous middle-class' family. When the play was published and performed, intervals between its scenes were extended: now only Act I took place in wartime, while Acts II and III occurred at Christmas and New Year, 1945–6, making it a narrative about the transition to peacetime.[44]

Frieda launched Millar as a playwright. Reviews of the stage production were nervous in tone because of the subject-matter, so he did not yet have a career-making success, but things changed when Michael Relph, the play's designer but also a key figure at Ealing, showed the script to Michael Balcon, who headed the studio. Balcon saw that *Frieda* would fit Ealing's social agenda, and promptly bought the film rights, assigning Basil Dearden to direct. Millar was contracted to write the screenplay, but since this was his first such effort he relied heavily on advice from Angus McPhail, Ealing's scenario editor, and was anyway soon lured over to Hollywood. Millar thus contributed storyline and essential elements of plot and character, but the collective involvement of Relph, Balcon, McPhail and Dearden made this a classic case of Ealing teamwork.[45]

In the play a careful balance of sympathies is kept, and Millar warned directors against presenting only Frieda as a victim. It was vital to underline the tensions within Aunt Nell, Frieda's chief tormentor within her new 'family' and advocate of the view that Germans should never be forgiven. For the film, the torment that Nell suffers before conceding that she had been wrong to reject her nephew's German wife was reinforced by casting the forceful Flora Robson in the role. The casting of Frieda was therefore crucial, and the question arose as to whether a German actress should be used. As early in the post-war years as 1946, it would have been difficult to find any German actress not associated in the public mind with the Nazis, for there were few émigrées available for female roles. As Millar puts it, 'the war was still an open wound and even if a German actress were to be granted a work permit, which was highly unlikely even by a Socialist government, we had seen no German artists on film since before the war'. Ealing therefore tested 'several admirable English actresses with carefully coached German accents', before deciding this would not work. It would have to be another foreigner, so Dearden and Relph flew to Sweden to try out Mai Zetterling. This seemed an unpromising option, for Zetterling spoke little English and loathed London ('damp, dark and unfriendly'). She was however signed up, triumphantly re-learned English at the gallop, and had just the right mixture of vulnerability and strength. Moreover, blond plaits and strong cheekbones fitted British preconceptions of what a German woman ought to look like: the *Sunday Graphic* thought that Zetterling contrived to look 'as touching and as German as a dachshund'.[46]

Millar and McPhail introduced significant changes between play and screenplay, while Dearden and Relph darkened the piece in their design and direction. Frieda's husband Robert treats her with near sadism, having no apparent motivation except that he married her from a sense of obligation (she helped him to escape) rather than for love, and now feels trapped. This personalised the idea that the British people ought to like Germans but so far did not. Back in Britain, Robert finds that his pre-war love is now free, her fiancé killed 'by' the Germans. Since Frieda's parents died during RAF raids, both families are war victims, but British victims are foregrounded, Germans just mentioned in passing. Nor are Robert and Frieda fully married, for their union is unconsummated. This allows for the arrangement and periodic postponement of an authentic British marriage, before the film's melodramatic climax, when Robert realises he loves Frieda, saves her from a despairing suicide and promises to name the date. In both play and film it is an ending that beggars belief. When the film ends, the British hero is about to penetrate German virginity – evoking the 1945 invasion of Germany rather than post-war harmony – and this happens because the British decide it is right. Nor is there any doubt that the family stands for the nation. Robert tells Frieda as they travel back to England that 'Denfield' is 'quite an ordinary town . . . just like any other'. The film was shot on location in Woodstock, typical of the small-town Englishness celebrated in 1940s national myth-making, and coincidentally the birthplace of Winston Churchill.[47]

Frieda remains ambiguous in confronting Germany's Nazi past and German culpability. In the first half Frieda is 'forgiven' for being German by her new family, while more outspoken anti-German remarks from the play have disappeared. Frieda plays Schumann to her relations, German music on a German piano. Apart from Nell, the only character who voices bigoted views has been maltreated in a

POW camp, so he will take longer to forgive, but for personal reasons. Christmas shows that Frieda has been accepted, though at the price of Aunt Nell moving out of the family home. Since Nell has meanwhile won a by-election on the platform of continuing to treat Germans as collectively guilty, we are reminded that Frieda's family are ahead of most British opinion. Robert, apparently fair and impartial, is all set to 'marry' Frieda.

The second half of the film challenges the comforting idea that time is all that is needed to bring enchantment. Frieda's brother Rikki arrives during the first peacetime Christmas, an unreconstructed Nazi. He gives his sister a swastika brooch, and rants about the rebirth of the Reich. *Today's Cinema* thought Albert Lieven 'the embodiment of all that is evil in the Nazi code', representative of everything implied by the word 'Belsen'. When Frieda resists, saying that both she and Germany have moved on, he reminds her that she had attended Nuremberg rallies and endorsed the regime. Her not contradicting him is an important silence, since all we knew about her past was that, as a nurse, she treated the war's victims. Rikki is recognised by the maltreated former POW and Robert beats him up in a pub, then calls off the wedding, telling Frieda that he cannot now marry her; hence, the melodramatic ending. Frieda is driven to suicide more by her loss of Robert than by her exposure as a Nazi, while Robert changes his mind because he loves Frieda, not just because he is able to accept her past. Her brother has meanwhile been arrested as a war criminal, so will be a scapegoat for the Nazi episode of German history. The issue of German culpability has been raised, side-tracked and left unresolved. As the American *Motion Picture Herald* noted, 'From England comes a film story of tolerance – tolerance towards Germans in these days of peace, despite their country's crimes in the time of war. As such it is a well-wrought but somber story which will cause many audiences to examine their own reactions to the question: who is to be held responsible for the war, the German people or their Nazi Government?'[48] Note the ambiguity of 'their', used here twice: were 'their' country's crimes and 'their' Nazi government things for which 'they' must be held responsible, or was it merely conventional syntax denoting nationality? The *Motion Picture Herald* was no more ready to offer an answer than the film. Britain's *Monthly Film Bulletin* likewise concluded that 'this is definitely a film with a theme which will set any audience thinking' but offered no advice as to *what* they should think. *Today's Cinema* noted that the pivot of this 'problem drama' came with the assertion that 'you cannot treat human beings as less than human, without being less than human yourself', words with which Aunt Nell recants her anti-German bigotry. Nevertheless, while its climax 'makes out a moving case for compassion', its acceptance 'remain[ed] a matter for individual mentalities'.[49]

Making a virtue out of necessity, ambiguity became Ealing's sales pitch. Ronald Millar remembered that after weeks of indecision about marketing, the head of the studio's press department 'came up with a brilliant gimmick. In a series of carefully chosen newspapers there appeared in bold lettering the simple question, WOULD YOU TAKE FRIEDA INTO YOUR HOME . . . The theatre-going public apart, no one knew who this person was or why, before taking her into one's home, a measure of caution was advisable. But they *wanted* to know.'[50] The press were cheekily assured that 'the question posed on the advertisements . . . is not a publicity stunt. It is the question posed by the film. More, it is a question that goes beyond the story of one family . . . The implications are international and affect the lives of us all.' Posters and newspaper advertisements added three more rhetorical questions: 'What would you do about Frieda? Would you take Frieda into your heart? Would you give Frieda a chance?' The second and third of these at least hinted at the positive answer the film eventually gave, but the added claim that it was 'a great controversy of our time – brought courageously to the screen' would induce more nausea than cogitation.[51]

The *Daily Express's* Leonard Mosley wrote that 'the advertisements ask "Would you take Frieda into your home?" When Frieda is the Swedish star Mai Zetterling, who is not only lovely but can make herself look like a tired and frightened kitten, the answer is "Yes, sir!"' In the same spirit the *Sunday Chronicle's* critic responded, 'I would take Mai Zetterling . . . into my home any day.' Presumably the craggy-faced Flora Robson would not have fared quite so well if the same question had been asked of Nell, which only shows how the film's casting manipulated audience response: the *Evening News* said that 'the beauty and sensitiveness of Mai Zetterling . . . do much to sway the balance in favour of the intruder' – but notice 'intruder'. Despite his flippancy, Mosley was at one with critics in seeing 'a well-made film that will make most people argue', and equally with them in failing to offer a contribution to the argument.[52]

Some reviewers did though manage to retain a critical distance. The *Daily Worker*, always the last to rehabilitate Germany, had a fair point: 'In the original play, Frieda comes to realise her political responsibility and decides to return to Germany to work out her personal regeneration. The film's happy ending does not solve the problem nearly so satisfactorily.' On the other side was the *Manchester Guardian*. Though noting that the film offered no answer to its central question that could be politically generalised, it decided that *Frieda* 'does at least give the answer so far as it need be given to individual British people when dealing with individual Germans. That answer is the obvious one – or at least it is the answer which is obviously dictated by Christianity. Indeed, the only fault of this worthy film is that it is all a little slow and a little obvious.'[53]

Between these opposites, most critics concluded that the film had got it about right, but came to that conclusion mainly by clambering onto the fence alongside it. In explaining this we need to pay heed to what trade reviews were saying. Most were sceptical as to whether the public was ready for such a film of forgiveness. Was it, asked *Kinematograph Weekly*, just 'too early' for talk about 'shaking our enemies by the hand'? Or, as *Variety* succinctly summed up its likely appeal to American audiences, this was a 'topically hot treatise on the Germans, OK for big urban centers, n[ot] s[o] g[ood] in nabes [suburbs]'. Middle America was no more ready than middle England to welcome Frieda into its homes. It is though testament to the speed with which opinion moved on that when *Frieda* was re-released in 1954, it was generally thought out of date, and to refer to a world of hatred that had long passed away.[54]

By then, Carol Reed had inexplicably ducked the issues raised by *Frieda* in *The Man Between* (1953). Here the location is contemporary Berlin, while the central characters include a British army doctor and his recently married German wife. We are soon told that they sleep in separate rooms, so this is another unconsummated Anglo-German alliance. In a film set among the rubble of a bombed city, Reed revisited the ravaged Vienna of *The Third Man* (1949), but the male lead, Ivo, is now a German who turned to racketeering not because he has no morals, like Harry Lime, but because his sensitivities have been outraged by his activities as a German soldier. The opportunity is there for a full examination of the war-guilt questions set by *Frieda*, but no such attempt is made. Crucially, the part of Ivo was handed not to a German but to James Mason, who had recently played Rommel in *The Desert Fox* and who was therefore thought to fit another German part. Since Ivo is 'the man between', this wrecks the film, especially when he delivers anguished lines about culpability for war crimes. *The Man Between* soon loses interest in such matters anyway, developing into a Cold War thriller. The marital sub-plot forfeits our interest once it becomes clear that tension arises from the German wife having accidentally married bigamously, believing her German husband dead. There is no personal discord between husband and wife and the problem is solved by Ivo getting shot while helping his sister-in-law to escape. This 'man between' dies in the no man's land between the communist, racketeering East and the democratic West, rather than between the German past and an Anglo-German future. Advising on the script, Graham Greene argued that 'a thriller about Europe today has surely got to have some significance about it and not simply end in long exciting chases'. On release, the film was panned by critics for its lack of meaning. The *Daily Worker*, again hitting the nail on the head with its hammer (and sickle), argued that Reed 'has taken his technique to one of the key points of the world and has shirked the challenge'.[55]

Such evasions had no part in *Bachelor of Hearts* (1958), a sequel in two senses. It was a natural attempt to cash in quickly on Kruger's success as *The One That Got Away*, and was modelled on *A Yank at Oxford* (1938); *Bachelor of Hearts* should have been titled *A Kraut at Cambridge*. In *A Yank at Oxford* Robert Taylor is pitch-forked among British eccentrics, class-ridden and ineffective. The first half hour is all mutual incomprehension, but by the end he has understood the bedrock qualities of the British and they have accepted him too. The film was made by 20th Century Fox to appeal simultaneously in its two biggest markets, but a story of harmony among the English-speaking peoples on the eve of world war also had international importance.[56] The decision to remake *A Yank at Oxford* twenty years on, but with a German now the estranged cousin, was thus a significant cultural moment. Setting the film in Cambridge also evoked

Leslie Howard's *Pimpernel Smith* (1941), a classic wartime propaganda piece about national identities, in which a Cambridge professor is supported against the Nazis by students very like those Kruger now encountered.[57] Rank's wish to harmonise post-war relations therefore had something in common with American studios' motivations in the late 1930s, as did its hope to improve sales abroad. The film was assigned to Wolf Rilla, an all-round director like Baker, not much noted for political views. He had made fifteen British films, none about Germany, but his émigré father had acted in British films in the 1930s, so the young Wolf (born 1920) had personally experienced being a young German in Britain, in Cambridge to be precise, where he was a student just when Robert Taylor fictionally attended Oxford.[58]

This being an original story, Rank turned to Frederick Raphael, already the author of two novels but not long down from Cambridge and destined for a writing career in which Britain's ancient universities would often feature. The writing credit was shared between him and Leslie Bricusse, later more known for lyrics than novels. Their original intention was to produce a Varsity comedy derived from *Love's Labour's Lost*, and elements of this survive in a pact among undergraduates not to make love to their girlfriends. In this version the hero would have been a British star, but Kruger now had to be incorporated. Raphael's initial reaction was that this might be a joke, but he and Bricusse did as they were told. They were after all being well paid, and wrote screenplays (as British writers usually have) mainly to finance 'serious' writing. It was anyway a comedy, so political overtones seemed insignificant. Raphael also thought that if anyone involved with the film *had* questioned the idea of comedically rehabilitating Germany in 1958, such a challenge would have been 'unthinkable' in the cinema of the time.[59]

After the 1950s, Raphael was to write often and with great insight about Germany and anti-Semitism, so there is something ironic about the way in which this early work treats Britain's recent enemy so superficially. Knowledge of German war crimes, including the mass murder of Jews, was then not much discussed, the word 'Holocaust' and all it encapsulates not yet in general use. Lord Russell of Liverpool's *The Scourge of the Swastika* tackled the issue head-on and was widely debated, as was Alan Bullock's *Hitler*, but

William Shirer's influential *The Rise and Fall of the Third Reich* was yet to come.[60] The media world though was not outside such debates. There was a furore in July 1958, just before *Bachelor of Hearts* was released, over an East German film about the survival of prominent Nazis in West Germany. *Holiday on Sylt*, a film about a former SS general who was now Burgermeister of a North Sea holiday resort, was to be shown on ITV, but was cancelled after the broadcasters consulted the West German Embassy and the Foreign Office. Newspapers as far apart as the Tory *Daily Express* and the Labour *Daily Herald* united to denounce ITV's craven submission to a Foreign Office 'appeasement' of post-war Germany (interesting choice of word). Labour MPs deplored censorship in the Commons, angry letters were written to newspapers, and film magazines devoted much attention to the story. As a sequel to *A Yank at Oxford*, *Bachelor of Hearts* might well have met similar resistance. That it did not can be attributed to more than one factor: it was a breezy comedy with any political implications submerged; it personalised its main theme in a warm-hearted love story; and in Kruger its German character was of an age that made wartime memories irrelevant.[61]

In *Bachelor of Hearts* Wolf Hauser (Kruger) comes to study at Cambridge on a student exchange. He is an able mathematician, but not much liked by male undergraduates (though already a hit with the women), and especially not by drones in a drinking club called the 'Dodos': Hauser the German is modern, Britain is not. He is keen to win acceptance, but the Dodos hold him at bay. Not a word is said about his nationality, but they dislike his stiffness, over-confidence and lack of humour, surely all signalling a cinematic 'German'. They exploit his wish to belong by giving him a leading role in their rag-day stunt, without explaining that he is to be a human sacrifice. Hauser is paraded through Cambridge dressed in a white sheet (symbolic German repentance?), doused in paraffin and set alight on a bridge over the River Cam. (Kruger becoming a Roman candle was cut when the film appeared on television in the 1970s, the idea of setting fire to a German by then deemed unacceptable even as comedy.) Fortunately, he is soon in the river and the fire is out, so another one gets away. Honours are about even, but there is neither affection nor real acceptance – he is part of the Dodos' circle but not a member of the club, symbolic of Germany's place in the international community in the 1950s. His tutor, though recognising talent, is nevertheless critical of Hauser's earlier education as mechanical, producing only a 'notebook mind': the German education system (and surely this again hints at more than education) has taught him *what* to think but not *how* to think; in Cambridge he must become his democratic self. This links fascinatingly with what Hardy Kruger was then saying about his own life: 'Until I was 15, I never met anyone who questioned that Hitler was right. I had been educated to believe in him. I knew nothing else. Then I met people who were against him and I began to think for myself.'[62]

Soon after escaping immolation, Hauser rescues the leading Dodo from rustication. Now he is accepted, but goes over the top in his desire to be British, wearing tweeds and a waistcoat (rather than the belted leather coat which had denoted Germanness), smokes a pipe like all 'good chaps' in British films, and obsessively entertains undergraduates to tea. Convergence is now personalised in his friendship with an attractive female undergraduate. Though he has initially lived up to the name Wolf, and been firmly pushed away with the reminder that in Britain men do not behave like that, they fall in love and personal attraction becomes the film's vehicle for integrating the intruder into the heart of Britain. Hauser knuckles down to the very 'German' practice of working hard, and duly gets a First as well as the girl. A journalist wrote of *Bachelor of Hearts* that 'sex knows no national boundaries', but ten years earlier that was exactly the statement that *Frieda* had failed to make. A nicely rambling conversation between two dons finalises Hauser's acceptance: the former 'strange chap' becomes 'a good man', semantics that say it all. Meanwhile, Kruger and his girl drift past on a punt and discuss getting married. However, in case the vision of a German hero clinching with a British starlet in the final frame was too shocking for audiences, he falls asleep and cannot quite strike the deal before the film ends.[63]

Reviewers were generally censorious about the film's depiction of the upper class at play, one exasperatedly thinking it 'difficult to avoid the feeling that such irresponsible behaviour by young people of a different social class would label them spivs or Teddy Boys', but even that reviewer called it 'a light-hearted comedy of charm and youthful appeal' in which 'Hardy Kruger's boyish charm is well in evidence'. *Kinematograph Weekly* felt that 'the foibles of both the British and the Teutonic temperaments are subtly contrasted'. *Variety* noticed that it was 'a switch on *A Yank at Oxford*', and thought it a much inferior copy, but then the film's producers had never expected to appeal to Americans. However, when *Variety* argued that 'US audiences are likely to be completely bewildered by the proceedings' it was surely also showing pique that an Anglo-American formula had been so successfully subverted.[64]

Rank's publicity for the film concentrated heavily on Kruger and his nationality, with the first paragraph of its press release asserting that 'The finest ambassador Germany has sent to Britain since 1945 is, undoubtedly, a young actor called Hardy Kruger. Tall, flaxen-haired, with piercing blue eyes, he is the very prototype of German manhood, but his slow, dimpled smile, quiet, firm manner, and wry sense of humour have won him the unqualified admiration of millions, regardless of nationality.' Cinema managers were offered Hardy Kruger postcards and urged to cooperate with newsagents, so that the cards could be slipped into women's magazines. Much of this was no more than the traditional hype any male star received, but the international issues were not neglected. There was a promotional tie-in with Lufthansa to encourage tourism in Germany. Raymond Durgnat sees Rank's contribution to the normalisation of Anglo-German relations as closely linked to its sales drive in Europe. With Curt Jurgens and Horst Bucholz following Kruger, 'the bright, eager, masculine, domineering, amiable young male asserted his German virility everywhere from Oxbridge . . . to Hong Kong (*Ferry to Hong Kong*)'. The journalist Thomas Wiseman knew even then that commercial motives explained a good deal: 'In the last few years, the German market for films has become one of the most profitable in the world, and such factors always inspire strong bonds of friendship: the profit motive being an infallible promoter of brotherly love.'[65]

German critics welcomed both of Kruger's films for Rank. There was admiring comment on the fact that he spoke good English, but was also dubbing his own voice for the German editions. There was even reporting of his comment that success in English would not mean he would forget how to speak German. With *Einer kam durch* (literally 'One Came Through', *The One That Got Away* in Germany), *Der Spiegel* seemed puzzled by its motivation: 'With almost pedantic fairness the English producers show in every detail how the cunning German airforce hero leads their compatriots and later the Canadians by the noses, until he finally escapes into neutral America. The *mecki*-faced Hardy Krüger, trained in such roles, seizes this grateful part as skilfully as probably any German actor could have done.' *Der Tagesspiegel* was also impressed with both Kruger and the fairness of the film, but mysteriously referred to it leaving out the 'tragic irony' of von Werra's death in neutral America. The real irony was that he had died in action after being welcomed home by Göring, not in America. When *Bachelor of Hearts* (as *Mit dem Kopf durch die Wand*) appeared, *Die Welt* reminded readers that Kruger was now 'the irrepressible herald of German youth'. It thought the film no more than 'a harmless and well-meaning' ninety-minute 'pastime', but another chance for Kruger to be 'a mediator for Anglo-German understanding'. *Der Spiegel*, punning on the German titles of both films, headlined its report 'Hardy Comes Through Again'. Manfred Delling found no trace of the usual British understatement, but reported that 'the many lovely girls among the premiere audience were very much amused by Hardy's smart-alecking. And (mainly) young and older women will certainly shriek with delight at every showing.' Nevertheless, he recognised that 'even if this movie does nothing for art, it does perhaps at least serve Anglo-German under-standing, so we had better be nice to it'.[66]

It certainly worked for Hardy Kruger, voted in a 1959 poll the most popular male star with British female audiences. His third film for Rank was Joseph Losey's *Blind Date* (1959), in which his nation-ality was not an issue, for he plays a Dutch painter in contemporary London, framed for murder by a Frenchwoman and cleared by the Welsh Stanley Baker. Kruger recalls how Baker's machismo forced him to make his Dutchman romantic and dreamy, to differentiate between them. But if nationality was no longer a problem, politics still got in the way. Losey originally signed Kruger to play in a Cold War melodrama about the nuclear bomb, but Columbia backed out because Losey and his writer had been blacklisted during Holly-wood's McCarthyite witch-hunts. *Blind Date* was substituted because it was cheap enough not to need American money, but when released *Variety* denounced a picture made by 'alleged Reds' and starring an 'ex-Nazi'. A German distribution deal netted forty thousand pounds, but it was only his own importance in the German market that enabled Kruger to insist that Losey got on-screen credit. Paramount then released *Blind Date* in America in a deal which made the producers twice what the film had cost, but after the British opening hostile picketing was threatened by the American Legion and Paramount abandoned plans for a US premiere, and then sneaked it into suburban cinemas on a double bill with a comedy. It is not clear whether resistance was really to 'alleged Reds' or an 'ex-Nazi'. Kruger had anyway been signed by then to play the lead in Howard Hawks' *Hatari* (1960), and continued his international career with the French *A Taxi to Tobruk* (1959). He now lived mainly in Switzerland but had built a bungalow-hotel in East Africa, where tourists could film – but not shoot – the local wildlife.[67]

When his career maintained international momentum after his British successes, life was not so easy for Kruger. Producers wanted him on screen as a wartime Nazi, and interviewers pried into what he had done as a teenager, his role in the Hitler Youth and how he had come to star in the propaganda film *Junge Adler* (1944). It was while making *Junge Adler* that Kruger first met people who had themselves rejected Nazism and participated in acts of resistance, the beginning of a process which opened his eyes about Hitler. Understandably irritated by all this, he has occasionally lost his characteristic cool with reporters. In 1984 the *Daily Express* – under the headline 'Stamping Out That Jackboot Nazi Image' – quoted Kruger saying, 'in only five of my sixty films have I played a Nazi, but I am sure people think I have a uniform at home to strut around in'. In 2003 he demanded, 'Why shouldn't I try to show the world that there had been friendly Germans? Take for example the former Chancellor Helmut Schmidt, a highly intelligent man full of integrity. He too did not voluntarily end up in the German army. He was simply drafted.' Back in 1958, it had been easier. Photographed for the *Evening Standard* with the caption 'Hardy Kruger: No Signs of Arrogance', he dealt intelligently with questions about his German past, though he did admit he was 'rather miserable about the line that our interview had taken'. War films were boring and by concentrating on individual heroics they invariably failed to remind viewers 'how horrible war is'. He would play a Nazi officer, 'in a film exposing Nazism', but such films could not be made yet in Germany, since Germans in the 1950s were

still too close to the events . . . There is such a mass of confused feelings in Germany about these things that it is impossible for a German
writer to give a really true and objective account of how a people
could come to do what we Germans did. I do not know the answer.
For the moment it must come from people who live outside
Germany. It is not possible for us to look at this objectively.

By 2003, he was no longer sure that it was only a matter of time, for
the French film *Le Franciscain de Bourges* (1967), in which Kruger
played a war-resisting monk drafted into Hitler's army, had still not
been shown in Germany. Asked in 1958 how he interpreted his success at the British box office in *The One That Got Away*, he smilingly
responded that 'the English are so sporting'.[68]

The fact that in *Blind Date* a star's nationality could now be
ignored in Britain, if not yet in America, shows how far cinematic
relations had normalised since 1945. A great deal was owed to Hardy
Kruger in this convergence between former enemies. Jacques Chirac
acknowledged in 2001 his equivalent contribution to Franco-German
understanding by awarding Kruger the Legion of Honour, only the
second German actor to be so recognised. He speaks with pride of
holding the same decoration as Marlene Dietrich, known for 'her
unshakeable stand against Hitler, his cronies and a nation who followed these criminals blindly', but is also proud that as the first
young German actor to work prominently in Britain after 1945, he
was able 'to stand before the British people as a German of the new
and responsibly living generation'.[69]

Likeable people whose careers are in the public eye can have a disproportionate effect on popular attitudes, and here the contributions
of Frederick Valk and Hardy Kruger can be laid alongside the less visible work of enlightened film-makers, Guy Hamilton, Michael
Powell and Roy Baker. Cinema in the 1950s both mirrored public
taste and helped to push it in a positive direction – if also, for understandable commercial reasons, trying hard not to get too far ahead of
its public.

9

'Bert Trautmann's helmet': English soccer and the German problem

In 1995 the Manchester City supporters' fan magazine changed its name from *Electric Blue* to *Bert Trautmann's Helmet*. The 'historic first issue' had its new title in Gothic script and as its logo a spiked helmet. This was an obvious tribute to British soccer's most famous German import – a man who had retired more than thirty years earlier. It was at the same time a deliberate act of defiance, for it had long been a joke among the fans of Manchester United that City had 'no trophy in their cabinet except Bert Trautmann's helmet'. The magazine argued that Trautmann 'better than anyone else embodie[d] the spirit of Manchester City (or at least the fans' perception of the spirit of Manchester City)'. Though Trautmann, as a Second World War paratrooper, had never actually worn a spiked helmet, the quintessentially German helmet just had to be there because Trautmann so represented Germany for fans. Even while he played for unfashionable City in the 1950s, fans had had to endure an earlier joke: 'Which team is "the Potters"? No, not Stoke. Manchester City, because it consists of ten mugs and a jerry.'[1]

Despite these jokes, Trautmann had become a revered figure in Manchester after his contentious arrival in 1949, and is considered by many to have been the finest goalkeeper ever to play in the English league; the legendary Russian keeper Lev Yashin famously claimed that there had only ever been two world-class goalkeepers, 'Yashin and . . . that German boy who played for Manchester'. Over a career that involved six hundred professional appearances in goal, Trautmann saved about 60 per cent of the penalties he faced.[2] Nevertheless, he has really remained famous for being a German whose previous career in Hitler's war machine made his acceptance into British football problematic, but who lived down bigotry and turned it into love. This was therefore an improbable story for early post-war Britain, not least because it centred on a city which had suffered greatly in the war, but also because the warmth of the City fans towards an unapologetically German ex-paratrooper was fortuitously matched in 1958 by similar demonstrations of tolerance from Manchester United. In both cases observers asserted without irony that sportsmen could rebuild relations between former enemies where diplomats laboured in vain. Unfortunately, the next two generations demonstrated exactly the opposite, football becoming rather a surrogate for war between former enemies, and its reporting the excuse for cliché-ridden reminders that in war – if rarely now in football – Britain had 'always beaten the Germans'. As George Orwell had put it, sport was 'war without the shooting'. Although this was driven by the market needs of newspapers, it was not a process in which ordinary supporters were passive. In 2000, during the final match at the old Wembley Stadium, England against Germany, the home fans sang 'The Dambusters' March' to the visitors (with appropriate arm movements to denote bombing). It was a gesture of gratuitous ill-will that bewildered German officials. In contemporary all-seater stadiums a variation on the same theme at England–Germany matches was for England fans to chant, 'Stand up if you won the war'. When Wembley was demolished, the *Sun* was defiant: although the Twin Towers must fall, the country would never forget the day when England had so comprehensively beaten Germany beneath them – with the towers reminiscent of the flak towers on the Möhne dam in 1943. The paper was furious to discover a few days later that Wembley would be torn down with German equipment, and only partly mollified by assurances that the demolition team would be British. Something clearly went very wrong after Bert Trautmann retired in the early 1960s.

The Trautmann story did not begin well as an exercise in Anglo-German rapprochement. When in October 1949 the Manchester papers splashed the news that City were about to sign a German paratrooper, until recently a prisoner of war, legally an 'enemy alien', all hell broke out. City fans, perhaps hundreds of them, indignantly sent back their season tickets, a pub fight broke out in Salford, there was violence on the terraces at the next home game and stones were thrown through some shop windows. Angry letters were sent both to the club and to the press, and one supporter warned the club's directors by telegram that if Trautmann played there would be a mass boycott of City by the fans. That threat, by a supporter signing himself '45 years a Jewish City supporter', promised to mobilise the British Legion and Manchester's Jewish community. 'No doubt you are aware that the Germans killed six million of my brothers and sisters in the last war, and the English public must have a short memory if it has forgotten the thousands of women and children killed in air raids.' A Jewish ex-servicemen's club argued that 'anybody who can watch one of Hitler's former soldiers pushing an Englishman out of a team must have forgotten the atrocities of the Germans'. Manchester took considerable pride in its contribution to the war, as recent celebrations to mark the admission of Winston Churchill as a freeman had shown; in those ceremonials Manchester was congratulated by Churchill on both 'taking it' during air raids and 'dishing it out' through its soldiers, sailors and airmen.[3] The festivities had been marked by some of the biggest Manchester crowds ever seen, and those same spectators were unwilling to watch a German given such an important place in the city, not just playing for one of the big Manchester teams, but filling the symbolic gap left by the retirement of the great Frank Swift – England's, as well as Manchester City's, goalkeeper. 'German Seeks Swift's Job' was the *Daily Express* headline. 'Trautmann Signs and Starts Big Controversy', reported the *Manchester Evening News*, while a letter to the paper signed by three Mancunian ex-soldiers argued that 'already I've heard plenty of people say they would not go and watch a German; City must be mad to think of signing him'. Letters to the press were signed 'Sieg Heil!', and many were too inflammatory to be printed anyway. So many letters on the subject were sent to the *Manchester Evening News* that the Post Office made special deliveries. As its chief football reporter Eric Thornton later recalled, 'more people lost their temper over Manchester City signing Bert Trautmann than they had ever done before, or since'.[4]

In legend at least, that anticipated mass protest is just what happened: Colin Shindler writes of Manchester later saluting Trautmann, while 'a vast proportion' of the city 'had wanted to kill the ex-prisoner of war when he first signed for City in 1949'. For Fred Eyre and Roy Kavanagh, Trautmann had 'defied British chauvinism and won British hearts with talent and good manners', making him 'a Teutonic, one-man United Nations'.[5] Yet the storm subsided as quickly as it had arisen – at least on the surface, though Trautmann had to endure Nazi salutes from opposing fans throughout his career. The quick defusing of the crisis can be attributed to four causes. First, there was always an undercurrent of fairness among Manchester fans, which ran in parallel with the chauvinism that was mainly remembered later. Many letters to the press were from fans who wanted Trautmann to be signed; they knew of the club's desperate need for a good goalkeeper, but they also saw no necessary connection between resentment of 'Germany' and fairness to individual Germans. Such letters made up the majority of those printed by the local papers, though not necessarily of those received. (The type of sentiment found in some of the unprinted letters may be deduced from one sent to Trautmann: 'I don't give a fuck what you are and where you come from as long as you can put some life into this fucking City team.') This positive response was no doubt reinforced by the second factor: City's counter-offensive on Trautmann's behalf, which used the club's weighty position in the community to great effect. The chairman issued a statement in which he admitted that 'there is no doubt that many people will be upset by our signing of a German, but I feel we must take the broad view. City need a goalkeeper, and we have excellent reports of this German as a goalkeeper, and as an individual.' When Trautmann arrived for training at Maine Road, he was welcomed by the club captain, Eric Westwood (himself an ex-soldier who had fought the Germans in Normandy), with assurances that there would be no war in the changing room. Trautmann was then carried around shoulder-high by Westwood and other players, everyone visibly embarrassed by an obvious stunt for the cameras. Both the captain's welcome and photographs duly found their way into the press. City were apparently also using their supporters' club to generate favourable letters to the press, having first ensured that leading members had met Trautmann and could provide

'excellent reports' of him 'as an individual'. This process was completed when Trautmann first appeared for the team, and Frank Swift
endorsed him: 'Good show. You'll do!' (a rave review for Manchester
in the 1940s). News was leaked that other league clubs had also hoped
to sign Trautmann (City had apparently snatched him from right
under Bolton's nose on the day before he was due to sign for them).
This made Manchester City's decision seem bold and successful
rather than a provocative gamble, adding to the overall sense that the
club had got it right. Trautmann was 'a City player because chairman
Walter Smith had the vision and courage to bring him to Maine
Road', crowed a Manchester journalist in 1956.[6]

The third factor was less obvious: the decision by leaders of the
Jewish community to boycott the proposed boycott. Within a few
days it was officially announced that 'the boycott is off', and most
later accounts have attributed this to the influence of liberal Jews in
the Manchester elite, notably Rabbi Altmann, whose public statement was notably generous:

> Each member of the Jewish community is entitled to his own opin-
> ion, but there is no concerted action inside the community . . .
> Despite the terrible cruelties we suffered at the hands of the Germans,
> we would not try to punish an individual German, who is uncon-
> nected with these crimes, out of hatred. If this footballer is a decent
> fellow, I would say there is no harm in it.

Dignity and generosity may not though have been the whole story.
The original proposer of a boycott soon abandoned it himself, telling
the *Manchester Evening News*, 'we have been thinking over the situation and have decided to let the occasion pass'. He was less guarded
with the *Evening Chronicle*, telling its reporter that his plans had
'caused a lot of anti-Semitic feeling. If I had known it was going to
do so, I would not have opened the matter at all.' The *Chronicle*,
with obvious relief, headlined the story, 'Maine Road Goalie Boycott
Now Off'.[7] But how had anti-German feeling produced an anti-
Semitic reaction so soon after the Holocaust? Clues are to be found
in those letters to the press opposing the boycott, quite a few of
which pointed out the Jewishness of its supporters. One ex-
serviceman wrote to the *Evening News* to express resentment at

Jewish attacks on British soldiers in Palestine, but did not propose to hold all Jews responsible, so Trautmann was likewise not responsible for all Germans. Liberalism and sporting pragmatism then beautifully combined in the remark that 'it would only matter if [Trautmann] were a fascist – or a poor goalie'. The anti-Jewish point was more brutally made by another correspondent: 'I do not refuse to enter a café because a Jew eats there, though they killed my pals in Palestine'.[8] Since 1945 there had been attacks on the British army by Jewish terrorists in Palestine, notably the blowing up of its headquarters in Jerusalem's King David Hotel and the angrily received hanging of two British sergeants in reprisal for the execution of terrorists. Reporting of these events revealed widespread anti-Semitism in the British press, and apparently among the public too. Disturbances were reported as far afield as Bethnal Green and Plymouth, but they centred on Lancashire, where there were riots and attacks on Jewish-owned shops in both Liverpool and Manchester. In November 1947 a jury at Liverpool Assizes refused to convict a newspaper editor who had published a venomously anti-Semitic editorial.[9] Memories of such anti-Semitism had fortuitously come to the rescue of Trautmann, and the leaders of Manchester Jewry had persuaded their zealots to back off when it was seen how nasty the backlash against a boycott might be; shops with stones through their windows were never identified in the press but were almost certainly those with Jewish names over the door. The last thing Manchester's Jews wanted so soon after Israel's successful establishment as a state was to be forced to choose between Britishness and Jewishness.

The final factor in defusing the row was Trautmann himself, for if he had proved 'a poor goalie', then neither the club nor its fans would have defended him. That was never likely, for observers of non-league soccer had known about him for some time; he was, as the *Daily Express* put it, 'good, spectacular in fact'. But the speed with which he now demonstrated his exceptional skills – catlike movement, rapid reactions and extraordinary powers of anticipation – against First Division forwards was nevertheless remarkable. After try-outs in the reserves, he made his first-team debut on 19 November 1949, and though the side was defeated he was thought to have done extremely well. The *Sunday Empire News*, which had already offered its readers a photograph of Trautmann in action against Barnsley reserves ('Ex-POW Saves a Goal'), now thought him 'a player in the first flight . . . If ever a player "stole" a match, Trautmann did this.' Two weeks later, although City lost 7–0, it concluded that Trautmann 'could not be blamed for any of the goals'. On 18 December Trautmann had 'alone held the Villa forwards at bay', and a week later he was injured when colliding with the goalpost, 'but Trautmann is tough and after a few minutes he returned . . . to resume normal duties'. His team-mates warned that trouble would arise when he first played in London, since Londoners had endured far more bombing than the north of England. The Fulham game early in 1950 was therefore pivotal, and Trautmann later recalled seeing with horror London's visible bomb scars on the way to Craven Cottage. As the game began, he imagined Fulham fans saying to each other, 'So that's him? That's the so-and-so Nazi, is it?' Yet when he put on another star performance, fans on both sides cheered him, and the Fulham players applauded him off the field. After half a dozen games, Trautmann had made himself indispensable, and the pattern had been set: he would always be standing alone against opposing forwards, a man unusually tough and brave, quick and athletic.[10] When the six-year-old Colin Shindler saw his first football match in 1955, 'Bert Trautmann, the German ex-paratrooper and the greatest of heroes to this tiny Jewish supporter . . . stood like Horatius on the bridge, repelling the barbarian Red hordes' (Manchester United).[11]

Who *was* 'Berg' Trautmann (for in 1949 even his name was a mystery, so quickly had come his celebrity status)? He had been christened Carl Bernhard, but acquired the nickname 'Berg' in the army, on account of his height. He was first called 'Bert' shortly before he came to Manchester, by younger female admirers – of whom he had many. After indecisive weeks in which the press variously called him Berg, Burg, Burt and Brett (and on one occasion even Burgermeister), it was Bert that he remained. The label had a homely English sound, but he pronounced it in a very personal manner, an accent David Downing aptly describes as 'like that of a Lancastrian playing a German in an English war movie'. Bert Trautmann was born in 1923 in Bremen. His father worked in the port, and the family were not particularly unwilling collaborators in the Nazi regime. Though a social democrat in earlier days, the elder

Trautmann was officially classified as a Nazi by the British occupiers after 1945. Trautmann's autobiography points out that this was mainly because his father had to join the Nazis in order to keep his job, and then had to wear a uniform in order to play in the works band. That is plausible, but it is harder to explain why the nine-year-old Bert was enlisted in the Hitler Youth before Hitler came to power, and long before it became compulsory. He enjoyed his time in that organisation, for it fostered physical effort, to which he was already attracted and in which he excelled. One of Trautmann's most engaging qualities has been lifelong innocence, which was certainly at work in his early association with the Nazis, though he witnessed anti-Semitic violence in Bremen. When as a prisoner of war he was shown film of Belsen, he was horrified and ready to apologise on Germany's behalf for the rest of his life. He could therefore be redefined, soon after he came to Manchester, as a 'good German'. The young Peter Chapman, growing up in Islington in the 1950s, was told by his father that Trautmann was 'a good bloke', like Rommel, 'one among the enemy who gave you hope'. Bert never took refuge in claims that he had only been following orders. Though that would not have been a convincing defence in his case; he was never very good at obeying orders.[12]

Discontented with life as a mechanic, he joined the Luftwaffe in 1941, before the age at which he would have been conscripted, so he volunteered for the war as well as for the party. He had an eventful war, for in addition to being buried alive when under shellfire, he was taken prisoner four times: by Russian partisans in 1942, by the French resistance in 1944, by the Americans and then the British in 1945. He was lucky to survive the first two captivities (from both of which he escaped by his own efforts), but it was only the British who managed to hang on to him. Trautmann's military career was a curious mixture of the exceptional, the naive and the insubordinate, which prefigured what was to happen in football. As well as winning five medals (including the Iron Cross, first class), and killing at least the Russian mentioned in his autobiography, he was court-martialled and sent to a military jail for misappropriating army property. When the war ended, he was a hardened veteran paratroop sergeant, the tough survivor on which the army depended as it struggled against defeat. When shipped to Britain as a POW, he was, like his father, classified as a 'Nazi', as were most surviving members of the German airborne elite. He was a POW for three years and remained under surveillance by military intelligence until 1953.[13]

Trautmann was therefore nowhere near being the type of German who could claim to have kept a low profile under the Nazis. The experience of another POW footballer, Alec Eisentrager, at Bristol City, makes the contrast clear, for Eisentrager was quickly accepted, and later recalled a career in which he had 'no problems because of my nationality'. But he had been an unwilling sixteen-year-old conscript when he joined the army in 1944, was still under eighteen when the war ended, and barely twenty-one when he joined Bristol City. On release from his POW camp he lived with a local family that treated him like a son – their actual son having fallen in the war – and was viewed as another of the war's victims rather than a war criminal. He was popular with fans, who turned out in force with blue and white scarves for his wedding to a Bristol girl, and continued to live in the West Country after retirement, having by then played two hundred times for Bristol City and scored many goals. Eisentrager effectively became British himself, though in this process his stature – five foot six, hardly that of an *Übermensch* – and cheeky, boyish personality clearly helped.[14]

Trautmann, on the other hand, had been an active participant in Nazi warmaking, and, though he was willing to denounce the Nazis after 1945, he remained proud of his nationality even when England tried to adopt him. *Steppes to Wembley*, the title of his 1956 autobiography, was not only a neat pun, but a reminder to readers that he had come from the Russian front in Hitler's war. The *News Chronicle* noted in 1956 that Trautmann, 'even though his own countrymen won't honour him, has a natural patriotism that prevents him becoming a naturalised Briton'. He was also wont to tell football interviewers that part of his success as a goalkeeper derived from a paratrooper's ability to land softly, so cushioning the ball after making a catch. It may indeed have been his determination to remain a German in England that made him an effective peacemaker between the two countries, though this left him always vulnerable. When his first marriage was collapsing, his wife hit on a cruel way of causing embarrassment: according to his biographer, when friends visited the Trautmann home, she would goose-step around shouting, 'Sieg Heil'.[15]

By 1949, he was already very different from the man captured at the end of the war. Re-educated out of unthinking support for the Nazis, he came to like Britain, thought most of his captors to be fair, and made friends with many Lancastrians who welcomed him into their homes. By the time of his release in 1948, he had decided not to return to Germany, finding work instead on a farm, and later with bomb-disposal workers. Increasingly, though, he devoted himself to football, a sport at which he had had a good deal of match practice in POW camps. Trautmann played as an amateur for St Helens, since, being still officially an alien, he could not take paid work without War Office approval (he was later limited to a weekly wage of just five pounds even when allowed to turn professional), but he also watched league football and developed aspirations to try it himself. When he arrived in Manchester in 1949, Trautmann was already a man with a split nationality. St Helens had paid for his first post-war visit to Germany in early 1949, so that he could reconnect with his family, the supporters' club collecting fifty pounds for his journey and a food parcel to take with him. He was horrified to see how Bremen had been devastated by bombing, but when he spoke warmly of his Lancashire friends, his brother angrily called him 'a bloody Englishman'. From then on, as his biographer put it, he was a man with 'a loyalty for two countries'.[16]

Right through the 1950s, as he kept goal for Manchester City, this dual identity remained. Team-mates ribbed him for his Germanness and his idiosyncratic way with English, while he reciprocated their gibes with further malapropisms and colourfully scabrous rebuttals of their crude efforts at humour. On one occasion, discussing a television documentary about the war ('Yes, we won again!'), one cheerfully asked, 'Did you see it, Trauty?' 'No, I bluddy didn't, you bastard.' When such rough humour got out of hand, Trautmann roared across the dressing room, 'It's like bluddy Bethle'em in 'ere!' But when his rising standard of living enabled him to buy a car, he drove a Volkswagen Beetle, an obvious personal statement. When a Birmingham player later called him in the heat of the moment a 'German bastard', Trautmann raced after him to retaliate, but when restrained by his team-mates grinned and said happily, 'Bluddy *English* bastard!' Trautmann was never one to apologise for himself, and he had anyway an explosive temper that opposing players and referees occasionally encountered; he was sent off, suspended and fined for misconduct, even while being regarded as a great sportsman, and was once fined by City for refusing even to try to save a penalty because he did not accept that it should have been awarded. His generally sunny disposition though made him the darling of fans, and he took pains to sign autographs for the younger ones, sometimes then driving them home when he thought they were out too late. On one occasion this reduced a small boy to happy tears, not only by making time for him when obviously late for another commitment, but by then signing his grubby autograph book, 'Your pal, Bert'. Trautmann took obvious delight in his own son, and when that son was killed in a traffic accident, there was a great outpouring of emotional support for the family. The press reported his unavailing attempt immediately to adopt a substitute, lookalike son – another 'blond blue-eyed German boy', as the *Daily Herald* unhelpfully put it.[17]

It was difficult to occupy Trautmann's intermediate status between two countries lately at war. German newspapers reported his prowess, and he was welcomed back to his country of birth when City toured West Germany in 1954 and 1955. Such tours were then very popular, not least because so many British fans were in Germany in the army; in May 1955 five British clubs were touring Germany at the same time. City were paid an additional five hundred pounds if Trautmann played in such matches, so clear was it that German fans too would want to watch him. Despite this, and foreshadowing disputes over remuneration which eventually soured Trautmann's relationship with City, he was still paid only the standard ten pounds for playing. Trautmann found it hard to motivate team-mates for friendlies in Germany, or even to take them seriously on the field. In one game Don Revie deliberately handled the ball in the penalty area so that Trautmann could entertain the crowd by saving a penalty. When he duly did so, there was an enormous roar from the crowd – perceiving a symbolic German victory – while British soldiers stationed near by were simultaneously cheering the goalkeeper who had denied a goal to 'Germany'. Trautmann could be equally unhappy with Germans, as on the 1954 tour when over-zealous Wuppertal policemen restrained both the players and their British-soldier fans with unnecessary force. When a local civic official defended their actions during a post-match banquet, Trautmann stormed out, shouting, 'I don't care if I ever play in Germany again.'[18]

But that was not true. The one real aspiration he still had was to play for Germany, and had he done so he might well have won a World Cup winner's medal for West Germany in 1954. The German footballing authorities refused though to select any player who did not play for a German club. Trautmann therefore, though one of the best goalkeepers in the world, only ever played in one international match, captaining the English League against the Irish League in a match of no significance whatsoever. He never played for 'his' country, though when Germany visited England late in 1954 he was recruited as a translator and tour guide. In 1966, after his retirement, he was official liaison officer for the German team in England for the World Cup finals, and took obvious delight in wearing their strip during training. He was crushed with disappointment by their defeat – by England – in the Wembley final (though City's Joe Mercer assured him that England would never have won if Trautmann had been in the German goal). As Trautmann himself told a Manchester reporter, 'although he had lived and played among Englishmen for some years, and had come to like their way of life and most of the folk he had met, there were times when the desire to meet his countrymen became so strong that he simply could not get it out of his system'.[19]

The British press thought Trautmann's inability to play internationally was due to Germany's petty vindictiveness, but no national coach would then have selected a player not available for training, when in that generation hardly any footballers played outside their own country. Trautmann could therefore play for Germany only if he was transferred to a German club, but this possibility, when it emerged in 1952, sparked a rather nasty incident. He had been approached by a mysterious middleman and expressed a guarded interest in the idea, but then let it be known informally that he would soon return to Germany, before any formal approach had been made to City. He apparently assumed that everything would be sorted out once he told people that he wanted to go. When a formal approach was made, the two sides failed to understand each other, for City demanded twenty thousand pounds for Trautmann (well above any transfer fee that had ever been paid for a goalkeeper), while the

Germans offered one thousand pounds (which was still higher than any German transfer fee yet paid). The mismatch between the two national systems and mutual failures of explanation left City feeling that FC Schalke had tried to get one of its key assets for almost nothing, while the Germans thought the English club had been utterly unreasonable and could not understand why it had not asked the player where he wanted to play. Manchester City, Trautmann himself noted, had paid St Helens only £550 for him three years earlier. Some of the correspondence in the Manchester papers suggested that chauvinism was still not far away: one fan thought City should replace Trautmann with Accrington's goalkeeper, since 'if he wanted to see his mother he would only have to go to Salford'. Trautmann, deeply disappointed by the outcome, appealed to the FA, FIFA and the Football League, but there was nothing that they could or would do. *Die Welt* concluded that 'the case of Trautmann cannot be solved on a judicial or political basis, but only by human understanding. If Trautmann is not released it would be at the least a cruel joke in the history of sport that England discovered a German player but would not allow the German to play football in Germany.' A cartoon depicted Trautmann as Odysseus, tied for ever to the mast of a ship called *Manchester City*.[20]

Despite these differences, Trautmann soldiered on, keeping Manchester City in contention in the early 1950s when they did not have a very good side. In the middle of the decade things looked up, and his involvement in City's best years helped cement his own reputation in Britain. The catalyst was England's shattering 3–6 home defeat by Hungary in 1953, a match which caused deep soul-searching throughout the conservative English game and allowed those who wanted to try 'continental methods' an overdue chance. Trautmann, already credited with introducing the low-cut 'continental' football boot to England, was still in touch with the way the game was played outside England and thought that English clubs had a lot to learn, though his attempts to educate readers of his ghosted column in the *Manchester Evening News* were generally frustrated by the editorial conviction that Mancunians were only interested in gossip about English players. For Manchester City, modernisation involved the 'Revie plan' of rapid passing, a scheme that hinged on the midfield play of the future England manager Don Revie, who had just joined the club. Trautmann was central to this system, for he was one of the first goalkeepers in England to contribute significantly to outfield play. Instead of always punting the ball upfield and 'clearing his lines', Trautmann often threw the ball out, a directed straight-arm throw of considerable range given his physique, which transformed defence into attack and caught opposition teams off-balance. Manchester City became for a time one of the leading English clubs and reached the FA Cup final in both 1955 and 1956, so giving Trautmann national exposure in the only game then regularly televised.[21]

In the 1955 final City were beaten, but Trautmann's team-mates had the pleasure of watching their German *kamerad* bowing to the Duke of Edinburgh; when reminded that this was the first German player to appear in a cup final, Prince Philip responded, '*Sehr gut!*' City's cup run in 1956 was even more successful, and owed more to the goalkeeper, his defence of the goal on a muddy pitch at Southend probably his greatest performance. It was personally more difficult during the semi-final, for Trautmann committed what most spectators thought a professional foul by bringing down a Spurs forward. Since no penalty was awarded and City won the game by a single goal, he was booed off the pitch, and both press and newsreels ('. . . and now see the German goalkeeper foul George Robb by holding his legs') found him guilty. By coincidence, City were due to play Tottenham in the league the very next week, and in the intervening period Trautmann received a great deal of hate mail. In the press the story did a good deal to rally support: the *Manchester Evening Chronicle* reported that 'the filth of fanatics' had been 'pouring through the Trautmann letter-box', but that it could only have come from people who did not know him, for 'to meet Bert Trautmann is to like him'. He embodied 'good fellowship' and showed 'deep affection for the land in which he lives and for its people'. The paper reinforced this claim by reporting support that Trautmann had offered to 'a crippled compatriot', while noting that he never refused requests for hospital visits or to be photographed with young fans on their birthdays. The personal side was clearly very important in Trautmann's ambassadorial role, as he himself noticed: people 'started to see me as a person with a mother and a father. It was all about the human touch.' Many British footballers of that era agreed. Newcastle United's Jackie

Milburn thought that Trautmann 'had the quickest reflexes I have ever experienced and he was a bloody nice bloke as well', while Preston North End's Tommy Docherty remembered that 'his consistent form, skill and ability won the hearts of all sports people after the terrible war'. For Jimmy Hill, 'the respect that he commanded for himself, and as a result the German nation, was perhaps the beginning of the healing of the wounds caused by the war. He was in fact far more than a brilliant goalkeeper.'[22]

Despite the fouling incident, after a contentious debate he was named Player of the Year by the Football Writers' Association, the first goalkeeper and the first foreign player to receive the award, facts that generated widespread comment. The *Daily Telegraph* reported that Trautmann was 'rated the finest goalkeeper in England', while the *News Chronicle* identified him as 'the man who came into English League football in 1949 when Nazi atrocities were still fresh in the public mind, and was met by a storm of abuse. There were boos and catcalls of "Get back to Germany!"' Yet by now Trautmann had become 'as Lancashire through and through as if he had been born at Wigan, St Helens, Bolton or Preston', and was generally to be seen off the field wearing a cloth cap and muffler, 'like a mill worker off duty'. Official endorsement was given when the secretary of the FA, Sir Stanley Rous, contributed a foreword to Trautmann's autobiography. The 'Player of the Year award', he noted, was 'not given solely for achievements on the field of play, but also for character and sportsmanship. Indeed, this German-born player owes so much of his popularity to his cheerful demeanour on the field and his determination to do well whatever the odds.' Rous complacently added, 'it is typical of football in this country that not only have we accepted Trautmann as a player, but we have come to praise his splendid goalkeeping and to admire his rich personality'. The myth was now fully in place – Trautmann had healed war wounds between the two countries, but in part this reflected the splendid tolerance of the English. Trautmann implicitly accepted this view, responding as Player of the Year with heartfelt thanks:

> Whatever success I have enjoyed in English football could not have been achieved without the co-operation, tolerance and sympathetic encouragement of the man who represents the backbone of your

national game – the chap on the popular side with his cloth cap and muffler, and penetrating voice. To him and his lady I owe more than I can hope to repay . . . Thank you to supporters all over the country for their many kindnesses to a German stranger in what was once an alien land.[23]

In view of the heroics that Trautmann performed at the 1956 cup final, it has often been assumed that he became Player of the Year in consequence of that game, but the honour preceded the match by a month and was based on what he had already done. The cup final merely cemented his reputation. He was knocked out cold during a collision with a forward, but refused to leave the field, and though hurt again in a second collision, he insisted on finishing the game. City duly went on to win. Trautmann therefore received in person a winner's medal from 'your queen' (as his autobiography described her). In the euphoria the BBC's Kenneth Wolstenholme told viewers that 'he's probably already forgotten about that bang on the neck', and when the Queen asked if he was all right, Trautmann responded, 'It'll be fine, Ma'am, thank-you.' Actually, he had broken more than one neck bone and was lucky to be alive, though it would be five days before this was spotted by a Manchester hospital. He spent months in hospital but made a full recovery, forced himself back to fitness, and played for Manchester City for another seven years. But thereafter, he would always be known as the German goalkeeper who played on with a broken neck. For Peter Chapman, 'if [Trautmann] was well-regarded before the match, there was no measuring his popularity after it. There could be no clearer example of a keeper who "took it", which is what the best British keepers were meant to do. [And of course not only goalkeepers.] Yet this one was a German, and people loved him for it. He hardly seemed foreign at all, and was really "one of us".' Every stage of his recovery was reported – 'Bert Is Out Of Hospital', blazed one national newspaper headline.[24]

Before Bert Trautmann's apotheosis, Manchester United had an opportunity to show that they too did not bear grudges for the war. United had pioneered England's association with the nascent European Cup, and in that context had to play in February 1958 in Belgrade. Their plane landed in Munich to refuel, but when attempting to take off in icy conditions the plane crashed, more than twenty players and reporters were killed and many others seriously injured. This 'Munich' air disaster of a British aeroplane returning from Yugoslavia therefore had very little to do with Germany until after the crash, though for many (as the novelist H. E. Bates explained in a radio broadcast) the very word 'Munich' produced instant reminders of the crisis of 1938. As the plane landed, the *News Chronicle*'s Frank Taylor had reflected that 'as with most Britons of my generation, I always associated Munich with Hitler and the Nazis'. The tragedy was also reminiscent of the war: for one fan, the silence that pervaded Manchester as the news spread was like 'the sharp intake of breath that greeted the aftermath of the Luftwaffe attack on Manchester, as the light of day revealed the destruction of the city centre'. After the crash, all reports of German responses were positive, with many accounts of the 'wonderful' hospital staff and of the injured being 'bombarded' with flowers from the citizens of Munich. In due course United's supporters' club reciprocated by sending the hospital eighteen pounds of chocolates. Almost all commentaries were though coloured by memories of 1939–45. As United manager Matt Busby lay for weeks in hospital, barely surviving his injuries, he pondered the fact that he had been a keen enough anti-fascist to volunteer for the British army even before the war began, while his father had been shot by a German sniper on the Somme. Now Germans were labouring day and night to save his life, and the experience changed his personal outlook: 'ironic isn't it, that until then Germans to me were Germans, the enemy if you like . . . you learn as you get older'. Frank Taylor, who remained longest in the Munich hospital, made there a close friend of a German called Richard Leppla, 'a blond square-jawed man' who expressed great interest in the history of the RAF, for he was a Luftwaffe veteran of the Battle of Britain. For Taylor too, national stereotypes drawn from the war would never quite work again. Survivors were internationally disorientated in all sorts of ways. Bobby Charlton, who had lost most of his clothes in the crash, had to buy a complete outfit in Munich: 'I guess they're OK. The shoes are a bit pointed. The overcoat would never hold up in Manchester weather.' On the other side of the fence, the chief surgeon who saved a number of their lives, Professor Georg Maurer, made his first decisive contribution by driving marauding British pressmen out of his hospital; even with some of their own in intensive care the journalists had been shamelessly shroud-chasing for good stories. In due course Maurer was awarded the CBE, and must have reflected on how unlikely this was for a man who had already received the Iron Cross from Adolf Hitler.[25]

Such ironies were far from the surface when, with most of the survivors back home and the team struggling back into the life that would see the new 'Busby babes' improbably win the FA Cup later in the year, Manchester sought to pay proper respect to Munich. The city council passed a fulsome resolution of tribute to the doctors and nurses of the Rechts der Isar Hospital, and commissioned the Lord Mayor to deliver the resolution in person. In the shabbiest traditions of British local government, the story then descended into farce. It transpired that Professor Maurer and his senior staff would be in Manchester themselves as guests of Manchester United and a Sunday newspaper. The relevant council committee rapidly withdrew its authority for the Lord Mayor to travel to Munich at the expense of the ratepayers, and when he protested that Manchester could hardly ask Munich to collect its own resolution of gratitude, he was told to go to Munich if he wished, but at his own expense. The fact that the Lord Mayor, Leslie Lever MP, was not exactly short of a bob or two only added piquancy to the story. Having exploited the issue for all it was worth as a means of embarrassing the town hall, the local papers then completely ignored Lever's visit to Munich, and concentrated instead on welcoming the Germans to Manchester.[26]

That welcome was ungrudging: one headline read, '60,000 Cheer the Munich Angels', and the phrase 'the Munich Angels' was then generally used. The German party was officially met by Lever and by the Mayor of Stretford, while during the evening reception in Stretford town hall the Union Jack and the West German flag flew side by side. The following day the guests toured the city, attended a match at Old Trafford and enjoyed a civic banquet. The local press publicised all these events, and people seem to have turned out in force to pay personal thanks. When they stepped onto the turf at a packed Old Trafford, they were overwhelmed by the physical impact of roared cheers, and again when Maurer took a personal salute before the match started. The *Empire News* reported that 'no one needed to whip up enthusiasm, for it was there, filling the great bowl of Old Trafford to overflowing'. It claimed indeed that 'the whole crowd rose – every man, woman and child – as Dr Maurer led his Angels onto the turf', that everyone joined in the singing, and that all the men stood bareheaded in tribute to the German visitors as the German national anthem was played. It is sometimes claimed even that the Manchester crowd sang the German national anthem, though there is no reference to this in the very full newspaper accounts of the time. Mancunians would surely not have known the third verse of the West German anthem (the only words used in the 1950s, and impeccably democratic), and they could hardly have sung, '*Deutschland, Deutschland, über Alles*', the only words they might possibly have known. They did though quite clearly sing to Maurer, with immense enthusiasm, 'For He's a Jolly Good Fellow', words that denoted as much goodwill as any national anthem, but which hailed an individual rather than a country and evoked no memory of either Adolf Hitler or Kaiser Bill.[27]

Maurer was shocked by the warmth of his reception, as were the German ambassador and the German press. The *Süddeutsche Zeitung* reported:

> surprises for the guests and for the hosts alike. The first one was the fact of the invitation to Manchester. To be sure, the footballers and journalists who were injured in the plane crash ... were selflessly cared for in the Hospital ... But – as the invited, from Prof Maurer to the youngest nurse, kept explaining time and again – they had after all done nothing but their usual duty. They would not have dreamed that they had earned special gratitude with this – and not at all that this gratitude would find its expression in a real frenzy of enthusiasm.

Maurer was visibly at an emotional loss for words, as were the civic leaders who replied. All expressed the hope that out of football and grief would come a better level of international understanding.[28] Nor did the goodwill evaporate with the immediate memory of the Munich crash. Maurer was again the guest of Manchester United at the cup final in April, while Manchester and Munich developed an exchange scheme for schoolchildren, with the specific hope that social contacts would reduce international suspicion. At a lower level new friendships continued too: when the footballer Bill Foulkes became a father for the first time, he and his wife received knitted baby clothes from Frau Maurer. There were then some lasting effects from 'the biggest show of gratitude this city has ever put on', as the Lord Mayor had described it.[29]

The climax of footballing goodwill came with Bert Trautmann's retirement. His special status was permanent after 1955–6, and comprised a diplomatic role as well as the fame of a great footballer. Even in 1955 his parents, visiting England for the cup final, had been amazed by their son's treatment. The *Manchester Evening News* reported that they saw him 'at that brilliant best, which had helped him break through the post-war hate barrier . . . and made him his country's finest ambassador'. His mother, having witnessed Manchester's reception for the beaten cup finalists, whispered amazedly, 'It is all so wonderful, so wonderful. How kind they all are. And they are calling for Bert too, my Bert.' She was also quoted as saying, not quite so positively, 'he even speaks German with a funny accent nowadays'. His father was yet more moved: 'I can't get over the whole week-end. I have seen the English people as they really are, and I am so proud and thankful. They seem to be very fond of you Bert, and you must never forget them and what they have done for you.' Then, turning to enter Manchester town hall, he smiled and added, 'You know, Hitler never had a reception like that!' Trautmann himself wrote that his success in 1955–6 proved that 'football . . . transcends all politics and racial hatred, and for a German to be considered worthy of the highest honours the English game can offer surely inspires the confident belief that on the sportsfields at any rate, there can be fostered the international peace and goodwill that are the objectives of all right-thinking people'.[30] He was elected president of the Anglo-German Fellowship, and worked hard to facilitate its exchange schemes for young people. A local paper noted that he was a special hero to visiting German schoolboys, but also reported that they had liked local policemen, though in terms that suggested that even the 'your policemen are wonderful' cliché was susceptible to national stereotyping: one German schoolboy confided wonderingly that 'in England the policeman is your friend and helper' – compared to what and where? The final local accolade may be thought to have come from the *Guardian*, which had not even reported the 1949 row over Trautmann's signing, and had given only cool coverage of the events of 1955–6, so limited was its interest in off-the-field soccer, even in its home town. In 1962, though, the *Guardian* decided that he was 'a popular hero, worshipped for the right reasons', recalled that 'because of his nationality life was never easy or pleasant during his early days' in Manchester, and concluded that he had always been the favourite of the fans – at least until Denis Law joined the club (the *Guardian* here exhibiting that fatal respect for truth which ruins even its best-intentioned pleasantries).[31]

Trautmann's 639th and final game for City was on 27 March 1964. It was a colossal number of appearances for a man who was already twenty-six when he arrived. Local pressmen had formed a committee to stage a testimonial match, and this provided the stage on which Manchester could bid a proper farewell. All the England players but one who were invited to form the visiting team agreed to come, and, amazingly, the Manchester team to play 'England' would be a joint City and United XI, for Busby had generously offered all his United players and the promise that none would ask for an appearance fee. Two very special sides therefore played in Trautmann's testimonial game, but the vast crowd reflected on Trautmann more than on the other twenty-one players, as did the ovation that greeted his appearance. The official attendance was 47,951, a record for any soccer testimonial game in England, but it was an open secret that the ground's official capacity had been ignored and more like sixty thousand people had squeezed through the turnstiles. They certainly got a good show for their money, for 'Manchester' beat 'England' 5–4. Whether Manchester should really have held on to its lead nobody will ever know, for the game ended unusually. With several minutes to go, small fans began clustering round Trautmann's goal to get a final autograph, and Trautmann began signing them whenever the ball was at the other end of the field. Gradually this pitch invasion accelerated and as the turf disappeared under a mass of spectators the referee tactfully blew the final whistle early, while policemen struggled to extricate Trautmann. Emotional speeches were then made, notably Trautmann's: 'I have had the honour of living among some of the best people in the world. Tonight I am very grateful and very humble. Not only on my own behalf but on behalf of myself and of the German people. I hope in some small way that I have contributed something to make the world a nice place to live in. God bless you all.' His gratitude was clearly reciprocated: so many fans had turned out that Trautmann collected over nine thousand pounds from the gate receipts. Next day, the press reported his speech at length, but they also printed tributes from others who had been present, including one from the sainted hero of English footballing, Stanley Matthews, who echoed Stanley Rous's 1956 claim that football was such a marvellous game because it provided the means by which former enemies could become friends. Years later, Matthews recalled for his autobiography that it had been 'a privilege' to play in Trautmann's benefit match, for he was 'an outstanding goalkeeper and one of the warmest and most endearing people I ever met in football'. The best tribute though was to be found among thousands of letters sent to Trautmann: a Manchester United fan wrote simply, 'Thank God you've retired!'[32]

After two unhappy years managing Stockport County, Trautmann returned to Germany, without his English wife, and then worked as a trainer for a couple of German teams, but he seemed unable to settle in his country of birth. His career as a footballing ambassador was not over, though, for from 1972 he was able at last to do something as a German for Germany, when appointed to a roving post within West Germany's overseas aid scheme, an imaginative programme that provided support for Third World countries' sports teams. In this role, he coached or managed over fifteen years the national sides of Burma, Tanzania, Liberia, Pakistan, Yemen and Malta, before finally retiring to Spain.[33]

How far did Trautmann have a lasting impact on Manchester and on Britain? For Peter Chapman, 'he did more than any other person for post-war reconciliation between Britain and Germany. In passing, he also performed the almost unbelievable trick of remaining an outsider while winning the acceptance of the crowd.' This was surely significant, for, although later German players coming to Britain, like Jürgen Klinsmann, received barracking from fans, they never had to face such hatred as was visited on Trautmann in 1949. Klinsmann had sufficient personality and confidence to meet the issue of his nationality head-on when signed by Tottenham in 1994. Knowing that he was arriving with the reputation of a man who got penalties unfairly, he enquired at his first press conference whether anyone could recommend a good diving school in London, and celebrated his first Spurs goal by 'diving' to the ground. That first goal was followed by

'Wunderbar Jürgen' flashed on to the electronic scoreboard, in the German national colours. When Klinsmann, like Trautmann, drove Volkswagen Beetles, it was not a declaration of nationality but a signal that he was an ordinary guy who had not let riches go to his head. In due course, he became a very popular player, and recalled after retirement that 'many of the greatest experiences of my career were in London where I was very happy'. In 1995 he became the first German player after Trautmann to be named Player of the Year; the goalkeeper was the guest of honour at the dinner to celebrate the striker's title. Time may well have had something to do with Klinsmann's popularity, but Trautmann himself was a factor too. Nor did British clubs, following Manchester United into European competitions, tend to see them as political battles; and the worst violence between club fans has been against Italians and Turks, rather than Germans. That was a positive trend, if of a limited sort, since it did not directly relate to political issues from either the past or the present, but unfortunately it was not replicated in international matches.[34]

Even in club football, not all German players had as happy an experience as Klinsmann and (eventually) Trautmann. The first German player in English soccer, Max Seeburg, played for Tottenham in 1908, but found himself interned as an enemy alien in 1914, though his brother was by then in the British army. Almost a century later, Dietmar Hamann was welcomed at Liverpool, but his earlier experiences at Newcastle United had included being given *Mein Kampf* by his team-mates at the club's Christmas party. Even at Liverpool, Hamann was subjected to a vicious verbal attack by a Charlton supporter, who was convicted of using 'racially aggravated threatening words and behaviour'. Perhaps the most striking point in Nick Harris's comprehensive survey of foreign players in English football concerns the actual numbers. Between 1908 and 2002, there were seventy-three 'German' players registered with English League clubs, the great majority when the international transfer market opened up in the 1990s. However, twenty-seven of these seventy-three had been born in Germany but did not have German nationality (quite a few were the sons of British soldiers). That leaves forty-six, which might still seem a lot, until a comparison is made with other countries. Denmark, Norway and Sweden each contributed more footballers to the English League than Germany, despite much smaller populations, while there have been about three times as many Dutch and French players as there have been Germans. The statistical evidence bears out Harris's conclusion: 'there is ultimately no bar to whom supporters will adore. It just makes it easier if they're not German, or, if they are, that they're like Klinsmann, and not only confound the stereotype from day one but are tremendously successful on the pitch too'.[35] Despite Trautmann's success, in other words, German footballers with English clubs still have a higher tolerance threshold to surmount than other foreign nationals.

At the international level, relatively friendly English sporting relations with Germany turned into a symbolic battle of the nations from the 1970s onwards. In the development of that hostility soccer even contributed to the idea of the Germans working deliberately towards war in 1939, through newsreel footage of a Zeppelin hovering over a vulnerable-looking Wembley Stadium while a match is played. This was the FA Cup final of 1930, and the Zeppelin was therefore a peaceful visitor to the London skies, the pilot having descended to 2000 feet so that his passengers could watch Arsenal defeating Huddersfield Town. But the regular recycling of that image on post-war television has invariably been intended to show the English at play while the Germans (apparently, but misleadingly) rearmed. As Harris notes, the commentary on such documentaries invariably describes the Zeppelin's presence over London as 'looming' or 'ominous'. In fact it was neither, and Germany was anyway a democracy at the time.[36]

Before the Second World War – for Britain a home draw followed by an away win – England had played full internationals against Germany only three times.[37] The first match, in Berlin in May 1930 (just days after that Zeppelin had hovered over Wembley), was a deliberate encouragement of Weimar democracy, and the reversal of antagonisms engendered by the Great War, since in 1919 the FA had decided that England must never play against Germany, Austria or Hungary. Now England played Austria and Germany on the same tour, apparently vindicating contemporary claims that 'sport is still the best League of Nations'. England's 3–3 draw in Berlin was thus a good result for diplomacy as well as an enjoyable event for spectators. The British press claimed that 'we was robbed', since the draw was achieved with only ten fit men, but it appreciated the gentlemanly behaviour on display. The *Daily Express* reported with relief, 'There was no congratulating the goal-scorers. On the English side, everyone's feelings were under perfect control. The Germans allowed themselves to go a little more, but always in good taste.'[38] Things became more fraught at club level, even before the Nazi revolution, as Everton discovered during a tour in 1932. After contentious preliminaries to the game in Dresden, including a nose-to-nose dispute between the captains about which football to use (resolved by the Everton player kicking the German ball out of the ground), matches were extremely 'physical'. Despite the presence of Hermann Göring, the Everton boys refused the Nazi salute, and were booed by the crowd. The climax came in Cologne, when Dixie Dean, seeking to rescue two team colleagues from threatening policemen after a lively post-match celebration, was beaten up by the police after crudely offering them a bribe, imprisoned and fined. Only the club chairman's paying the fine that Dean indignantly refused to acknowledge as just avoided a nasty international incident.[39]

The second international, a 3–0 win for England in London in December 1935, was overshadowed by worries about Nazi Germany and the propaganda possibilities of sport that would soon be highlighted by the 1936 Berlin Olympics. The British government maintained that the game had been 'privately arranged without our knowledge', rejected TUC demands that the match be banned, and feared violence against ten thousand Nazi fans in London. Such fears proved unfounded, for the game was played in a sporting atmosphere, but the FA chairman officially apologised to the German players for the TUC's protest march. German fans contributed to this harmony by laying a wreath, 'in memory of the British dead, from fifteen hundred German football supporters'. The leader of Germany's Olympic organisation asserted that German footballers had come to London 'as apprentices to the masters', though he also expounded Germany's cult of fitness under National Socialism. The *Observer* reported that the German supporters left for home with 'perfect peace in all London', and another paper claimed it had been 'almost an affair of friendship rather than football'. Fourteen people had actually been arrested during violent demonstrations outside the ground and after clashes between Blackshirts and Communists at Victoria Station, as German fans departed.[40]

Perfect peace was rather less the mood when England played in Germany in May 1938, for by now football could not be divorced from the country's foreign policy of appeasing Germany, even though it was well understood that Goebbels would use the match as propaganda. The British ambassador in Berlin, Nevile Henderson, urged care 'in advocating contests between British and German individuals and teams. The Nazis are looking for easy opponents to boost their regime. It is their way of claiming a super-race.' The Foreign Office now urged the FA to make sure that 'Britain' (*sic*) put up a 'first-class' performance, which was 'really important for *our* prestige'. On the instructions of Henderson the FA ordered the English team to give the Nazi salute which British athletes had refused at the 1936 Olympics, arguing that this was merely the politeness required of visitors. Henderson explained, 'when I go in to see Herr Hitler, I give him the Nazi salute because it is the normal courtesy expected. It carries no hint of approval of anything.'[41]

The English players received this order with alarm, having already acquired negative personal impressions of Nazi Germany on the previous day in Berlin. Stanley Matthews later recalled players being 'livid and totally opposed to it, myself included', yet they had little option but to give the salute, even though they recognised that press photographs would cause uproar back home. They had two ways of getting their own back. As they lined up for the ceremony before the game, some noticed a few English supporters waving a Union Jack amid the 110,000 Germans gathered from all over the country. As the word passed along the line, some players opted to look at their own flag while apparently saluting the Nazi anthem. It was apparently not noticed, for a Berlin paper reported: 'Then the English "God Save the King" sounds, saluted by everyone with the German greeting. Then our anthems resound across the pitch – saluted by the English national team with the German greeting. Thunderous applause thanks them for it.' More obviously, they could simply go out and win the match. Angered by being dragged into a political gesture, the players were up for it, led in their determination to win by Matthews' dazzling performance on the wing. Their general mood can be seen in the reaction to Len Goulden's twenty-five-yard drive which settled the match: the terraces were 'as lifeless as a string of dead fish', but as Goulden raced past Matthews he shouted into the silence, 'Let them salute that one!' Since England won 3–6 – rather different from the outcome expected by the German paper which predicted that 'there will probably be few goals but instead we will get to see ninety minutes of chess on the pitch' – there was little that the Nazi propagandists could do except praise the sporting spirit in which the match had been played. Henderson also had personal revenge for the difficulties to which he had been subjected: seated next to a Göring ablaze with medals, Henderson wore old tweeds, so undermining any significance the occasion might have, but when the English team established its dominance, his ornithologist's binoculars were offered solicitously to Göring: 'What wonderful goals! You really ought to get a better look at the game.' He then had the satisfaction of watching the Nazi leaders leave before the game ended rather than see their team beaten. Popular memories of this 1938 match were clearly near the surface of the 1981 film *Escape to Victory*, and the mood of Matthews' appeal to go out and beat the Germans is very close to Michael Caine's 'Come on, we can win this one!' in the film. Back in 1938, the FA formally thanked Neville Chamberlain on the success of his policy in preventing war. The planned return fixture, an England–Germany game in London during the 1939–40 season, was though replaced by a rather different contest.[42]

When war came, it affected footballers like everyone else: seventy-five professionals were killed, hundreds lost their livelihoods and six years when no serious competitive football was played. It would hardly be surprising if they had borne grudges, but as we have seen from Bert Trautmann's experiences in the 1950s, few of them did. Bristol City had Alec Eisentrager on its books even before City signed Trautmann in 1949, and Leeds United had an ex-POW too; the sports press reported that fans accepted both as footballers rather than rejecting them as Germans. As we have also seen, British clubs were soon touring Germany again, and post-war international matches resumed in 1954, by which time West Germany were the world champions, but they were nevertheless reassuringly defeated 3–1 by England. According to the *Daily Mirror*, 'it could just as well have been 10–1 or 20–1 or 30–1'. Ten thousand German supporters came to see it happen, and *Bild* had told its readers that fifty million Englishmen were on tenterhooks, hoping for a German defeat; the German players, told by their ambassador that they might have to be good losers, had no time to visit Wembley before the game, for they were waiting outside Buckingham Palace in the rain, hoping to see the Queen. The German national anthem was received in deadly silence by both nationalities, its first playing in London since the war, but the *News Chronicle* decided that the German fans were the world's most disciplined supporters, and another paper paid tribute to 'conscientiously prepared Teutons' in the team. That 1954 victory largely set the pattern, for England did not lose to any German team until after the 1966 World Cup. (The BBC commentator pointed out that fact three times during the first fifteen minutes of the 1966 final against West Germany.) While this was a matter of pride, international fixtures, except for 'home internationals' against Scotland, Wales and Northern Ireland, attracted little attention. The FA battled with the isolationist Football League for room in the annual programme for internationals, while even the best clubs were inward-looking, with English teams only reluctantly entering European club competitions. There was television coverage of some international matches, but no proper England supporters' organisation, and few fans travelled to watch away games. However, television soon started to make a difference: the sight and sound of Brazilian fans supporting their national team during an England visit in 1959 started English fans singing in home matches (though it was only in that generation that singing by fans also became a regular feature of club football). The BBC recording of the 1966 World Cup final suggests that many fans learned to chant and sing for the England team only as that key game progressed. The limited importance attributed to internationals did not though mean that either fans or journalists expected England to lose them. Unexpected defeats by Hungary in 1953–4 were a shock, albeit not for long; the national team's early exits from the World Cup in 1954 and 1958 did not occasion much disappointment either, since England could still beat the Scots, which was what had always really mattered. Such insularity changed only under the combined impact of clubs playing in European competitions, increasing television coverage, and the accelerating ease of travel. Then in 1966, with the World Cup finals hosted by England, interest in England's performance in 'the national game' finally took off. When England won the tournament, their becoming world champions completed the process, and raised expectations of

English success replaced the relative indifference of the first two-thirds of the century. The fact that England reached that pinnacle of success by beating 'Germany' in a battle watched by millions of viewers added a good deal of satisfaction to the process.[43]

The 1966 World Cup final was one of the great days in British (and especially English) sporting history. Although there was an inescapable whiff of wartime memory about, it could hardly have been otherwise when England were contesting the championship of the world with Germany, only a generation after they had been at war. Jack Charlton, at the heart of the English defence, found himself thinking it surreal: 'we had waged a war for six years against Germany . . . and now we were preparing to do battle on the football field'. The BBC's John Humphrys, a Welshman far from addicted to soccer, recently recalled it as the last complete football game he had watched: 'I did so because it had almost nothing to do with football and everything to do with the war. The Germans were still the enemy and we had beaten them again.' The England captain, Bobby Moore, had been born in the East End of London during a 1941 air raid, and the manager, Alf Ramsey, had lost six years of his playing career to army service. The goalkeeper, Gordon Banks, had served in the British Army of the Rhine (what *Bild* still called 'the British occupation forces') and had a German wife who now had divided loyalties. The BBC commentator, Kenneth Wolstenholme, had flown a hundred bombing sorties over Germany and won the DFC. At the end of the final, Wolstenholme, as Ian Wooldridge put it, 'ad-libbed five words into a microphone . . . that were destined to be re-broadcast more times than Winston Churchill's "We shall fight them on the beaches . . ." exhortation'. But in 1966 virtually nothing was said overtly about the war by any of these men. The press was less careful, and German papers were irked that a sporting event should be reported 'with a steel helmet and a gas mask'. They deplored attacks on German players for alleged cheating: 'Some of these comments sound like war reports. That four players have so far been sent off during games against Germany is not of course the responsibility of those punished but of the evil Germans.' One even printed a spoof report of Germany's win over Switzerland as if written by a British paper: 'Eleven German football players have masterfully sawn the Swiss cheese to pieces. They proved that Wilhelm Tell's shot was nothing compared with our goals . . . These people should ski, tend cows on the alpine pastures or milk goats.' Vincent Mulchrone in the *Daily Mail* wrote in just that tone, 'if Germany beat us at Wembley this afternoon at our national sport, we can always point out to them that we have recently beaten them twice at theirs'. David Downing has suggested that the German players were aware that

> the weight of the past fell more heavily on them . . . It was they who had been spurned by their opponents at the beginning of the century and they who had been disgraced and defeated in two world wars. If the West Germans went into the 1966 final with something of an inferiority complex – and their tactics suggest that they did – then it was one borne out of more than football.

Wolstenholme insistently reported the good spirit in which the match was played: 'The final itself was a real carnival, with not a single trace of animosity, despite two disputed goals, and despite the absence of fencing in of spectators.' There is though a comforting assumption of English superiority in his memory of the team's sportsmanship, and his concession that 'perhaps there was a little animosity towards the Germans, but it was shown mainly by those people whose countries had been occupied during the war. In fact, some of the European commentators draped the Union Flag from the front of my position and added, "You mustn't lose this one."'[44]

That 1966 triumph encouraged complacency in English football, marking the beginning not of a golden age but of frustration on the pitch and derision on the sports pages. The inherited expectation that England would win was increasingly at odds with the reality of England losing; taking refuge in war nostalgia was the national defence mechanism. The idea that the British were in their international identity, and not only in football, 'prisoners of the past' was well illustrated in *Escape to Victory*, a 1981 film that blended memories of the 1966 World Cup with books and films about German POW camps: wartime prisoners beat the German army in a high-profile soccer match and then escape too. The *Financial Times* reviewer thought it *Match of the Day* crossed with *Stalag 17*; another suggested 'Tinseltown meets Ipswich Town', since real footballers (some from Ipswich) appeared alongside actors. The 'World' team is led by

Englishmen to victory over Nazi brutality and German cheating, the accents of London and Manchester predominating both in the dressing room and on the pitch.[45]

The idea had clearly been to make a killing with two discrete box-office audiences. Since it could boast both major acting names and international footballers – Bobby Moore and Michael Caine in one film – *Escape to Victory*'s reception was therefore a disappointment; as an article in *Empire* recently recalled, in Britain it was 'released to critical derision and Vauxhall Conference box office', though some concede that the film is so terrible that it has acquired a curious cult status, and is 'unwatchable and unmissable in equal measure'. Yet it did not do too badly in the first place, except for those who had unreasonable expectations. Michael Caine's memoirs get it right: he had expected the film to be 'death in America and fine in Europe, which is exactly as it turned out'. America's *Variety* had those expectations at the time: this 'soccer-themed World War II escape drama should boot big b[ox] o[ffice] abroad, less domestic'. It certainly did well in Britain, running for seven weeks at the Empire, Leicester Square, where it was the top-grossing film of the year, and had similarly extended runs in most other cities. Though *Variety* was surely unfair when suggesting that the film had spent so much time extolling the virtues of honourable Germans only because 'the German market represents a big share of the global grossing potential', it did do rather well in West Germany.[46]

Caine's biographer draws attention to the *Daily Mirror* reviewer saying that the last twenty minutes, the football match itself, 'compensates for the flabby screenplay . . . Small boys will love it.' In a similar way *Screen International* was critical of the script's confusions, the directing and the acting, but also expected that it would attract not only soccer fans but 'a much wider audience of regulars and not so regulars who enjoy the audience involvement in an upbeat story that will raise their spirits'. The highbrow film buffs did not like the film, though they agreed that others would love it. The distinguished critic Andrew Sarris, who thought little of its acting or direction, and considered Sylvester Stallone's performance enough to send him into hysterics of laughter and disbelief, had nothing but praise for the football scenes. 'When the Allied players pass up a chance for freedom in order to finish the match the probabilities of psychology and history are outrageously violated, but the sport-loving beast in all of us is satisfied.' Richard Schickel, similarly unimpressed, nevertheless thought that in its climax, '*Victory* achieves its goal, and anyone who does not find himself yelling along with the extras should probably have stayed at home with his Proust and bitters'. This was because the film had but one aim, successfully achieved, which was 'to convert a movie audience – typically composed of individuals lost in private fantasies – into a sports crowd, in which singular preoccupations are submerged in communal joy as the home team is cheered on in a transcendence everyone shares'. In later years the film even achieved a rising critical reputation. Will Buckley noted in 1996 that it 'is routinely panned by the critics who snidely damn it with the faintest of praise: "It's so bad, it's almost good". Codswallop. The movie is a classic. It contains a fast-paced plot, some crisp dialogue, and a football match that the commentator rightly describes as "a sizzler".'[47]

It probably made little difference what reviewers said about this film, though, for it was a PR man's dream. Newspapers devoted more space to such attention-grabbing pictures as Bobby Moore surrounded by Nazi guards and barking Alsatians than they did to reviewing it. 'The goal is freedom', reported the *Daily Express* three months before the film was released. 'The great moral issues of World War Two are fought out on a football field,' said the *Sunday Times*.[48] One consequence was that the BBC paid a million dollars for the television rights, promising an additional fee based on turnover, reportedly equivalent to British box-office receipts over half a million pounds, which must have cost it dearly when the film did so well in the cinemas. Over at ITV, the film buyer Leslie Halliwell predicted that it would cost the BBC as much as *The Sound of Music*. Inevitably this meant that the Corporation would show the film early in its life and often thereafter, to recoup its investment. It was first shown at prime time on BBC1 on Boxing Day 1984, and has been a regular feature on TV screens ever since. Since it shadows POW films made three decades earlier, but invests them with special accessibility through its football stars, it has passed on time-warped images of Germany to younger generations.[49] David Castell recognised when reviewing it in 1981 that it had contemporary relevance in Britain, because it reinforced existing prejudices. 'For all its daftnesses, the picture's image of the soccer field as a battleground is one that

modern audiences will not have difficulty in recognising.' As the
screenwriter Yabo Yablonsky wrote, describing the film's climactic
soccer game, 'it was more than just a game – it was combat'. These
were sentiments that fitted easily into every England–Germany
match report by the 1980s.[50]

It was easy to be magnanimous about England–Germany matches
when winning them in the 1950s and early 1960s, when British people
complacently viewed Germany as a country treated with far greater
generosity than Hitler would have applied to Britain had the great
referee's decision gone the other way in 1940. For the early period
after 1945, this was also an easy position to adopt because the utter
destruction of Germany – much of it by Kenneth Wolstenholme
and his pals – made Germans hard to see as threatening rivals: even
when English teams had nasty shocks against Hungary, they never
lost symbolic contests against Germany.

England–Germany Soccer Internationals[51]

Period	Won by England	Drawn	Won by Germany
1900–14[52]	5	1	0
1930–66	7	1	0
1968–99	2	2	9

What the statistics show though is that the 1966 World Cup final
was the fulcrum between two very different periods: England dominant until 1966 but Germany afterwards. In the sixteen World and
European championships held between 1968 and the end of the century, England finished lower than Germany every time. With
Germany by the 1970s a major economic competitor which overtook
Britain in export markets, and for some at least a political threat too,
international football matches took on an added symbolism, and the
language and rhetoric of the world wars were increasingly used to
describe them. When Duncan Edwards was christened 'Boom,
Boom' by newspapers in the 1950s because the power of his shot

reminded them of the 'Big Bertha' gun, it was a joke; but when a generation later Franz Beckenbauer became 'the Kaiser', the soubriquet had a darker tone. A hint of what was to come had been noticed by club sides playing in Germany in the 1960s. Manchester United's Bill Foulkes recalled in 1965 German reactions after a 1957 drawn game in Düsseldorf, when, despite a fist-fight in a working men's club to which both teams had repaired after the match, 'the people there were incredibly hospitable and warm-hearted'. His next game in Germany was not until 1964, when 'things were very different. Whereas before we had enjoyed the family party, as it were, with beer and pies, this time it was very different. Now that the German teams have made the big league, their super League, the atmosphere is very formal, and far less friendly.' It was much the same the other way round: a Liverpool goal against Bayern Munich was greeted soon afterwards by a Scouse voice bellowing, 'That'll teach yer for bombing ower 'ouse!'[53]

No wonder then that England's increasingly regular defeats by German national sides were received so badly in a country that no longer felt so comfortable alongside a Germany whose footballing and economic power had overtaken Britain in both fields at once. As Peter Chapman outrageously puts it, describing the 1970 World Cup in Mexico, 'One well-timed leap by a veteran German footballer had done more than the Luftwaffe managed in years of aerial warfare. Uwe Seeler's flick found Peter Bonetti unable to get back to his line and set events on course to the demise of old industrial Britain.' The first English defeat by Germany in a 1968 friendly game was of limited importance, but increasingly after the 1960s the defeats were not just regular but irritatingly coincident with key games in international competitions. Seeler's 'flick' helped to knock England out of that 1970 World Cup, and the match was so shattering to some Britons that it was seriously offered as explanation for Labour's failure to win the general election a few days later. Rather as the young Peter Chapman could not quite believe it when Germany even scored against England in 1956 – nor could the radio commentator believe the manic cheering of the Berlin crowd, as if they thought they might actually *win* – so when England were roundly defeated in 1970 fans and journalists refused to believe that the match could have been fair. Surely, the mysterious stomach bug that laid low Gordon Banks must mean that he had been poisoned, so that he would be ruled out for the German game? Such fevered inventions were one-tenth serious at most, even to those who claimed to believe in them, but testified to the conviction that England just should not lose to Germany. For Geoff Hurst, who had scored a hat-trick in the 1966 final, England's defeat in Mexico was 'the most disappointing day of my life'. It cannot have helped that a popular Mexican paper headlined the story 'Blitzkrieg!'[54]

English supporters also found it especially hard to accept the way in which German footballing dominance in the last third of the twentieth century appeared to confound national stereotypes just then being reinforced by *Escape to Victory*. For while the teams of 'Kaiser' Beckenbauer and his successors displayed what Dave Bowler calls 'the Germans' trademark efficiency and organisation', they also showed an alarming propensity to play with flair and initiative – supposedly British characteristics that were alien to the automaton-like Germans. As J. B. Priestley had assured radio listeners in 1940, the Dunkirk evacuation would have been impossible for the Germans: 'That vast machine of theirs can't create a glimmer of that poetry in action which distinguishes war from mass murder.' In 1972, writing under the headline 'Night That Changed the German Image', Ian Wooldridge described Germans playing with grace and winning in style: 'This was a German team to make nonsense of the pulp magazine conception of the German national character and to make a few million adults realise that their prejudices are as obsolete as Bismarck's spiked helmet.' In 1990, echoing these sentiments for the next generation, David Lacey argued in the *Guardian* that 'the Germans have all the qualities that the English hold dear: strength, speed, spirit, character and an undying will to win'. From the 1970s onwards, German national teams were good at avoiding defeat even when neither well prepared nor playing particularly well, another cherished aspect of the British self-image derived from episodes of history ranging from the Spanish Armada to Dunkirk. Important English defeats were given added force when they twice occurred after penalty shoot-outs, which seemed to prove that the Germans also kept their nerve better under pressure. For Jürgen Klinsmann in 2000, this was indeed a matter of national 'mentality', to be explained by Germans having had to 'build up our country [twice]' after shattering defeats in successive world wars. Memories of the war could thus become a German rather than a British psychological asset as the century ended. Nail-biting finishes in penalty shoot-outs produced scapegoats and a general sense of England being robbed of victory by the weakness of individual non-scorers – Stuart Pearce and Chris Waddle in 1990's World Cup semi-final, Gareth Southgate in 1996's European Championships semi-final – communal moments of mass-participation national failure, with almost twenty-five million people in the UK watching each of the two defeats.[55]

'Please don't get so excited, Mein Führer –
it's only a game of football.'

England's defeats at the hands of Germany had by now started to arouse strong feelings outside the immediate significance of the matches themselves. When it became known in 1998 that George

Cohen, a World Cup-winner in 1966, was selling his medal to raise money for his retirement, he was roundly attacked in the press for being insufficiently patriotic, as if pride could pay his bills. In 2001 Geoff Hurst was signed up to comment on a match for a German rather than a British broadcaster, no British company having invited him to the microphone, and this too was thought unpatriotic in some quarters. A few years earlier a planned friendly match between the two countries had to be cancelled because it had inadvertently been scheduled to take place on Hitler's birthday, which it was feared might lead to crowd trouble. It was British newspapers that noticed the date's significance.

German newspapers now routinely commentated in advance on their British counterparts' entirely predictable coverage of football matches. In 1990 the German press was sharply critical of the violence associated with the World Cup semi-final: the *Frankfurter Allgemeine Zeitung* reported that 'in the resort of Brighton five hundred English troublemakers chased some three hundred German language students until the police intervened and found them security in a nightclub. Subsequently the Germans were taken to their lodgings in buses . . . In parts of London cars with German number plates were the preferred focus of violent Britons. In other towns businesses run by Germans were ravaged.' It all sounds rather like 1914, the disturbances having produced one fatality, scores of injuries and six hundred arrests, yet while British papers told their readers that the Queen Mother had watched the match and other such trivial details, the riots were 'more of a marginal topic . . . presumably because they are just as much part of the football here as are victory and defeat'. The *Süddeutsche Zeitung* quoted the sociologist David Hill describing 'the typical ugly Englishman: "Of white skin colour, male, a descendant of those who served as cannon fodder in the [First] World War. Brought up to use his muscles rather than his brain, without much prospect of social advancement" . . . It is telling, to Hill's mind, that their father "fought not against the Nazis but against the Krauts".' Approaching the Euro '96 semi-final rather warily, the *Frankfurter Allgemeine Zeitung* noted:

The steel helmet has become fashionable again in England this summer. But whom does that surprise? Whether the 'auld enemy' from the north, 'Juan' from the peninsula or 'Fritz' from the country of the Huns – whoever dares challenge the Empire in Wembley first needs to survive the attacks from publishing outposts in the gutter. Headlines in military style are traditional on the island. And the Englishman preserves things that have tradition . . . These stereotypes for which only England still provides a market elicit responses of mild despair from the serious press . . . Having enlisted Culloden and the Armada against the Scots and the Spaniards, now with the Germans it is the turn of the Second World War and one can only recommend not taking these things too seriously.

The *Süddeutsche Zeitung* learned of Germany being drawn to play England in the 2002 World Cup with resignation and irritation: 'The Panzers will be rolling again across English newspaper columns. Perhaps footballers will be urged to strike at the evil *Krauts*. English newspapers love writing about war when the subject at hand is football, especially when Germany is involved.'[56]

Yet there had been that remarkable, convergent period of relative innocence in the 1950s, when wartime antagonisms seemed to be dying away. 'Bert Trautmann's helmet', still proudly on display in Manchester City's notional trophy cabinet, and Trautmann himself, loudly cheered during recent visits to Manchester, are evidence of the fact. That 1950s convergence was highly conditional from the British viewpoint, but it is striking that Manchester's welcomes to Trautmann after 1949 and to Georg Maurer in 1958 were both loudly echoed in the national press, and by the evening and Sunday newspapers of the city. Newspapers then encouraged existing tolerant, fair-minded opinion and helped to ensure that it predominated; it was journalists who arranged the Trautmann testimonial match, crowned his career with a popular triumph, and provided the enormous local audience for his retiring paean to Anglo-German friendship, a view that they reported in full and explicitly endorsed. In later years none of these favourable circumstances continued to operate as the background to English football – or more widely in Anglo-German affairs either.

10

'People to people, there is a problem'[1]

Reviewing Anglo-German relations in 1964, Donald Watt was cautiously optimistic; attempting the same task ten years later, in *Our German Cousins*, John Mander was less sanguine. Mander was a prolific writer on German history who believed that Britain and Germany must be friends: 'since we cannot live without them, we must learn to live with them'. However, quoting a recent poll showing that Germans were among the British people's least popular foreigners, favoured by only 13 per cent, while the majority saw Germans as 'violent, lacking in tolerance, and unfriendly', he added that 'the age-group which finds the Germans least friendly is the 18–24 year olds'. It might still be too soon, for men whose lives had been scarred by the Nazis were still around; and, although West Germany had established a functioning democracy, 'is there a single one of Germany's neighbours who, deep down, is confident that this mood will last?' He thus concluded that 'there *is* a "German problem"; and perhaps there always will be', though 'the Germans are rather *more* capable than other people of changing their spots'. British opinion remained within the overall European context, if at the suspicious end of the spectrum, and he allowed himself optimism about the future. Thirty years later, his view that Germans are better at changing than their neighbours has acquired a different resonance. German democracy flourishes, now incorporating all Germans, not just the West. Most neighbouring peoples recognise that fact, and

British distrust of Germans is one more aspect of Western Europe's odd man out. The gap between elite perceptions and popular prejudices has remained wide open: Britain's diplomatic relations with Germany are close – warmer anyway than relations with France – and in 2005 Chancellor Angela Merkel could plausibly claim that after disastrous wars in the first half of the twentieth century, the two countries had 'walked the path towards a peaceful and united Germany side by side'. Yet popular distrust of 'the Germans' remained widespread. During a visit to Britain in October 2004, ahead of yet another royal visit to Germany intended to terminate antagonisms, Germany's Foreign Minister Joschka Fischer explained his country's growing irritation. The two governments wished to extend contacts exemplified by two thousand twinning arrangements and exchange schemes, but goodwill was obstructed by the British media: 'If you want to learn how the traditional Prussian goose-step works, you have to watch British television . . . My children are 20 and 25, and when they watch Germany in some of the British media they think this is a picture they have never seen in their whole lifetimes. Germany has changed in a democratic, positive way.' Diplomatic relations were 'excellent [but] people to people, there is a problem', said Fischer. The media reported his speech at length, often delighting to note that when discussing possible Turkish membership of the European Union Herr Fischer had himself made reference to D-Day – no question of 'don't mention the war', then. Yet, as a *Daily Telegraph* editorial concluded sixty years after VE Day in May 2005, 'we are a nation fixated with the Second World War and are becoming more so . . . Thirty years after Basil Fawlty got into a terrible state for mentioning the war once, we have become a country that can hardly stop mentioning it.'[2]

Without doubt, the German government had grounds for complaint, for British culture continued to be saturated in products memorialising British victories over Germany. It would be simplistic to blame the media: not only do newspapers mirror public opinion in addition to shaping it, but the phenomenon goes far wider. Popular literature, invasion tales, television, children's books and history courses, as well as the xenophobic lead given by politicians and newspapers, all contributed to the popular mindset. We need though to begin with a distinction and a prospective explanation: Germanophobia was increasingly an English obsession, rather than the wider British view that it was in 1915 and 1950; and this suggests the explanation. As the British Empire was liquidated in the 1960s, and Britain's economy went into steep decline compared to those of her European partners, there was a generally perceived identity crisis; Britain had not found a post-imperial identity. Rudyard Kipling had demanded, 'And what should they know of England who only England know?' but if England alone remained, who *were* the English? For Scotland and Wales, the sinking of nationality into a 'British' imperial mentality, as the British Empire emerged during the eighteenth century, facilitated the post-imperial shift back into older identities when it collapsed; for Northern Irish Protestants, being let down by Westminster encouraged a similar retreat into the siege mentality of the Pale, while for their opponents self-identity had always been Irish. Whatever the constitutional arrangements involved in devolution, the 'United Kingdom' all but ceased to exist for those born in the last quarter of the twentieth century. When white undergraduates were asked in the 1990s to define their own identity, hardly any offered the word 'British', preferring English, Welsh or Scots (and occasionally 'European'); only ethnic minority students continued to call themselves British (though with a hyphen, such as 'British-Asian'), pre-eighteenth-century nationalities having for them no relevance. The Union Jack was flown on the terraces when England won soccer's World Cup in 1966, but by 2005 English sports crowds generally waved the older flag of St George; commentators increasingly pointed out the absurdity of singing the British 'national anthem' for English teams, but 'Flower of Scotland' for the Scots and 'Land of my Fathers' for Wales; increasingly English fans adopted their own anthems for international matches – though rarely choosing anything with much Englishness about it.[3]

It is a commonplace among students of nationality that collective identity is established by differentiation from the 'other'. Kipling put it rather well: 'All the people like us are we, / And everyone else is They.' 'They' exhibit characteristics quite different from 'us', as Britishness was in 1800 epitomised by Britain fighting wars against France: free, Protestant, Germanic Britain contrasted with sub-servient, Catholic, Latin France; we loved plain roast beef while

Frenchmen ate 'made-up' dishes dripping with garlic. In post-imperial Britain, Scots and Welshmen had no difficulty identifying their 'other', since long campaigns for devolution explicitly promised to end centuries of domination by England. For the English, no local 'other' easily offered itself, but history could produce one. For geographical reasons – proximity to continental airfields – English cities were more bombed during the world wars than the rest of the United Kingdom, and the English have mainly perpetuated what Angus Calder dubbed 'the myth of the Blitz'. That myth casts Londoners/English/British as victims, Germans as aggressors, and 'proves' that 'we' could 'take it', being true Brits. 'Our finest hour' is not to be understood though without the parallel myth that 'we', murdered by unprovoked aggression, also won the war and 'saved Europe'. As Adrian Thrills noted in 1998, 'No team from Continental Europe ever plays at Wembley without being serenaded with at least one chorus of "If it wasn't for the English, you'd be Krauts",' a version of the Second World War that post-imperially ignores the Scots, Irish and Welsh, as well as the Red Army, the Commonwealth and the Americans. Neither fans nor press approached German games against Scotland or Wales in this spirit: needle matches for the Scots were played against England, national honour at stake just as when England plays Germany. For Wales and Ireland, something similar occurs in rugby matches against England, while English cricketers have faced an equivalent determination to beat former masters from Australia and other ex-colonies. None of these contests has excited either fans or the media to the hysteria routinely accompanying England–Germany games on the soccer field.[4]

During the 1990s, historians challenged Britain's wartime folk memories, and such ideas as the total national unity of 1940 took a few knocks. Yet however objectively true or untrue such 'memories' were, the myth was believed for several generations and remains largely intact. The more the Second World War was served up in novels, films and television programmes, the more it reinforced inherited assumptions. Sheer familiarity through repeated exposure thus carried deeper into the national mentality, and into generations unborn in 1945, the idea that Britain and Germany are natural enemies, that 1940 showed who we were when it mattered most, while concentration camps showed what 'they' are capable of doing. When

Britain went to war in the South Atlantic in 1982, the language and attitudes of the 1940s effortlessly reasserted themselves, to the dismay of liberals and leftists. The comedian Bernard Manning urged our boys to remember 'two world wars and one world cup', a phrase that had nothing to do with Argentina and everything to do with Germany. When the conflict ended in victory, street-parties were held as mass-participation community events all over the country, in self-conscious emulation of 1945, and Vera Lynn was exhumed to sing for England at the official victory concert; the Church of England even re-enacted 1945's spat over whether to hold triumphalist celebrations in the churches.[5]

Long after the event, thrillers highlighted the Second World War. As David Sexton argued in the *Guardian* in 1995, 'Hitler and the Nazis remain one of the great resources of the bestseller list. Every rack of airport novels includes at least one cover emblazoned with an eagle, a dagger, Gothic script and an embossed swastika.' In 1998 Robert Harris (who better to understand this than the author of *Fatherland*?) explained that, for middle-aged men, 'there's a hole in our lives where a war should have been'. The *Observer* quoted this remark in 1999 when analysing the popularity of computer games, allowing players themselves to defeat Germany. Michael Burleigh exasperatedly argued in 2003 that, 'oblivious to mounting disquiet (and distaste), the Hitler industry is recycling anything that publishers can dredge up and decorate with a swastika'.[6]

Len Deighton's *Funeral in Berlin* was the precursor to Frederick Forsyth's *The Odessa File* (1972), where Nazis remain a dangerous foe in the near present. Using the cunning mixture of fact and imagination that had been dazzlingly successful in *The Day of the Jackal* (1970), Forsyth here described an SS old-boy network in 1963–4, not only protecting comrades from prosecution by a nerveless West Germany, but infiltrating that state to restore Nazi rule. The hero, Peter Miller, is unaware of the Nazi period and the Holocaust, so better-informed authority figures must read him regular history lessons on 'what actually happened'. During the 1960s, Forsyth recalled thirty years later, in German schoolbooks 'the whole of the Second World War was about five lines. Some war to be covered so superficially.' For post-war Germans, the Second World War had remained 'blanked out for roughly 20 years', though he conceded that 'there is now a complete admission by the German people of what happened'. That concession was in an interview with his biographer, but the novel, still in print, is unchanged. Nor could recent readers separate documented realities like the Nazi-hunter Simon Wiesenthal from the fictional storyline. Advance publicity planted the idea that Forsyth had done extensive research, Wiesenthal's files providing essential data on Edouard Roschmann, the 'Butcher of Riga', who is the book's Nazi target. Soon after the film of *The Odessa File* was released, an Argentinian told police that Roschmann lived in his street; he was arrested, bailed and fled, dying from a coronary while crossing into Paraguay. When Roschmann was reported dead, Wiesenthal did not believe it, thinking it another escape into a new identity, just as in the novel. Austrian policemen took to Argentina not only fingerprints but a copy of Forsyth's book, concluding that the dead man was indeed Roschmann partly because Forsyth mentioned that he had lost two toes crossing the Alps in 1945. Life and art inextricably intertwined. Forsyth had originally treated tales about conspiracies by former SS men 'with a pinch of salt', but agreed to see one informer, who told him about 'this mysterious self-help organisation' ODESSA (Organisation of Former SS Members). The author's researches were frustrated by the German authorities meant to track down ex-Nazis (exactly Miller's experience in the book). In 2000 his only regret was not placing more emphasis on the Nazi gold in Swiss banks, but he was proud that his novel had helped to squeeze a billion pounds out of Zurich to compensate Holocaust victims.[7]

Imaginative use of the Israeli intelligence community and the 1967 Arab–Israeli War (which was indeed 'history' before his novel appeared) provided another pull towards fact within fiction. According to Forsyth, *The Odessa File* was 'the serious one' among his first three novels: 'it is a reconstruction and carries a strong message'; newspapers often reviewed it as if it were investigative reporting rather than a thriller. An 'author's note' thanks ex-SS men for helping him, some of whom must needs remain anonymous, placing the book within the same conspiratorial realm as its plot, a Germany fearful of Nazi retribution. Finally, although the hero unmasks the conspiracy and survives multiple efforts to kill him, Nazi villains escape to safety, their protectors among West German policemen remaining unchallenged. *The Odessa File* was on the British best-seller lists for a year; Forsyth had already had the largest-ever British advance for a novel, and for the film received 'an altogether astronomical six-figure sum' (according to *The Times*). *The Odessa File* was a movie seen all over the world in 1974, carrying the message to a wider public. Its first British television showing was on New Year's Day 1979, watched by an enormous family audience, and when re-shown in 1981 it was again one of the week's top ten BBC programmes. Novels do not make an individual impact (not least because financial success tempts others to exploit their themes): *The Odessa File* fell for cinema reviewers within a new cinematic obsession with Nazi Germany, typified by *The Night of the Generals* (1967) and *The Night Porter* (1974), while its conspiratorial assumptions were shared by Ira Levin's *The Boys from Brazil* (1976, filmed in 1978).[8]

The same mood pervaded Cold War thrillers, as in Len Deighton's 'Game, Set and Match' trilogy: as the urbane East German von Munte observes in *Berlin Game*, 'we Germans find reassurance in tyranny. That's always been our downfall.' The novels make continuous links between the present and the Nazi past, for example in descriptions of the geography of Berlin. The hero, Bernard Samson, often thinks of something as 'typically German' or 'berlinerisch', but from a perspective we must think well informed. Lisl Hennig, in whose house he grew up, displays photographs of the Kaiser, and there is even a space where Hitler's portrait used to hang; she reminisces about Goebbels, and plays bridge with Herr Koch, a former secret policeman. Samson's best friend since his own Berlin childhood, Werner Volkmann, is victimised (he believes) by West Berlin policemen: 'Bloody Nazis. They picked me because I'm a Jew.' All Samson's Berlin friends have a past rooted in the black market, transformed into corrupt East–West trade across the same border that the spies penetrate. Even when fleeing from the Stasi, Samson notices that picnickers by a Berlin lake are 'smoking and drinking in silence, with a dedication that is unmistakably German'. Stereotypes create the cumulative impression that Germans are different from us, the war still part of their lives. The fact that Len Deighton then produced six more Samson novels suggests that Bernard retained his public interest right to the end of the century.[9]

Pausing to reconsider the prehistory of wartime Berliners in *Winter: A Berlin Family, 1899–1945*, Deighton's picture offers few hints of spring to come. The family has Jewish relations whose fate under Hitler is horrifying: Pauli, one of two brothers, is complicit in the SS empire that works Jews to death, while Peter is a late and unconvincing convert to resistance. After Peter escapes to America, his wife tells Pauli that people won't mistreat him: 'It's only you Germans who have that deep-down fear and mistrust of foreigners that makes you treat strangers so badly. That's how the whole Hitler business got started.' Brian Samson, Bernard's father, scoffs at the resistance: 'The army! Don't tell me about the bloody army. Those spineless bastards didn't discover that there was anything wrong with Hitler until the Red Army started showing them how to fight battles, and the RAF started bombing their precious German towns. Now they've decided that they want to get rid of him. Typically German, that; fair-weather friends the Germans.' As the story reaches its post-war climax at Berchtesgaden, where the Winters have a villa, Samson reminds himself that this was 'the view Hitler had from the terrace of his Berghof. Why did the Germans love to hide themselves in such mountain scenery? . . . Was it something to do with their fundamental paranoia?' Deighton has both the Winters killed in obscure circumstances, good and bad German dying together.[10]

When he resumed Bernard Samson's story in the 'Hook, Line and Sinker' series, Deighton's enthusiasm for Germans had not enlarged. In *Spy Hook* Lisl's sister gives Bernard 'the standard answers that people who lived under the Third Reich give to foreigners and strangers of any kind'; at a London dinner party, nobody argues with a British teacher just back from Bavaria – in 1987 – when he announces that 'you see these mean little German kids and you understand why the Germans have started so many wars'. In Berlin Bernard notices that Bendlerstrasse, 'from which the Wehrmacht marched to conquer Europe, is re-named after Stauffenberg, architect of the failed anti-Nazi putsch. [But] is there some militaristic ambition burning deep inside the town planners who keep Bendler Bridge still Bendler Bridge?' Crossing into the East, he reflects on East Germans' Marxism: 'Why not? Who could doubt that the Germans, who had given such unquestioning faith and loyalty – not to mention countless million lives – to Kaiser Wilhelm and Adolf Hitler, would soldier on, long after Marxism had perished at its own hand and been relegated to the levelled *Führerbunker* of history?' That observation places Hitler within rather than outside German history. In *Spy Line* Werner Volkmann exhibits 'ingrained Germanic thinking' through 'mild paranoia', and by being 'provincial and narrow-minded, in the way that Germans are prey to being'.[11] Even in the final Samson trilogy, written after Germany had been reunited, though set in the late 1980s, Erich Honecker's East Germany seems the continuation of Hitler's dictatorship and of other violent episodes from German history. Yet British agents despise 'that bloody man Kohl . . . a snake in the grass', for his efforts towards unification. Stereotypes of Germanness continue, with Bernard revisiting areas famous for war crimes perpetrated by 'the Germans'. Finally acquiring a desk job as MI6's deputy chief in Berlin, he is rescued from neglecting paperwork by a secretary who stands over him, but rarely understands his jokes: 'she was very German'. The bloody climax takes place at a luxury villa on the Wannsee, where it is rumoured that Heydrich once lived: 'coming downstairs for a midnight snack you might rub shoulders with a natty-uniformed blond ghoul with blood on his hands' – surely a reflection on more than a house.[12]

Deighton's tenacity makes him the outstanding example of a writer whose work kept Nazi Germany in the British mind, but others contributed too – Victor Canning in the 1960s, Jack Higgins in the 1970s, Robert Harris in the 1990s, each finding different German nightmares with which to confront readers. Similar fantasies can be found in books by Eric Ambler, Ken Follett, C. S. Forester, Hammond Innes, Robert Ludlum, Alistair Maclean, Nevil Shute and Elleston Trevor, to name but a few.[13]

Victor Canning's *The Whip Hand* (1965) launched his 'Rex Carver' novels about a hard-boiled British private eye. When visited with an offer of employment by the blond, fleshy 'Herr Stebelson' on the first page, we are straight into stereotypical Teutons, while Carver's partner provides an assessment of post-war Germans: 'He looks prosperous but he's not a gentleman. There's something flashy about him.' Such pigeonholing continues throughout: German holidaymakers all look 'brown, beefy and self-assured', racial types described in Nazi theories that Carver finds still current in a contemporary German book. The gangsters are hunted by a Jewish survivor of the Holocaust, but East German agents are unreformed ex-Nazis. The gangsters turn out to be Nazis relaunching Hitler's quest for world domination, centred on a 'blond Siegfried' who believes himself the son of Hitler and Eva Braun, with a shrine containing Hitler's corpse as their Valhalla. A powerful shadow Nazi group, the Atonement Party, has infiltrated West German democracy, pretending to preach contrition for the German past while planning a new war of terror. Those attending a secret conclave where the conspiracy is outlined provide another negative image of 1960s Germany: successful men who know 'about compromises, and profits . . . about nice, clean commercial murders, and the way to push them out of mind and conscience when they went back to the bosom of their families'. Their pledge to unite for 'a new Europe' had a sinister ring in the very years when Britain first sought to join the European Community. Carver wonders why, with all the world's espionage agencies on the track of these new Nazis, the story 'hadn't . . . got to Bonn. It wasn't like them to miss the smell of drains in their own backyard.' But the novel says that it was, for neo-Nazi groups have influence enough to protect themselves in Germany. Carver falls hopelessly for Katerina ('beautiful, blonde and German'), but discovers that she is the Aryan chosen to produce Hitler's grandchildren. Katerina almost flogs him to death with an SS whip; Nazi violence having reached half time in 1945, the second half will now be played. The hero learns on the final page that 'they really want a new Germany, you know . . . There's no racial discrimination these days. Just cooperation.' That view has arisen from nowhere, however, and does not convince Carver himself, while the Nazi thugs have escaped to fight another day. H. F. R. Keating thought that, 'for sheer bloody enjoyableness, Canning is hard to beat'. In 1965, at the height of his powers, while another of his novels was being filmed by Alfred Hitchcock, he thought the Nazi chapter of German history far from over.[14]

With Jack Higgins, sleight of hand operates in space rather than time: Nazis come to Britain rather than reappearing in Germany. Writing in 1996, Higgins claimed that *The Eagle Has Landed* (1975) 'changed the face of the war novel', for until then 'all Germans, both in the cinema and the novel, were seen as rampant Nazis intent only on rape, pillage and murder. Having worked with many German Army veterans of the Russian front during my service with the Royal Horse Guards during the Cold War, I had discovered that the majority were much like us.' His publisher, though, when offered a novel in which German paratroops jump into Norfolk in 1943 to kidnap Winston Churchill, thought it 'the worst idea he had ever heard [for] how could you identify with a bunch of Nazis'. The book was published in America first, and appeared in Britain only after doing well abroad. It sold twenty-six million copies in fifty-five languages, 'a publishing legend and a major film', but the idea that *The Eagle Has Landed* showed Germans as 'much like us' is open to question. Like Forsyth, Higgins did serious research before writing, and like Forsyth he created ambiguity between fact and fiction. The 1943 story is framed by chapters in which Higgins himself learns that German paratroops did indeed invade Britain in 1943; long-suppressed 'truth' in the rest of the book therefore gains credibility. An author's note claims that 'fifty per cent is documented historical fact', and in a postscript he describes the fate of the 'historical characters' (but cannot resist continuing the fictional lives of invented characters too). Without a close knowledge of wartime events, the reader is hard pressed to know what is invented and what is not, yet a recent reviewer decided that 'since plots a lot stranger than this actually did happen in the shadows of World War II (some of them inspired by the sneakiness of Churchill himself), it's not at all difficult to buy the premise lock, stock, and barrel'. This matters because, as Higgins himself put it in 2000, 'It was a special book indeed; one of those that comes along and all of a sudden is read by people who don't often read.' He takes pleasure from visitors to Norfolk asking for directions to Studley Constable, where Churchill was almost kidnapped – yet no such village has ever existed.[15]

The novel shows German paratroops as tough soldiers but not Nazis, whereas wartime intelligence knew there were plenty of party members in such units; British defenders are invisible and American Rangers fight like rank amateurs. As their commander points out, the Germans' raid fails only because one dives into a river to save a British child from drowning, during which his German uniform becomes visible. That commander, Colonel Steiner, is from Prussian military stock, his father a general who is being tortured to death by Himmler for plotting against Hitler. Their collaborators in Norfolk are a Boer who has hated the British since 1900, and the IRA man Liam Devlin, a professional hitman who also hates British imperialism. Higgins did after all hail from Belfast and understood such

feelings, but the film of *The Eagle Has Landed* reduced the Irish executioner to a comedy Celt. Yet the German characters, knowing the
war is lost, continue to work for the Nazis and delude each other to
that end: the war hero Radl tells Steiner that if his raid succeeds his
father will be saved for he has Himmler's word for it, though he
himself does not believe anything Himmler says and knows that if the
raid fails they will all die to cover the SS's tracks. Nobody except the
elder Steiner considers resistance, and his has already failed. With the
failure of their mission and the certainty that they will be killed, the
raiders refuse surrender, and fight to the last man, just as Hitlerian
Germany went down in 1945. Steiner may 'regret' the necessity to
shoot Churchill, but he does it anyway, and it is hardly his fault that
'Churchill' is an actor on display while the real Prime Minister flies
to meet Stalin at Tehran.[16]

   In the sequel, *The Eagle Has Flown*, written in 1991 after demands
from thousands of 'fans of my work', Higgins takes a similar line.
Steiner somehow recovers from being shot dead – when so much is
invented, why not? Liam Devlin returns to rescue him from a British
prison. Again a framing device suggests fact within fiction, including
the murder of an American Ph.D. student who discovers the 'truth',
killed presumably by British intelligence since nobody else knows
that truth. Steiner and Devlin behave with bravery and chivalry, with
the full backing of Germany's armed forces. With no Churchill
kidnap plot to give the tale real clout, we have Himmler planning to
kill Hitler, a plot that will collapse if Steiner can be released and
bring to Hitler his loyal soldiers. So the book's 'good' Germans, those
who are 'much like us', must employ remarkable moral gymnastics:
better to keep Hitler alive, since he is losing the war, while Himmler
would make things even worse. Nobody ever expresses the view of the
actual conspirators in 1944: that Germany must be freed from such
impossible choices by driving out all Nazis. The good guys escape
from England and Hitler is saved; this time it is the Germans who
will deny that anything ever happened, while Steiner, had he not to
flee to Ireland to escape Himmler's vengeance, would have fought for
Hitler until May 1945. Any sense of their being a moral chasm
between Germans and Nazis has vanished.[17]

   With *Fatherland* (1992), Robert Harris produced one of the best-
ever first novels, though he had already written non-fiction works,

including one about the forged 'Hitler Diaries'. Like Forsyth, Harris sets his story in a 1960s Germany that knows little of Nazi crimes, this time because Germany has won the war and written the 'history'. Continuities with the actual Nazi period remain, despite a normalised post-war framework: the hero Xavier March works for the criminal police, whose duties range from burglary 'up to murder' – and mixed marriages. The story depicts his work as a detective and an 'unreliable' (as his indoctrinated son points out); an unidentified corpse in a Berlin lake turns out to be just one victim of a murderous plot to suppress all evidence of the Holocaust. Harris mixes together real people and invented characters, using documentary material captured in 1945, but changes events from 1942 onwards to fit into his counter-factual tale. Much post-war reality remains, but subtly altered: a twenty-year Cold War reflects nuclear stalemate between the German Empire and America, although détente is being promoted by President Kennedy – but Joseph Kennedy, the admirer of Hitler, not JFK. Harris's discussion of the Wannsee conference, detailed knowledge of which had indeed survived only because a participant disobeyed orders by filing the minutes (the same Martin Luther who is a murder victim in *Fatherland*), gives force to the idea that 'history' can be 'made' in more than one way. (The same documents underpinned HBO's film *Conspiracy* (2001), Kenneth Branagh contributing a terrifying performance as Heydrich.) Yet, at the end of *Fatherland*, March's resistance to the Nazis has failed, and the SS are torturing him to death. We are unsure whether his accomplice escapes abroad with the evidence and tells the free world about the Holocaust; even if she does, Germany will not find out, though Harris suggests that Germans know anyway: 'You can't build on a mass grave,' asserts March. Nor can we know whether Joseph Kennedy's America would publish such documents, whether the need for peace with Germany will dictate suppression. There is then no closure, just *Nacht und Nebel*.[18]

There are darker suggestions about German history even within that fog of uncertainty. Early in the story, while taking his son around Albert Speer's monstrous Berlin monuments, March notices extravagant claims made by the guide: the triumphal arch is bigger than the Arc de Triomphe, the dome higher than St Peter's. 'Higher, longer, bigger, wider, more expensive . . . Even in victory, thought March, Germany has a parvenu's inferiority complex.' He later takes a secret package to the Grünewald, reflecting that, 'from these forests, five centuries before Christ, the warring German tribes had emerged, and to these forests, twenty-five centuries later, mostly at weekends, in their campers and their trailers, the victorious German tribes returned. The Germans were a race of forest-dwellers. Make a clearing in your mind, if you liked; the trees just wanted to reclaim it.' Germany is so dominant as to have established a trading bloc of twelve members, a European parliament, a single currency, a blue flag with gold stars, and a European anthem based on Beethoven's Ninth Symphony. These were probably viewed by the author as jokes indicating how much remains 'the same' even if one variable changes. Nevertheless, in a decade when politicians spoke of Germany's intention to achieve through 'Europe' the domination of Europe which Hitler had sought, it was surprising stuff from a man close to Tony Blair and Peter Mandelson.[19]

Fatherland was a hugely popular book, winning ecstatic reviews and prizes (rightly including the annual W. H. Smith prize for a 'Thumping Good Read'); within weeks it was out in eight languages and had made Harris a dollar millionaire. It sold four million copies in three years, and the vogue for such counter-factual fiction as Peter Preston's *Fifty-first State* (1998) has been attributed to *Fatherland*. By 2004, the book had been in the Nielsen lists of best-sellers for ten years, one of only twenty-nine titles to achieve that success. It was still selling between eight hundred and a thousand copies a week in Britain in 2000. As Thomas Sutcliffe put it in the *Independent*, Harris 'did to the international bestseller lists what the Nazis did to Poland'. 'Say what you like about Adolf Hitler', Harris joked in 1996, but 'he's always been good to me'. Embarrassment occurred when Harris's German publisher Bertelsmann turned out to have a Nazi past denied in its own carefully crafted alternative history, but it had been a struggle to find any German publisher for *Fatherland*, which was initially printed in German only in Switzerland. *Vaterland* hit the headlines when Hamburg police impounded paperbacks displayed by a bookshop, objecting to the swastika on the cover (illegal in Germany, but ironically not elsewhere); although, by then, the hardback had already attracted neo-Nazis. It was obviously a valuable film property, but here the ability to 'make history' was demonstrated again. Columbia wanted a big-budget Hollywood movie, but ran into trouble over the script: Harris claimed that 'the studio bosses consulted the target audience, 16- to 21-year-old Americans, and discovered that they did not even know that there had been a Second World War, let alone who had won it'. Their reluctance to proceed probably also owed something to the difficulty of making an American film with a pro-Nazi President Kennedy, however well documented from history. HBO thus transformed the project into a made-for-television quickie, with amusing results and a happy ending that contradicted everything the novel did so well. With the Dutch Rutger Hauer as March, the studio looked as usual for British actors as villains, but since Hauer had a Dutch accent, those Brits must have 'German accents' too, or the audience would be confused: several fine actors came close to Herr Flick in 'Allo, 'Allo while others just couldn't be bothered. Nevertheless, the story retained its power to shock, and when re-shown on television in 2002, *The Times* thought it 'an intriguing slice of alternative history'.[20]

Alternative history became popular in the post-war period, and the historian of these allohistorical fables about the war, Gavriel Rosenfeld, has analysed around a hundred examples from books, films and television. Although these were found all over the world, four out of five were British or American, and hence accessible to British readers and viewers; Britons and Americans were happier than anyone else to re-imagine the war, having been its winners, and 'speculating about alternative outcomes to the Nazi era has become a notable phenomenon in Western popular culture'. The fact that 'the Third Reich is the most commonly explored subject in alternate history' indicates how far Hitler's era was seen as 'pivotal', and since alternative history is essentially a 'presentist' genre, exploiting the past only to illuminate the present, this tells us a lot about the speculators and their own societies.[21]

Within that Anglo-American fascination with re-imagining the 1940s, it was the British who mainly concerned themselves with a hypothetical Nazi invasion of Britain: four-fifths of British alternative histories supposed a Nazi victory, compared to under half of American fables and only a third of German ones. The readiness to see Britain fictionally conquered drew on earlier traditions of invasion literature and linked back to the first era of Anglo-German rivalry:

An Englishman's Castle, a 1978 ITV mini-series depicting a successful German invasion, had a title blatantly stolen from the Edwardian invasion play *An Englishman's Home*. Usually such tales ended by reasserting the wartime myth in one form or another, with a fight-back much like those offered by William Le Queux and Saki. One of the first to venture into the field after 1945 was Noel Coward, whose play *Peace in Our Time* appeared in 1947, conceived when he visited post-war Paris and found his flat vandalised by German occupiers, while friends awaited trial for collaboration. He staged the effect of defeat through a Chelsea pub; Churchill has been shot, the King imprisoned at Windsor, the Isle of Wight is a concentration camp, and the Savoy Hotel open only to Germans (this last probably the worst disaster Coward could imagine). Leftist intellectuals collaborate but workers stand aloof, forming resistance groups and 'fighting the bloody Germans', triumphing when the Commonwealth, the Americans and the Free French liberate Britain from what *Might Have Been* (the play's original working title). The invaders are uniformly repellent; their chief spokesman, the Gestapo officer Albrecht Richter, proclaims a racial affinity between Britain and Germany, before killing one of the pub's regulars. When a German artist visits, he is ironically congratulated on his 'quite remarkable' modernist designs for *Der Rosenkavalier* at Covent Garden. He hopes that a few decades of German rule may bring Britain up to date, oblivious to the sarcasm when a local replies, 'it's too sweet of you to take the trouble to teach us. We've been trying for centuries to acquire a little "kultur" but without the slightest success'. That joke is heavy-handedly underscored when another character quotes a patriotic speech from Shakespeare, 'This royal throne of kings . . . ' The play was one of Coward's few flops, the public not yet ready for such a nightmare; many critics hated it and audiences stayed away in droves. Nevertheless, the same theme was taken up in the 1960s and 1970s in three very different products: *Daily Mail* articles by C. S. Forester (1960); *It Happened Here* (1964), made by Kevin Brownlow and Andrew Mollo; and Len Deighton's *SS GB* (1978). Forester's, as might be expected from the creator of Hornblower, was a patriotic version, concentrating on how a possible invasion would have fared militarily and concluding that it would have failed, shortening the war by hastening German defeat. He had though already told readers what

Nazi rule would be like in a book of Third Reich short stories, *The Nightmare* (1953), presenting the 1944 resistance as half hearted and indecisive and war criminals after 1945 as unable to grasp that they had done anything wrong.[22]

It Happened Here was conceived by a pair of inexperienced teenagers, one of whose pacifist views sat oddly alongside the other's fascination with Nazi uniforms, and was a labour of love that took almost a decade to complete. The film is set in 1944, after the Germans have occupied Britain, and centres on an Irish nurse; she is initially non-political but recruited to the British fascists, only to be repelled by their using her in the euthanasia of consumptive Polish slaves. The film begins and ends with indiscriminate shootings by the British resistance, and in the central section a British resister explains that the worst thing about fascism is that you have to adopt its methods to crush it. This is a relativist standpoint: Britons collaborating with Germans, the resistance as bad as the occupiers, though they are winning. Although the heroine is Irish there are enough solidly English characters among the collaborators to push home the moral. That message is anyway shockingly reinforced by the film's visual impact, which suffers less from loose structure and woodenness of execution than do the acting and the plot. There is a brilliant pastiche of a wartime German newsreel, in which John Snagge (voice of the BBC) recounts Britain's defeat and explains her racial affinity with Germany, while the camera shows German soldiers fraternising with girls in Trafalgar Square, photographing the Albert Memorial (a neat Anglo-German point), and generally behaving like the Wehrmacht in Paris. While this was an anti-fascist film, it does not say much about Germans except to demonstrate the moral and physical consequences of becoming their victims. Since British viewers already knew plenty about what the German army and Gestapo had done to the Dutch and Danes, merely showing them swanking round London was effective enough, notably when a British bobby cycles without concern past a German tank, it being an everyday sight. Such moments created incident during filming, as when real German soldiers, on leave from training in Wales, watched 'German' conquerors ceremonially marching around Parliament Square. It was not quite so funny when ex-POW extras debated where an SS officer should wear his gun, until an actor who had been in the SS himself ruled that the original actor had got it right – and nobody argued. Brownlow's aim was to humanise Germans, making them seem no better or worse than the British; he was unimpressed by the fact that he had to pay £360 to a 'respected German music publisher' for the right to use the '*Horst Wessel Lied*'. But the film did not show any Germans resisting fascism, and their ubiquitous presence on the London streets was a continuous visual reminder that all this misery began with a German invasion. German troops, *circa* 1944, marching past a London bus, Big Ben in the background, visually told that story to great effect.[23]

Even before completion, Brownlow's film was raided by the *Daily Mail* to provide illustrations for its Forester articles, but when finished it had a hard road into the cinemas, and was only commercially shown after a scene in which British fascists expounded their views had been cut. Though the directors thought these fascists condemned themselves out of their own mouths, others thought the film pro-Nazi: for the *Jewish Chronicle*, 'it was like viewing a Mosley meeting'. Others were more complimentary, as the film made its way around European festivals, though audience members in Mannheim complained that it was 'unfair to Germans [and] disgusting that this film should be shown in Germany at this time'. Did they really only enjoy films when Germany lost? Once it had been edited, *It Happened Here* played in a prestigious London cinema, but it attracted mixed reviews and never went on general release; it acquired cult status later only through showings on television and in art-house cinemas.[24]

SS GB reflected historians' shifting view of Nazi Germany, now seen not as a monolithic autocracy but as an anarchy of competing forces. Deighton's German conquerors are a pack of ruthless competitors, with the chief rivalry between the SS and the army. Collaboration with the conquerors is presented in ambiguous shades of grey, compared to the stark black and white of earlier invasion fantasies. Descriptions of familiar places under German rule nevertheless have some of the impact of their visual equivalents in *It Happened Here*, just as in books by Le Queux: Buckingham Palace, the Victoria Palace music hall and the Dorchester Hotel lie in ruins; British bobbies work for the occupiers, the Gestapo run Scotland Yard, and British POWs remain in German camps as hostages; veterans reminisce about heavy fighting around Colchester and Cheam, both now uninhabitable; a mass round-up of civilians involves holding centres at the Albert Hall, Earl's Court exhibition hall and York Way goods depot, with the residents turned out of Dolphin Square to provide offices for interrogations; Churchill has been executed and the King shot dead while escaping German captivity in the Tower of London; collaboration, informing, the black market and moral collapse are universal, while 'Teutonics' lord it and German military bands patronisingly play 'Greensleeves'. Yet though they fall out among themselves and amorally contend for nuclear secrets, neither the good nor the bad Germans ever express the slightest regret for coming to Britain in the first place; death, misery and moral ambiguity underline collective guilt. Reviewers commented on the novel's plausibility, though this will have made it more shocking to British readers, while traditionalists regretted Deighton's refusal to condemn Nazism. During the 1990s, exactly as the myths of the 'People's War' were being exposed by historians, further invasion fantasies provided critiques from Left and Right on what would have happened after a successful invasion. The atypical case of the Channel Islands, which did have Nazi occupiers, was hugely over-investigated both in literature and on television, interesting in itself but telling us nothing about what would have happened to London or Liverpool. The invasion issue was much revisited, with reminders in each decade since the war that Britain had in 1940 come close to unspeakable horrors, from which both vicarious pleasure and moral lessons could be learned through their re-enactment. This was after all the history of what did *not* happen, and the effect was generally to reinforce support for what actually occurred.[25]

It was no accident that *It Happened Here* gained its audience through television, for British TV has unrelentingly offered reminders of the Second World War over the entire period since it resumed broadcasting – with a 1946 victory concert. In addition to re-broadcasting old films, which served up reheated portions of outdated attitudes as weekly nutrition, all television channels found audiences for programmes of their own, factual and documentary, fictional reconstructions, and even comedy. In September 2005 Channel Four reported that eleven of the hundred all-time top-grossing films in Britain were about the Second World War; an earlier poll rated half a dozen among the greatest films ever made (which, given the quality of war movies in general, suggests some favouritism). In the same week, when no anniversary fell and no special wartime memory was celebrated, free-to-air channels carried on average more than one programme a day about the war, and the cable networks three or four each day. A dedicated viewer with a VCR could spend his spare time watching the Second World War daily. Some probably do.

Among Second World War television dramas, a few stand out, but sheer ubiquity has been the most important factor: *All Our Yesterdays* (1960–73), *The Valiant Years* (1960), *1940* (1965), *A Family at War* (1970–2, the eighth most popular programme in 1971 and 1972), *Colditz* (1972–4, the seventh most popular programme in 1973), *The World at War* (1973), *The Evacuees* (1974), *The Sullivans* (1976–83), *Secret Army* (1977–9, the eighth most popular programme in 1979), *Enemy at the Door* (1978–80), *Danger UXB* (1979), *Kessler* (1981), *Tenko* (1981–4), *We'll Meet Again* (1981–3), *Fortunes of War* (1987), *Wish Me Luck* (1987–8), *The Camomile Lawn* (1992), *The Nazis, a Warning from History* (1997), *War of the Century* (1999), *World War II in Colour* (1999), *Band of Brothers* (2001), *Foyle's War* (2002–), and *Colditz* (2004). Most of these series have been repeated at least once, the older titles now featuring regularly on cable channels like UK Gold, and almost all became available on video, though the BBC was in the early 1990s reluctant to put war programmes into renewed circulation. Even from that incomplete list, a chronological pattern emerges: there was a concentration on the war in the 1970s, which eased but then resumed in the 1990s, when television companies also gave in to demand and released on video series like *Secret Army*, previously kept in the vaults. *Secret Army* makes a good representative example of the genre.

A carefully researched tribute to the Belgian resistance, *Secret Army* centred on 'Lifeline', the network spiriting RAF flyers back to Britain through Spain, based on 'actual persons and events', according to the script editor. In the first series action increasingly focused on the Brussels café that provides the network's base and the livelihood of its organiser, Albert Foiret. By the second series, Foiret has a new café popular with German officers, so he and his friends can eavesdrop on their conversations, but the writers had become increasingly interested in the Germans anyway, and by the third series they are central to the story. German characters are differentiated between a 'good German' in the Luftwaffe police and SS Standartenführer Kessler, sent to Brussels to 'use any methods you like that will produce results'. In principle the series maintained balance between Germans and Nazis, though both were usually outwitted by the resistance, who hate 'the Germans'. Not until the end does any German suspect that their favourite café also harbours their deadliest foe. Even before this climax, 'good' Germans are ineffective and misdirected, lamenting that Germany is losing, seeing whose fault that is, but doing nothing about it. Meanwhile, Kessler reminds viewers of long-running German stereotypes: respect for order and 'correct behaviour'; obsessive bureaucratic tidiness; a cruelty that inflicts 'excruciating torment' on prisoners; sentimentality. Though he loathes Kessler's Nazi views, a subordinate reflects that 'the man really was convinced and dedicated to his beliefs. It was a curious loyalty to an idea that at least half of the Germans could not wholly accept' – but which that majority could not mitigate, even as it dragged them into the abyss.[26]

The 1945 climax takes the German side of the story further. As German units retreat towards Belgium, Kessler maintains that the Führer will achieve a victory with secret weapons, rounding angrily on any other view as traitorous defeatism; the book of the series dwells on his Aryan features and suspicious nature, searching the desks of subordinates, 'clicking his heels, as a good German should'. When Major Reinhardt tells him that Albert Foiret organises Lifeline, he at first refuses to believe it, but when convinced he orders Reinhardt to kill Foiret, even though Brussels will be evacuated that day. Reinhardt is also ordered never to surrender, while Kessler has already made plans for his own escape, sentimentally taking his Belgian mistress with him. Reinhardt confronts Foiret, who admits his guilt, but then the German officer surrenders to the café owner, rather than arresting him, and they drink to the end of the war. With Belgians liberated, Kessler and Reinhardt fetch up in the same POW camp, Kessler no longer in SS uniform. Seeing Reinhardt, he denounces him to the senior German officer and demands his court martial for disobeying a direct order not to surrender. Though the senior officer is a Prussian of the old guard, he orders the trial and keeps Kessler's identity secret; he manages even to get permission to execute Reinhardt in the camp, the Canadian commander deciding that 'if they want to kill themselves, why in hell not? They're crazy. The whole race, just plumb crazy. I almost wish they would make a break for it.' Reinhardt is thus shot by Germans while Kessler escapes, a Canadian sergeant bribed to allow him just to melt away. So the good German comes to a pointless end while the Nazi personifies how guilty Germans evaded punishment in 1945. Since it is Canadians who take all the wrong decisions, the British and the Belgians have clean hands, while complicity by the aristocratic Prussian commander is a reminder of the German army's refusal to disobey Nazi orders. The producers pointed out that a real German POW had been executed in a Dutch camp, but it was nevertheless their decision to use this as the climax of the series. The happy ending of liberation is undermined and as Kessler and Madeleine escape, 'there would be a place for them in the new Germany'.[27]

It was inevitable in the decade that generated *The Odessa File* that the story would not end there, and in due course the BBC produced a sequel, showing what happened to *Secret Army's* characters after the war. Yet, although there were scenes that showed how Albert and his friends fared up to the 1970s, the focus was on one character, and the title was *Kessler*. The scriptwriter explained that this was because Kessler 'became so popular with viewers, and, indeed, entered into the mythology of World War II in such a way as to be possibly more real and memorable than the persons upon whom he was based'. Viewers wanted to know 'what happened to Kessler?' so after research they now offered a story 'much nearer to the truth than has ever hitherto been portrayed'. In view of these claims it is significant that the series showed Kessler, under an assumed name, as a West German industrialist, and one who 'holds the key to the vast and powerful web of neo-Nazi organisations', the Kameradenwerk. The new plot begins when investigative reporters identify Kessler: Britain's MI5 expect 'the Jerries to put their own house in order', but Kessler is tipped off by West German intelligence and decamps to Paraguay. There he encounters Martin Bormann and Josef Mengele, and a crisis develops when these refugee Nazis discover that Kessler has inadvertently led Israeli agents to their hiding-place; the exiles are confidently awaiting *'Der Tag'* when the Fourth Reich will arise. Kessler is now court-martialled by the Nazis but eventually commits suicide when Mossad captures him. He has a bad conscience about what he did to Reinhardt, a capable officer – for Germany needs all her resources for the next war – but regrets the Holocaust only as bad for Germany's image abroad.[28]

Kessler was not the only sequel to *Secret Army*, for although the location shifted from Belgium to France, another spin-off was the comedy series *'Allo, 'Allo* (1984–1992). As Michael Portillo argued in October 2004, when urging the Queen not to apologise to Germans for anything Britain did during the war, 'both *Fawlty Towers* and *'Allo, 'Allo!* are vintage television productions . . . Undeniably there is a huge output of British television histories of Hitler: few subjects can rival the Führer for viewing figures. Somehow, too, it is true that we find the Third Reich funny . . . and it is a remarkable feature of the British psyche that we are still laughing about the Nazis.' In *'Allo, 'Allo* the brave Albert Foiret becomes the harassed café proprietor René Artois, there are always RAF escapees in hiding (whom the Germans never find), German officers are bumblers rather than honourable men racked with indecision, and the Gestapo's Herr Flick terrifies everyone in quite ineffective ways; comedy accents abound and taste is absent. The public loved it, even accepting the 'outing' of the actor who played René and sending him flowers when he was injured in a car crash; at its height each episode attracted twelve million viewers. The *Telegraph* reported when the show ended that it had acquired 'unlikely fans. Lord Rees-Mogg, chairman of the Broadcasting Standards Council and champion of politically correct broadcasting, startled the public on his appointment by confiding that *'Allo, 'Allo* was his favourite programme. The Queen Mother is also believed to be an enthusiast.' The general mood is caught by Herr Flick's comment when a new commanding general arrives: 'Von Schmelling has crossed swords with the Gestapo many times in the past. This is why he wears an eye-patch and a wooden leg.' When the BBC cashed in on the success of the series by issuing *The Complete War Diaries of René Artois*, they reminded viewers of past glories: the entry for 31 December 1942 refers to 'Herr Flick's traditional yuletide interrogation. He holds it in his dungeon immediately after Hitler's Christmas speech.' The sexually ambiguous Leutnant Gruber sings, 'I'm going to wash that man right out of *Mein Herr*,' and General von Klinkerhoff gets the Italian War Hero Medal, which is 'very rare'. Quite what was made of this when *'Allo, 'Allo* was shown in Germany is hard to fathom, let alone the reference to the SS's exploitative wartime business activities: they advertise 'Gestap-o-grams' ('Male SS strippers . . . Naughty Hitler Youths . . .') – 'if anyone is cheaper, they will be shot'.[29]

'Allo, 'Allo was one of many comedies about the war, which, as Portillo suggested, has remained a topic thought suitable for humour; one of Britain's most popular club comedians, the Mancunian Bernard Manning, did his national service guarding war criminals at Spandau Prison, but made regular references to German stereotypes during racially provocative routines, and kept at home a bust of Hitler ('as an investment'). Comedians and scriptwriters were usually on the patriotic side. *Dad's Army* (1968–77), while concentrating on geriatrics defending Britain, allowed its characters to express uninhibited opinions about the enemy, more often 'the Hun' than 'the Nazis'. On the rare occasions when Germans appeared they were sent up no more than the British, but these moments were few and far between, for the overall theme was inoffensive Britons defending their homes against German aggression. Beyond situation comedies set in wartime, to which we could add *Goodnight, Sweetheart* (1993–8), there have been obligatory references to the war during almost every other successful situation comedy. *The Likely Lads* (1964–6) conveniently ended with one of the eponymous lads accidentally joining the army, so that when the BBC launched *Whatever Happened to the Likely Lads?* (1973–4) Terry returns to County Durham with jaundiced opinions of Germans gained at München Gladbach; the writers marry him to a German wife, so providing material for many anti-German jokes. In *Till Death Us Do Part* (1965–75), Alf Garnett bangs on about the East End being bombed by 'the bloody Huns', while the film spin-off included not only wartime scenes but also Alf abusing Germans on the football terraces in 1966: when Germany score first, Alf responds, 'Same as in the war, mate. Same as in the war. Started off well but got clobbered in the end, din't ya?' When Hurst's second goal goes in for England, Alf shouts, 'He's done it again, hasn't he, mate? Bleeding Blitzkrieg, eh?' BBC Comedy's website reports that the show did well abroad. 'A German version of *Till Death Us Do Part* was less successful, however. In this, the local producers had made the Garnett character resemble Hitler and the series was taken off by public demand. [The writer] then received a letter from the head of German TV that explained

"We just haven't got the racial bigotry in Germany that you have in England."' Rigsby in *Rising Damp* (1974–6) harps on his 'war wound', but if neither Garnett nor Rigsby was envisaged by their creators as a role model, Warren Mitchell and Leonard Rossiter made them such awful men that they drew big audiences to their bigotry. In *Are You Being Served?* (1973–83) one episode features a 'German week' in the store, decorated with German flags, signs and music, German products pushed onto reluctant customers. The first day goes badly and the resident characters voice doubts: 'some of us have long memories'. For Mrs Slocombe the memory is of 'being flung flat on my back on Clapham Common by a landmine! And the German air force was responsible.' All comedy series based on sketches, like *The Dick Emery Show* (1963–81) and *Morecambe and Wise* (1961–83), had their moments in which humour relied on a spiked helmet, a German accent or a comedy Nazi, while Barry Humphries offered viewers *The Rise and Fall of the Third Reich* as a musical, years before *The Producers* unveiled 'Springtime for Hitler'.[30]

The most treasured comedy was John Cleese's *Fawlty Towers* (1975–9), its 'The Germans' episode forever associated with Basil Fawlty's self-ignored injunction, 'Don't mention the war! I did once, but I think I got away with it.' In 1997 this was chosen in a poll as the twelfth-greatest comedy sequence ever; the tenth-anniversary repeat drew twelve million viewers, though almost everyone must by then have seen it. Within two years of its appearance, the first series (including 'The Germans') had been sold all over the world, and went on to radio, LP, cassette, video and DVD editions. The series-book claims that 'all the audiences, not excluding the Germans, relished the six programmes', which may not be quite true: when the series was remade by German television in 2001, 'The Germans' was quietly dropped (though German viewers apparently loved the violence Basil visits on Manuel). 'The Germans' was an oddly structured episode, the first half covering a different subject altogether; then Basil gets concussed, which 'explains' his appalling behaviour when later serving German tourists in his hotel dining room. Other residents are unhappy to have Germans even under their roof, the clubbable Major Gowan thinking them 'bad eggs', to which Basil replies, 'Still, forgive and forget, eh, Major? Though God knows how, the bastards!' He responds when the new guests try to make themselves understood with: 'Oh, Germans! I thought there was something wrong with you.' Despite his 'Don't mention the war!' Basil insults and degrades his guests with offensive remarks, and John Cleese reprises his 'funny walk' from *Monty Python* as a goose-step while pretending a Hitler moustache. The Germans are reduced to tears, but when they argue and one shouts, 'Well, we did not start it!' Basil replies, 'Yes you did. You invaded Poland.' His parting shots are 'You stupid Kraut!' and 'Who won the war, anyway?' As the doctor finally leads him away, the Germans murmur, 'However did they win?' Whenever interviewed, Cleese has been keen to explain that the aim was to educate his audience by showing bigotry's ugly face, claiming that Germans well understood this; in Hamburg, a voice apparently shouted across a hotel foyer, 'Hey, Mr Cleese, don't mention zee war,' which Cleese thought 'terrific. It's taken a little time. But I felt really good about that. That chap had got the whole point of the episode.' It is less clear that British viewers over three decades got that same point.[31]

Alongside programmes there was German stereotyping in adverts too, notably two Carling Black Label ads which relied on folk memory of the Dambusters' raid, but linked to disputes around Mediterranean swimming pools and football; one was voted among the twenty best adverts seen on television. Another brewery produced the most anti-German off-screen advertising: Shepherd and Neame for their 'Spitfire' ale ('the bottle of Britain'). The promotional material incorporated images of Churchill's V sign ('Two more pints, please'), and slogans included 'Downed all over Kent, just like the Luftwaffe' and 'No Fokker comes close'. Relentless programming reinforced British memories with a drip-feed of serious and unserious, fictional and factual reminders of 1939–45. There has been no compensating material presenting Germans positively, as Frenchmen were shown as incomprehensibly eccentric but basically all right, for instance in *French Fields* (1989–91) and *A Year in Provence* (1993). Television programmes set in Germany, like *Auf Wiedersehen, Pet* (1983–4, 2002–4) and *Redcap* (2001–), rarely allowed Germans to develop as characters. When in 1997 Germany's ambassador deplored Britain's reluctance to forget the war, a correspondent fired off a letter to the *Daily Telegraph* arguing that it was 'his' country, rather than 'ours', that was 'tainted by history', as anyone would know if they were currently watching the 'revealing' BBC2 series, *The Nazis, a Warning from History*.[32]

Children and teenagers are over-represented in television audiences, so young Britons will have seen plenty of TV that accentuated the negative in British relationships with Germany, but other sources specifically aimed in their direction: comics, military models and juvenile fiction. Michael Paris and Mark Connelly have each shown that war comics remained popular with boys long after the war; though from the 1980s they celebrated heroes of the Falklands and Gulf wars too, the chief source of material remained 1939–45. Paris gives a typical illustration from a 1976 edition of *Battle Picture Weekly*, in which the heroes butcher 'Jerries' with grenades. Germans are 'bullet-headed', whether drawn in pictures or described in prose, they swear and bluster, but are worsted by 'our' modest good chaps. Connelly cites the 1980 *Victor* annual, the cover of which showed Hurricanes and Heinkels over London, while inside the back cover British planes bomb Cologne.

> Between these scenes the annual contained fictional stories about an RAF fighter pilot, a Royal Navy torpedo boat mission, an Eighth Army raid on the Afrika Korps involving troops on camels, RAF bombers over Italy, 'Pasty' White in a daring spying mission, and Joe Bones, 'the human fly' and scruffiest soldier in the British army, climbing a sheer cliff to sabotage German coastal guns. Story and history merged in these annuals.

Even when such works were read in the 1950s and 1960s, it was by boys whose adult careers ended only around the end of the century, but, as Paris puts it, 'even in the late 1990s, the pilot of a Dornier bomber is made to exclaim "Himmel, ein Englander Fighter!" and dive away in panic as a Fleet Air Arm ace comes in to the attack.' Paris and Connelly also point out that many readers of such works were familiar with a Dornier, probably having made one from a plastic kit, for although Airfix and its competitors offered ships, aeroplanes and model soldiers from the entire twentieth century, products from the Second World War were at the centre of their output; the 1940 Spitfire was Airfix's first product and its best-seller ever since. In the IT-orientated 1990s comics and models were reinforced by computer games that also focused on the war. Take the course, read the book, see the film, watch the television programme, laugh at the jokes, play the game, make the model; this was a multi-media teenage cultural experience, none of it calculated to present Germans as much fun.[33]

Recent teenage fiction has been less anti-German than in the 1900s or 1950s, but even here there have been continuities. To take one archetypal example, Captain W. E. Johns' 'Biggles' remained a force to be contended with in his struggle against the evil Prussian Erich von Stalhein: in the very first book Biggles tells recruits that 'if you can get two Huns – Germans – before you go, you are one up on the enemy and you've helped to win the war for England' (rarely 'Britain' in such books, it should be noted). Johns, though a British pilot in 1914–18, was a dedicated pacifist when he put Biggles into the air in the 1930s, but the onset of the Second World War changed all that, first with updated versions of books about the Great War showing the same enemy behaving in just as dastardly a fashion. Ten further Biggles novels followed by 1945, and though the prolific Johns added, in deference to the inclusive People's War, the heroine Worralls, Biggles remained the core of his appeal to young readers, and von Stalhein the perfect German heavy, there being little attempt to distinguish Nazis from other Germans. In principle Biggles' anti-German life came to an end in the late 1940s, as thereafter he worked for the Special Air Police (an airborne UN peacekeeping force) or flew Cold War missions against the Russians; in *Biggles Buries the Hatchet* (1958) he even rescues von Stalhein from the Reds, providing fascinating evidence of the Cold War's capacity for transforming allegiances. Yet for boys growing up in the 1950s and 1960s, world-war Biggles stories remained more popular, easy to obtain through public and school libraries, and passed down from one generation to the next; readers, rather than writers, determine which books are read. Then, in the 1980s and 1990s, Biggles books were reissued, and he again became a hero for the young; by 1993, there was a *Maniac's Guide to the Biggles Books*, telling young readers about the man's 'career', and how to get hold of out-of-print titles; there was again a Biggles Club and a quarterly magazine. Omnibus editions included at least one novel set during the war, a comic-strip version of *Spitfire Parade* appeared, and in 1993 ten novels were reissued as paperbacks, including *Biggles Defies the Swastika*, first published in 1941 and now available for grandsons of the original readers. These new editions included a preface, first penned by Johns in 1939, explaining that 'Hun' was merely a word for Germans that British flyers used in 1914–18, but Biggles and his chums shoot down 'Huns' without remorse, and the Germans in the stories continue to shout, '*Donner und Blitzen!*' Answering its readers' 'frequently asked question' as to why Biggles had once languished only in second-hand bookshops, the *Maniac's Guide* is unrepentant: 'Well, it's partly because many years ago some people complained about them. They said that the Biggles books were not very nice to people from other countries. Well, it was true that Biggles knocked out von Stalhein with the butt of his gun, but what did they expect? He asked for it?'[34]

Situation comedies and comedians' jokes can also be matched in their assumptions of Anglo-German antagonism by 'funny history' books, again aimed at children in the market place of 'horrible Huns' and 'crafty Krauts'; alliteration breeds contempt too. In *The Complete Bloody History of Britain, Without the Boring Bits* (1999), John Farman loses few chances to express anti-German opinions. He manages even to have the Russians (rather than the Prussians) appearing, 'like the cavalry in a cowboy film', at Waterloo; maybe he just could not believe Germans would be late? Victoria marries Albert, but 'it beats me why they always seemed to marry Germans (fat lot of good it ever did us)'. British pleasure at French defeat in 1871 was a big mistake, since 'better the Frog you know than the Kraut you don't. This, you see, really was the beginning of the German Empire, and we all know what fun they were going to be.' The Great War section is headed *1914 – Trouble with Germany Again* and argues that 'Germany was still up to its old tricks, trying to expand its Empire and bullying defenceless little countries', so Britain defended Belgium, 'as it had done years before when France and Spain had done the same thing'. The Allies win the war, so 'Germany was on its knees. By 1918, they'd lost the war, all their colonial Empire, a big slice of their European territory, and all their money – and it jolly well served them right. But did it teach them a lesson? Wait and see!' Even the abdication of Edward VIII sets the author wondering why he could not marry an American, since 'I'd have thought anything was better than a German'. Nazi support sweeps through Germany 'like Beatlemania' and Hitler achieves 'almost godlike status among the sheeplike Krauts'. The author regretfully concludes that the Holocaust has no place in a 'funny' book, but nevertheless argues that 'one can say that, years after, the rest of the world finds it very difficult to trust Germany again'. Though Germans, fighting a 'rotten cause', produced many 'astounding soldiers', it was 'the ghastly Germans' who introduced the most indiscriminate terror weapons, such as V1 rockets. Come 1945, 'the horrible Hun was beat, Good had triumphed over Evil [and] our young chaps took a break from Kraut-crushing'. Readers learn nothing about post-war democracy, but Farman naturally deplores German reunification: 'From now on all the rest of the world had to look out for was funny men with little black moustaches.[35]

Such books could make an impact largely because of what children learned – and especially what they did not learn – at school. There has been a running battle between German ambassadors and the British press over the way history is taught in British schools. When reviewing the record of Ambassador von Moltke in 1999, *The Times'* Berlin correspondent wrote, 'another German ambassador is leaving Britain with his heart broken by the cruel gibes of the tabloids, the implacable ignorance of British teenagers . . . They all break in the end.' In an interview on his departure, von Moltke said, 'one has the impression that the teaching of history in this country stops at 1945', and regretted the reluctance of young Britons either to learn German or visit Germany. Though *The Times* thought von Moltke had overreacted, since 'the war happened' and it was 'not unreasonable' that children should learn that 'the Germans committed some of the most dreadful crimes of the century', it agreed that British teenagers showed a 'stunning lack of interest' in all things German except football and Hitler; a recent survey showed that British children regarded Germany as 'the most boring, unattractive and poorest country in Europe', with even Bosnia a more attractive holiday destination. The effect was obvious to pupils of the German school in Richmond, since they were called 'Nazis' on the bus, their football team christened 'the Hitler boys'; Helmut Kohl's son had been chased through Brighton by 'youths making Hitler salutes'. Yet few letters to the paper took von Moltke's side, one pointedly arguing that ending history teaching in

1945 was 'deeply regrettable [but] no worse than the practice, adopted in some foreign countries, of not teaching what actually happened between 1939 and 1945'.[36]

Von Moltke's successor, Thomas Matussek, was soon in the same trenches, regretting almost on arrival the exploitation of war memories by Eurosceptics; Britain and Germany had a 'solid partnership', and a relationship that was 'quite dynamic, if not excellent'. With Matussek in post, the campaign against British history-teaching resumed: in December 2002 he told the *Guardian* that he was 'very much surprised when I learned that at A-level one of the three most chosen subjects was the Nazis'. It was right that teenagers should learn 'as much as possible about the Nazi period and the Holocaust. But what is equally important is the history of Germany in the past 45 years and the success story of modern German democracy.' His speech was widely reported, not least because it followed an attack on two German youths in south London, and prompted more sympathetic responses. An A-level student from Southampton wrote to the *Telegraph* to endorse Matussek's views, since 'for the past four or five years of my academic life, the focus has been overwhelmingly on Nazi Germany', covered in Year 9, again for GCSE, and finally for A-level. 'Frankly, I am tired of the Nazi period.' Such responses and further promptings by the ambassador eventually produced a government reaction, when Education Secretary Charles Clarke flew to Bonn in October 2003 to hear the view of his opposite number. Emerging from that meeting, Clarke denied that British schools distorted German history and assured journalists that Hitler would stay on the curriculum, but promised to 'look at ways to update Germany's image in classes', for Germans were 'making a perfectly fair point and we are certainly having to think about it'. Having, as *The Times* put it, 'tried out his O-level German in a few stumbling phrases' during the meeting, Clarke also called for more foreign-language teaching in Britain and launched a scheme for partnerships between British and German schools.[37]

The resulting teacher exchanges got off to a rocky start, for a six-day trip to Germany by twenty British teachers in 2004 was widely reported as wasting fifty thousand euros. 'Why not?' riposted a Sussex teacher interviewed by the *Guardian*: 'You don't get many freebies in teaching . . . Quite frankly, who wouldn't?' Another, amazed to be staying in a five-star hotel at taxpayers' expense, whispered, 'we discovered later that even the mini-bar was free'. The teacher-tourists had visited the Reichstag and the state opera, 'astonished at the lavish hospitality provided by the German government', but doubted if it would change their teaching. That Sussex teacher observed that 'kids find the Nazi period interesting. A lot of things happen. There is plenty of violence.' This was useful in keeping up numbers for what was after all only an optional subject beyond the age of fourteen. Post-war German history was, by comparison, 'more sophisticated and convoluted and is therefore harder to teach'. Asked if he could teach Germany's reunification period, he replied, 'It's all a bit dry, isn't it.' A colleague from a Newcastle comprehensive thought his pupils 'bigoted and uninterested. The general impression is that Germans are all Nazis who steal sun loungers. This is all a cartoon-style view. The problem is that if you ask them seriously they have no view of Germany at all.' A grammar-school teacher from Torquay concurred, blaming it on the national curriculum, for 'Europe disappears entirely after the Norman invasion and only reappears in the Twentieth Century.' The problem with Nazis was 'they are sexy. Evil is fascinating.'[38]

The Qualifications and Curriculum Authority (QCA) also got involved, following Clarke's initiative of the previous year. Their report on German history blamed teachers for 'playing safe', covering mainly subjects about which pupils already knew something, to ensure high grades, hence teaching them about Hitler several times. Yet this can have been at best half true, for repeated coverage of Nazi Germany was often a matter of student choice, and it was in the selection of options at GCSE and A-level that bias was most apparent. Universities were not within the QCA's remit, but they would have found similar bias in higher education too, with some pupils opting for courses in familiar fields, and hence analysing Nazism for the fourth or fifth time in ten years. Since such options were a matter for teachers and pupils, the curriculum authority could do little but exhort and encourage. In spring 2005 Ambassador Matussek returned to the attack, while deflecting embarrassing questions about Prince Harry attending a party in Nazi uniform. He would not dream of advising the royal family on what was suitable behaviour, but 'if it were a normal teenager, I would like to create an opportunity to tell him what Germany is really about'. Britain and Germany were 'drift-ing apart' because of 'dangerous misunderstandings' fed to British children. Typically, the *Sunday Telegraph* went to the British Legion for a quote with which to conclude its report: the ambassador had it wrong, responded a veteran, for 'we move on, but we don't forget'. Its sister paper reported three days later that the sixtieth anniversary of VE Day celebrations had been a difficult week for Matussek, since the media had been fuller than usual of material about the war. Yet a leading article concluded that 'he has certainly got a point' and agreed that something should be done about it in the schools. But it would be unwise to hold one's breath while waiting for this to happen, since the problem is already half a century old, and the best of inten-tions have constantly been frustrated; declarations of intent by successive education ministers have likewise failed to reverse the falling number of teenagers who learn German.[39]

From early in the post-war years, there was criticism of German history teaching in British schools, but although British representa-tives paid lip-service to resolutions passed at conferences organised by UNESCO and the Council of Europe, little changed. E. H. Dance reported in 1970 that although most British schools taught some German history within 'European history' courses, they tended to teach only those parts which forced themselves into an Anglocentric agenda; just as the 'Irish question' was about how British politicians treated Ireland when unrest forced them belatedly to notice it, 'the German problem' was covered when it affected British foreign policy or involved war. There was little teaching of Germany (or indeed Ireland) in a broader context: no wonder that pupils came to think of the Irish as troublesome and the Germans as aggressive. School his-tory was in decline in the 1950s and 1960s, paralysed by old-fashioned books and out-of-date methods, before the trend was halted by 'the new history', with its emphases on social and economic issues, per-sonal experience and documentary sources. Yet a 1984 survey found that syllabuses remained overwhelmingly political, as did examina-tion papers. History was by then attracting forty thousand A-level candidates a year, with the concentration of specialised study on Tudor and Stuart Britain plus modern Europe. Recent examination papers showed the value of focusing on personalities rather than themes: almost every examination board demanded knowledge of

Bismarck and Hitler but few enquired about any other Germans. The consequence was that Germany was still studied only during epochs of military aggression.[40]

This was neither an accident nor a consequence of schoolteachers question-spotting to get good results for pupils, for British historical writing has been notable for emphasising personality, and for the weakness of its theoretical foundations; it is no coincidence that biography is the most important non-fiction genre in the British book market. British textbooks, noted a German researcher in 1987, 'remain narrative and concrete', with an emphasis on the national past by then unusual in Europe, while 'the history of her continental neighbours is hardly mentioned'. British schools still used updated editions of textbooks first published before the war ('unthinkable' in Germany), and were less geared towards political education. The assumption of British separateness from Europe was paramount, there being only limited awareness of what could be learned comparatively. This made it 'impossible' for British pupils 'to understand why constitutional development took a different course in Germany than in Britain – impossible, that is, without attributing to the Germans a particularly large amount of political stupidity and political immorality'. Germans stumbled from one crisis to another, never achieving political maturity. The paradox was that textbooks were actually very favourable to Germans, and 'none of them leave any doubt about the fact that the Germans are among the most educated, the most efficient, and the most cultured of European nations . . . Precisely because in their modern historical existence the Germans are not portrayed as "barbarians", notions to the effect that "German uncertainties" are still with us cannot be got rid of completely.'[41]

Such roadblocks barring British partnership with Germany could in principle have ended with the national curriculum in the 1980s, since it gave ministers unprecedented powers to determine what is taught. Educational historians point to an irony here, for Kenneth Baker claimed for the Secretary of State powers which would have been unconstitutional in Germany, where the Allies reserved such decisions to local authorities precisely because centralised power had been abused by the Nazis. In practice the national curriculum made little difference, for those who drove it through were advocates of a *greater* emphasis on national history. Nor was Baker likely to challenge the emphasis on personalities, for he believed that 'young children need heroes': history showed 'virtue continuously triumphing over wickedness, courage over cowardice, and that a good little 'un can beat the big bad 'un', a perception that had obvious relevance to the 'myth of the Blitz'. His successors have generally been too distrustful of teachers to encourage teaching of contemporary history. Von Moltke's 'suspicion' was thus correct, but pupils' ignorance was wider than he appreciated, for post-war Germany is not alone in being excluded from pupils' attention, there being little teaching about anywhere at all after 1945. Where A-level courses include post-war topics, they make only a quick dash through the Cold War and European integration, but since this was new to most history teachers (not having been part of either previous teaching or their experience as students), there was greater reliance on textbooks, which, argued William Marsden, tended towards bias through selection, simplification and compression. They were anyway written by 'less expert historians', so bias was sometimes not evident even to their authors. Another recent study found that while history textbooks now contain less 'unbridled patriotism . . . banal nationalism and xenophobia', there remain 'vestiges of traditional ideas of "heroic sacrifice" and "the righteousness of the cause", stimulating pride in being British . . . predisposing pupils to hold negative stereotypes of Germans'. As studied, the Cold War presents Germany as a spectator, her 1945 division a temporary solution to the 'German problem', NATO a reassurance to her understandably worried neighbours. European integration at least presents Germany in a continental context, but textbooks rarely mention that democracy has become firmly established there.[42]

Textbooks thus remain personality-based and bring Germany into focus only when things go wrong; a study in 2001 found that much of British textbooks' concentration remained on Bismarck, Wilhelm II and Hitler, all pre-eminent when Germany went to war. One set of A-level revision notes, much reprinted since 1985, describes Bismarck as a man with a 'talent for diplomacy', but few German politicians since, 'if any', showed the same skills. German nationalist feeling after Bismarck aimed to make Germany 'pre-eminent' in Europe. The Weimar constitution was fine 'at face value', but flawed in practice, and was anyway wrecked by there being too many German anti-democrats. Hitler, found attractive by 'the German people', exploited Germany's grievances over Versailles, and came to power because democratic politicians could not offer Germans 'a credible alternative', once the treaty failed to solve the 'German problem'. Post-war European diplomacy revolved around 'the problem of Germany', since 'a revived Germany was likely to produce certain anxieties within other nations'. None of these statements is necessarily untrue, but each is dangerously over-simplified, and cumulatively they present Germany as a rogue state; there is no mention of German democracy after 1945 to modify that impression. A similar view, even more dependent on personality-centred interpretations, emerges from another text: however 'inevitable' German unification may have been, 'it happened as it did and when it did largely as a result of Bismarck's actions'; had he lived he would have been 'distraught' by what followed his fall, yet 'Bismarck's spirit has continued to haunt German history'. Keith Crawford found in 2000 that British history teaching of the Second World War remained 'ethnocentric', while in subtle ways textbooks continued to condemn the Germans: when discussing the Holocaust British texts stress Germany's anti-Semitic past, thus placing Nazism within German traditions; accounts of the Second World War rarely dwell on the German resistance and mention at most one of the seventeen attempts on Hitler's life; British texts justify and sustain a nationalist response to 1939–45.[43]

Distortions exist even in books aimed at children aged seven to eleven. Rachel Wright's *World War II* for the 'Project Homework' series makes little distinction between Germans and Nazis, emphasising the experience of the British Home Front under indiscriminate German attack. The same publisher produced novels for history juniors: eight of the ten twentieth-century stories were set in the Second World War, including bomb disposal during rocket attacks in 1944, and Jewish children in Nazi Germany – all were about victims of Nazi/German aggression. *Escape from Germany* recounts a Jewish girl's terrifying time during *Kristallnacht*, after which 'Margot and her family are no longer safe in Germany'. The narrative concludes reassuringly that although Germans treated Jews with 'appalling cruelty', this made the rest of the world even keener to defeat Germany (which is, to say the least, an odd comment on 1938). These are remarkably negative attitudes to pass on to generations who will not lead the country until the 2040s. As William Cowper suggested in 1784, 'From education, as the leading cause, / The public character its colour draws'. But for those educated in Britain, Germany's 'colour' remains the black of SS uniforms.[44]

When ambassadors complained, they put tabloid newspapers in the dock alongside schools, and here too they had a point, though they confused general xenophobia with anti-German bias. Since Rupert Murdoch turned the *Sun* into a populist tabloid, there has been an irresistible downmarket pressure on all other papers, but mainly on the *Daily Mirror*, the closest market rival. The *Sun* initially stole a march on the *Mirror* by being brighter and more politically incorrect when the *Mirror* had become a touch too lacking in fun; having been launched in 1969, the *Sun* overtook the *Mirror* as the biggest seller in 1978 and has remained the market leader ever since. Its daily sale of almost four million copies in the 1990s implied an enormous readership. It was not, suggests the *Sun*'s historian, 'written for *Guardian* readers or eggheads who enjoy delicate debate. Its whole style depends on telling readers what they think, reflecting what is being said in pubs, on factory floors, in bus queues and over back fences throughout the land.' Murdoch declared that the *Sun* would speak for 'middle England commonsense', since 'we understand working-class values'. A former assistant editor put it rather differently, though accepting that 'it's not a consensus paper', while Roslyn Cruse thinks 'reading a *Sun* editorial is like being kicked with a steel-capped boot'. Irreverent humour has been at the heart of its success, as has outrageous simplification of issues; it is written to be comprehensible with a reading age of ten, and so uses only a limited vocabulary, but it assumes extensive awareness of the Second World War, through phrases, images – and agreed villains. Yet it also appeals to readers in the A, B and C1 social groups, and is said to be read by more 'top people' than any of the quality papers, which must therefore also compete for customers.[45]

How far the paper tells people what they think, tells them what *to* think or simply appeals to their lowest instincts is a moot point, but it is certain that, as Cruse puts it with commendable understatement, 'by and large the *Sun* does not like foreigners'. Nor is it concerned if its aggressive banner headlines ('Up Yours, Delors!' addressed to the president of the European Commission) embarrass the British government or upset Europeans who have less experience of such rough handling by their domestic press. As Ralf Dahrendorf suggested in 1982, 'the British love the outrageous and the eccentric, and positively relish being politically incorrect, without always appreciating that they may be taken more seriously abroad than they themselves take the world beyond the Channel, which they insist on calling "Europe"'. There was indeed a view, widely current in the 1990s, that the ownership of British newspapers by non-Europeans with business interests outside Europe prevented Britain from conducting a rational debate about the Community. When that was argued in 2000 by the British ambassador in Berlin, Sir Paul Lever, he was so violently attacked by the press itself that both he and the Foreign Office rapidly retreated. This prompted an *Observer* columnist to declare that 'don't mention the war' was really a euphemism for 'don't mention the Holocaust', which should be often mentioned; 'we have', argued Carol Sarler, 'no reason yet to forgive or forget or embrace or completely trust' Germans. The *Mirror* was less Eurosceptic than the *Sun*, but they apparently united in despising Europeans. There were scathing articles on France during trade disputes, and the *Sun*'s editor Kelvin Mackenzie was famous for his 'Frogophobia', yet neither cartoons nor headlines had the same capacity to wound France that they had with respect to Germany, for there was no recent memory of fighting to reignite. When in 1987 stories surfaced about disturbances between British and German tourists on Spanish beaches, the *Sun*'s cartoonist showed German military men methodically planning to 'occupy ze sunbeds here at precisely 5 a.m.'. These gibes were answered by Germany's *Bild* newspaper, so the *Sun* promptly mobilised every cliché of 1939–45. A headline screamed, 'The *Sun* Invades Germany', next to a photograph of Churchill, captioned 'He would have been so proud of our brave invasion platoon'. In 'Operation Klobber the Krauts' *Sun* journalists would visit to teach Germans their 'holiday manners' and 'give those Krauts a lesson to remember'; an accompanying map, parodying the credits of *Dad's Army*, showed arrows advancing from Wapping into the heart of the Fatherland (one marked place being 'Lüneberg', where German armies surrendered to Montgomery in

1945). The paper was disappointed that Germany's 'scumbag press' refused to fight back, so the story quickly ran out of steam. The theme continued, though, as when in 1990 Ambassador von Richthofen visited the paper's offices: 'The *Sun* Meets the Hun'. Three years later a columnist argued that 'I still don't like the Germans, they haven't changed except that their desire for conquest and occupation is now focused on something more innocuous like sunbeds'. The approach was especially seen in the paper's coverage of football: the *Sun*'s cartoonist showed Hitler haranguing the 1990 German football team with 'Victory or the firing squad!' This was just one among the *Sun*'s nostalgic romps through prejudice, but other papers followed its lead, often in a similar quest for humour. The *Mail* printed in 2001 a photograph of a white cat that lived in a Guernsey pub, black fur along its upper lip. The caption was 'Adolf Kitler', a feline which produced regular sallies from customers: 'Don't mention the paw' and 'Herr, kitty, kitty!'[46]

The *Daily Mirror*'s 'war on Germany' came in 1996, when a head-line declared 'ACHTUNG! SURRENDER. For You Fritz, Zee Euro '96 Championship Is Over'. The diary of the *Mirror*'s editor Piers Morgan shows how far this was a marketing ploy: if England beat Spain, they would play Germany in the semi-final, and 'most football fans in the country will instantly be thinking – great, we can knock the Krauts out again'. He regretted that he was not 'a normal football fan, but a national newspaper editor with a certain amount of respon-sibility'. Morgan had already offered readers '10 things you did not know about the Spanish' (number one being their bringing syphilis to Britain), but anticipated better opportunities, for 'Germany always brings out the worst xenophobic juices in tabloid editors'. He notice-ably used 'Hun' for 'German' in his diary, just as in editorials and headlines; parodying a Winston Churchill speech in an editorial, he stopped only just short of 'we shall fight them on the terraces', but came close enough for *Mirror* readers to work it out. Stunts abounded, including sending a reporter to 'invade' the German team's swimming pool and put Union Jack towels on the loungers. To Morgan's amazement, the reaction was not laughter but condem-nation of his apparent encouragement of hooliganism. The *Frankfurter Allgemeine Zeitung* suggested ironically that after two world wars and British beef's sad tale, British reporting was 'still rather tame'.

Chastened by a worried management and a thousand protest letters, Morgan called off other planned stunts, which would have included sending a Spitfire to 'bomb' German footballers when training, and parking a tank outside the Berlin offices of *Bild*. Even when forced to apologise with a Harrods hamper for the German captain, Morgan ensured that it included frozen peas, so that he could head the apology 'Peas in Our Time'. He spent the rest of the week worried that there might be violence for which the *Mirror* could be blamed, and was relieved that 'the only reported incident of any significance concerned a young Russian who's been stabbed in Brighton by yobs who thought he was German'. In due course Morgan was awarded a prize by the Anglo-German Forum for the year's 'Least Constructive Contribution to Anglo-German Relations'; he declined to attend the prize-giving, where his deputy admitted helping to write the offending editorial, but claimed he had been 'only obeying orders'. A month later, a drunken group of the paper's executives was confronted by German bankers in a Sussex hotel: 'I regret to say that when one of the bankers shouted, "You started zis!" I [Morgan] shouted back, "No ve didn't – you invaded Poland!" I'm not John Cleese and they didn't laugh. In fact more of them started swinging punches.' Unrepentant – once Morgan knew that the management blamed the Germans just as Basil Fawlty would have done – the *Mirror* riled Germans whenever the chance arose. The *Mirror*'s unsubtle view remained as it had been in a 1990 cartoon: Germans were aggressive, bullying and too stupid even to understand why others disliked them.[47]

Alongside unhelpful images and memories, Britain experienced in the 1980s and 1990s more open anti-German prejudice among her rulers than at any time since 1945. Within the broader aim of reasserting Britain internationally, Margaret Thatcher and some of her senior ministers harboured deep personal suspicion of everything German. Though these were mainly open secrets to be deduced from their pronouncements, in 1989–92 they erupted to the surface. Unlike near-contemporaries who themselves had fought against Germany and come back keen to ensure that no such war should ever happen again, Thatcher never got over the experience of being a civilian threatened by the Luftwaffe. As Prime Minister she was constantly amazed that those around her did not share her views and sought

CHARLES GRIFFIN, *DAILY MIRROR*, 17. 7. 1990

'Vell, Englander, answer ze kvestion! Vy do you not like us?'

advisers who did, notably her private secretary Charles Powell. When consulting historians chosen for their expertise on post-war Germany, she lectured them on what they ought to be advising her to do, generally what she already intended; after witnessing one such meeting, Douglas Hurd noted in his diary that 'none of [the academics] shared her extravagant suspicions of Germany but this just makes her flail about more. All good humoured, but they are half amused half depressed by her prejudices.' Nor did she ever get on well personally with her German opposite number after 1982, Helmut Kohl. When she visited Kohl in his native Rhineland in 1989 and he made great efforts to show her around, her reaction on the plane home was 'my God, that man is so German!' Challenged for her views, she announced that she did not believe in 'national guilt', adding, 'but I do believe in national character'. Reminded of the size of Germany's contribution to the EU budget, she responded, 'it's always been a misnomer to say that the Germans are the paymasters of Europe. The Germans have been simply paying reparations for all the things they did during the war.' Nor was she comforted by West Germany's economic strength, which had sustained democracy since 1945, for she 'never believed that German nationalism was dead'; younger Germans were sure to seek reunification and make their country again the dominant force in Europe. For her foreign policy adviser George Urban, Thatcher's views on Germany were close to the 'Alf Garnett version of history'. Germans were not reassured when supporters defended her views, as the columnist Peter Jenkins did in 1990; she was not really 'subliminally anti-German', just typically English and 'subliminally anti-European'.[48]

These views were not very different from those held by Harold Macmillan as Prime Minister twenty-five years earlier – except that Macmillan kept his opinions to himself until he wrote his memoirs, while Thatcher was less careful. A quarter century of German democracy might anyway have transformed perceptions, but as Hurd recalls, 'her firm idea of Germany . . . was not based on any understanding of the new German political system', and she had rarely taken part in such 'bridges' to Germany as Königswinter conferences or the Conservatives' own meetings with Christian Democrats. She was unlucky therefore to be the premier forced to carry out the pledge to support the reunification of Germany given by her post-war predecessors, some of whom, like Macmillan, had not meant a word of it at the time. Struggling to obstruct the process, she argued like the victors of 1945 that German unity was simply too big an issue to be decided by Germans for themselves, but received backing of consequence from nobody who mattered. When Russia, America and France all accepted German unity, she had little option but to recognise what had happened, but even then assented only when assured that 'sizable' British, French and American forces would remain on German soil, to contain not a Soviet threat but a hypothetical German one. This was, as she put it in her memoirs, 'one instance in which a foreign policy I pursued met with unambiguous failure'. The arguments she advanced against joining the rush towards German unity included fears that Gorbachev's Russia would be destabilised and *Glasnost* imperilled. As a Eurosceptic she was not convinced by French intentions to accelerate the unification of Europe, to 'bind' united Germany to democracy. At heart, though, it was German 'national character', and therefore fear of a powerful Germany, that lay behind worries about 'all those Prussians and Saxons who are now joining West Germany but had no experience, since 1933, of any political system other than Nazism and Stalinism'. Discussions with hand-picked historians at Chequers demonstrated that she was almost alone in her views, but she kept replying, 'Yes, but you can't *trust* them.' Even as unification went ahead, she told a German diplomat that 'it would take at least another 40 years before the British could trust the Germans again'. In her memoirs she added in retirement a new barb to the repertory of Germanophobia: 'the true origin of German *angst* is the agony of self-knowledge'.[49]

She had barely given her ungracious blessing to German unity when the 'Ridley affair' burst into the open. One of her closest supporters, the Industry Secretary Nicholas Ridley, had given an interview to the *Spectator* and ranted about the German threat once the interview was officially over, but without making it clear that his remarks were off the record. Ridley suggested that the EU was 'a German racket to take over Europe [and] you might just as well give it to Adolf Hitler, frankly'. This the *Spectator* underlined with a dramatic cartoon, of Ridley painting a Hitler moustache on a poster of Kohl. Ridley and Thatcher deplored publishing private conversations (which this was not), and at first thought that withdrawing the offending words would be enough; neither seems to have grasped that to think such things or to say them in private was almost as offensive as voicing them in public. Despite Party Chairman Kenneth Baker's efforts to repair the damage ('Nick had been very frank . . .'), the row rumbled on, though German politicians did limit the impact by hinting that Ridley must have been drunk. Since Ridley was so close to Thatcher, Foreign Secretary Douglas Hurd's position became impossible, since no German politician would believe promises of friendship while the Prime Minister's confidant espoused such views and remained in the cabinet. Ridley therefore had to resign and take the blame with him, but again Thatcher's memoirs show her real opinions: Ridley's 'gaffe' was just 'telling an inconvenient truth'. Even that strategy failed, for within a few days minutes of the Chequers meeting leaked into the headlines. This record bore little resemblance to the memories of historians who had attended, nor indicated the Prime Minister's isolation. Among the 'abiding part[s] of the German character' identified by the meeting, according to Charles Powell's minutes, were 'angst, aggressiveness, assertiveness, bullying, egotism, inferiority complex, sentimentality', while further discussion had added 'a capacity for excess' and 'a tendency to over-estimate their own strengths and capabilities'. The *New Statesman* pointed out that most of these qualities were attributed to Thatcher herself, even by admirers. Ridley, now on the backbenches, received thousands of letters deploring the fact that he had been forced out, and his views were supported by half the Tory backbenchers contacted by Channel Four. Polls suggested that a third of the public agreed with him, too, especially older people – as they did when similar polls were conducted in Denmark and the Netherlands.[50]

The Ridley affair, and public support for the disgraced minister, appears in hindsight an early flowering of the xenophobia that would flourish during the Maastricht debates and in the UK Independence Party as an electoral force, but in the short term the effect was to contribute further evidence of Thatcher's inflexible opinions to a party majority desperate for her retirement, which it secured later in the year. Her successor, John Major, supported moves to improve relations with Germany, launched by Douglas Hurd from the Foreign Office and by the Party Chairman. Major worked hard at building a rapport with Kohl, and delivered a key speech, promising to put Britain 'at the heart of Europe', to the Christian Democrats in Bonn. If he was unsuccessful in prising Germany away from its alliance with France, then he merely failed where every prime minister for forty years had failed. Yet during Major's second year in office divergences over economic policy prompted another Anglo-German crisis. From the perspective of British ministers, locked into the Exchange Rate Mechanism (ERM) that constrained exchange rates, the escalating cost of integrating the reunified Germany produced high interest rates internationally and unpopular consequences within Britain. By September 1992, with German interest rates staying high to restrain inflation there, the ERM strained to bursting point. At a meeting in Bath there was a confrontation between the British Chancellor of the Exchequer, Norman Lamont, and the head of the Bundesbank; stuck in Balmoral, Major heard one of his staff shout over a poor line, 'I don't think that we can rely on the Germans', at which his police guards responded in chorus, 'Dead right!' The situation worsened when the Bundesbank president made incautious comments about the need for further currency revaluations after Italian devaluation, and his refusal categorically to withdraw the remarks launched a speculative attack on the pound until, on 'Black Wednesday', sterling crashed out of the ERM. During that dramatic day repeated demands that German banks support the pound produced only inaction, though British ministers showed little awareness of the Bundesbank's constitutional independence when urging Kohl to order it to help. This was a public disaster for British policy, and it was tempting to blame it on Germany, in view of how it had come about, apparently confirming within two years the worries about German power that Thatcher and Ridley had voiced. For a time intergovernmental relations were strained, and the press on each side unhelpfully heated a boiling pot. Ralf Dahrendorf noticed that Thatcher and Kohl would barely even speak to each other at the next Königswinter conference, even though the whole point of such meetings was to foster harmony; each sat by the chairman, but turned away and conversed animatedly with the person on their other side. Even sending the Queen to Germany did not work now, for both crowds and enthusiasm were less than before, except in East German cities like Leipzig that had never seen her before.[51]

JAK, EVENING STANDARD, 21. 10. 1992

'... And this is your tenth cousin three times removed!'

European partnership and NATO required that the September 1992 spat be put behind Britain and Germany, but on both sides comments made in the heat of the moment continued to rankle, stoked up by newspaper speculation as to whether Kohl had or had not wanted to be invited to the fiftieth anniversary of D-Day in 1994; in either case he was not there. In due course Major re-established warm relations with Kohl, listing him on the fiftieth anniversary of VE Day as one of the architects of modern Europe, alongside Churchill and de Gaulle. In 1997 the British and German foreign offices jointly published Thomas Kielinger's *Crossroads and Roundabouts: Junctions in German–British Relations*, an interesting review of the past, which nevertheless offered only reassuringly bland visions of an increasingly harmonious future, something regularly contradicted by what successive German ambassadors were saying in London. The joint Conservative Party–Christian Democratic Union book *German–British Relations* (2005) managed the remarkable feat of being yet more bland; in the process two eminent media professionals had to write about the British press and television without actually discussing how negatively these media portray Germany. It was by then though already clear that the effect of German unification would not be the immediate emergence of an economic superpower, but in the short term a transition during which German growth would lag behind Britain's. Many German commentators adopted a self-confident tone during the Ridley affair, as did Gina Thomas, when noting how atavistic Britain had become:

> This has as much to do with economics as with politics. The image of the 'ugly German' developed even before the First World War when towards the end of the nineteenth century the Kaiserreich rose up to become a great economic power and threatened to compete with the British Empire. Today the anti-federalists, who cling to Britain's crusty institutions, would rather accept marginalisation than European integration.

Such views soon seemed remarkably dated, not in the British context so much as the German, and partly for that reason Major, Tony Blair, Kenneth Clarke and Gordon Brown all enjoyed warmer relations with their German opposite numbers than had often been the case for British ministers in the past. Blair did not fall out with Chancellor Schroeder over Iraq in 2003 as he so publicly did with France's President Chirac, though the policy disagreement was much the same in both cases. Britain had by then achieved a higher standard of living than Germany and the gap was widening; as in the 1950s, an economically weak Germany was less visibly a threat to the United Kingdom than in the years between, when Britain envied German wealth and Germans occasionally sneered at British reluctance to work hard. Now, it appeared, Germans were the ones clinging to the comfort blanket of outdated trades union practices while the British relished free competition. *Plus ça change*, but were Germany again to establish the economic dynamic of the 1960s, it might soon be *la même chose*. British fears in 1990–2 were deep-seated and will not simply have gone away, though there has seemed no reason to articulate them in the meantime. The way in which British cartoonists responded to German unification says much about core beliefs, since cartoonists reduce complex issues to single images, persuade their editors to print them, and must make them acceptable to the public. The *Daily Star* offered in February 1990 a sequence of images, through which the map of two Germanies gradually transforms into a marching Nazi soldier, the Fourth Reich. Nor did such images disappear once unification was done and dusted. When the first Gulf War was fought in 1991, and Germany proved reluctant to offer soldiers, a *Sunday Express* cartoon showed Kohl (with Iron Cross) offering instead German expertise, consisting of books by Hindenburg, Ludendorff, Rommel and Rundstedt. *Today* showed two images, first a German soldier of 1941 singing '*Deutschland über Alles*', then a German arms exporter singing in 1991 '*Deutschland über Allies*'. After Black Wednesday, the *Guardian* depicted a booted Deutschmark, carrying a beer stein and waving two fingers in victory, trampling over the defeated pound sterling, and the same paper showed a bloated Germany, eating in bed (which is itself a giant Hohenzollern eagle), but his pudding is a globe: 'tomorrow the world'. In the *Daily Telegraph* in 1994 a Brünnhilde-like Germany, lying on Freud's couch, dreams of Hitler and concentration camps. In 1997 Peter Brookes of *The Times* drew successive British coins, the first three bearing the changed profiles of Queen Elizabeth since 1953, but the fourth showing the profile of Helmut Kohl in '20??'. Such hostile images appeared in all British papers, and were picked up and reprinted in German papers as evidence of British attitudes.[52]

During the uproar that followed Ambassador von Moltke's parting shot about British Germanophobia, a reader wrote sadly to the *Independent* to point out 'how difficult it is for British people to obtain access to information about holidays in Germany'. He loved Germany, his daughter had been born in Bavaria and was taking German A-level, but he found it hard to plan German holidays, and 'the impression' gathered was 'that Germany had little interest in opening up her domestic holiday scene to others'. It was quickly pointed out that two generations of self-promotion by Germany had made little impact on the British market, so both the German tourism industry and British travel agents had directed their efforts elsewhere. This is important, for personal contact has so often been the most effective way of removing the impact of folk memory. The 2003 *Travel Trends* survey showed that

1953   1985

1998   20??

PETER BROOKES, *TIMES*, 23. 10. 1997

UK residents made sixty million foreign visits a year, but only 3 per cent of these were to Germany, the largest country in Europe. Since equivalent German statistics aggregate the UK, Ireland and Scandinavia, which together make up 5 per cent of German travel, the reverse pattern seems much the same. British visits to Germany ran at the same level as to small countries like Belgium, and were half the figure for the USA, one-sixth of the number for France and a seventh of those going to Spain. Nor was the trend encouraging, for over the previous four years, when cut-price airlines facilitated a 15 per cent rise in travel, the figure for British visits to Germany remained static; as a British business travel and holiday destination, Germany was behind America, France, the Netherlands, Spain, Italy and Greece, and could on current trends fall behind Turkey and Cyprus. The survey also indicated that British trips to Germany were short, and that spending had not kept up with inflation. All this mainly shows is that British holiday-makers (like Germans) prefer Mediterranean sun to cooler northern weather, and exotic locales rather than scenery like Britain's own. But it also shows that within the thriving 'city-break' market, no German city has attracted British tourists like Paris, Amsterdam and Prague, a preference that has nothing to do with beaches, sun or exoticism. The same pattern exists in overseas home-ownership, which rocketed in the last decade. There are now a quarter of a million Britons with second homes abroad: France and Spain make up half the total and America comes third, but Germany barely registers. Travel to Germany must anyway be inflated by the British military presence there, but while at one time the British army ensured that large numbers of conscripts saw Germany before anywhere else abroad, it is now mainly the long-term residence of a smallish number of career soldiers, while civilians vote with their pounds sterling for other destinations.[53]

The negative impact of German unification on British opinion emerges in poll figures quoted by Jürgen Krönig. In 1986, 26 per cent of British people had seen Germany as Britain's best friend in Europe, but by 1992 that had fallen to 12 per cent. When asked in 1986, 'In case of war, to what extent could we have trust in Germany as an ally?' 28 per cent trusted Germany 'a great deal', 18 per cent 'not at all'; in 1995 only 10 per cent trusted Germany 'a great deal', while 35 per cent trusted her 'not at all'. The issue behind such fears emerged from a third question: asked in 1977 'Do you think there is or is not much chance that Nazism or something like that will again become powerful in Germany?' 23 per cent said yes, 61 per cent no; by 1992 the pattern had reversed, with 53 per cent voting yes, and only 31 per cent no. Nothing in German politics had provided any cause for that reversal, but deep British prejudice had floated to the surface.[54]

Reports like this have continued to appear, for though hostile poll figures have eased somewhat, German polls worry some as much as British ones. In 1994, noting that the German recession had encouraged memories of the Weimar Republic, the *Daily Telegraph* anxiously reported that '58 per cent of east Germans and 53 per cent of west Germans had called for a "strong leader".' A 1996 Goethe Institute survey found that Adolf Hitler was the best-known German among British schoolchildren, heading a short list that also included Goebbels and Göring. Asked in 1997 if they thought any one country would dominate Europe through a single currency, the proportion of Britons naming Germany was 85 per cent. Mind you, 83 per cent of French and 81 per cent of Italians similarly suspected Germany, and though Germans themselves generally denied that any one country would predominate, for those who were prepared to name a country, Germany came out ahead there too. Another

Goethe Institute poll, in 2003, the background for a 're-branding' of Germany in the UK, made equally gloomy reading, by demonstrating sheer ignorance among young Britons: while 81 per cent of young Germans could name a living British celebrity (often Robbie Williams), three out of every five Brits could not name a single living German, Klinsmann, Becker and Graf apparently having dropped below their radar. As *The Times* reported,

> 42 per cent of British teenagers justified their hostility for 'cultural reasons' – that is the Second World War, Nazis, bad food and bad football. A further 34 per cent objected to right-wing extremism in Germany, racism, arrogance, rudeness and lack of humour. In other words, the war conflates with a more general distaste for what is seen as the German personality. Yet a broad majority of British people have never been to Germany or had contact with Germans – they are working on basic prejudice . . . The fact is that Germany is one of the few European countries to deal openly, honestly and unremittingly with its wartime past – sometimes under outside pressure, but always (to risk another ethnocentric cliché) thoroughly.

In summer 1995, commenting on a poll about British self-identity, Anthony King noted that 'The nation's history is also a central theme. People attach special importance to Britain's defiance of Nazi Germany in 1940.' That poll showed that 'Britain's defiance of Nazi Germany in 1940' was cited by 59 per cent as very important and 28 per cent as fairly important in defining their own Britishness, though not many by then remembered 1940. The only factor ranking higher was 'British people's right to say what they think', which was also a comment on traditional perceptions of British differences from Germany; 40 per cent mentioned the British people's ability to 'take it', 42 per cent the Royal Navy, 31 per cent 'Land of Hope and Glory'. Pubs, warm beer, double-decker buses, red telephone boxes and cricket were all well down the list. George Orwell and John Major, eat your hearts out. Taking all these things together, with obvious relevance to 1940 and fighting Germans, 86 per cent were proud to be British.[55]

What they actually felt about Germans themselves was demonstrated by a YouGov poll for the *Telegraph* late in 2004. When the British were asked where they would most like to take a holiday,

Germany ranked twenty-second out of twenty-three options, between Israel and Kenya, both of which had experienced recent terrorism. Germany was admired for producing reliable goods, high-quality public services, and (surprisingly) a strong democracy, but was ranked below average in 'deserving international respect' and having attractive food and landscape; it was well down for 'friendliness of the people'. Only 4 per cent of Britons wished to live in Germany (compared to 27 per cent aspiring to move to the USA) and only 3 per cent liked even the idea of a visit. Yet if they would not go there, how would they ever learn?[56]

In these circumstances it is not surprising how overboard the British went when the twenty-first century began with England's crushing soccer defeat of Germany in Munich in 2001. The tabloids approached the contest in a spirit far removed from 1966. The *Sun* hired an 'oompah band' to play outside the German team hotel before the game: England's opponents would be kept short of sleep before the big day. But it was in reporting the result that newspapers really showed their colours. The *Sun* devoted twenty-three pages, of a 'Special Souvenir Edition: Germany 1, England 5', to the match, almost every page making brutal war references. Under the headline, 'Oh Mein Gott, Germans Suffer Their Wurst Nightmare', the writer gloated about despair in the German press, '1–5, *Grausam!*' being *Bild am Sonntag*'s headline. The match report spoke of 'capitulation . . . followed by evacuation and eventual resignation', while a German player said, 'this was the worst night ever in German sport. We have stepped back into the Stone Age because of this.' The *Sun*'s back page echoed Lord Haw-Haw with 'Germany Falling'; the *Daily Mirror* offered 'Their Finest Hour', and the *News of the World* 'Don't Mention the Score'; while the *Mail on Sunday* announced that England was 'Über der Moon' (its readers presumably not knowing Germans have a word for 'moon'). On the morning of the match, Ian Wooldridge used his *Daily Mail* column for nostalgia: 'long before the Archduke Ferdinand, Field Marshal Haig, the Versailles Treaty, Chamberlain, Colditz, Bomber Harris and Dresden became components of the great game that led to a paranoiac state of antagonism between the two countries, there was a time when England and Germany could meet at sport without all this frightful jingoism'. This was pretty disingenuous, for it launched an article celebrating the occasion in 1901 when 'we gave the Germans a 12–0 lesson in goal-scoring'. The paper also carried two pages about previous matches, 'Stars Who Shook the Germans', while three further pages of advance coverage had the headline 'We Will Win!'[57]

After the match, perfectly sane people all over England seemed suddenly to become mad with joy. Simon Barnes in *The Times* ('For once the nation's jam butty has landed jam-side up') thought, 'it is not just that a traditional sporting foe has been defeated. It is as if the hostile Universe has turned benign.' A *Guardian* reader commented despairingly that 'England won a football match and people thought it was everything that mattered.' Even during the match, BBC Television's John Motson crowed, 'I think this could be our best victory over Germany since the war,' which might have been better put.[58]

There was by now a general expectation that the tabloids would behave that way, and not only for international matches as such. Richard Littlejohn in the *Sun* greeted 1999's 'head to head' European Champions' League final between Manchester United and Bayern Munich: 'Britain against Germany – two world wars and one world cup' (thirty years of English failure had vanished from memory, as it did for thousands of fans who belted out that mantra from the terraces). 'You couldn't ask for a more perfect clash of cultures. Cool Britannia versus the master race. Bayern might field a Ghanaian and the Brazilian Elber. But they are probably the only black men in Munich, the crucible of Nazism.' *Die Zeit's* Jürgen Krönig warns against a resigned 'well, that's just the tabloids' response, quoting an *Observer* column on the 1998 World Cup:

> Like Greek tragedy, the World Cup is based on a series of timeless, dramatic principles. The final has to feature and ideally be won by the tournament's most cheating, jammy and negative side, or to put it another way – Germany . . . The Germans are unappealing, nasty. And in the finest traditions of that country's humour, only the inhabitants are laughing.

In 1999, when England were drawn against Germany in Euro 2000, the *Frankfurter Allgemeine Zeitung* reported on how 'the English press had commented on the pending duel with old revenge slogans': the *Sun* had 'England out for revenge', and the *Mirror* 'Fritz for our boys. The whole country gasped for air when it realised that our worst enemy represents the greatest hurdle on the way to the 2002 world championship.' Yet 'respectable papers too showed themselves warlike': the *Independent* hailed 'the chance for retaliation' for past defeats, and *The Times* headlined 'England Craves Revenge'. Ancestral war-memory was not even limited to games against Germany, though it made most impact there. In May 2002 Judith Mackrell wrote in another 'respectable paper', the *Guardian*, of David Beckham celebrating a goal against Argentina by 'zooming across the pitch, arms flaring out behind', looking 'like a little boy flying an imaginary Spitfire. Was it too fanciful to imagine that Becks, at that critical moment, was summoning his very own ancestral spirits, the fighter pilots of the Battle of Britain?' Maybe fans who sang 'The Dambusters' March' when Germans visited England summoned up the same ancestral spirits to evoke Lancaster bombers that devastated Germany in 1943–5? Or maybe they just remembered old films on television? That 1–5 victory in Munich drew quality papers and broadcasters into the tabloids' chauvinistic view, often reporting what the tabloids themselves were saying as if *this* were the news story. The *Daily Telegraph* discussed the *Sun*'s oompah band without a hint of disapproval, and reported fans trying to present England's (Swedish) manager with an urn containing 'the ashes of German football'. The effect may be seen in Sven-Göran Ericksson reporting that before the game he was 'constantly accosted by people exhorting him to "just beat the Germans"', exactly the recollection that participants had of what was said before the 1966 World Cup final – but not then by the British. A few days later, *The Times* reported that, in one week, a quarter of a million Britons had spent ten million pounds buying the new national strip *after* the game. 'A "woman's fit" that makes allowance for the female form is already on offer, while customised jerseys with a picture of the Munich scoreboard are also proving popular', as were Dambuster ringtones for mobile phones; the tills were alive with the sounds from Munich, and public participation was widespread and enthusiastic. Four years later images of that 1–5 Munich scoreboard were still on sale as mobile-phone logos, screensavers, badges, prints, posters, postcards and T-shirts; by summer 2005, a Google search instantly found 1270 web-pages including the phrase 'Germany 1, England 5'; searching for 'Deutschland 1, England 5' produced only a fraction as many pages posted by Germans.[59]

A century after antagonism began, the defeat of Germany, the reassertion of the legend of 'two world wars and one world cup', seemed still to be essential to the English sense of who they are, and how they got here. Joschka Fischer was right: people to people, we do have a problem. In 1965 *Private Eye*'s cartoonist Hector Breeze drew a British housewife, comfortably knitting as her husband enters the room, dressed as Hitler and giving the Nazi salute. So little has changed that the cartoon is as apposite now as it was forty years ago.[60]

HECTOR BREEZE, *PRIVATE EYE*, 16. 4. 1965

'Why don't you ever dress up as Albert Schweitzer?'

Select Bibliography

The note section can be found on the Internet at
www.johnramsden-dmtw.co.uk

Anthony Aldgate and Jeffrey Richards, *Britain Can Take It: The British Cinema and the Second World War* (Blackwell, Oxford, 1986)

Michael Balfour, *Propaganda in War, 1939–1945* (Routledge & Kegan Paul, London, 1979)

Peter Beck, *Scoring for Britain* (Frank Cass, London, 1999)

—— '"The Relevance of the Irrelevant": Football as a Missing Dimension in the Study of British Relations with Germany', *International Affairs*, 79 (2003)

Robert Birley, *The German Problem and the Responsibilities of Britain* (Burge Lecture, SCM Press, London, 1947)

Douglas Botting, *In the Ruins of the Reich* (Allen & Unwin, London, 1985)

Tom Bower, *A Blind Eye to Murder: Britain, America and the Purging of Nazi Germany* (Paladin, London, 1983)

Dave Bowler, *Three Lions on the Shirt: Playing for England* (Orion, London, 2000)

Kevin Brownlow, *How It Happened Here* (Secker & Warburg, London, 1968)

H. N. Brailsford, *The German Problem* (Common Wealth, London, 1944)

Robert Bruce Lockhart, *Comes the Reckoning* (Putnam, London, 1947)

William Buchanan and Hadley Cantril, *How Nations See Each Other* (Greenwood edn, Westport, CT, 1972)

Peter Buitenhuis, *The Great War of Words: Literature as Propaganda, 1914–18 and after* (Batsford, London, 1989)

Kathleen Burk, *Troublemaker: The Life and History of A. J. P. Taylor* (Yale University Press, London, 2000)

Angus Calder, *The Myth of the Blitz* (Pimlico, London, 1991)

F. L. Carsten, *Britain and the Weimar Republic* (Schocken Books, New York, 1984)

Peter Chapman, *The Goalkeeper's History of Britain* (Fourth Estate, London, 1999)

I. F. Clarke, *Voices Prophesying War: Future Wars, 1763–3749* (Oxford University Press, Oxford, 1992)

L. J. Collins, *Theatre at War, 1914–1918* (Macmillan, London, 1998)

Mark Connelly, *We Can Take It: British Memory of the Second World War* (Longman, London, 2004)

Keith Crawford, 'History Textbooks and the Construction of National Memory: A Comparative Analysis of Teaching the Second World War', *Curriculum*, 21, 1 (2000)

Nicholas Crowson, *Facing Fascism: The Conservative Party and the European Dictators, 1935–40* (Routledge, London, 1997)

David Dilks, ed., *The Diaries of Sir Alexander Cadogan, 1938–1945* (Cassell, London, 1971)

David Downing, *Best of Enemies: England v. Germany, a Century of Football Rivalry* (Bloomsbury, London, 2000)

Raymond Ebsworth, *Restoring Democracy in Germany: The British Contribution* (Stevens, London, 1960)

Martin Evans and Ken Lunn, eds, *War and Memory in the 20th Century* (Berg, Oxford, 1997)

John Farman, *The Complete Bloody History of Britain, without the Boring Bits* (Ted Smart, London, 1999)

Henry Faulk, *Group Captives: The Re-education of German Prisoners of War* (Chatto & Windus, London, 1977)

David French, 'Spy Fever in Britain, 1900–15', *Historical Journal*, 21 (1978)

Franklin Reid Gannon, *The British Press and Nazi Germany* (Oxford University Press, Oxford, 1971)

Martin Gilbert, *The Roots of Appeasement* (Weidenfeld & Nicolson, London, 1966)

Peter Gillman and Leni Gillman, *Collar the Lot: How Britain Interned and Expelled Its Wartime Refugees* (Quartet, London, 1980)

David Gilmour, *The Long Recessional: The Imperial Life of Rudyard Kipling* (John Murray, London, 2002)

Victor Gollancz, *Shall Our Children Live or Die?* (Gollancz, London, 1942)

—— *In Darkest Germany* (Gollancz, London, 1946)

G. P. Gooch, *Germany* (Ernest Benn, London, 1926)

Richard Griffiths, *Fellow Travellers of the Right: British Enthusiasts for Nazi Germany* (Oxford University Press, Oxford, 1983)

Nick Harris, *England, Their England: Foreign Footballers in the English Game since 1888* (Pitch Publishing, Hove, 2003)

Duff Hart-Davis, *Hitler's Games: The 1936 Olympics in Berlin* (Century, London, 1986)

Arthur Hearnden, *Red Robert: A Life of Robert Birley* (Hamish Hamilton, London, 1984)

—— ed., *The British in Germany: Educational Reconstruction after 1945* (Hamish Hamilton, London, 1978)

Nevile Henderson, *Failure of a Mission* (Hodder & Stoughton, London, 1940)

Karen Herrmann *et al.*, eds, *Coping with the Relations: Anglo-German Cartoons from the Fifties to the Nineties* (Goethe Institute, London, 1993)

John Horne and Alan Kramer, *German Atrocities, 1914: A History of Denial* (Yale University Press, New Haven, CT, and London, 2001)

Samuel Hynes, *A War Imagined: The First World War and English Culture* (Bodley Head, London, 1990)

Images of Germany: United Germany in Cartoons Abroad (Stiftung Haus der Geschichte der Bundesrepublik Deutschland, Bonn, 1994)

Ronald Jasper, *George Bell, Bishop of Chichester* (Oxford University Press, Oxford, 1967)

Jerome K. Jerome, *Diary of a Pilgrimage* (Alan Sutton, Gloucester, 1982)

—— *My Life and Times* (Folio Society edn, London, 1992)

—— *Three Men on the Bummel* (Penguin edn, London, 1994)

Wolfram Kaiser, *Using Europe, Abusing the Europeans: Britain and European Integration, 1945–63* (Macmillan, London, 1996)

Dexter M. Keezer, *A Unique Contribution to International Relations: The Story of Wilton Park* (McGraw Hill, London, 1973)

Paul Kennedy, *The Rise of the Anglo-German Antagonism, 1860–1914* (Humanity Books, Amherst, NY, 1980)

J. M. Keynes, *The Economic Consequences of the Peace* (Macmillan, London, 1984 edn)

Thomas Kielinger, *Crossroads and Roundabouts: Junctions in German–British Relations* (Foreign Office, London, 1997)

Ivone Kirkpatrick, *The Inner Circle* (Macmillan, London, 1959)

Jürgen Krönig, 'The Mass Media in the Age of Globalisation: Implications for Anglo-German Relations', Reuters Lecture, University of Kent, 1999

William Le Queux, *Spies of the Kaiser: Plotting the Downfall of England* (Frank Cass, London, 1996 edn)

Ian Maclaine, *Ministry of Morale: Home Front Morale and the Ministry of Information in World War II* (Allen & Unwin, London, 1979)

John Mander, *Our German Cousins* (John Murray, London, 1974)

Hartmut Mayer and Thomas Bernd Stehling, eds, *German–British Relations, and the 'Spirit of Cadenabbia'* (Konrad Adenauer Stiftung, Berlin, 2005)

Patricia Meehan, *A Strange Enemy People: Germans under the British, 1945–50* (Peter Owen, London, 2001)

Piers Morgan, *The Insider: The Private Diaries of a Scandalous Decade* (Ebury Press, London, 2005)

Benny Morris, *The Roots of Appeasement: The British Weekly Press and Nazi Germany* (Frank Cass, London, 1991)

Alfred Moss, *Jerome K. Jerome: His Life and Works* (Selwyn & Blount, London, 1928)

A. J. A. Morris, *The Scaremongers: The Advocacy of War and Rearmament, 1896–1914* (Routledge, London, 1984)

George Orwell, *Collected Essays, Journalism and Letters* (four vols, Penguin, Harmondsworth, 1970)

Norman Page, *Auden and Isherwood: The Berlin Years* (St Martin's Press, New York, 1998)

Alan Palmer, *Crowned Cousins: The Anglo-German Royal Connection* (Weidenfeld & Nicolson, London, 1985)

Michael Paris, *Warrior Nation: Images of War in British Popular Culture* (Reaktion, London, 2000)

Ben Pimlott, *Hugh Dalton* (Cape, London, 1995)

Terence Prittie, *My Germans, 1933–1983* (Wolff, London, 1983)

Nicholas Pronay and Keith Wilson, eds, *The Political Re-education of Germany and Her Allies after World War II* (Croom Helm, London, 1985)

David Ramsay, *Lusitania: Saga and Myth* (Chatham Publishing, London, 2001)

Nicholas Reeves, *Official British Film Propaganda during the First World War* (Croom Helm, London, 1986)

Keith Robbins, 'Protestant Germany through British Eyes', Annual Lecture, German Historical Institute, London, 1992

Norman Rose, *Vansittart: Study of a Diplomat* (Heinemann, London, 1978)

Gavriel Rosenfeld, *The World Hitler Never Made* (Cambridge University Press, Cambridge, 2005)

Alan Rowlands, *Trautmann: The Biography* (Breedon, Derby, 1990)

Lord Russell of Liverpool, *The Scourge of the Swastika* (Cassell, London, 1954)

Andrew Sharf, *The British Press and Jews under Nazi Rule* (Oxford University Press, London, 1964)

K. R. M. Short and Stephen Dolezel, eds, *Hitler's Fall: The Newsreel Witness* (Croom Helm, London, 1988)

Robert Skidelsky, *John Maynard Keynes, Vol. I: Hopes Betrayed, 1883–1920* (Macmillan, London, 1983)

Daniel Snowman, *The Hitler Emigrés* (Chatto & Windus, London, 2002)

David A. T. Stafford, 'Conspiracy and Xenophobia: The Popular Spy Novels of William Le Queux, 1893–1914', *Europa*, 3, 3 (1982)

Roland Stromberg, *Redemption by War: The Intellectuals and 1914* (Regents Press, Lawrence, KS, 1982)

Matthew Barry Sullivan, *Thresholds of Peace: German Prisoners and the People of Britain, 1944–1948* (Hamish Hamilton, London, 1979)

Bert Trautmann, *Steppes to Wembley* (Hale, London, 1956)

Ian D. Turner, ed., *Reconstruction in Post-war Germany* (Berg, Oxford, 1989)

George Urban, *Diplomacy and Disillusion at the Court of Margaret Thatcher* (I. B. Tauris, London, 1996)

Robert Vansittart, *Black Record: Germans Past and Present* (Hamish Hamilton, London, 1941)

Stuart Wallace, *War and the Image of Germany: British Academics, 1914–18* (John Donald, Edinburgh, 1988)

Wesley Wark, *The Ultimate Enemy: British Intelligence and Nazi Germany* (Oxford University Press, Oxford, 1986)

D. C. Watt, *Britain Looks to Germany: British Opinion and Policy towards Germany since 1945* (Wolff, London, 1965)

Richard Weight, *Patriots: National Identity in Britain, 1940–2000* (Macmillan, London, 2002)

Alan Wilkinson, *Dissent or Conform: War, Peace and the English Churches* (SCM Press, London, 1986)

E. E. Williams, *'Made in Germany'* (Harvester Press edn, Brighton, 1973)

Index